LITERARY
LAND
CLAIMS

Margery Fee

LITERARY
LAND
CLAIMS

The "Indian Land Question" from
Pontiac's War to Attawapiskat

**WILFRID LAURIER
UNIVERSITY PRESS**

This book has been published with the help of a grant from the Canadian Federation for the Humanities and Social Sciences, through the Awards to Scholarly Publications Program, using funds provided by the Social Sciences and Humanities Research Council of Canada. Wilfrid Laurier University Press acknowledges the support of the Canada Council for the Arts for our publishing program. We acknowledge the financial support of the Government of Canada through the Canada Book Fund for our publishing activities. This work was supported by the Research Support Fund.

 Canada Council Conseil des arts
for the Arts du Canada

Library and Archives Canada Cataloguing in Publication

Fee, Margery, [date], author
　　Literary land claims : the "Indian land question" from Pontiac's war to Attawapiskat / Margery Fee.

(Indigenous studies series)
Includes bibliographical references and index.
Issued in print and electronic formats.
ISBN 978-1-77112-119-4 (paperback).—ISBN 978-1-77112-100-2 (epub).—
ISBN 978-1-77112-099-9 (pdf)

1. Canadian literature (English)—Indian authors—History and criticism. 2. Indians of North America in literature. 3. Colonization in literature. 4. Indians of North America—Canada—Claims. I. Title. II. Series: Indigenous studies series

PS8089.5.I6F43 2015　　　　　　C810.9'897　　　　　　C2015-902042-5
　　　　　　　　　　　　　　　　　　　　　　　　　　　C2015-902043-3

Cover design by Martyn Schmoll. Front-cover photo © 2007 Katrina L. Coombs katrina@outsideinstyle.net. Text design by Sandra Friesen.

This book is printed on FSC® certified paper and is certified Ecologo. It contains post-consumer fibre, is processed chlorine free, and is manufactured using biogas energy.

Printed in Canada

 MIX
Paper from
responsible sources
FSC® C004071

Contents

CONTENTS

List of Illustrations

Acknowledgements

I thank the Musqueam Nation, on whose unceded territory I have worked and lived for the past two decades, and the other nations whose lands have supported me and my family. At the suggestion of my series editor, Deanna Reder, the title of this book comes from a paper I wrote for *The Native in Literature: Canadian and Comparative Perspectives* (1987), edited by Thomas King, Cheryl Calver, and Helen Hoy. I thank Deanna for the title and Helen, Cheryl, and Tom for inviting me to contribute to this early and important collection.

I wish there was enough space to thank all those whose kindness and patience led to my slow learning over the twenty-eight years between writing that paper and this book. I was fortunate to teach English at the Native Friendship Centre in Victoria in 1986–1987. The students, despite having to cope with crazy bureaucratic demands, constant financial and family emergencies, and their very white, very middle-class teacher, generously taught me a lot about the damage done by colonization and the extent of my privilege.

When I arrived at UBC the welcome of Jo-ann Archibald and Madeleine MacIvor at the First Nations House of Learning made it possible for me to imagine teaching First Nations literature at the university level, which I began to do in 1996–1997. I thank the English Department, which had hired me to teach postcolonial studies, for letting me veer off that track. This flexibility likely had something to do with the early intervention into the field of Indigenous literary studies of my colleagues, Bill New and Laurie Ricou, with the special issue of *Canadian Literature* that became *Native Writers and Canadian Writing* (1990).

I thank all the students in successive classes who questioned my assumptions and broadened my horizons. The chance to supervise and to be on the committees of graduate students working on Indigenous topics has been a gift:

their engagement with their projects has helped me see the field from many different perspectives. UBC set up the First Nations Studies Program in 2001 when I was an associate dean in the Faculty of Arts: this happy accident made it my duty as well as my pleasure to work with colleagues to produce the initial curriculum and hire the first staff and faculty for that program. They and the faculty and staff since hired have all been part of my education, particularly Linc Kesler, the first program director, who has forged strong community links and mentored a generation of amazing students. Their projects help UBC remember and fulfill its responsibilities to the Indigenous peoples whose land it occupies. Musqueam 101, a UBC–Musqueam program that has met weekly during term time at Musqueam since 2001, was the brainchild of Leona Sparrow and Michael Ames. My participation has enabled me to spend time with elders and other members of the community, to hear their opinions, and to learn about their experiences. This friendly collaboration continues the long traditions of Musqueam hospitality. The chance to begin to learn hən̓q̓əmin̓əm̓ (Musqueam Salish) with elder Larry Grant and Patricia Shaw further allowed me to learn about the place where I live and work.

Sneja Gunew and Susan Gingell have both engaged me in constant intellectual conversation for several decades, helping me to think more critically and read more widely. Charlotte Townsend-Gault and Patricia Shaw have helped me cross some disciplinary boundaries. For invaluable advice on various draft chapters, I thank Julie Cruikshank, Carole Gerson, Janet Giltrow, Sneja Gunew, Daniel Heath Justice, June Scudeler, and Wendy Wickwire. Karen Dearlove kindly provided me with a tour of Chiefswood outside the regular season. The work and friendship of many other colleagues has been a wonderful privilege. I also thank the anonymous peer reviewers for their suggestions and comments, which helped me to clarify the aims of the book.

I end with heartfelt thanks to my family, who have always supported me. Of course, the opinions (and mistakes) in this book are mine alone.

Introduction

> Our lands along James Bay were "given" to the Hudson's Bay Company by the king of England. How did he acquire these lands to give them to a company? This company, in turn, "sold" the land to the Dominion of Canada, even before the treaty was signed. I could interpret this as us being sold as well …
>
> *Jacqueline Hookimaw-Witt, "Keenebonanoh Keemoshominook Kaeshe Peemishikhik Odaskiwakh / We Stand on the Graves of Our Ancestors,"*
>
> *1998 (3)*

How does literature claim land? For Romantic nationalists, a national literature constitutes a land claim.[1] In the introduction to his 1889 anthology, *Songs of the Great Dominion*, William Douw Lighthall says that the poems capture and convey a sublime wilderness: "Through them, taken all together, you may catch something of the great Niagara falling, of brown rivers rushing with foam, of the crack of the rifle in the haunts of the moose and the caribou." Lighthall's ideal poet-Canadian was young, brave, and manly: "The tone … is *courage*;—for to hunt, to fight, to hew out a farm, one must be a man!" Further, Lighthall promises, readers will hear in these poems "the lament of vanishing races singing their death-song as they are swept on to the cataract of oblivion …" (Introduction xxi). In this scenario, Indigenous people conveniently vanish, leaving their land behind for new arrivals.

Ironically, E. Pauline Johnson had submitted her dramatic monologue "A Cry from an Indian Wife" to Lighthall for his anthology (Gray 120–21)—instead, two of her lyrics were chosen. Despite the presence of poems by an indisputably living Mohawk woman poet in the collection,[2] the section

1

entitled "The Indian" might just as well have been called "The Vanishing Indian." Johnson's Indian wife encourages her husband to fight against the theft of their land; Lighthall's own poem, "The Caughnawaga Bead-work Seller," features a Mohawk woman resigned to the inevitable:

> They are white men; we are Indians;
> What a gulf their stares proclaim!
> They are mounting; we are dying:
> All our heritage they claim. (49)

Johnson likely had some scornful remarks to make about this representation when she got her copy of the book.[3]

For over a hundred years, until Indigenous and other "minority" writers began to make their critical and literary voices widely heard in the 1980s and 1990s,[4] many "majority" English-Canadian writers and literary critics produced versions of this story that Indigenous peoples would vanish, should vanish, or already had vanished.[5] Not everyone in Canada found this narrative compelling.[6] The works I analyze here by John Richardson, Louis Riel, E. Pauline Johnson / Tekahionwake, Archibald Belaney / Grey Owl, and Harry Robinson express dissident positions that derive from their distinctive experiences in particular histories, places, and social configurations. John Richardson was inspired by his (step-)grandmother's eyewitness tales of Pontiac's siege of Detroit. He fought in the War of 1812 alongside Tecumseh. Louis Riel brought Manitoba into Canada in 1870 and was hanged for high treason in 1885. Johnson became both a canonized poet and a celebrity performer in Canada and toured in the United States and Great Britain. Grey Owl's books, speeches, and films made him famous; the discovery that he was an Englishman made him notorious. Harry Robinson lived through almost the entire twentieth century in Okanagan territory. His origin story draws on the long history of Indigenous activism in British Columbia and deploys the diplomatic skills of Coyote to work out how best to share land. All these works are—inevitably—marked by the history of colonization. Their critical and public reception reveals conflicts about whose claims to land can be taken seriously or even heard at all. Reading their words along with some critical responses reveals the outlines of the powerful but dynamic discourses that stabilize the colonial claim to land.

These people had varying relationships to Indigenousness and therefore to land. John Richardson's biological grandmother was said to have been an Ottawa woman, but if so, he never acknowledged it. Louis Riel's mother was from a Quebec-French family; his Métis ancestry came from his father, whose grandmother was Chipweyan. The Métis were acknowledged to have claims to land in the Manitoba Act (1870), but only since the Constitution Act (1982) have they been classified as Aboriginal. E. Pauline Johnson's mother was English; because the Haudenosaunee trace clan relationships through the mother, in traditional terms Johnson was not Mohawk even though her father was a hereditary member of the Iroquois Confederacy Council. By Canadian law, however, she was a Status Indian. Archibald Belaney was an Englishman, although he lived most of his life as a "half-breed" trapper, claiming his mother was Apache. Only Harry Robinson's identification as Syilx (Okanagan) is without controversy. The variety of their identifications, ancestry, and life experiences allows me to consider how the concept of identity is connected to land rights.

Over the two hundred years between Richardson's birth in 1796 and Robinson's death in 1990, social norms and legal concepts of identity changed. These norms and laws constrained these writers' ability to identify in certain ways; changes in the norms and laws affect their subsequent literary reception. Agonizing discussions about who is authentically Indigenous often overwhelm discussions about the content and quality of what people actually did, said, or wrote. I believe that no one has a pure or innate identity. Identity always is produced through discourse, law, social convention, and embodied experience and then anchored by the belief that authentic identities exist—impossibly—outside of power relations. Where is the line between biological ancestry, experience, and cultural attainments to be drawn? Who should draw it? Who has the power to draw it? I deliberately chose to include speakers and writers who are difficult to place in the "same" category. They cannot easily be categorized as Indigenous or Canadian if the categories themselves are artifacts of colonization. Neither the Canadian state nor the Canadian literary canon can easily include or even categorize all these speakers and writers. The state and the canon are challenged by their words and their histories.

Some object to the phrase "land claims" as applied to Indigenous land rights, since it implies that these are debatable. After all, if I use the word "claim" in reported speech—"He claims he knew nothing about the crime"—I also warn listeners that the speaker may be lying. Here I use the phrase "land claims" in the context of colonization. How did it become obvious to most people living here and worldwide that the territory that is now called Canada belongs to the Crown? How have Indigenous people been put in the position of having to claim their lands even if the state has wrongly appropriated them? How has the formation of a Canadian literature been complicit in the colonial process of occupying and claiming land?

STAKING THE CLAIM

Edward Hartley Dewart compiled his anthology, *Selections from Canadian Poets*, to demonstrate that the colony of Canada had what it took to become a nation, intellectually, spiritually, and politically. By 1864, when the anthology was published, the ideas he confidently mustered were mainstream clichés:

> A national literature is an essential element in the formation of national character. It is not merely the record of a country's mental progress: it is the expression of its intellectual life, the bond of national unity, and the guide of national energy. It may fairly be questioned, whether the whole range of history presents the spectacle of a people firmly united politically, without the subtle but powerful cement of a national literature. (ix)[7]

The literature needed to unify a people and form a national character did not have to be overtly patriotic, but it did have to capture the essence or spirit of the nation. Such a literature, evidence of both civilization and distinctiveness, would allow the new nation to take its place among the older nations, implicitly those of western Europe. European nationalist thought claimed land by pointing to the long history of the people who lived on it and their distinctive languages, cultures, and literatures, from folk tales, through oral epics, to written literature. This literature was the voice of the people, channelled by great poets and firmly grounded in a distinctive national territory (see Benedict Anderson; Fee, "English-Canadian Literary Criticism"; Hulan). This ideology did not translate seamlessly to settler colonies. A colony by definition has trouble distinguishing itself from the imperial power with which it shares a language and cultural traditions. In Canada, two imperial traditions have to be acknowledged, those of France and Britain. The looming power of the United States, with its shared English language and British cultural origins, poses a further obstacle to finding national distinctiveness. And then there are the "inconvenient Indians" and their prior and continuing presence in the land the newcomers claim as their own (King, *Inconvenient*). A hallmark of Canadian nationalist literary criticism (and that of other settler nations) has been its flexibility in negotiating multiple contradictions, as becomes clear in its treatment of Indigenous peoples and the issues of land ownership. These contradictions explain some of the strange qualities of imaginary Indians, who flicker in and out of public view.

Northrop Frye's Canadian literary criticism, collected in *The Bush Garden: Essays on the Canadian Imagination* (1971), along with Margaret Atwood's *Survival: A Thematic Guide to Canadian Literature* (1972), supported the establishment of Canadian literary studies in high schools and universities.[8] Both books are important examples of the continuing utility of the ideas mobilized in the works of Dewart, Lighthall, and most other earlier critics. Together these books inspired a generation of literary-critical work that used a nationalist frame, what Frank Davey calls "thematic criticism" or "paraphrase" because of its focus on recounting national themes (the frozen North, the hardy pioneer, the transcontinental railway) discovered in literary works that themselves were inspired by nationalism ("Surviving"). Davey describes this criticism as a series of "messianic attempts to define a national identity or psychosis" ("Surviving" 6). Despite its recursive, even tautological nature, Romantic nationalism was extremely influential. In its first year in print, *Survival* sold thirty thousand copies, an unheard-of number for a book published in Canada, let alone a book of literary criticism (Atwood, Introduction xvi). I own first editions of both *Survival* and *The Bush Garden*, heavily annotated and falling apart. Second editions of both books have appeared; neither has ever been out of print. Both are infused with Romantic nationalist critical ideas that focus on the distinctiveness of Canada, particularly its landscape. Frye describes the difference between arriving in the United States ("a matter of crossing the ocean") and Canada ("being silently swallowed by an alien continent") and quotes Rupert Brooke's remark about the "unseizable virginity" of the country's landscape (222). These images, Eva Mackey argues, depict Canada as "a devouring, dangerous and alien female" (60) who implicitly needs to be brought under control. Although Frye does outline a Canadian pastoral myth, he follows Lighthall in highlighting less domesticated landscapes. However, unlike Lighthall, he argues that the Canadian imagination is characterized not by courage, but by a "deep terror in regard to nature" (227). Here Frye follows the British literary critic and politician Edmund Burke, who argued that "terror is in all cases whatsoever ... the ruling principle of the sublime." For Burke, this emotion was best evoked by "the great and sublime in nature," which, in turn, inspired the greatest literature, for example, John Milton's *Paradise Lost*. If Canada was to achieve a great national literature, it would begin with this response to nature, a nature usually characterized as "wilderness."[9]

Atwood's *Survival* similarly represents Canadians as subject to, even victims of, a variety of threatening forces, from the bitter cold of the North[10] to "Nature the Monster" to US imperialism. Again the link between settler and land is emphasized. The land itself forms the national character, for which literature becomes the primary evidence. The Canadian imagination and identity will be formed by the struggle to survive in a cold wilderness, and that distinctive identity, formed by the land (autochthony), then becomes the title (entitlement) to the land itself.

In his much-reprinted conclusion to the *Literary History of Canada* (1965), which also concludes *The Bush Garden*, Frye writes, "It seems to me that Canadian sensibility has been profoundly disturbed, not so much by our famous problem of identity, important as that is, as by a series of paradoxes in what confronts that identity. It is less perplexed by the question 'Who am I?' than by some such riddle as 'Where is here?'" (222). The identity of a nation of diverse immigrants must be tied to the new land. Frye describes Canada as "a vast country sparsely inhabited" (225). He notes that "[t]o feel 'Canadian' was to feel part of a no-man's-land with huge rivers, lakes and islands that few Canadians had ever seen" (222). This description of Canada as a "no-man's-land" resonates with a powerful land-claiming narrative: the legal concept of *terra nullius*, Latin for "land belonging to no one." Frye's description vanishes the Indian even more thoroughly than Lighthall's. Frye also echoes Lighthall in his description of the Canadian writers "who have found their way back to the headwaters of inspiration" as "heroic explorers," men who claim land imaginatively rather than literally (236). Canadian writers, according to Frye, were unable to make any connection with Indigenous mythology; rather, Indians "were seen as nineteenth-century literary conventions" (235). As a result, the implicitly male and white Canadian writer had to develop a new mythology from the beginning: "He is withdrawing from … a country without a mythology into the country of mythology, ending where the Indians began" (240). Writing becomes analogous to the discovery, exploration, claiming, and mapping of actual territory. The heroic author takes over from the vanishing Indians to form a new indigenous mythology for the newcomers, who thus become indigenous themselves.

In *Survival*, Atwood takes the mapping metaphor further: "Literature is not only a mirror, it is a map, a geography of the mind. Our literature is one such map, if we can learn to read it as our literature, as the product of who and where we have been. We need such a map desperately because we need to know about here because here is where we live" (18–19).[11] The "we" in this passage clearly excludes Indigenous people. The passage imagines a new map of an implicitly empty territory. In fact, overlooking Johnson and other early Indigenous writers, Atwood remarks that "[u]ntil very recently, Indians and Eskimos made their only appearances in Canadian literature in books written by white writers" (91). If Indigenous people don't write literature, they cannot contribute to the map of the Canadian national imaginary. And if we subscribe to Romantic nationalist ideas, their lack of a literature means they had no claim to nationhood or land in the first place. In 1990, by which time Indigenous writers such as Jeannette Armstrong, Marie Annharte Baker, Beth Brant, Tomson Highway, Basil Johnston, Thomas King, Lee Maracle, and Beatrice Culleton Mosionier had all achieved public success, Atwood wonders how she could have overlooked Pauline Johnson in 1972. She accounts for it this way: "Perhaps because, being half-white, she didn't rate as the real thing, even among Natives" ("Double-Bladed" 243). Here, Atwood does not recognize Johnson as Indigenous and presumes that unnamed but implicitly authentic Indigenous people would likely agree with her. Indigenous writers are either invisible or, if visible, not "the real thing." As we will see, such demands for an impossible authenticity are characteristic of much writing about Indigenous people and, by undermining their claim to a valid identity, also discount their rights to land. Published just after Canada's Centennial celebrations in 1967, *Survival*'s logic then seemed impeccable. Many Canadians—me included—figured as victims rather than colonizers, were inspired to work their way out of victimhood by contributing to that "desperately needed" national map.

Indigenous storytellers describe the land as speaking, as telling its own stories in every rock, stream, and headland; this narrative map was already in place when explorers conscripted Indigenous people as guides through a supposedly empty wilderness. Their discourses of autochthony, not surprisingly, differ from those produced by settlers. Indigenous people have not characteristically described themselves as transfixed by a deep terror in response to nature or as heroes for overcoming it: unlike incoming settlers, they have lived on and with the land for millennia.[12] Jeannette Armstrong writes, "[T]he flesh that is our bodies is pieces of the land come to us through the things that the land is. The soil, the water, the air, and all the other life forms contributed parts for our flesh. We are our land/place" ("Community" 57). In "Land Speaking," she writes,

All my elders say that it is land that holds all knowledge of life and death and is a constant teacher. It is said in Okanagan that the land constantly speaks.... Not to learn its language is to die. We survived and thrived by listening intently to its teachings—to its language—and then inventing human words to retell its stories to our succeeding generations. (178)

Marilyn Dumont, in her poem "Not Just a Platform for My Dance," declares that "this land is not / just a place to set my house my car my fence … this land is / my tongue my eyes my mouth" (46). Bonita Lawrence describes the basis for Algonquin land ownership this way: "Algonquin jurisdiction derives from a knowledge of the land, the teachings related to it, and duty to be responsible for its welfare" (*Fractured Homeland* 151). The epistemological difference between seeing oneself as separate from a terrifying Nature and identifying with it is huge. How land is represented as living kin or dead matter, home or territory, spiritual resource or real estate is mediated by these differences. So although contemporary Indigenous writers like Armstrong, Dumont, and Lawrence make what look like literary land claims, often in literary forms familiar to the mainstream, their notions of land and the human relationship to it are grounded not in Romantic nationalism but in Indigenous epistemologies tied to specific stories, languages, communities, histories, and lands.

The settler's terror produces the conservative mindset Frye calls the "garrison mentality" (*Bush Garden* 222). Here Frye evokes the situation that John Richardson uses to great effect in his novel *Wacousta*: a small number of British soldiers surrounded by hostile Indians in a vast wilderness. Frye captures a persistent ideological strain: although Indigenous people live scattered across Canada in small groups, whenever "they" cause any "trouble," mainstream Canadians retreat to the mental garrison. This disproportionate reaction results from the fear of opening up the dangerous question of Indigenous rights to land. Frye explains it otherwise: "[T]he terror is *not* for the common enemy, even when the enemy is or seems victorious, as in the extermination of the Jesuit missionaries …" (228; italics added). For Frye, the terror is caused by the "vast unconsciousness of nature," which he sees as inimical to human moral values (227). Despite his disavowal, in this passage he situates the Iroquois both as the enemy and also, in their apparently unreasoning violence, as part of nature. Frye references the Iroquois negatively a second time, commenting on "the destructive force in the Nazis and the Iroquois who martyred Brébeuf, the capacity in man that enables him to be deliberately cruel" (248). Here he himself follows nineteenth-century conventions in distinguishing good settlers from evil savages. Linda Hutcheon writes in her introduction to the second edition, "I have no doubt that Frye, were he writing today, would not write as unselfconsciously as he does in some of these early pieces in *The Bush Garden* of Indian primitivism, brutality or ferocity" (xvii). I suspect she's right. Atwood's position has certainly shifted: her remark about Johnson was made in an early and enthusiastic article about the work of Thomas King. What Frye's remarks certainly do make clear is the tenor of the dominant discourse at the time he wrote these words around fifty years ago.

In repackaging some reviews and occasional essays by Frye, who was by that time internationally famous for his *Anatomy of Criticism* (1957), and then following it with a popular book by an acclaimed poet and novelist, the House of Anansi focused a collectivity already formed by nationalist discourses to justify the recognition and study of Canadian literature. As Atwood herself astutely points out, this nationalist focus appropriated the position of the Indigenous people as victims of colonization for their white Canadian colonizers: "In fact, white Canadian identification with the Indian-as-victim may conceal a syllogism something like this: 'We are to the Americans as the Indians are to us'" (*Survival* 100). At the end of the chapter "Early People: Indians and Eskimos as Symbols," she notes that such identifications obscure Indigenous people as "real inhabitants of a land" (105). Atwood clearly acknowledges the ethical problems generated by her project, although this insight didn't change her focus. Faced with institutions that strongly favoured British and American literature and fostered a colonial mentality in Canadians, she was more concerned with making the settler-nationalist case.

Imaginary Indians were said to be vanishing, but they never quite vanished. Instead, they have been wheeled in as necessary, either to demonstrate what Eva Mackey calls the "mythology of white settler innocence" (39) or to provide resources for settlers to indigenize themselves. After all, even if real Indigenous people actually did vanish from the notice of the general public,[13] representations of the settler cannot do without those of the Indian, in relation to which the settler's identity has been defined. In *White Civility: The Literary Project of English Canada*, Daniel Coleman describes the production of the idealized identity of the white British settler in English-Canadian literature under the rubric "white civility." This civility defined itself against savagery, thus consolidating the stereotype of the Indian as generally more primitive and more cruel than settlers, albeit leavened by the occasional noble exception (see Dickason; Ellingson on the noble savage; and Fulford on the Romantic Indian). Thus those designated Status Indian or Eskimo were excluded from citizenship altogether: defined as uncivilized, they could not be citizens. The 1876 Indian Act used this logic to exclude Indigenous people from pre-empting land: "No Indian or non-treaty Indian ... *shall be held capable* of having acquired or acquiring a homestead ..." (Canada; italics added). In the act, which obsessively repeats the words "land" and "lands," the main objective is to sort humans into "persons" and "Indians" and then to distribute the land taken from "Indians" to those designated as "persons." The land base allocated to Indigenous people, described in the Royal Proclamation of 1763 as generous "hunting grounds," was over time restricted to hundreds of scattered "postage-stamp" reserves, often unproductive lands that they did not choose and that could not support them.

Thus, the white British settler became the normative centre of the colonial relationship. Everyone else became "hyphenated," albeit to differing degrees. Fred Wah comments on the power of the hyphen in "Half-Bred Poetics":

> Though the hyphen is in the middle, it is not in the centre. It is a property marker, a boundary post, a borderland, a bastard, a railroad, a last spike, a stain, a cipher, a rope, a knot, a chain (link), a foreign word, a warning sign, a head tax, a bridge, a no-man's land, a nomadic, floating magic carpet, now you see it now you don't. (73)

To be saddled with a "partial" identity as Canadian is to be marginalized.

French speakers in Canada, while a long-standing problem to homogenizing national visions based on British norms, had to be accommodated because of their priority and their numbers. Further, political alliances between Ontario and Quebec were necessary to govern the country. The French in Canada called themselves *Canadiens*; this name was appropriated from them along with transfer of the territory called Canada. They became hyphenated French Canadians.[14] However, the label Canadian was applied grudgingly or not at all to other racialized groups. Because of their dangerous originary claims (something that the label First Nations picks up on), and the white settler's need to appropriate the legitimacy conferred by priority, the imaginary Indian was situated directly as the Other of white civility. They may have always been here, but their nomadic habits and supposed inability to form a national imaginary meant that they had never really been here except as migrants.

The formation of the settler/Indian binary obscured the presence of many other racialized groups who arrived in Canada early in its history. They, like Indigenous people, were excluded from the dominant notion of who could legitimately own land or assert citizenship, as were all women (see Binnie-Clark; Chambers).[15] Many recent critical and literary texts engage directly with a discourse that excludes the experiences of those deemed to be not white, not civil, and not legitimately connected to the land. And these experiences were accommodated differently in different parts of Canada. Renisa Mawani argues that in British Columbia, although "some racial Others (aboriginal peoples) could be tolerated in the settler regime and eventually civilized through moral training, there were Others (Chinese and mixed-bloods) who were deemed to be too distant from the values of European modernity to be improved and assimilated and who thus needed to be expunged" (*Colonial Proximities* 20). The creation of and reactions to racialized difference have varied across the country, depending on local histories, and these differences require detailed comparative study, something I cannot manage here.

Fortunately, those racialized out of mainstream Canadianness are reconfiguring the national discourse, although, as Roy Miki pointed out in 1998, CanLit is often "still narrated through the historical projectile of (white) Anglo-European 'settler' culture" (161). Further, as Sneja Gunew points out in *Haunted Nations: The Colonial Dimensions of Multiculturalisms*, complex social struggles emerge in settler colonies around "who may lay claim to 'our natives' where the debates are conducted in terms of ... who 'owns' or is able to legislate upon the representations of the 'Native'" (45). The white settler claim to control both land and "Indian" leaves others who played important roles in the early history of Canada out of the picture. F.R. Scott makes this point in response to E.J. Pratt's nation-building epic poem "Towards the Last Spike" (1952). Titled "All the Spikes but the Last," Scott's poem begins, "Where are the coolies in your poem, Ned? / Where are the thousands from China who swung / Their picks with bare hands at forty below?" (64).[16] The railway itself became a symbol of the (white settler) nation while the Chinese and Irish men who laid the rails were excluded.

This settler culture quickly imposed its particular worldview, including notions of gender and sexuality, on Indigenous people who sometimes adapted and sometimes resisted. I will use the title of Mark Rifkin's book *When Did Indians Become Straight? Kinship, the History of Sexuality and Native Sovereignty* (2010) as shorthand to indicate how scandalized incoming settlers attempted to, in Jean Barman's words, "tame Aboriginal sexuality" and impress, as Sarah Carter's title puts it, *The Importance of Being Monogamous* on cultures with very different sex-gender systems. Queering settler heteronormativity by reclaiming and reimagining the histories of these different systems is part of the project of Indigenous sovereignty. That said, it is dangerous simply to see incoming settlers as repressive and traditional Indigenous cultures as less so, since this retains the stereotype of settlers as self-controlled and Indians as wild. Further, the conversion of many Indigenous people to Christianity cannot be seen as coerced assimilation in every case.[17] Strong dissenting voices speak in both Indigenous and incoming cultures; dominant discourses both produce and channel much conflict and contradiction.

Lighthall's long-established and resilient binary—white men/Indians—certainly implicates me and my white British settler ancestors in the narratives of difference that support colonization. I do not want to use my ancestry to ground a privileged relationship to Indigenous people or to the national imaginary, but rather to write out of my own standpoint as clearly as I can in hopes of getting others to engage with the issues I raise as well as to note what issues my embodied subjectivity has blinded me to.[18] All of those whose ancestors immigrated here or who have recently arrived face the land question, albeit from different political and historical perspectives. Responses from many different and even apparently incommensurable standpoints, including those from many Indigenous nations, are now at play in the discussion. The resistance at Oka/Kanehsatake in 1990, not to mention the 500th anniversary of the "discovery" of the Americas, makes the 1990s a useful symbolic end date for my case studies. A critical discourse dominated by Romantic nationalism promoted by the descendants of white settlers has since that decade featured many dissident voices coming from an array of cultural, political, institutional, and theoretical sites.[19] Nonetheless, my conclusion does examine the persistence of long-standing colonizing discourses in the recent debates around the hunger strike of Chief Theresa Spence of Attawapiskat, the Idle No More movement (see Kino-nda-niimi), and the Indian Residential School Truth and Reconciliation Commission hearings. The framework produced by the discursive opposition of white civilization and primitive savagery remains a sturdy resource in the face of long-standing attempts to destabilize it (see LaRocque).

I have chosen the works I write about here because they all talk about what used to be called "the Indian land question," an old-fashioned phrase, but one that would have resonated with all five of the selected writers and

speakers that I consider. They work from particular experiences and identifications that bear on their attitudes to the land and on Canada's claim
to nationhood. The histories described in these works and the lifespans of
their speakers and writers range across the period roughly between Pontiac's War (1763–1765) and 1990, when an armed struggle between the
people of Kanehsatake and the town of Oka, the Sûreté du Québec, and the
Canadian army made it perfectly clear that the Indian land question was
unresolved. Despite this time span, the book does not provide comprehensive historical or geographical coverage, although the notes send readers to
other sources that do better. However, examination of these works and the
nationalist responses to them allows for some insight into the ways that the
relationship to land was represented in various periods. What these writers
and speakers have in common is their position in what Mary Louise Pratt
has called "contact zones," which she defines as "social spaces where cultures meet, clash, and grapple with each other, often in contexts of highly
asymmetrical relations of power, such as colonialism, slavery, or their after-
maths as they are lived out in many parts of the world today" ("Arts" 34).
However, texts produced in contact zones, as Pratt points out, are "heter-
ogenous on the reception end as well as the production end" (37). I do not
read them as telling an integrated or progressive narrative about the development of an ideal and homogeneous "national imaginary," even if modified by words like "mosaic" or "multicultural." Rather, I read these texts with
some of their critics to find the points of friction where they rub against
both the dominant discourses of their times and those of their more recent
reception.

The life story of John Richardson (1796–1852), born near Detroit into a
fur-trading and slave-owning military family, has been interwoven with
the reception and interpretations of his writing as an exemplary Loyalist literary forefather. His novel *Wacousta* (1832) deals with Pontiac's War.
Its sequel, *The Canadian Brothers* (1840), is set during the War of 1812, in
which Richardson fought as an underage officer. Although the War of 1812
was declared a British victory, the Indigenous men who fought alongside
Tecumseh, including E. Pauline Johnson's grandfather, did not recover the
land they lost after the American Revolution. Richardson's heavy use of
gothic conventions reveals his pessimistic outlook for Indigenous people
without Tecumseh's leadership. Although Richardson has long been read
into a nationalist narrative as the founder of Canadian literature, I read
him as a disaffected, pessimistic, and even traumatized chronicler of a dark
time in colonial history. Because he lived through the period during which

Indigenous people were transformed from military allies and trading partners into wards of the state, he was able to see how Canada had forgotten its earlier more honourable relationship with them, symbolized for him by his memory of shaking hands with Tecumseh just before that leader's last battle.

I next consider the transcribed speech of the two addresses to the court made in 1885 by Louis Riel (1844–1885). He was forced by a carefully selected charge of high treason into a difficult choice: to silently accede to his lawyers' defence of insanity or to proclaim his sanity, defend his political vision, and risk hanging. Although these addresses have been read as incoherent, I argue that this judgment is a response not to the difficulty of his language but to the originality of his vision for the future of Canada. He justifies his leadership of two armed resistances to the Canadian colonization of the plains, speaking not only as a Métis but also as a son of the North-West and, indeed, as a Canadian. One of Canada's first acts as a nation was to hang a leader whose principles were profoundly democratic, someone who had been elected three times to the House of Commons. Ironically, he figures as both the founder of the Red River Métis nation and—because of his role in negotiating the constitution of Manitoba—a Father of Confederation. A five-volume edition of his collected works in English and French was published in 1985, but his voice is barely overheard in literature classrooms. A rhetorical study of his addresses shows how his vision for sharing the land with Indigenous people and an array of incomers from many countries differed profoundly from that of Prime Minister John A. Macdonald.

E. Pauline Johnson / Tekahionwake (1861–1913) did not speak "from below," as her inclusion in *Songs of the Great Dominion* makes clear. As the daughter of a Mohawk chief and an Englishwoman, she was formed by the powerful social circles and discourses of both cultures. Her career as a performer made her a Canadian literary celebrity. Johnson's reception demonstrates how the Indian/white binary pervaded thinking about identity in Canada. She enacted the problem, reciting in evening dress for one half of her performance and in buckskins for the other. Her loyalty to the Crown and Canada did not prevent her from regularly pointing out that Indigenous people faced starvation, injustice, racism, land theft, and continuing colonization. Discussions of her as a poet and a performer usually attempt to pin down her "real" identity. She, like Riel, did not see herself as having a "part" or "half" identity. She is better seen as performing the work of "disidentification," that is, "a strategy that tries to transform a cultural logic from within" (Muñoz 12). Her gender made this work especially complex, since she performed during the time when Indigenous women were, as Barman bluntly puts it, "sexualized as prostitutes" ("Taming" 243).

Archibald Belaney / Grey Owl (1888–1938), like Johnson, appeared on international stages in buckskins; both were working in the long-standing tradition of performing Indians exemplified by Buffalo Bill Cody's Wild West shows. Belaney identified with the imaginary Indian as a child growing up in a middle-class British home and performed this identification until his death. He wrote in a Romantic tradition, but learned to survive with those who taught him about Ojibwa, Cree, and Mohawk perspectives in a world where humans respected other-than-humans. His life and work transgressed the Nature/Culture divide, as he moved from trapping beavers as commodities to learning from them as kin.

Finally, I read Harry Robinson (1900–1990), examining a transcribed oral origin story that explains Indigenous relations with whites from the beginning of time. This story is preoccupied with the relations between literacy and land ownership: Robinson is working to articulate the problems posed by a white culture obsessed with "paper." Robinson's transcribed oral stories might be deemed to belong to anthropology.[20] Indeed, his distinctive English makes them an unlikely focus for literary critics working in a discipline that favours polished language. Literary scholars are still struggling with how to approach oral texts (see Gingell and Roy; McCall). Despite these difficulties, we should respect Robinson's desire that his stories reach a wide audience, "white or Indian" (*Living* 89).[21]

Each chapter focuses on a different aspect of the colonizing discourses in which these writers and speakers worked. In reading Richardson, I focus on how his critical reception has generally overlooked his use of parody and paradox to reflect his conflicted desire for the Canadian conciliation of Indigenous people. Theories of rhetoric and genre are helpful in understanding how Riel conveyed his vision for a new cosmopolitan and egalitarian nation in the North-West. Performance theory and feminist theory help illuminate Johnson's work and how she furthered her political vision as a Mohawk while fostering the the lyric and sentimental sensibility that rendered her intelligible to the mainstream. Belaney, over time, learned not only to "look Indian," but also to "live Indian," and finally, to some degree, to "think Indian." I examine how the Indigenous attitudes he began to understand differ from the dominant view that frames a feminized Nature as outside the social world of "culture" formed by men. Robinson was a master storyteller who nonetheless saw literacy as a political necessity. His stories spotlight the "Great Divide" constructed by settler scholars between orality and literacy, a theory that either romanticized those without writing as authentic or classified them as savages in need of civilization. In his story, the illiterate Coyote, backed by God, forces the king of England to agree to write laws that will restore the honour of the Crown. The honour of the Crown, a legal phrase, is in question in all the works I consider. In them, Indigenous people are repeatedly shown to have been treated dishonourably, particularly when they persist in stating that they own the land claimed by the colonists.

One of my goals in reading these narratives is to situate them in a decolonizing discipline of Canadian literary studies that will respect all cultural production.[22] The focus of this book on written texts or transcribed speech demonstrates just how many subdivisions the academy has for "culture": I am not writing about music, art, dance, or ceremony here. These topics are the academic turf of other people housed in other university buildings who attend different conferences and publish in different journals. Such specialization may lead to depth of insight, but at the expense of connection, both human and philosophical. Indigenous people generally do not separate these activities from each other or from "politics."[23]

Treating others with respect, even those others we disagree with, by paying close attention to what they say, is an ethic worked out over generations by Indigenous people.[24] The right to freedom of speech in mainstream society often does not appear to include the right to be heard. From Tecumseh's handshake to Coyote's diplomacy, the texts I examine attempt to represent respectful ways to work through the disconnect between white settler logics and Indigenous worldviews.

Chapter One

"How Can They Give It When It Is Our Own?": Imagining the Indian Land Question from Here

I arrived in Musqueam territory in 1993, an univited and oblivious guest; I thank the Musqueam people for welcoming me anyway, and for the chance to get to know some of them in language classes, at ceremonies, on committees, and in conversation. Part of their land was handed over to the University of British Columbia by the provincial government in 1910, but the first buildings did not appear until 1925 (Norman). Lately, they have been getting some nearby land back (Yonson). I still remember the first time— around 2003—that I heard a president of the university, Martha Piper, acknowledge publicly that the university occupied traditional Musqueam territory. Now this phrase is firmly incorporated into the life of the university: the chancellor says it at every convocation. Musqueam people have been saying these words over and over again, persistently reminding listeners of their title to this point of land at the mouth of the Fraser River, which pours into the recently renamed Salish Sea. Such persistence creates a river of words (including those of the lawsuits Musqueam is famous for); slowly a delta rises, land that people can inhabit.[1]

GROWING UP IN AN UNJUST SOCIETY

So when did I realize that there was a problem? In the fall of 1968, I had the good fortune to meet and talk to many Native activists at a student-run conference held at Glendon College of York University in Toronto. These activists were organizing against the White Paper of the Trudeau government,[2] a major manifestation of what Harold Cardinal called "the unjust society" in his book of that title. I even got to drive Cardinal in from the airport. Although I was impressed by his beaded buckskin jacket and his amazing way with the audience, he was too earnest for my taste. (I had just turned twenty; he was twenty-three, and had just been elected leader of the

FIG. 1 Today Your Host Is Musqueam, Native Hosts, 1991–2007, Hock E Aye vi Edgar Heap of Birds (Cheyenne/Arapaho). Photo Margery Fee.

Indian Association of Alberta—I had no idea how impressed I should have been by that!) Another activist impressed me even more. Tony Antoine was the spokesman for the Native Alliance for Red Power (see Fidler; Josephy, Nagel, and Johnson). Wearing his red beret, he ripped up the Indian Act and demanded his land back, a piece of guerrilla theatre that made a huge impact.[3] Chatting nervously with him later, I asked him where his land was. When he said, "Vancouver," I replied, inanely, "Oh, I don't think they'll give you that back, not with all the buildings." He looked right at me: "We don't want the buildings." This abrupt comment has shaped my thinking and my career, testimony to the power of Indigenous pedagogy.[4]

Now, although I do acknowledge Indigenous ownership of the land I live and work on, what this acknowledgement means remains to be worked out, and not just by me. This work has to be done collectively, by everyone living on the territory now designated as Canada. Indeed, the work may extend beyond that, since Canada has signed many international conventions, including—belatedly—the UN Declaration on the Rights of Indigenous Peoples in 2010.[5] What follows is my best attempt to write through some of the issues that I have struggled with in my career of teaching Canadian literature, postcolonial literatures, and, since 1985, Indigenous literatures. This book, then, is situated knowledge, coming from the lifelong perspective of someone who can be categorized as a "white settler/invader." I acknowledge this label as a useful check on any desire for an easy national identification. Nonetheless, however useful such labels may be in assessing someone's likely knowledge or standpoint, I regard them as (powerful) sociopolitical constructs that can be changed. Although I recognize the dangers of writing as an oblivious Canadian nationalist, enthusiastic white wannabe, or absolution-seeking colonizer, I persist in writing to attempt decolonization. Destabilizing established frameworks, stereotyped identity categories, and dominant discourses is an effort that is bound to lead to mistakes and misinterpretations. Still, I hope this book will complicate purist notions of identity and land ownership and help shift debates around land and identity in Canada into a better place.

ON NOT SHARING THE WEALTH

As someone whose ancestors all arrived from Britain at least three generations ago, I know that my current high level of education, income, and privilege results from their access to cheap land and resources.[6] Canada's national prosperity also comes from these assets. And I have benefited from having a life history and appearance that align me with the dominant idea of what it means to be a "proper" Canadian. These privileges have not been extended to Indigenous people or communities. Although Indigenous people make up less than 5 percent of the total population, a quick visit to Statistics Canada's *Aboriginal Statistics at a Glance* reveals headings announcing that Aboriginal people are more likely than other citizens "to live in houses requiring major repair" and "to have trades and college certificates" rather than degrees, and to have a "lower median total income." They are "still less likely to be employed" and to be "over-represented in custody." If the Indigenous population is considered separately from the Canadian population as a whole on the United Nations Human Development Index, it ranks at the level of countries like Panama, Malaysia, and Belarus (see Daschuk 18). Indigenous life expectancy lags that of the rest of the population.[7] So why isn't there enough prosperity to go around? Why do many Indigenous people live in material conditions that are routinely described as "Third World"?[8] These are colonial conditions that in the past inclined them to agree to treaties that were manifestly unclear and unjust. These conditions continue to make it difficult for them to organize against continuing encroachments on their land (Lawrence, *Fractured* 70). Restorative justice takes time, energy, and lawyers.

LITERARY LAND CLAIMS AND LEGAL LAND CLAIMS

Although law is a narrative discipline like the other humanities disciplines I have relied on to write this account, literary land claims should not simply be collapsed into legal ones. Law, as Pierre Bourdieu explains, operates in a separate cultural field. For law, unlike the other humanities disciplines, interpretation is not an end in itself. Rather, the legal decision has the effect of an act: "The judgment represents the quintessential form of authorized, public, official speech which is spoken in the name of and to everyone. These performative utterances, substantive ... decisions publicly formulated by authorized agents acting on behalf of the collectivity, are *magical* acts which succeed because they have the power to make themselves universally recognized" (Bourdieu 838; italics added). When E. Pauline Johnson spoke the words of her "Indian wife" on stages across Canada—"By right, by birth, we Indians own these lands"—she was performing a performative. However, in order to work, the "magic" requires the authorization not just of an audience but also of a large collectivity. There is a big difference between applauding a stage performance and agreeing to transfer land title. When Johnson spoke, Indigenous opinions rarely reached the mainstream; few had the privilege of a platform or a press. However, this situation has been changing as more and more Indigenous people have used their talents to move into locations where they can make their opinions and those of their communities public. The law is usually represented as fixed, graven on stone tablets; it gets its stability from the collectivity that authorizes it and after that does not resist it. However, despite the collectivity's implied or explicit assent, the law's institutionalized power obscures its violence from the "ordinary Canadians" that form the majority. Dissent is inhibited through the use of carceral spaces such as reserves, residential schools, and prisons to produce governable subjects, thus serving the law's aim to preserve "peace, order and good government" (Constitution Act, 1867, sec. 91). Those working in the creative and narrative disciplines can expose this violence and chip away at the assumption—often conveyed by literature, literary criticism, history, and many other narrative forms—that the "Indian land question" was fairly settled long ago and once and for all.

SANCTIONED IGNORANCE

In fact, one of the most serious conflicts faced by Canada is foundational, between Indigenous land ownership and the claim asserted by the Crown. Even reserve lands have been under constant pressure. In 1911, the Indian Act was amended to allow Indigenous people to be forced off a reserve without their consent if it was located within the borders of an incorporated town or city with a population of over eight thousand. Prime Minister Wilfrid Laurier described such reserves as "a source of nuisance and an impediment to progress" (7249).[9] There is a reason why Indian bands were barred between 1927 and 1951 from hiring lawyers.[10] (Some of this history features in Chapter 7 in my discussion of Harry Robinson's origin story.) In *R. v. Sparrow* (1990), the Supreme Court justices provide a brief overview:

> For many years, the rights of the Indians to their aboriginal lands—certainly as *legal* rights—were virtually ignored.... For fifty years after the publication of Clement's *The Law of the Canadian Constitution* (3rd ed. 1916), there was a virtual absence of discussion of any kind of Indian rights to land even in academic literature. By the late 1960s, aboriginal claims were not even recognized by the federal government as having any legal status.

In 2014, in *Tsilhqot'in v. British Columbia*, after generations of Indigenous activism, the Supreme Court of Canada asked this question: "How should the courts determine whether a semi-nomadic indigenous group has title to lands?" adding that "[t]his Court has never directly answered this question." The decision to grant the Tsilhqot'in title to their traditional hunting territories, rather than restricting it to village sites or reserve lands, provides a direct answer.

The Supreme Court stated in 2004 that "Canada's Aboriginal peoples were here when Europeans came, and were never conquered" (*Haida Nation v. British Columbia*; see also Foster, Raven, and Webber). Further, the Government of Canada "recognizes the inherent right of self-government as an existing Aboriginal right under section 35 of the Constitution Act, 1982" (Canada, Aboriginal Affairs and Northern Development Canada).[11] These statements likely come as a surprise to many readers. The dominant discourse in the country that reflects and influences the opinions and behaviour of most Canadians is certainly not in line with them.[12] Nor, many would argue, are the actions and intentions of federal politicians or bureaucrats. In fact, Canada is filled with people who firmly believe that Canadians are among the most tolerant and most civil in the world and that "their" government treats Indigenous people well—even too well (Kalant 200). Little is taught in Canadian schools and universities that might fill the huge gap between what "ordinary" citizens believe and what many white scholars and judges, not to mention Indigenous activists and intellectuals, are now saying (see Godlewska, Moore, and Bednasek).

This "sanctioned ignorance" (Spivak, *Critique* x) depends on the production over hundreds of years of a set of ideas about Indigenous peoples and their land. Many of these ideas have been widely transmitted by mainstream literature because of the status accorded it by Romantic nationalism, not to mention literature's intrinsic aesthetic appeal and rhetorical power. Gauri Viswanathan has shown how the rise of English literature as an academic discipline tracked the colonization of India, setting into place against India's older civilizations and cultures a "superior" model to be emulated. Other narrative disciplines such as anthropology, history, philosophy, politics, and law have also participated in producing and naturalizing a settler land claim to North America.

Filling in the knowledge gap for mainstream Canadians requires a huge amount of discursive work in all disciplines, not just the humanities. In the chapter on Grey Owl, I discuss how the construction of the material world as Nature situated Western science as outside Nature and, thus, as the only way to know, understand, and conceptualize it. The disciplines that structure the Western academy have been produced along with colonization; decolonization requires interdisciplinary investigation because the foundational tenets of academic disciplines do not recognize the intellectual output of Indigenous people.[13] The discipline of anthropology was founded on the idea that "primitive" people were without law, history, philosophy, literature, science, or religion. Their cultures were not comparable to that of the "civilized." This disciplinary segregation was matched by the relegation of their cultural production, defined as craft rather than art, to museums rather than art galleries. Similarly, the concept of canonical written literature has been strongly complicit in defining what counts as civilized discourse, a demarcation that excludes those speaking or writing "from below."

In the academy over the last century, literature has replaced religion as the most humanizing of discourses,[14] and science has replaced religion as the closest to truth. At first, Indigenous peoples did not have the true religion; converted, they were deemed not to have literacy in a European language or the high culture it transmitted; literate, they are still deemed not to have science. The elevation of science over other cultural productions has led to the idea that the only form of science that matters "belongs" to the West. This notion serves to disempower all those cultures supposedly without this form of knowledge (Latour, *Modern* 99).[15] Consistently depicted as lacking what the mainstream culture values most, Indigenous people have always been represented as in need of salvation or tutelage by the so-called civilized.

UNLOCKING LOCKE

The *Report of the Aboriginal Justice Inquiry of Manitoba* (1999) notes that European states "have sought to justify and legitimate" the taking of Indigenous land "through the use of the doctrines of discovery, occupation, adverse possession, conquest and cession."[16] It continues, "On the whole, domestic courts have either ignored or generally misapplied and misinterpreted these doctrines in their discussions of 'Aboriginal title,' thereby upholding the status quo of Aboriginal dispossession" (Manitoba). Further, it argues,

> The precise legal nature and effect of Indian treaties in North America are uncertain under international law, but the validity of many of the treaties could be easily questioned and rendered uncertain at common law, in light of both the questionable tactics used by the Crown's representatives in inducing Aboriginal groups to sign and the failure of the Crown to honour its obligations.

In "The Struggle for Legitimacy and the Image of Empire in the Atlantic to c. 1700," Anthony Pagden notes that in legitimating their appropriation of land, the British relied heavily on the political philosophy of John Locke. In his *Second Treatise on Government* (1690), Locke, extending the Roman idea of *terra nullius*, argued that "[b]ecause Amerindians merely roamed and foraged across the land, they did not *own* it" (Pagden 46). Tellingly, three hundred years after Locke made this argument, in his 1991 decision in the land claim case *Delgamuukw v. British Columbia*, British Columbia Chief Justice Allan McEachern concluded that the plaintiffs' "unsettled habitation in those immense regions cannot be accounted a true and legal possession" (qtd. in Culhane 239). According to Locke, settlers made their claim to land through labour, for example, by plowing fenced fields:

> God gave the World to men in Common, but since he gave it them for their benefit, and the greatest Conveniences of Life they were capable to draw from it, it cannot be supposed that he meant it should always remain common

and uncultivated. He gave it to the use of the Industrious and Rational (and Labour was to be his Title to it). (sec. 34)[17]

Here Locke constructs a group of Industrious and Rational men prepared to "cultivate" the land and who are thereby entitled to appropriate the resources of others who are, by implication, Lazy and Superstitious. This idea grounded the whole system of land distribution to settlers, who had to "improve" the land they pre-empted. As McEachern put it, "land must be used or lost" (qtd. in Culhane 300). However, his definition of "use" was based only on British practice and legal traditions and ignored the forcible means employed to prevent Indigenous people from using their lands in any way under any definition. He also quoted from Thomas Hobbes's *Leviathan* (1651): "[T]here is no doubt ... that aboriginal life in the territory was, at best 'nasty, brutish and short'" (qtd. in Culhane 236); that is, the primitive should be grateful to be colonized. That he based his judgment on the ideas of seventeenth-century British political theorists, while failing to hear the words or arguments of those Indigenous people speaking in his courtroom, shows the power of established discourses.[18] The Supreme Court, who heard the appeal, decided that this failure to hear or credit oral testimony invalidated his decision. They did not decide about the land, however, but ordered a new trial.

THE ROYAL PROCLAMATION OF 1763

I was disconcerted to discover recently that Canada has absent-mindedly built its national capital on land that it failed to secure by treaty from the Algonquin people. It is even more disconcerting to discover that a settlement is imminent (Ontario, "The Algonquin Land Claim"). In fact, as Bonita Lawrence makes clear in *Fractured Homeland: Federal Recognition and Algonquin Identity in Ontario*, many of those Algonquin people have been kept in the dark by confidentiality rules, which doesn't accord with the process laid out by George III in his Proclamation:

> [I]f at any Time any of the Said Indians should be inclined to dispose of the said Lands, the same shall be Purchased only for Us, in our Name, at some *public* Meeting or Assembly of the said Indians, to be held for that Purpose by the Governor or Commander in Chief of our Colony respectively within which they shall lie. (italics added)

One can see why the "subtle but powerful cement of a national literature" is so useful in maintaining a land claim that, in legal terms, is slightly dodgy (see Macklem).

The shaky quality of the colonial claim has been persistently pointed out by Indigenous people. The Royal Proclamation of 1763 is now widely accepted as a foundational legal document for land claims and treaty making in Canada.[19] Indigenous people questioned it from the beginning. Addressing George Croghan, deputy Indian agent from 1756 to 1771 for the northern British colonies, Nimwha, a Shawnee diplomat, said, "You think yourselves Masters of this Country, because you have taken it from the French, who, you know, had no Right to it, as it is the Property of us Indians" (qtd. in Dowd 216). George Copway's best-selling autobiography, published in 1847, describes the treaty made with the British by his people, the Mississauga Ojibwa, in 1818, the year he was born near Rice Lake, Ontario:

> As they could neither read nor write, they were ignorant of the fact that these islands [in Rice Lake] were included in the sale. They were repeatedly told by those who purchased for the government, that the islands were not included in the articles of agreement. But since that time, some of us have learned to read, and to our utter astonishment, and to the everlasting disgrace of that *pseudo* Christian nation, we find that we have been most grossly abused, deceived and cheated. Appeals have been frequently made but all in vain. (66)[20]

Similarly, Poundmaker/Pitikwahanapiwiyin, Plains Cree chief and signatory to Treaty 6 (1876), declared, "This is our land! It is not a piece of pemmican to be cut into pieces and given in little pieces back to us. It is ours and we will take what we want" (qtd. in Stonechild and Waiser 15). His metaphor gains more power from the knowledge that Plains chiefs signed treaties only because their people were facing starvation. The government refused to issue adequate rations when famine hit, although the treaties had promised such support (Lux 48–51; see Daschuk). Despite protests, the colonizers' might made their claim into right.

British Columbia, which entered Confederation in 1871, was the last province of Canada to be colonized.[21] In 1888, two Canadian men were sent out to talk to some North-West Indigenous people about land: Joseph Phrys Planta, acting for British Columbia, and Clement F. Cornwall, acting for the Dominion. Like all nations, those they met with had a system for managing their territories and for sharing them with other people—indeed, of welcoming other people into them. David Mackay, a Nisga'a man from Greenville (now Laxgalts'ap), presented a short, succinct, and logical account:

> What we don't like about the Government is their saying this: "We will give you this much of land." How can they give it when it is our own? They have never bought it from us or our forefathers. They have never fought and conquered our people and taken the land in that way, and yet they say now that they will give us so much land—our own land. These chiefs do not talk foolishly, they know the land is their own; our forefathers for generations and generations past had their land here all around us: chiefs have had their own hunting grounds, their salmon streams, and places where they got their berries; it has always been so.... Years ago, among the Indians, it was the way if any strangers went on our grounds to hunt or to get their berries, or get their salmon from our streams, without paying the owners, it was to cause fighting and bloodshed. There is only one thing that can give peace among people, that is payment for anything. When we get that land we just spoke of, we wish the Government to pay us for the land outside that we wish secured to us. We wish to get a yearly payment for it, and we wish it to be written down. (British Columbia, *Condition of the Indians* 436)

Here, David Mackay is asking for a proper negotiation, not for history to be reversed. He was not speaking English when he made this case. He had likely not heard of Hobbes or Locke, although he quite possibly had read the Bible. He was speaking from a standpoint based on his traditions, applied in new and challenging circumstances. Thus, it would be a mistake to think that in asking for payment, he held the same ideas about land as did the two commissioners (see Kramer 720–21). The popular idea that Indigenous people did not believe that land could be sold or owned has been taken to mean that they therefore regarded it as open to everyone, rather than to be used and shared in particular ways, including by nation-to-nation treaty. For Mackay, control did not rely on fences or clearly demarcated borders, but on protocols where incomers asked permission to travel on the land or use its resources, generally in the expectation of a welcome from the nations, clans, or families who controlled it (see Thom). Such permissions usually entailed the exchange of gifts and ongoing ceremonial and diplomatic contact, practices that were maintained by the French and, to some degree, by the British (see White). Every work I examine in this book, however, notes the refusal or failure of settler governments to keep promises about land to Indigenous people or to deal justly in the allocation of land.

SOVEREIGNTY, SPEECH ACTS, AND PERFORMANCES

In formulating the notion of "discourse," Michel Foucault does not separate words from the social world: discourse is made up of "signs" (words and what they signify), but these signs are also "practices that systematically form the objects of which they speak" (*Archaeology* 49). Thus, to speak of "Canadian literature" serves to produce and legitimate a field of cultural production and academic study. Similarly, to speak of "Indians" and "white settlers" reproduces these groups although those assigned to these categories are disparate peoples with perspectives and allegiances that overlap or contrast in ways that may mean they do not fit easily or at all into the "proper" category. Intellectual work often consists of taxonomy, devising and defining categories and then determining their membership. Bruno Latour calls this "the work of purification"; it invariably conceals as much as it clarifies (*Modern* 11). Ter Ellingson remarks, "[T]he 'Savage' and the 'Oriental' were the two great ethnographic paradigms developed by European writers during the age of exploration and colonialism ..." (xiii). The "savage savage"/"noble savage" binary made colonization both necessary (because "savage savages" *should* be violently suppressed) *and* virtuous (because "noble savages" require protection from savage savages and unstoppable incoming settlers) (see Ellingson; Dickason). The civilized, who were (except for a few bad apples) presumed to be at a stage of development "above" and "ahead" of the primitive, had a duty to carry out these important tasks.

The binary between primitive and civilized was set into motion by the idea that all human societies developed in fixed stages: the myth of progress. In lectures delivered in 1762 and 1763, Adam Smith defined these stages as "1st, the Age of Hunters; 2dly, the Age of Shepherds; 3dly, the Age of Agriculture; and 4thly, the Age of Commerce" (qtd. in Brewer). This schema, which he elaborated in *An Inquiry into the Nature and Causes of the Wealth of Nations* (1776), was widely disseminated and used to categorize all Indigenous people as hunters (although all traded and many farmed as well), fated to work their way through all these stages while the already civilized raced ahead.

Emma LaRocque describes the pervasive binary at the root of these narratives as the "civ/sav" distinction (37–58) and discusses how it has been deployed to naturalize the claim to Indigenous lands and resources made by white settlers. Binaries, or to widen the concept, distinctions or categories, are useful to think with (because humans think with them) and bad to believe in (because categories are always culturally constructed and therefore never pure).[22] Despite their name, "dominant" discourses are often creatively (mis)read as individuals pick and choose among a vast array of ways of situating themselves in complex social interactions. As the authors examined here make clear, there are multiple ways to ground a claim to a place in Canada. However, only some of them can, on thoughtful examination, be widely agreed upon as just and good. The Supreme Court of Canada is guided by what is called the Badger test, after *R. v. Badger* (1996):

> The honour of the Crown is always at stake in its dealing with Indian people. Interpretations of treaties and statutory provisions which have an impact upon treaty or aboriginal rights must be approached in a manner which maintains the integrity of the Crown. It is always assumed that the Crown intends to fulfil its promises. No appearance of "sharp dealing" will be sanctioned. (qtd. in Lindberg 136n)

When Canadians proudly sing in the national anthem of "our home and native land," they assert a claim that Indigenous people have been rewriting into "our home *on* Natives' land." Since the Supreme Court decision in *Calder et al. v. Attorney-General of British Columbia* in 1973, underlying Aboriginal title has been acknowledged by Canadian courts. The Crown's honour, then, requires that the land be justly shared, a project that is still unfinished. That the Court had to warn that "sharp dealing" should be avoided was an admission that sharp dealing has often characterized legal relations with Indigenous people.

WHITENESS, AUTHENTICITY, AND RIGHTS TO LAND

Susanna Moodie's disgusted depiction of a capering Irishman at Grosse Isle, crying out, "Shure we'll all be jintlemen," marked both her arrival in North America in 1832 and her introduction to the reconfiguring ethnic, racial, and class hierarchies of her new home (15).[23] As the Irishman's aspirational cry revealed, immigrants who identified with a variety of ethnicities and religious denominations arrived in North America in hopes of joining the category "white," an identity linked to discourses of superior civilization forged in Europe and implicitly the group best suited to own land and govern it. The Irishman, however, was (re)marked by his behaviour, nationality, and accent by Moodie, who simply assumed her superiority as an Englishwoman, a citizen of the nation that had colonized Ireland long before. White is not a skin colour, but a position of privilege that generally goes unmarked and unremarked. At the centre of whiteness in Canada were Protestant immigrants from England and the Scots who were the mainstay of the fur trade. Many groups are still demarcated as Other, despite a long history in Canada (see Backhouse). The very terms "settler" and "immigrant" mark a hierarchy based on priority, albeit one that does not admit Indigenous people or French settlers to priority over the dominant British and Protestant white settler (see Povinelli).

Binaries are abstractions that serve to organize and produce a social hierarchy that people use in the struggle to claim cultural and physical space. Gunew puts it this way: "The Other ... rather than having essential alterity, may more correctly be perceived as being located in difference as part of a signifying chain" (*Haunted* 101). Moodie's representation of the Irishman ridicules his aspirations and places herself firmly above him in the social hierarchy. She provides a good example of how the civ/sav binary is maintained by disagreements about who fits in which category. Her progressive political views meant she thought of Indigenous people as "noble savages" and Black people as unjustly oppressed (but see Antwi); she found the Irish and Americans she met in the bush intolerably vulgar. Gillian Whitlock points out that like all autobiographers, Moodie "scripted" herself "not through oppositions so much as through adjacencies and intimacies, through associations and dissociations that are complex and ongoing" (43). To the degree that my narrative is autobiographical—and all narrative is to some degree—I am scripting myself and reading others as producing themselves in similarly complex and shifting ways. However, the discursive work done in the past to produce "white civility" means that my claim to Canadianness and thus to the land scarcely requires any maintenance, while that of others—including that of Indigenous people—is often questioned.

Because of their difference from mainstream representations of proper Canadianness, for example, Indigenous people are often configured as immigrants. One of my Indigenous students told me that a fellow student had told her if she didn't like Canada she could go back to where she came from; fortunately, she found this argument hilarious (see Cardinal, "A Canadian"). Those who don't look or sound like me are often faced with two questions by those who do: "Where are you from?" and, if the answer is something like "Toronto" or "Halifax," then, "No, where are you *really* from?"

The idea of authenticity, however, is not confined to white stereotypers. Although no one is born with an essential identity (at least from my secular and deconstructionist viewpoint), anyone assigned to a "minority" is by definition seen as lacking. And such social sorting does constrain what kinds of social space those assigned to a minority category can move into without bar. Despite the idea of the Freudian unconscious, which posits that humans cannot know themselves in any comprehensive or final way, the fantasy of a necessary, complete, consistent, and essential identity is widespread. This notion means that those of Indigenous ancestry may, on the one hand, feel they are lacking authenticity, or, on the other, may claim to be more authentic than others (thus forms the chain of alterity). Two books with the same title, *Real Indians*, one published in the United States in 2003 and the other in Canada in 2004, both by women of Indigenous ancestry, Eva Marie Garroutte and Bonita Lawrence, make this point. Their publication shows that the notion of what makes a "real Indian" is undergoing scrutiny in the twenty-first century. Both examine how notions of authenticity have supported a variety of "divide and conquer" tactics deployed by politicians and governments, Indigenous and not, in both countries.

Marilyn Dumont's poem "Leather and Naugahyde" is a brilliant short example of how someone can be located in difference as part of a signifying chain and how notions of authentic identity can work to move someone from insider to outsider in the space of a brief conversation. The speaker is "having coffee with this treaty guy from up north." They are bonding against the "mooniyaw" (whites) in the city; authenticity is marked by their shared knowledge of the Cree term. Then "the conversation comes around to where I'm from" and "I say I'm Metis like it's an apology." Suddenly she does not fit into the category the "treaty guy" assumed she belonged to. Suddenly, she is an imposter who must understand that someone else has the power to categorize her as inferior:

> ... he says, "mmh," like he forgives me, like
> he's got a big heart and mine's pumping diluted blood and his voice
> has sounded well-fed up until this point, but now it goes thin like
> he's across the room taking another look, and when he returns he's
> got "this look," that says he's leather and I'm naugahyde. (58)

These small power-laden transactions, Dumont notes, are common in "underground languages": the conversation "comes around to where I'm from ... in the oblique way it does to find out someone's status without actually asking" (58). Janet Giltrow has examined similar expressions of "politeness" (like the "mmh" that supposedly expresses a "big heart") to include "tacit gestures by which people recognize one another in their range of social distinctions, by which people indemnify themselves and sustain advantage" (214). Authenticity is granted or refused in brief interactions that can lead to feelings of belonging (united in laughing at the *mooniyaw*) or feelings of exclusion and inauthenticity ("I'm naugahyde"). These feelings are extreme, affect-laden, and hard to articulate, although Dumont has succeeded brilliantly in articulating them. Although the treaty guy "wins" this brief transaction because he is more like the "Indian" of the dominant white/Indian binary, his identity has nonetheless been constructed within a wider discourse that marks him as Other. He wins because he is a "treaty guy," presumably with Status and a state-endorsed stake in a particular if limited territory. He consolidates this identity by scoring off someone who belongs to a group he sees as even worse off in the authenticity contest.[24] These tiny interactions are how dominant ideas are disseminated and how they do the work of social sorting. Foucault's idea of a "microphysics of power" adds such transactions to the overall picture of how social discipline operates, rather than seeing all power concentrated "above," in elite institutions (*Discipline and Punish*). Dumont "lost" this transaction—but then she wrote the poem.

The lack of approved social categories (authenticity) for those who are not clearly "Indian" (whether defined by the federal government or the community) have left many people of Indigenous ancestry with a troubled relationship to their family past, which in fact was often suppressed because of widespread racism. Bonita Lawrence, for example, recounts growing up in a "British" family. After her British father left, her mother, identified as "dark, French-speaking and Catholic," but even so excluded by the Montreal francophone community, fought to keep the family together by denying any Nativeness (*Real* 2–3). Children who can pass as something other than the least favoured racial category are often kept in ignorance of their heritage, out of shame or out of fear that they will suffer from racism or that social welfare agencies will remove them from their family. Not surprisingly, these children may grow up into artists, writers, and scholars trying to make sense of the confusing secrecies of their childhood. The documentary film *Women in the Shadows*, based on Christine Welsh's life (dir. Norma Bailey, NFB 1991; see also Welsh), and Warren Cariou's *Lake of the Prairies* recount such histories. Thomas King's "You're Not the Indian I Had in Mind," Eden Robinson's *The Sasquatch at Home*, and Drew Hayden Taylor's "Pretty Like a White Boy" all examine paradoxes imposed by notions of authenticity.

For Lawrence, it is always dangerous to aspire to an identity legitimated by the state. If the final definition of who is "authentically" Indigenous is left in the hands of a federal government always eager to save money and demonstrate efficiency, then a kind of bureaucratic genocide by (re)definition can be set into motion (see Neu and Therrien). One goal of successive administrations has been to reduce the number of Status Indians and, thus, any obligations to them, by excluding various groups from how status is defined: the work of purification with a vengeance. In the past, education and military service could move men and their wives and children out of Status through "enfranchisement"; women were also moved out of Status if they married a non-Status man, as were their children. Similarly, the different categories devised for Indigenous people in Canada by the Constitution Act, 1982—Indian, Métis, Inuit—categories from which many people with Indigenous ancestry have been excluded, ultimately can pit these groups against each other for what have been made into scarce resources by the state. Despite the force of the historical argument that the treaties and other nation-to-nation agreements validate Indigenous sovereignty, Lawrence shows how even this argument can operate as a "divide and conquer" tactic (as demonstrated by Dumont's "treaty guy"). She argues for a return to traditional alliances so that the unit of governance is larger than the reserve band council that often represents only a few hundred people. John Borrows's response is to see Canada as always already Indigenous, despite the intrusions of colonization, and in need of "recovery" by Aboriginal people. It is time, he says, for "Aboriginal control of Canadian affairs" (*Recovering* 140). Decolonization theory has always argued that sovereignty must be performed, rather than wheedled out of or even demanded from the dominant power: the Musqueam people welcome visitors to their land at all important university functions and have provided carved figures that symbolically welcome people landing at the Vancouver airport, coming on to the UBC campus, and visiting the Museum of Anthropology. Thus, they situate themselves as hosts and benefactors.

PROBLEMS OF REPRESENTATION

We are born into a web of ideological discourses and make sense of the world through them. Self-representations are made out of and feed back into these discourses. The word "representation" itself has two meanings, as Spivak has pointed out—making portraits of or speaking for others (*Critique* 257–64). Both these acts mark others as unable to speak for or portray themselves, and those who make the representations as more powerful and, usually, more virtuous. Marking the other as "vanishing," as in the case of Indigenous peoples, made both these processes of representation seem urgent as well as desirable, with anthropology, for example, moving to "salvage" both oral tradition and material culture from what was seen as the burning building of Indigenous culture. Painters like George Catlin (1796–1872), Paul Kane (1810–1871), and Cornelius Krieghoff (1815–1872); photographers like Edward S. Curtis (1868–1952); and anthropologists like Franz Boas (1858–1942), as well as travel writers, historians, collectors, poets, and novelists, all participated in the salvage that moved Indigenous cultural legacy into colonial writings, homes, museums, and archives. Certainly, these ventures preserved irreplaceable cultural goods, but only by appropriating them from their creators. This work was supported by the premise that Indigenous peoples, backward and beleaguered Others, require "rescue" by brave, virtuous, and competent white people, a rescue that almost invariably involves forcing or at least expecting Indigenous people to vanish into Western models of time, space, and culture by becoming Christian, adopting capitalist ideas, and moving into the "modern." Rudyard Kipling famously named this model of virtuous rescue "The White Man's Burden" in a poem that hailed young British men to risk their lives in colonial wars. The dominant culture authorizes this "burden," allowing those who take it up to avoid reflection on their actions while dedicating their lives to others who may neither want nor need such dedication. Lenore Keeshig-Tobias ends her poem "The White Man's Burden" this way: "PUT DOWN THE LOAD, STUPID" (267).

REPRESENTATIONS CRITICISM: TARGETING STEREOTYPES

What might be called "representations criticism" is a large and important body of work on stereotypes of Indians that sets out to rescue Indigenous peoples from bad representations (see Chamberlin, *Harrowing*; Francis; Goldie; Monkman; Thérien). These works quite rightly point out that Indigenous people are not the stereotypes about them, and that "Indians" were created by the fantasies of non-Natives in order to consolidate themselves as white. Atwood puts it this way: "The Indians and Eskimos have rarely been considered in and for themselves; they are usually made into projections of something in the white Canadian psyche, a fear or a wish" (*Survival* 91). This perspective, however, enables the critic to focus only on mainstream representations, rather than considering Indigenous people's perspectives and responses, which have often been seen as non-existent, inaccessible, or incomprehensible. For example, Terry Goldie declares in

Fear and Temptation: The Image of the Indigenene in Canadian, Australian, and New Zealand Literature (1989), "Regardless of Arnoldian claims for the freedom of the disinterested liberal critic, I question the right of any person to judge another's representation of his or her own culture" (217). This relativist stance dodges some arrows by refusing the unmarked position of privileged white judge, but it also absolves critics from the task of reading or hearing the Other's words, since one cannot do this without using some sort of judgment.[25] Without such interaction and judgment, however, the walls between "cultures" become higher and thicker, the categories they demarcate more and more "real." Every culture is seen as a pre-existent and separate homogeneous category unaffected by others, with which it should not be compared. Nor do dominant cultural producers in this relativist model have to justify their ways of thinking in relation to those of non-dominant groups. Despite the value of representations criticism in the early stages of trying to decolonize the minds of the majority, it may suggest that the stereotype masks a true representation, that these critics can reveal it (or, like Goldie, refrain from doing so), and that once the false representations are debunked, the authentic Indigenous person will magically appear (see Latour, "Why").

Debunking stereotypical representations has positive effects, but this way of reading can quickly isolate the values and people it is intended to promote in ways that replicate the apartheid of the reserve system. Representations critics do not actually have to convey what they have learned from those they position as victims: indeed, part of their victimhood (or subalternhood) is their inability to speak or be heard. In other words, such criticism may be blind to the risk of reconsolidating the Us/Them binary, placing Us (the implied white readers) on the side of the knowledgeable rescuer, and Them as authentic, an Essence that will appear once we have cleared away the bad representations. This (fantasy) Authentic Indian then will stabilize the identity of the (fantasy) Authentic (white) Canadian.

Whiteness studies scholars note that this virtuous production of the Other is one way that whiteness is consolidated (Wiegman 159–60). (Other ways are more obvious, such as racial insults or violent attacks.) Julie Rak warns against "a kind of discourse that works to make the non-native author invisible while forcing the native 'object' of knowledge to perform in visible ways" (153). Indeed, as Robin Wiegman points out in *Object Lessons*, entire fields of study can work this way. What she calls "identity-based fields of study ... emerged as a consequence of the rise of identity as a social force in the twentieth century" (2). Among these fields were women's studies, queer studies, ethnic studies, and Indigenous studies. She describes their "daunting" hope: "[I]f only we find the right discourse, object of study or analytic tool, our critical practice will be adequate to the political commitments that inspire it" (3). Unfortunately, as she demonstrates, these fields also consolidate and authenticate identities in the problematic ways described above. One can see these fields as institutions formed out of the desire to forward social justice for oppressed groups, a desire that also produces a virtuous white identity. As part of their nearly invisible work, these discourses reinstall the (implicitly white) academic critic and the university itself on the moral high ground as central to the achievement of social justice. That said, despite the inertial weight of academic traditions, positions are now being filled in the academy by students, staff, and professors from Indigenous backgrounds who present a range of perspectives previously excluded from the institutional discourse.

PERFORMANCE AND PERFORMATIVITY

Performance theory has emerged as a way to rethink the fixity of the identity model. If sovereignty is not simply something one *has* but rather something that one performs, as Indigenous thinkers like Taiaiake Alfred, John Borrows, Glen Coulthard, Bonita Lawrence, and Tracey Lindberg argue, the conversation moves along. Rather than being authenticated by such supposedly fixed markers such as appearance, blood quantum, or legal status, individuals will move into the social and political world as political actors who *choose* to articulate a particular standpoint (see Harding, *Sciences* 37). This means that Belaney can be seen as having lived most of his adult life as if he were "part Indian," rather than as a fraud who "really" was an Englishman. Similarly, Johnson's career can be read as a performance of the problems with ideas of fixed identity that faced her and other Indigenous women. This perspective accords with the notion that no one has a fixed identity, but rather that we produce our identities within the constraints of our family histories and our social locations, mobilizing our desires to connect with a variety of communities in complex ways. Of course, this shift brings with it new complications, as we shall see.

As Foucault explains his method, which he calls genealogy, "Genealogy does not seek to define our unique threshold of emergence, the homeland to which metaphysicians promise a return: it seeks to make visible all those discontinuities that cross us" (*Foucault Reader* 95). This resistance to the idea of pure homelands allows those people previously disenfranchised by colonization from an "authorized" identity the chance to work themselves into one *after* the moment the egg meets the sperm. Indigenous people who were adopted out or who grew up in foster care, whose parents concealed their background, who went to residential school and had their cultures and languages denied and insulted, or who ended up on the street in cities without any kin network should not be further disqualified from Indigenousness by those more fortunate, or at least with more boxes ticked on some invisible authenticity checklist. The conception of identity as performance allows people to self-constitute as Indigenous, as many cultural producers and scholars have actually done, performing themselves into existence by "making visible" the "discontinuities" that they face in daily life in Canada. That the idea of "having" an "authentic" identity can be a divisive trap explains Judith Butler's move to envisage political solidarity outside identity categories: "The foundational reasoning of identity politics tends to assume that an identity must first be in place in order for political interests to be elaborated and, subsequently, political action to be taken. My argument is that there need not be a 'doer behind the deed,' but that the 'doer' is variably constructed in and through the deed" (*Gender Trouble* 181). The retroactive work of rethinking this discourse of authentic identity and its relationship to land, a rethinking that involves recognizing Indigenous epistemologies and political positions, remains to be done.

The main fear of deconstructing the notion of authentic identity is, of course, that this move will further erode Indigenous claims to land by blurring what have been seen as real categories grounded in law or biology. However, the state has managed to use these categories to disenfranchise individuals with strong—even impeccable—claims to Indigenous rights. To rely on such categories to determine Indigenous rights without contextualizing them in past histories and legal agreements is also dangerous.

Of course, the easiest way out of these entanglements for settlers is to claim that one's love for (a stereotyped) Indigenous culture makes one Indigenous; Goldie has called this quick and easy way to collapse the difference between settler and Indian "indigenization" (13). Others have labelled this move, less politely, "white wannabeism." In this move, the settler vanishes the Indian by self-constituting *as* Indian, claiming Indigenous knowledge and Indigenous land along with this "magic" of identification. Carried out at the personal level, this move, which I discuss more fully in the chapter on Grey Owl, can have consequences ranging from trivial to serious.

Versions of this move, however, also ground some institutions. In a sense, the founding of anthropology as a discipline was a high-level form of this move: civilized white people were situated as able to know more about

Indigenous cultures than Indigenous people could ever know about themselves.[26] This book, like all books by non-Indigenous people about Indigenous issues, negotiates this problematic ethical ground. My hope is to reveal the discontinuities that cross me by reading particular texts, rather than to consolidate an identity or claim a homeland. I try to resist producing my own set of "performing Indians" by clarifying my investments insofar as I can. What knowledge this book contains is written from the standpoint of someone raised as a white settler Canadian, however much reading I have done. Of course, my readings emerge from a set of constraining discourses, just as the texts I read have been. I read the texts I discuss as open to further interpretation, rather than closed by my authoritative judgments. I read the critical reception of these texts over time to show how critics are often heavily invested in consolidating white settler nationalist identity and ideas. I try to foreground my impulses to rescue, control, and homogenize conflicting and unruly texts to produce a consolidated imaginary homeland.

As Louis Riel demonstrated, one can speak boldly to disagree with others and still maintain an attitude of respect for them. He argued for conversation rather than critique, for putting things together rather than tearing them down (see Latour, "Compositionist"). To do this, I have had to engage in wide interdisciplinary reading. As a result, I am often out of my depth in conversations with political theorists, geographers, historians, legal scholars, and anthropologists, as well as several distinctive Indigenous national cultural and intellectual traditions. Despite my focus on land and land claims, I found I could not read such a variety of textual genres (novels, courtroom addresses, spoken poetry, animal tales, autobiography, oral story, and contemporary historical, literary-critical, and theoretical accounts) produced across such a range of time by such different writers and speakers all in the same way. One danger of hewing to a single theoretical perspective is that critical approaches evolve historically in ways that can hide continuing colonization. For example, Gayatri Spivak (*Critique* 1, 7), Rey Chow (*Protestant* 15), and Thomas King ("Godzilla" 184–85) have pointed out that postcolonial literary criticism can easily become an alibi, a way of consolidating one's identity while distancing oneself from any connection to colonial oppression. Feminist standpoint theory argues that "strong objectivity" is achieved by testing ideas from multiple perspectives, rather than by purifying them of the marks of the social struggle that produces all important ideas (Harding, *Feminist Standpoint* 127–42). Hubert Zapf, a cultural ecologist, argues that "the evolutionary principle of ecological diversity should be recognized for ... different forms of knowledge as they have evolved historically, both between and within cultures" (850). A diverse range of textual forms clearly can be adapted to staking or resisting a land claim. Thus I have used approaches grounded in deconstruction, new rhetorical genre theory, feminist standpoint theory, postcolonial theory, eco-critical theory, and science and technology studies, as well as theories now being formulated by Indigenous scholars, such as Indigenous literary nationalism and kinship criticism. Often, because it formed me, I find myself writing both with and against Canadian literary nationalist approaches.

The question of the land has not been resolved. So at this point, the dilemma is whether to continue to insist that there is only one viable law, British, now Canadian law, or to admit that there were nations with law on this continent before Europeans arrived. To do so entails decolonizing Canadian law (see Borrows, *Drawing*), because as the Supreme Court points out, "the Crown must act honourably. Nothing less is required if we are to achieve 'the reconciliation of the pre-existence of aboriginal societies with the sovereignty of the Crown'" (*Haida Nation v. British Columbia*). That the Supreme Court feels obligated to state these principles with such force is grounded on a fact that Richardson and all the other writers I discuss make clear: the Crown (that is, its fallible human representatives) has not behaved honourably. If the honour of the Crown cannot be restored, we remain a society where might and money trump honour and the rule of law. At this point, I may seem to have strayed far from literature. However, literature, as we shall see, deals with such issues all the time. Recent books of Canadian literary criticism with titles that contain the words "unsettled," "haunted," "worrying," and "troubling" certainly attest to this power (Goldman; Gunew, *Haunted*; Kerzer; Reder and Morra; Sugars and Turcotte). But to feel haunted is not enough (nor do these critics suggest as much, I quickly add). Daniel Coleman, paraphrasing Slavoj Žižek, argues that settler Canadians have worked on "the elaboration of a symbolic history that masks its obscene supplement, what he calls its spectral, fantasmatic history" (*White Civility* 28). This obscene supplement is the history of colonization. If literary studies are to take Indigenous oratures and literatures seriously without either appropriating them or segregating them into the corners of the curriculum and the margins of research, the discipline will have to consider how its borders and its methods have been formed as part of the production of this symbolic history. If we cannot rethink the Romantic nationalist critical ideas that have had such a firm grip on Canadian literary studies for so long, we support continuing colonization. If we do not accept that there are other worldviews that we need to learn about and respect, we support continuing colonization. Iroquois people were reading *Paradise Lost* and Pope's translation of Homer at the turn of the eighteenth century (B.F. Edwards, *Paper Talk* 86): literary scholars in Canada need to demonstrate a reciprocal critical interest.

Chapter Two

"Why Did They Take Our Hunting Grounds?": John Richardson (1796–1852) Laments for the Nation

> When we go to the Rockies we may have the sense that the gods are there. But if so, they cannot manifest themselves to us as ours. They are the gods of another race, and we cannot know them because of what we are, and what we did. There can be nothing immemorial for us except the environment as object.

> *George Grant,* Lament for a Nation *(17)*

TALE OF TWO WARS

Writing *Wacousta* (*W*; 1832) in London, John Richardson was immersed in discourses depicting Indians as exotic savages.[1] He could imagine settler–Indigenous relations differently from the discourses of the imperial centre, however, because of his experiences in Canada, growing up immersed in stories of Pontiac's War, the American War of Independence, and the War of 1812. He said his inspiration came from James Fenimore Cooper's *The Last of the Mohicans* (1826), stating that he "absolutely devoured" the novel "three times" (*W* 581). However, his interconnected novels, *Wacousta* and *The Canadian Brothers* (*CB*; 1840), unlike Cooper's, hit an impasse with respect to the future. This impasse is marked at the end of *The Canadian Brothers* by images of abjection: the death of Tecumseh and the vision of the "picked and whitened bones" of his hero, Henry Grantham, lying unburied at the bottom of the Niagara gorge, mingled with those of his killer (2: 473). For Richardson, these deaths marked the end of Indigenous sovereignty and of the nascent Canada, its distinctiveness as a nation destroyed by its inability to maintain an honourable relationship with Indigenous peoples. Even the title of *The Last of the Mohicans* suggests that the disappearance of the Native American sets the stage for the birth of a new nation. Richardson's logic based the survival of Canada as distinctive from the United States on the continuing honourable treatment of the Native American. He made the distinction rest on Canada's enacting a more ethical relationship than what he called the American "war of extermination" against Indigenous people (*CB* 1: 20). Once that distinction disappeared, a distinction that depended on the survival rather than the extermination of Indigenous people, so did Canada.

That these novels and many of Richardson's other works, literary, historical, and autobiographical, focus on the relations between Indigenous peoples and the British is hardly surprising, since his maternal grandfather, the fur trader John Askin (1739–1815), had lived and worked in the "contact zone" near Detroit since arriving in North America as a young man. Richardson grew up listening to the tales of his (step-)grandmother, who had been in Fort Detroit during the siege led by Pontiac (*W* 585).[2] Richardson and sixteen close relatives, including his father, a British army surgeon, fought in the War of 1812, all but one of them on the British side (Quaife 12). Richardson tells the story twice of his last contact with Tecumseh, leader of the Indigenous allies. In his history, *War of 1812*, Richardson writes that just before the Battle of Moraviantown, Tecumseh "pressed the hand of each officer as he passed, made some remark in Shawnee, appropriate to the occasion, which was sufficiently understood by the expressive signs accompanying them, and then passed away forever from our view" (212). In *The Canadian Brothers*, he writes, "Tecumseh passed along the line, expressing in animated language the delight he felt at the forthcoming struggle, and when he had shaken hands with most of the officers (we fancy we can feel the generous pressure of his fingers even at this remote period) he moved into the dense forest where his faithful bands were lying concealed" (2: 436). This encouraging and long-remembered handshake preceded an ignominious defeat for the British; a traumatic year as prisoner of war for Richardson, who had just turned seventeen; and Tecumseh's death. Released and his health recovered, Richardson boarded a troopship bound for England in 1815, arriving just too late to fight against Napoleon at Waterloo. He returned to Canada only in 1838, sent to report on the rebellions of 1837–1838 in the Canadas for the *Times* of London.[3] Richardson, like his character Colonel D'Egville, felt "pride in having received my being in a land where every thing attests to the sublimity and magnificence of nature" (1: 41). However, his pride was conditional on the just treatment of Canada's loyal allies. For him, Tecumseh's handshake symbolized the honourable relationship between Indigenous people and white settlers that Canada would prove unable to maintain in the face of American influence.[4]

MAJOR JOHN RICHARDSON.

FIG. 2 Major John Richardson, Knight of San Fernando,
Frederick Lock, 1848; Engraving (after 1902), Library and
Archives Canada MIKAN 4310431.

Wacousta and *The Canadian Brothers* together recount the history
of two wars and of two Indigenous leaders, the Ottawa chief, Pontiac (c.
1720–1769), and the Shawnee chief, Tecumseh (1768–1813).[5] Pontiac was
the most famous of the leaders of the war against the British after the Conquest of New France in 1759. Tecumseh recruited and led the largest group
of Indigenous allies of the British in the War of 1812. Each novel includes a
discussion of the rights and wrongs of the war by leaders from both sides.
In *Wacousta*, Pontiac and the governor of the besieged Fort Detroit engage
in parley, surrounded by their men (186–207, 223–33). In *Canadian Brothers*, the discussion takes place at the dinner table of Colonel D'Egville, the
fictional "superintendent of Indian affairs" and a Canadian (87), with some
of the historical British leaders of the War of 1812 and a fictional American

prisoner, Major Montgomerie. Tecumseh and his fellow chiefs are present (1: 67–94). In *Wacousta*, Colonel de Haldimar and Pontiac converse in Ottawa (187); in *Canadian Brothers*, the chiefs are hampered by their lack of English (1: 84). In the fifty years between the two wars, Indigenous leaders have been moved out of any direct participation in the lively political conversation about the Indian land question.

Still, it remains possible to recompose these novels to see beyond the end that Richardson predicted for Indigenous people here: "With … the death of Tecumseh, perished the last hope of the Indians to sustain themselves as a people against the inroads of their oppressors" (*CB* 2: 437). Since the war was essentially a stalemate, this defeatist conclusion refers to more than the enemy Americans: implicitly these "oppressors" are also Canadian. Rather than succumbing to the apocalyptic paroxyms of white guilt represented by Henry's plummet off the cliffs of Niagara, however, perhaps it is possible to return more patiently to a new conversation about the problems of racialization and land rights that have not vanished since Richardson struggled with them.

Despite the depressing ending of *The Canadian Brothers*, Richardson clearly hoped that his writing would move Canadians to resume earlier practices of treating Indigenous people as equals under the British Crown, as in annual gift-giving ceremonies.[6] This treatment, obviously, is not the same as admitting their sovereignty, but neither is it the same as reducing them to wards, the policy that led to the passage of the Act to Encourage the Gradual Civilization of the Indian Tribes in 1857. Richardson's work can usefully be revisited to examine the impasse he encountered and to see how his work has been written into a continuing literary discourse on Canadian identity.

CANADA'S GOTHIC HISTORY

Wacousta is a mix between a thrilling gothic romance and a historical novel. Ann Radcliffe, queen of the gothic, died in 1823; Scott's *Waverley*, the first British historical novel, was published in 1814. Despite Richardson's admiration for Cooper, critics have noted how different *Wacousta* is from *The Last of the Mohicans* (1826; see Ballstadt, *Major* 3). One major difference is Richardson's use of gothic tropes, best exemplified by the curse itself, whereas in Cooper's more realist account, success is built on Natty Bumppo's practical knowledge. Described as racially pure "without a cross" (63), "the honest but implacable woodsman" (197) provides a model for white American identity, whereas Richardson's two novels provide less straightforward identifications for Canadian readers. Dennis Duffy comments, "The prophecy, in reality a curse, indicates how hollow are the promises of new moral eras" like Cooper's (*World* 20). He notes that "Cooper offered Richardson a linear model of progress; Richardson would warp it into an arc of disillusionment" (36). This arc can be connected to larger patterns in Canadian literature.

Robert Stacey has suggested that Georg Lukać's model of the historical novel, which requires an organic link between past and present, does not fit Canada, where "declarations of an essentially pathological relationship between history and cultural production are not at all uncommon" (53). Richardson's use of the gothic to offset the historical may well reflect this pathology. Earle Birney's famous poem about Canadian literature suggests that it suffers from the repression of colonial history: "[I]t's only by our lack of ghosts we're haunted" ("Can. Lit."). Many of Canada's ghosts are the ghosts of those, both white and Indigenous, killed in a land grab.

The difficulty critics have found in interpreting Richardson's mix of gothic and "national epic" arises from the difficulty of Richardson's attempted social action. Carolyn R. Miller, a new rhetorical genre theorist, argues that genre is a form of social action: "[A] rhetorically sound definition of genre must be centered not on the substance or the form of discourse but on the action it is used to accomplish" (151). Richardson wrote not only to celebrate the origins of settler Canada, but also to celebrate the vital role of Indigenous people in the early history of British colonization and of Tecumseh and his allies in saving Canada from becoming part of the United States.[7] By 1840 this viewpoint was not welcome; by this time tropes of savagery had frozen into truths supportive of the dispossession of all Indigenous nations, irrespective of their histories. Richardson's use of the gothic undercut the clear trajectory of the historical novel from past to present; in his novel, identities are unstable, concealed by disguises; the sequence of events becomes arbitrary, even nightmarish. The excesses of the gothic move the text into the parodic and allow readers a shadowy glimpse of the otherwise imperceptible limits of the dominant discourse.

In new rhetorical genre theory, genres form out of recurrent situations (Lloyd Bitzer's "exigences"), which in this case are the continuing moral and political conflicts arising out of the colonization of North America. Many critics have pointed to the prevalence of the gothic in Canadian literature, most notably Northrop Frye, with his characterization of Canadian literature as marked by a "deep terror in regard to nature" (*Bush Garden* 225).[8] However, this terror has not often been explicitly tied to the obliterated history of settler/invader land theft and related injustices. Cynthia Sugars and Gary Turcotte, however, remark in 2009 that "[g]othic projections onto a purportedly unsettled 'wilderness' were often used to express the settler-invader's alienation from the New World territory that had been appropriated by illegitimate means" (xii). Frye acknowledged this appropriation only indirectly when he said in 1977 that "[w]e are no longer an army of occupation and the natives are ourselves" (*Divisions* 69). Presumably this movement from terror to identification would require the taming of both wild nature and sovereign ("wild") Indigenous people: "we" would finally have overcome our "garrison mentality." But Frye's oracular statement bases this amazing transformation on the evidence of a few settler writers who have appropriated Indigenous themes. Nor does he report any opinions from the Indigenous people who are no longer, apparently, native. Did they go voluntarily?

Some critics, unsurprisingly, are not so sure that this transformation has taken place. Just after the Kanehsatake resistance against the town of Oka, the Sûreté du Québec, and the Canadian armed forces in 1990, Lee Maracle wrote, "Canadians must get out of the fort and imagine something beyond the colonial condition" ("Postcolonial" 206). Getting out of the fort means both imagining and enacting decolonization. In the gothic, living humans attempt to communicate with the spectral dead, a communication that cannot succeed using reason alone. As Jodey Castricano notes, the gothic was, even in its heyday, "an aesthetically disavowed and morally repudiated genre," not least because it "deals in the epistemological and ontological aporias apparent in the totalizing gestures in Enlightenment value and thought." Richardson's depiction of the forest outside the forts in *Wacousta* as terrifying only for the British, while the Indigenous people and the French travel freely through it, makes it clear that for him the fort represented the constructed sociopolitical distinctions that had led to the genocidal nightmare of colonial wars of extermination. Since these distinctions rationalize rather than settle the claim to land, the dead from these wars cannot rest, cannot be accommodated by national history. And so they continue to haunt us.

Like George Grant in his *Lament for a Nation* (1965), albeit for different reasons, Richardson wrote despairingly that the moment for Canada to become a nation had already passed.[9] In his case, the despair came from his feeling that Canadians had become no different from Americans in their racism. As with Grant, some writers and critics found his depressive stance inspiring of a reconfigured nationalism. As Coleman puts it in *White Civil-*

ity, Richardson's "jeremiad of botched origins" could inspire by its negative example "a reassertion of the nation's better self—its higher, whiter enterprise" (67). Even though Richardson made it clear that the British victory depended on the Indigenous men they recruited as military allies in the War of 1812 (*CB* 1: 88; see also Colley 231), his novels can be read as establishing an early version of the self-justifying belief of white settler Canadians that "we" have always treated "our Indians" better than the Americans treated "theirs." Nationalists made a virtue out of this military necessity. Frye, for example, remarks in 1977, "Canada does not have quite so heavy a burden of guilt toward red and black peoples as the United States, and the French record with the Indians is rather better than the British or the Spanish record" (*Divisions* 68).[10] However, what Atwood describes as Canadians' "slightly better track record" (*Survival* 92) than the Americans in the historical treatment of Indigenous people was for Richardson ultimately not enough to keep the distinction between the two nations from collapsing.

TRANSATLANTIC INDIANS

Richardson's work emerged from a rapidly changing literary and sociopolitical discourse on both sides of what Timothy Fulford and Kevin Hutchings have called the "Indian Atlantic" (1) and David Armitage and Jace Weaver the "Red Atlantic." "Romantic Indians" flourished between 1756 and 1830, according to Fulford, during a period when "generic and idealized noble savages" of earlier literary representation became "complex, ambivalent, and detailed portraits" (17; see also Dickason; Ellingson; Liebersohn). A wide array of writers—including Samuel Taylor Coleridge, Samuel Johnson, Tom Paine, Robert Rogers, Robert Southey, and William Wordsworth—wrote positive portraits that aimed to inspire the British elite with a more enlightened attitude toward colonization and the people with a model of courage and resistance to tyranny (Fulford 24). However, the terror in France turned the Romantic writers from a revolutionary to a reform model of change (205–7), and the War of Independence turned the British public against using "savages" as allies in wars against the Americans, who, after all, were fellow Britons.[11] Indigenous people began to be depicted either as innately bloodthirsty or as pitiably weak and corrupted. A nascent scientific racism incorporated them into its taxonomies (Baum; Hudson). To destabilize the stereotype of the savage, even with the currency of Richardson's personal experience, was a near-impossible task. Even more difficult was finding uptake for a history that made Tecumseh and his fellow chiefs into founders of Canada when the settler elite was hastily obliterating Native land title.

THE CANADIAN CRITICAL RESPONSE

Richardson's complex works have received contradictory interpretations. D.M.R. Bentley, for example, comments on "his highly sympathetic view of the Native peoples as essentially blameless victims of European aggression" (*Mimic* 145), while others see his depictions of them as almost entirely negative. Indeed, Emma LaRocque argues that *Wacousta* should not be taught at all except as an example of hate literature (59). This disparity in reception may well reflect Richardson's own ambivalence about the settler–Indigenous relationship.

According to Michael Hurley, *Wacousta* and *The Canadian Brothers* can be seen as together forming both a "national epic" *and* its "parody" (24). This idea is connected to Linda Hutcheon's notion that parody can "both legitimize and subvert that which it parodies" (*Politics* 101). Critics from Alexander Clark Casselman (1902) to Daniel Coleman (2006; *White Civility*) have taken up the nationalist implications of these novels. Few, however, have read them as parody. Both novels are situated in the genre of the "prophecy" in their subtitles (*The Prophecy: A Tale of the Canadas* and *The Prophecy Fulfilled: A Tale of the Late American War*). The prophecy is, in fact, a dramatic curse of extermination laid on the descendants of Colonel de Haldimar, and by extension, on the nascent nation of Canada itself. Hurley asks, "Fourteen hundred and thirty pages later, is this 'national epic' telling us that there is no nation and no story to tell?" (25). However, presumably because of the anxiety around Canadian identity and claims to land, particularly during the formation of the field of Canadian literature in the 1970s, many readings skip or scant the "Indian land question" and read these novels into a positive settler-nationalist narrative.

Carl Ballstadt's introduction to *Major John Richardson: A Selection of Reviews and Criticism* (1972) notes that the early critics, both British and Canadian, "are all aware of the ambiguity of Richardson's Indians," which, he continues, is "testimony to the conviction and complexity with which he wrote. There are no simple romantic heroes and villains in *Wacousta*. Even though the plot of that novel and others may pivot on Indian massacres, the Indians are never one-dimensional, but are participants in a precarious struggle with other ambiguous characters" (3). In fact, other critics did find it possible to read Richardson's Indians as one-dimensional or even to overlook them. Much Canadian criticism was impelled by a desire to connect

Richardson to a progressive national literary history. James Reaney, who wrote a play titled *Wacousta!*, says he fell "in love with any and all of Richardson's stories" in part because he "had always been searching for a father figure to reverence as the progenitor of our tradition here in what Richardson calls 'the land of the Canadas'" (Afterword 586).[12] Like Reaney, critics often use Richardson as a point of origin (Moss 50; Michael Hurley 1–2), seeing his Loyalism as a "natural" precursor to their nationalism (Parkinson 454). His legacy is handed down from literary father to literary sons, a figure that incorporates the "natural" inheritance of land. Edward Parkinson points out that although troubled by the issue of distinguishing the truly loyal from the merely "land-hungry," critics "misrepresent how both desires are derived from the same structure of imperialism. The landowners participated in an economy of British mercantilism which has always been concerned with mapping, trading, mining, and acquiring land as property, so that to be 'loyal' is by definition, to be 'land-hungry'" (454). This distinction has always proved useful, however, in rationalizing why loyal representatives of the Crown have somehow never able to protect Indigenous people from the depredations of uncontrollable land-hungry settlers or, more recently, developers and resource extraction companies.

Loyalism and nationalism both require the naturalization of land ownership through literature, which explains both the title and the subtitle of Frye's *The Bush Garden: Essays on the Canadian Imagination*. Settlers transformed bush into garden while Canadian writers produced a national imaginary out of the "empty" wilderness. David Staines continued this narrative by using Frye's subtitle as the title of his important early critical collection, *The Canadian Imagination* (1977). For Romantics in Europe, the existence of a singular national imaginary (the *Volksgeist*) embodied in a great literature proved one's title to the land, a title figured as spiritual rather than material. Thus, literature demonstrated that one was not "land hungry," but rather spiritually tied to it, and, therefore, fit to govern justly. In settler colonies, a "haunted" land title combined with the lack of a unified culture or a sovereign state made the production of the required homogeneous national imaginary a complex and anxious process. Thus, there was a need for literary forefathers, particularly those who were writing in genres deemed most appropriate for a nation-building story such as the epic poem or the historical novel.

In 1978, Robin Mathews writes, "*Wacousta*, the first major novel to be written by an author born in this country, is at the centre of the Canadian imagination" (13). For Mathews, the novel works between the poles represented by its two major white characters, the noble Wacousta/Morton, representing American individualism/anarchism, and his enemy Colonel de Haldimar,[13] representing British law and order: "That is why Canadian experience and Canadian literature reveal that the battle is not between garrison and wilderness—a polite way of saying white man and native. The battle is between an alien exploiter or imperialist class and the settlers or community builders" (19). What is interesting to nationalist critics is the story of the emergence of a unified Canadian identity, often a story that simply avoids the whole issue of "garrison and wilderness" that was so important to Richardson's vision of Canada.

Other critics, like LaRocque, see Richardson's depiction of Indian characters as wholly negative. In 1981, Leslie Monkman writes, "The Indians in Richardson's novels are cast as demonic savages if they oppose whites' territorial designs" (11). After quoting a gruesome passage from one of Richardson's late novels, *Wau-nan-gee; Or, the Massacre at Chicago*, he concludes, "Intensifying the identification of the red man as savage in sensational images of animality and cannibalism, Richardson repeatedly exploits the threat and circumstances of Indian massacres for the same effects as those of contemporaries such as Goldsmith and Howe" (11).[14] Duffy, who has written extensively on Richardson, agrees with LaRocque and Monkman. He argues that *Wacousta* gives little or no explanation for Indian discontent, reducing their actions to the "predictable gestures of programmed robots" acting out of "motiveless malignity." He notes that "words like 'demonic' and 'infernal' sprinkle the text," assuring the "audience that no one needs to speculate on the motives for Indian-white enmity in the novel" (*Tale* 45–46). Of *Canadian Brothers*, he states, "Richardson's allies, a group that includes the hero Tecumseh, will be demonized. Their gestures become predictably violent, their conduct barbarous, their allegiance unreliable" (46). In *World under Sentence* (1996), he writes, "One side alone is capable of atrocity in Richardson's fiction. Any possibility for a display of humanity and reciprocity between the two races, unless it stem from (forbidden) erotic yearning or temporary alliance, goes missing. Not even evil is a matter for exchange between races. Rather it remains locked up on one side" (141). Given that Wacousta is, after all, the disguised Reginald Morton, a British nobleman who commits many atrocities while fighting as one of Pontiac's warriors, Duffy's assertions are rather sweeping. And indeed, it is the actions of the governor of Fort Detroit, Colonel de Haldimar, that elicit Ellen Halloway's curse. Ellen calls upon God to avenge his "devilish deed" (*W* 154)—the execution of her innocent husband—and it is avenged, with the last De Haldimar forced over the cliffs above Niagara Falls in the death grip of her and Morton's son, Jeremy Desborough (*CB* 2: 473). Evil is certainly not locked up on one side, if these three white men's actions count for anything at all.

Duffy's move here of taking over the moral high ground from Richardson with respect to his representation of Indians is a commonplace and tempting one in any field that deals with racialized relationships: "He not only repeatedly refers to Indians as savages ... but displays other racist habits of mind. This is why Pontiac and his confederates cannot mount the uprising on their own, but need a white advisor ... when that advisor goes, the Indians return to their usual aimlessness" (*Tale* 58). The word "racist," like "savage," is a morally and rhetorically loaded word intended to halt further discussion. But paradoxically, by situating Richardson's representations as one-sidedly racist, Duffy ends up repeating the act that he ascribes to Richardson. He reduces all the Indian characters in the novel to cardboard demons warring on the margins. In fact, Richardson points out that Pontiac and his allies fought to secure a relationship with the English that was as good as the one they had previously had with the French (*W* 250). Pontiac is depicted as making peace because he is pragmatic, rather than innately ferocious, misled, or aimless (250).[15]

ATTEMPTING AN IMPOSSIBLE RECONCILIATION

Perhaps not surprisingly, given their length and complex plotting, critical readings of these novels sometimes become self-contradictory. However, contradiction seems inherent in the colonial relations that both critics and novelist are all living with and writing about. What, then, would it mean to try to explain both these critical readings *and* the novels using the chiasmatic structure that Gayatri Spivak has called the "crossing of a double contradiction," a figure of (attempted but impossible) reconciliation between opposites ("Who Claims Alterity" 274–75)?[16] In *Native Heritage,* for example, Monkman's interpretation reveals a chiasmatic structure. Despite his remarks about "demonic savages," he does note that in *Wacousta* "positive and negative values are not simplistically assigned to white and red orders; what is important is the distance separating them" (22).[17] Then, like Duffy, he argues that Pontiac plays "only a secondary role": "The figure who transforms the savages into a 'legion of devils' and 'fiend-like bands' is Wacousta. This man, so consumed that he crossed the barriers between the civilized and the savage, becomes a larger-than-life satanic figure, exploiting the worst instincts of the savage Indians" (23). This statement shows the power of the established binary between "civilized" and "savage"; Monkman undermines its force by making it clear that a civilized, educated member of the minor nobility can both be *and* become a savage, and at the same time reinforces it with "barriers" and "distance" between the two states. Further, his statement shows how a pejorative name, "savage," makes it difficult to distinguish a people from a disposition to behave cruelly. Named thus, Indigenous people are condemned as a group, no matter how individual members behave. Wacousta, although more cruel than even the most cruel Indian, has to "cross the barriers" from civilized into savage territory in order to undertake his atrocities. Once there, he corrupts the Indians, who nonetheless are granted innate *instincts* that he arouses. (Monkman follows Richardson himself in ascribing "savage instincts" to the Indians [*W* 207].) Richardson cannot be looked to for a resolution, but rather, as Monkman's interpretation demonstrates, is better thought of as enacting, even forcing, contradictions that he cannot discursively resolve because his society is unwilling to resolve them. To resolve these contradictions would be to represent the British as savage invaders, something that even the disillusioned Richardson was unable to do, at least not until he had struggled to defer any such realization for fourteen hundred and thirty pages.

PERFORMING SAVAGERY

Spying on Wacousta as Pontiac recounts his plan to capture the fort, Frederick, the governor's son, "thought that he had never gazed on any thing wearing the human shape half so atrociously savage" (*W* 252). Discovered and captured, he addresses Wacousta, "There is no country in Europe that would willingly claim you for its subject. Nay, even the savage race, with whom you are now connected, would, if apprised of your true nature, spurn you as a thing unworthy to herd even with their wolf-dogs" (267). Wacousta's riposte is that he will be "the first to drink [Frederick's] blood" (269); Frederick retorts, "[F]iend! Monster! Devil!" (270). Notably, Richardson makes it clear in this passage that the "savage race" is, in fact, less savage than this disloyal British nobleman, since they would spurn him if they knew his past. Yet Wacousta still in many ways not only is savage, but represents the Savage, as well. His disguise and performance take on a reality even more powerful than that of the "real" Indians like Pontiac. Judith Butler argues that the excess of performances like drag or blackface reveal the constructedness of naturalized identities (*Gender Trouble* 146). The excessive language in this exchange, during which Wacousta does not drop his stereotypical mask, reveals how extreme the stereotypes of Indians had become, driven by the incomers' need to justify their own savagery and to maintain support for brutal (and expensive) colonial wars.

Discursive binaries bedevil any reading of Indigenous–white relations, in part because these categories are constructs that enforce a moral charge: the instant the categories are invoked, the ethical war begins. Monkman talks about Wacousta crossing the barrier between civilized Briton and savage Indian, but dressing and acting as an Indian do not *make* him an Indian— so, in fact, his actions should show that the binary is purely imaginary. But if we agree with Butler that identity is performed rather than innate, he *is* an Indian to the degree that his performance is convincing.[18] That his savage nature is seen *as* "Indian" in recent literary criticism shows the power of particular performances or representations of identity. David R. Beasley writes, "The Indian side of Wacousta's personality expresses the deep restless hatred of the Indian tribes for the militant whites usurping their lands" (*Canadian Don Quixote* 65). Apparently, all his negative emotions come from the "Indian" persona that he has adopted purely in order to take revenge on De Haldimar. John Moss says, "Wacousta, himself, is virtually a half-breed" (107). Jennifer Andrews refers to him as "the man who has become part-Indian" (211), and says that for Michael Hurley, "he epitomizes the Native Canadian outsider" (213). All these remarks describe a British man who was savage long before he donned buckskins. Yet his "savagery" still clings to the "Indian" side of the binary, which in turn attaches to real Indigenous people, assigned to this category no matter what their opinions or behaviour might be. Critical assertions such as the ones I have quoted demonstrate how this discursive binary acts to preserve the blamelessness of colonizers, even those who perform vicious and brutal acts.

Wacousta's performance also works inside the text. Pontiac, following the Ottawa custom of adopting captured women and children and those men who demonstrate the requisite courage, makes him his heir. He has been brought into the kinship network just as were Alexander Henry, whose Ojibwa brother Wawatum saved his life during Pontiac's War (Armour), and the Cherokee Scot John Norton, who fought in the War of 1812 as Joseph Brant's heir (Klinck, "Biographical" xliv). Richardson's depiction of the performance of identity, one that entails "Indian acquirements" (*W* 527), is working the notion of identity as learned, performed, and socially legitimated against the notion of identity based on ancestry, blood, or birthright. His fascination with these issues may derive from his upbringing in a culture that accepted marriages (variously defined) between Indigenous women and European men and allowed far greater flexibility in social roles than the highly stratified society he found in Europe, grounded on legislated blood relationships and social hierarchy and full of what he termed "English exclusive[s]" (CB 1: 67) and "Bond Street exquisite[s]" (1: 22).

Hurley, despite his insight into how gothic excess produces what he calls "break boundaries" similar to chiasmus, concludes that Richardson is depicting a "balanced pull" between opposites (31–32): "[T]he Europeans are as doomed as the Indians" (154). He does not even mention Pontiac or Tecumseh as individual fictional characters. In the context of Cooper and Scott he says,

> Wacousta's focus is not on the last of the Mohicans or the Jacobites, the last of the Ponteacs or the Oucanastas (who live on); it is the last of the De Haldimars and Mortons, the twin founding families of a precarious culture. Both perish in the War of 1812, a battle which Richardson, to his lasting dismay as veteran, historian, and artist, realized should have catalysed, but did not, a sense of separate national identity. (154)

This reading ignores Richardson's assertion that the death of Tecumseh marked the end of Indigenous sovereignty. Hurley represents the Indians as "living on" while the "precarious" founding families perish, almost suggesting that colonization did not actually happen. These critical readings enact the power of a long-established binary to direct interpretation in purifying ways.

THE ABJECT IMPASSE OF SAVAGERY

In Wacousta, the word "savage" is often used as the "neutral" or "unmarked" descriptor it had by then so usefully become. This neutrality is indicated in its frequent re-marking with negative modifiers, as in "black savages" (64) or "blood-thirsty savages" (309). The term is also frequently applied to Wacousta, even after the reader suspects he is a European (he is described as having the "sun-burnt skin of one of a … temperate clime" rather than "the copper-coloured flesh of the Indian" when first described in the novel [134], and he speaks in "the purest English accent" shortly afterwards [154]). Even after his "true" identity has been revealed, he is described as a "vast savage" (244); he even calls himself "a savage in both garb and character" (270), thus drawing attention to the slippage in the word between a descriptor for a people and for any cruel person motivated by rage and hatred.

The stereotype of the savage, whose name implied innate violence, allowed the violence enacted by the colonizers to be overlooked as an exception or rationalized as driven by "higher" goals. As David Murray points out, the "gifts" of the Christian religion and Western civilization were seen as so valuable that they outweighed the cruelty of the colonizers (18, and *passim*). One of the first plays acted in the New World, *Le théâtre de Neptune*, written by Marc Lescarbot and performed in 1602 for Samuel de Champlain and other leaders at Port Royal, already uses this logic. In one scene, Indians give gifts to the French leader: "The four gifts represent the natural wealth of New France (game, furs and clothing, precious stones, fish) which the natives are characterized as willingly offering in return for the blessings of European 'civilization' and aesthetic refinement" (Castillo 164).[19] The colonizers, acting in the name of these immaterial blessings, could also overlook their own dependence on Indigenous people for food and their use of a vast array of knowledge and technologies that were "borrowed" from Indigenous cultures without acknowledgement (see Newhouse, Voyageur, and Beavon; Weatherford). This view of the history of colonization as ultimately and inevitably positive, even if temporarily vicious and cruel, cannot be countered simply by pointing to white atrocities and depicting Indigenous people as blameless victims (that is, by flipping the binary), but must be rewritten to show Indigenous–white relations as complex, mediated, and situated in specific localities. This, I argue, is how Richardson tried to work, bolstering and nuancing the position set out in his literary works in his history, *War of 1812* (1842), and his autobiographical writings, *Eight Years in Canada* (1846) and "A Trip to Walpole Island and Port Sarnia" (1849). One of the ways he rewrites the story of settler colonization as the gift of civilization to an inferior race is by drawing an analogy between the Jacobite Rebellions and the Indigenous wars, and granting the Indigenous people the same rights to defend their lands as those of any other nation. The hero of Upper Canada, General Isaac Brock, defended the rights of the Indigenous allies to fight as "men, [with] equal rights with all other men to defend themselves and their property when invaded" (qtd. in Richardson, *War* 19). In *The Canadian Brothers*, the Canadian leader Colonel D'Egville states that Tecumseh is struggling "for his country's liberty" (1:79). "Liberty" was a word that resonated, given not only its allusion to the American Revolution, but also the rebellions that broke out in Upper and Lower Canada just before Richardson's return.

THE THEFT OF INDIAN LAND

Of *Wacousta*, Carole Gerson says that "local history forms only the skeleton of Richardson's novel, which he fleshes out with a romantic narrative motivated entirely by rivalries transplanted from Europe" (*Purer Taste* 86; see MacLulich for a similar opinion). However, colonial histories and European rivalries are not easy to separate. The history of Canada and the romantic plot vitally converge in the character of Reginald Morton/Wacousta. Although Morton is motivated purely by his desire for vengeance on Governor de Haldimar for "stealing" his fiancée, his personal goals align with the Indigenous warriors' fight to protect their land. And the plot of his personal revenge in *Wacousta* is itself closely tied to another continuing colonial struggle over land, that between the Scots and the English.

Morton's desire for revenge dates from a time when he and Charles de Haldimar, both junior British officers, were serving in Scotland to maintain peace after the Jacobite Rebellion of 1745. The rebels had aimed to end the Union of England and Scotland and put "Bonnie Prince Charlie" on the Scottish throne. Morton discovers the beautiful Clara, a near prisoner on the estate of her father, a reclusive veteran of the 1715 Jacobite Rebellion. With her consent and the expectation of marriage, he carries her off. He asks his friend De Haldimar to take care of her, saying she is his cousin, so that he can make wedding arrangements. Instead De Haldimar quickly marries her and then has Morton court-martialled to silence his protests. Since Clara dies before Morton can enact his revenge, he vows to kill all three of the De Haldimar children, Frederick, Charles, and Clara, in front of their father, a threat that he very nearly fulfills. Only Frederick survives to marry his cousin Madeleine, a happy ending that is overshadowed by the prophecy (although only for those readers who persist with the sequel). The gothic revenge plot and the historical plot run together, in that Morton/Wacousta figures both as part of a European homosocial triangle (see Sedgewick), where he contends with De Haldimar for Clara, and an Indian plot, where he is Pontiac's most powerful warrior and chosen heir, opposed by Oucanasta and her brother, as well as De Haldimar and the British. These plots can be pulled apart only by recognizing him as British and motivated by personal revenge, something that is revealed only well into the novel.

This dishonourable taking of a woman and the discrediting of a friend and fellow officer by "the book," rather than through a face-to-face confrontation, Morton argues, is wrong. Pontiac similarly protests against British behaviour in taking Canada. Pontiac's main complaint, which he makes directly to De Haldimar, is that the English did not honour their promises:

If the settlers of the Saganaw have fallen, it is because they did not keep faith with the red skins. When they were weak, and not yet secure in their strong holds, their tongues were smooth and full of soft words; but when they became strong under the protection of their thunder, they no longer treated the red skins as their friends, and they laughed at them for letting them come into their country. (*W* 198)

The failure to keep promises is at the heart of the Indian land question. Thus, the marriage plot can be read as allegory of colonization on several grounds. Clara's Jacobite father was one of those who saw the Act of Union of 1707, an agreement endorsed by both parliaments, as nonetheless invalidated by English bribery and threats. If Clara symbolizes Scotland, her marriage to De Haldimar represents its "legal" takeover. However, Morton believes that he has been betrayed. Although his anger and brutality are clearly condemned in the text, they are motivated, he argues, by De Haldimar's underhandedness. For Morton, personal honour and loyalty are more important than the letter of the law, which can always be perverted by power. Although analogies between events in Scotland in 1715 and 1745 and those in Canada in 1763 and 1812 might not occur to modern readers, when Richardson published his novel the Jacobite Rebellions were still a vivid memory. And anyone who read novels at all read Scott's *Waverley* (1814) and *Rob Roy* (1817) (see Bautz).

Richardson makes it clear at the beginning of *Wacousta* that Pontiac's War began over land; increasing settlement caused "numerous tribes of Indians" to move west, rendering "all the more central parts of those stupendous wilds ... doubly peopled" (8). The issue of land in *Wacousta* is presumably "settled" as it was in the historical negotiations that followed the war. Land theft hovers over the plot, however, at the metaphorical level. As Annette Kolodny points out in *The Lay of the Land*, the conquest of a feminized territory by men is a commonplace literary trope. Indeed the representation of nations as allegorical women (Britannia, Liberty, Marianne, Janey Canuck, etc.) and their relations to male citizens as analogous to patriarchal heterosexual relations drives the logic of war. Thus, young men are encouraged to defend their feminized country against "rape," and, by implication, to rape ("possess") the women of the enemy (figured as the "property" of men), as well as to conquer and possess their enemy's country. As noted, critical discussions of *Wacousta* have often delinked the "personal" gothic plot deriving from the sexual rivalry of Morton and De Haldimar and the "political" historical plot set in Canada. Such delinking also recurs frequently in literary criticism of works dealing with Indigenous claims to land (see Fagan, "Tewatatha:wi").

However, the competition of Morton/Wacousta and De Haldimar for Clara can be read as analogous to the struggles of colonization. Morton's seduction of Clara, a woman figured as one with nature in the Scottish Highlands, her pet stag reminiscent of the North American forests, can easily be read as analogous to the seizure of land. Her shift from her father to Morton requires his personal physical and mental daring in leaping across the crags to and from her remote bower and in finally carrying her off. De Haldimar, in contrast, captures her legally through the book of the marriage service and then renders Morton an outlaw through the book of the court martial. Clara states that she decided to marry De Haldimar because she loved him better (490), but the issue of female consent is simply ignored by Morton, just as the issue of Indigenous consent was ignored by colonizers. It is hard to stomach Morton's assumption that he "owns" her by right of discovery and capture, but it is also hard to accept that De Haldimar made her a good husband, given his cold and haughty nature. Neither man appears to be the right husband, just as the land itself remains subject to conflicting, improper, and unresolved claims.

In *White People, Indians, and Highlanders: Tribal Peoples and Colonial Encounters in Scotland and America*, Colin G. Calloway has laid out the ways in which Highlanders and Indigenous North Americans were seen as similar tribal peoples and indeed how they themselves recognized strong cultural similarities. Timothy Fulford has laid out the literary history of this trope, explaining how Scott was working with these notions as he wrote "The Lady of the Lake," published in 1810 (Fulford 7–11; see also Ellingson 5; McLaren).[20] This famous poem begins with the hunt of a stag, but bears on the dispossession of the Highlanders, "the Gael," by the Lowland "Saxons":

> These fertile plains, that softened vale,
> Were once the birthright of the Gael;
> The stranger came with iron hand,
> And from our fathers reft the land. (canto 5.7)

John Askin, Richardson's maternal grandfather, was said to be a relative of John Erskine, the Earl of Mar, who led the failed Jacobite uprising of 1715 (Beasley, *Canadian Don Quixote* 9; Farrell). Richardson's father's family was involved in the Jacobite uprising of 1745 (Beasley, *Canadian Don Quixote* 10). Thus, the capture of Clara, the daughter of a Jacobite, by two English soldiers, first Morton[21] and then De Haldimar, can be read as analogous not only to the capture of Highland territory by the "Saxons," but also to the British capture of Indigenous lands in North America. Richardson, the descendant of those dispossessed in Scotland by colonization, reveals his sympathy with the Indigenous people. This sympathy does not mean he repudiates his Loyalist devotion to Britain, no more than Tecumseh or Norton did; what they wanted in return for their military alliance and loyalty was a secure land base on which their people could govern themselves. They and their followers had clearly decided that the only way to achieve this goal was through the power and honour of the British Crown (see Fulford for more on Norton's failed project).

The conciliation depicted between the Highlands and the Lowlands in Scott's poem did not seem possible in Canada. Scott, like Richardson, had been brought up in or close to both of the cultures he wrote about; he played an active role in healing the rifts between Lowlands and Highlands and between Scotland and England. For example, he organized a huge pageant to welcome King George IV to Edinburgh in 1822, the first visit of a Hanoverian monarch to Scotland since that line took over from the Stuarts in 1714. Scott's efforts were central to the production of a national culture for Scotland (Trevor-Roper 29–30). Richardson, however, did not achieve a similar uptake in his attempt to write Native claims into a future discourse of Canadian prosperity and harmony, probably because, unlike Scott, he failed to write a bestseller or to make lasting political connections (Beasley, *Canadian Don Quixote* 133–42), and because Indigenous people were no longer either a political or an economic force to be reckoned with. And even if he had succeeded, it might have made little practical difference. The Highland Clearances continued unabated as Scott wrote, demonstrating that his apparently inclusive national myth did little to prevent the brutality of the landowners or to slow the emigration of the dispossessed survivors to North America. The trappings of the mythical Highlands were appropriated by the Lowland and English elites, along with the land. In Canada, Indigenous symbols have been similarly appropriated by the nation that aimed at making real Indigenous people disappear through colonization.[22]

The theft of Indigenous land was a theft carried out "by the book": by Charles II in the charter granted to the "adventurers of England trading into Hudson's Bay" in 1670 and by George III in the Royal Proclamation of 1763. Richardson's account of the encroachments of the settlers, however biased against the Americans, is front and centre in the introductory pages of the novel. He also makes it clear that the English policies pursued after the Treaty of Paris violated the expectations of the Indians, whose relationship with the French had always been based not solely on colonial rule or economic profit, but on an intercultural exchange of courtesies and gifts figured as part of kinship relations. In their first parlay, Pontiac asks Colonel De Haldimar, "Why did the Saganaw come into the country of the red skins? … Why did they take our hunting grounds from us? Why have they strong places surrounding the country of the Indian?" (*W* 196). Pontiac further accuses the British of violating an agreement made with the Ottawa that they came in peace, seeking "only to remove the warriors of the pale flag [the French], [so] that he might be friendly and trade with the red skins" (197). Pontiac justifies the killing of British settlers as a result of the breach of this understanding (198). Duffy writes, "Pontiac alone presents the (rather compelling) Indian case against white encroachment" (*World* 35).[23]

In this central scene, Richardson makes clear that the Indigenous leaders had a practical goal: to restore the trading relationship between friends and equals that they had with the French so that "instead of being treated with the indignity of a conquered people, they would be able to command respect" (*W* 250). For the Indigenous peoples, diplomacy, ceremony, and trade were intermixed (Gibb 33). In the actual history of the interior at the time, understanding these interconnections was crucial. The historical General Jeffery Amherst was in charge of the transfer from French to English; his policy was to treat the Indians as a subjugated people, a policy he did not have the troops to enforce.[24] The result was Pontiac's War; Amherst was recalled to England (White 289). Amherst's actions had broken the Covenant Chain that had governed British–Indian relations since 1677.[25]

THE ROYAL PROCLAMATION AND THE IDEAL OF CONCILIATION

The Royal Proclamation was intended to establish control of lands ceded by France and to regularize British–Indigenous relations. Although it embodies the realization that the Indigenous nations could not be controlled by force, it asserts the Crown's power over the land at the same time as it acknowledges Indigenous rights of ownership: "[G]reat Frauds and Abuses have been committed in purchasing Lands of the Indians, to the great Prejudice of our Interests and to the great Dissatisfaction of the said Indians." Then it sets aside areas reserved to Indians as "their Hunting Grounds." Here the Crown situates itself as the protector of the Indians while at the same time asserting ownership of their territory, some of which it then, beneficently, concedes that they may continue to use. Nonetheless, the Proclamation acknowledges past and continuing Indigenous title and lays out a process for treaty making that includes compensation for land. The Proclamation was ceremonially enacted in a meeting between government officials and over two thousand chiefs and other leaders from more than twenty-four nations, a ceremony that involved the distribution of wampum belts and gifts (Borrows, *Recovering Canada* 124–27). Richardson himself saw the court as an important audience for his novel, as he successfully ensured that William IV read *Wacousta*, and was prevented from dedicating *The Canadian Brothers* to him only by the king's death in 1837 (Preface, *CB*). Although the interest of the court would certainly promote Richardson's career as a writer, he may also have hoped to inspire changes in colonial policy.

Although Wacousta justifies his revengeful behaviour in part by characterizing De Haldimar as both a martinet and a time-serving bootlicker, De Haldimar does not carry out the policy that Amherst favoured. De Haldimar felt that "it was absolutely essential to the future interests of England that the Indians should be won over by acts of kindness and confidence" (*W* 18). In fact, policies like Amherst's are implicitly blamed for the siege. The narrator points out early in the novel that conciliatory policies were the only practical ones given the weakness of the defenders in the fort, but that "so little disposition had hitherto been manifested by the English to conciliate that every thing was to be expected from the untameable rancour with which these people were but too well disposed to repay a neglect at once galling to their pride and injurious to their interests" (18). This point is repeated later, as De Haldimar's younger son Charles remembers that "[h]is father ... had all along manifested an attitude of conciliation towards the Indians, which, if followed up by the government generally, must have had the effect of preventing the cruel and sanguinary war that had so recently desolated this remote part of the British possessions" (253). Richardson, in other words, depicts the Indians as motivated by something other than innate savagery. Further, he consistently contrasts the more conciliatory policies toward the Indians developed by the British after Pontiac's War with the American "war of extermination" against Native Americans (*CB* 1: 20). The success of these policies of conciliation cemented the allegiance of the Indian allies in 1812, an allegiance that was vital to the British success in a close-fought war in which British attention was mainly focused on Europe and Napoleon.

The idea of conciliation is also raised several times in the debate around the D'Egville dinner table in *The Canadian Brothers*. Here it is noted that the relationship between D'Egville and Tecumseh is not purely pragmatic, as D'Egville has a "strong personal attachment" to Tecumseh (1: 73).[26] De Haldimar, however, at first represents the rigid British approach to justice with respect to his men and his children; he is conciliatory with the Indians only because this is the sole practical choice. He changes his attitude toward both his men and his children only when his son Frederick reveals that he ordered Frank Halloway to open the gate of the fort. Realizing that his execution of Halloway as a traitor was wrong, the governor softens his haughty demeanour (428), even embracing his flagrantly unmilitary son Charles for the first time since Charles became a soldier (409). Later he dies of grief over his children's deaths. Thus an instrumental system of justice is abandoned for something more connected to human feeling.

REWORKING KINSHIP

Paternal intransigence here may mirror the strictness of Richardson's own father (Casselman xiii), but it also represents the intransigence (often coupled with incompetence) of a British colonial authority represented by leaders like Amherst and General Proctor, under whom Richardson served. Proctor was court-martialled for retreating from the Battle of Moraviantown, where Tecumseh was killed and Richardson captured. De Haldimar's embrace of Charles and his forgiveness of Frederick can be seen as analogous to Tecumseh's handshake, received by the author as a young officer, described by the older author to demonstrate the power of respect, feeling, and sympathy in human relationships. This symbolizing and memorializing of a handshake between an older officer and a younger one can also be read as a restructuring of filial relationships, severing them from a strict biological father and a British military hierarchy that ruled "by the book," and shifting them to Tecumseh, depicted as a far more effective and charismatic leader. Adopting others as kin was the central form of Indigenous diplomacy, which entailed personal relationships of mutual respect (see Justice). Unfortunately, as Richardson realized on his return to Canada, such relationships between settlers and Indigenous people had been abandoned.

Arnold Krupat points out that the fate of the Indigenous people in North America had to be figured as a tragedy in order to produce the narrative of the settlers as a comedy, with Indians cast primarily as "blocking characters" standing in the way of an inevitable and productive happy ending (135). Richardson does produce the expected happy ending in *Wacousta* with the marriage of Frederick and Madeleine. However, *The Canadian*

Brothers takes this happy ending into a death spiral that includes Indians and settlers alike. Coleman notes that the "fraternal allegory" invoked by the title of this sequel had no "ability to propagate itself" (*White Civility* 75). Richardson takes the tragic, via the gothic, into the excess of parody, and even further, into the realm of the abject—a free fall into oblivion. Margot Northey remarks of *Wacousta* that "it is by falling into the abyss below the bridge that Wacousta and Clara meet their death; contributing to the gothic horror in *Wacousta* as in other gothic tales is this sense of a precarious foothold, insecure and menaced, with a continuing danger of the fall into the abyss of spiritual or cultural doom" (24–25). Richardson clearly conveyed the tensions of living on stolen land. Indeed, the ending of *The Canadian Brothers* can be read as a form of narrative suicide, given that Henry is a version of the author (Beasley, *Canadian Don Quixote* 15n) and, like Richardson, a proud Canadian (*CB* 1: 34). In the end, enveloped in the loathsome clutch of Desborough's American corruption, Henry's Canadian pride falls to its doom near "the stupendous falls of Niagara," already a world-famous symbol of the natural sublime.

Chapter Three

"That 'Ere Ingian's One of Us!": Richardson Rewrites the Burkean Savage

"These lands ... are ours. No one has a right to remove us, because we were the first owners; the Great Spirit above has appointed this place for us...."

Tecumseh, qtd. in Benjamin Drake, Tecumseh and His Brother the Prophet *(92–93)*

Reginald Morton and Charles de Haldimar shift from brother officers and friends to enemies: the vengeful and elusive Wacousta confronts the rigid governor. The Canadian brothers, Henry and Gerald Grantham, also diverge in their moral paths. The grandsons of Frederick and Madeleine de Haldimar, they are both subject to the working out of the prophecy. Gerald becomes fascinated by Matilda Montgomerie, introduced first as the niece of the captured American Major Montgomerie. She proves to be Morton's granddaughter, her father, Jeremiah Desborough, the son of Wacousta and the mad Ellen Halloway (*CB* 2: 417). Gerald's fascination leads to his corruption, which is symbolically represented in his death. His own brother Henry shoots him at the Battle of Queenston Heights, convinced by his uniform that he is an American (2: 466). The move from brother to enemy is repeated. Richardson illuminates the nature of binary oppositions: although reason requires them, they contain a trap. To move, or worse, to find oneself moved from one side to the other, from good to bad, friend to enemy, is a constant risk. The rigid structure of morality and law (the fort) barely holds against a welter of dark affect and emotion (the wilderness).

The fear of disloyalty is thematized earlier in the novel when Gerald, taken prisoner by the Americans, is threatened with being shot as a spy because he is not wearing the uniform of his own regiment (2: 363–65). Uniforms, intended to represent one's identity, authenticity, and loyalty, are the reverse of disguise, which is intended to conceal these things, but here, as with many other binaries in the novel, Richardson shows how one can flip into the other. Richardson himself was fearful of being shot as a spy after he was taken prisoner at Moraviantown because he had taken a dead American's boots for the long walk south. Duffy analyzes a nightmarish scene in Richardson's history where he describes struggling to get them off his swollen feet. The use of tight boots to convey panic that one is turning into the enemy is masterful (Duffy, *Wacousta* 42). A consistent theme in the novel is betrayal: the fear that individuals can be seduced or coerced to betray their moral principles or their country. The fluidity of identity and morality, the constant sense that something is not what it seems to be, that one cannot trust or even recognize one's brother or worse, oneself, is a feature of the gothic. And yet, compromise is a requirement for conciliation and peace. Richardson's novels are haunted by the wavering line between compromise and betrayal.

Richardson's heroes certainly do not manifest the innocence of what Mary Louise Pratt calls "anti-conquest," which she defines as "the strategies of representation whereby European bourgeois subjects seek to secure their innocence in the same moment as they assert European hegemony" (*Imperial Eyes* 7). Rather, the brothers project a strong fear of contamination, not by the Indians but by other white colonizers. This is the same apprehension Joseph Conrad describes in *Heart of Darkness*, where at the end of the novel Marlow lies to Kurtz's Intended about Kurtz's last words. He preserves her innocent belief in Kurtz's love and honour by telling her that Kurtz spoke her name, rather than what he actually said, "the horror, the horror" (148). Marlow remains unable to describe Kurtz honestly to her, in part because of his own homosocial investment in both the man and his corrupted venture. The truth, he says, "would have been too dark—too dark altogether" (148). Gerson notes of Wacousta that "[a]s a pseudo-Indian he outdoes the natives in savagery, indicating how closely Richardson intuited the critique of colonialism later articulated as Conrad's *Heart of Darkness*" (*Purer* 87). But perhaps Richardson went even further into the darkness than Conrad.

Richardson used the deaths of Tecumseh and the Canadian brothers to represent the death of the nation, the end of an ideal of conciliation. And indeed, historians see the 1815 Treaty of Ghent as marking a decisive historical shift. Despite their loyalty, no lands were allocated to the Indigenous allies by the treaty. With each shift in power comes what Ernest Renan calls a necessary forgetting; this, for the French he wrote about, was the massacres of the Cathars in the thirteenth century and the Huguenots in the sixteenth. The state is founded on what is represented as necessary violence followed by necessary amnesia. This same forgetting took place in Canada after 1815.

Richardson was part of the forgetting and revision of history. Both he and Conrad were loyal to Britain; both could characterize the practices of another colonial power (Belgium, the United States) as genocidal, but struggled to extend that insight to Britain. In the introduction to *Wacousta*, Richardson says that "the colonies of America, now the United States" pushing "their course of civilization westwards" caused Pontiac's War (8). Of the regions around Detroit, he says that "the English colonists ... had never ventured so far" until after the Treaty of Paris in 1763 (9). The problem with this point is that, of course, the United States did not exist in 1763, and so those colonies and their settlers were British too. His representation in 1832 of British colonial incursions as solely American marks the Americans as bad colonizers and the British as good ones: he projects their national difference back in time in order to favour one side over the other.[1] Further, he describes the French as instigating the war by "artfully suggest[ing] to the Indians, that their new oppressors were of the race of those who had driven them from the sea, and were progressively advancing on their territories, until scarcely a hunting ground or a village would be left to them" (10). Here, the truth—that it was the British who were the colonizers of the territories south of the Great Lakes before 1775—is characterized as "wily suggestions" of the untrustworthy French. Then the reassuring authorial narrator notes that British policies of conciliation north of the American border have subsequently transformed relations with the French Canadians, but even more importantly, with the "Indian tribes," who have "been gradually weaned from their first fierce principle of hostility," and, in fact, their former hostility to the British has been transferred to "the inhabitants of the United States" (12). Historically, this transition was demonstrated by the allegiance of both Indigenous people and French Canadians to the British in the War of 1812, an allegiance that had been previously untested, since the border between the United States and Canada had existed for barely a generation. That said, Richardson himself exemplifies the ways in which those born in North America began to distinguish themselves from the British. Richardson distinguishes Canadians—that is, the British born in Canada—from the Americans—that is, only recently the British born in southern North America—on the basis of the *British* ability to conciliate both the French and the Indigenous peoples after 1763.[2] His shifting distinctions perform a kind of nation-building sleight of hand.

Richardson was born and grew up in what he describes as "those extreme and remote points of our Canadian possessions," where nonetheless big game was nearly extinct from over-hunting by 1688 (White 47) and which had been the site of trade dating back to the early 1500s. The result of this long-standing trade was a whole intercultural world, which Richard White calls the middle ground, where, he argues, both cultures worked to further their own goals, maintaining their "alliance through rituals and ceremonials based on cultural parallels and congruences, inexact and artificial as they originally may have been. These rituals and ceremonials were not the decorative covering of the alliance. They were its sinews. They helped bind together a common world to solve problems, even killings, that threatened the alliance itself" (93). For Richardson, any hope of such a middle ground (idealized or not) vanished in Canada after Tecumseh's death and the failure to deal with the land question. Others agree: "The major watershed in Indian-White relations in Upper Canada coincided with the 1830 transfer of Indians from the military authority to the civil government in each of the Canadas.... Once the Indian's usefulness as an ally had passed, his civilization became the ideal" (Wilson 65–66). This "civilizing" process presumed the inferiority of the Indian.

What Richardson had hoped for was the treatment of Indigenous people as equals, something that he depicts Brock as inspiring: "The dinner party at Colonel D'Egville's was composed in a manner to inspire an English exclusive with irrepressible horror. At the suggestion of General Brock, Tecumseh had been invited, and, with him, three other celebrated Indian chiefs" (*CB* 1: 67). By the time Richardson had moved back to Canada in 1838, the focus was on Christianizing and "settling" Indigenous people, who responded by arguing for decent education, a secure land base, and self-government. They faced officials who saw education as a tool for assimilation and land as an economic resource that should be logged off, fenced, and farmed (Coleman, *White Civility* 15, 56). Maureen Konkle notes that in the United States before 1830, the notion of Indigenous "racial difference" was new; by 1840, "the normalizing of Indian racial difference was complete" (40; see also Vandervort 74–76). Indigenous people were no longer required as allies or trade partners; furs were on the decline as settlement and lumbering cleared the forests and fashion dictated silk rather than beaver hats. Tellingly, John Jacob Astor moved out of the fur trade into New York real estate in 1834 (Peyer 228). In the United States, Andrew Jackson's government passed the Indian Removal Act in 1830; Native Americans began walking the Trail of Tears the following year, although there were wars to come on both sides of the border.

Arnold Krupat writes, "Indian removal could finally be written into law and enforced in the 1830s because by that time, a certain *story* about America and about 'civilization' had become sufficiently acceptable that it could be used as ideological justification ..." (132). This story, which had its Canadian variants, was the discursive formation that Richardson was writing within. Countering such a powerful formation could not be done straightforwardly, perhaps not always even consciously, as his frequent use of chiasmus and parodic excess makes clear. Although some of his Indigenous characters, like Tecumseh, depended heavily on the trope of the noble savage, he also created Indigenous characters whose behaviour was neither noble nor demonic. He also worked to show that the savage behaviour ascribed solely to the Indian—torture, scalping, the murder of prisoners and women and children—was widely found on both sides of the conflict. As recent historians have also made clear, such atrocities were also routinely carried out by British and American troops (Dowd 117; Richter 190–91).

CONTESTING "NATIVE CRUELTY"

During the War of Independence, the British use of Indigenous allies against the Americans was decried by Whig politicians, particularly Edmund Burke. In 1778, in what was described as his finest speech to the British House of Commons, "[h]e inveighed against the Indians' 'native cruelty' which 'consisted in human scalps, in human flesh, and the gratifications arising from torturing, mangling, roasting alive by slow fires, and frequently even devouring their captives'" (Fulford 184). In this speech, Burke drew extensively on a large ethnographic literature from the early eighteenth century that had already developed these stereotypes (Gibbons 108n52). While Richardson certainly drew on the conventions of the Burkean sublime, he can be seen as writing against Burke's characterization of Indians.[3] Burke's support for the British Americans explained this characterization, as he had argued fervently for conciliatory policies toward the colonists before the War of Independence broke out. His use of "atrocity discourse" to mark the Indian as Other would have fallen on deaf ears in Richardson's Loyalist family. Because of his personal experiences before and during the War of 1812 and his admiration for Tecumseh, Richardson was able to see Indians as allies, something that affected his depiction of them even in his account of Pontiac's War, where they were enemies of the

British. At some level, then, the two novels can be understood as an argument with Burke over the nature of Indigenous people.

That said, Indian warriors are definitely represented as demonic in *Wacousta*, described as "devil" or "devils" (49, 61, 65, 69, 316, 236, 492, 534); "devilish" (308, 318, 402); "fiend," "fiends," or "hell-fiends" (333, 358, 405); "fiendish" (317); "fiend-like" (60); "infernal" (50, 402); and "demons" (63, 312). Richardson dramatically evokes the desperate situation of the British soldiers, outnumbered and isolated in their tiny forts. Like many Romantic writers, he uses John Milton's *Paradise Lost* to good effect. Burke admired Milton's description of Death: "In this description all is dark, uncertain, confused, terrible and sublime to the last degree" (Burke). *Wacousta* opens with just such a compelling midnight scene. Several other scenes in *Wacousta* where the British can hear, but not see, what is happening in the forest reduce the Indians to a soundscape and the setting to Pandemonium, the dark capital of Milton's Hell.

These descriptions, of course, support the interpretations of those who see Richardson's Indians as wholly negative stereotypes. The use of Milton's Satan by Romantics was more complex, however, in that his rebellion against God was seen as parallel to the just uprising of the people against tyranny (McLaren 54). William Blake's remark in *The Marriage of Heaven and Hell* reflects this idea: "The reason Milton wrote in fetters when he wrote of Angels & God, and at liberty when of Devils & Hell, is because he was a true Poet and of the Devils party without knowing it." In an era of revolution, drawing an analogy between Indians and demons was not necessarily to condemn them. As Fulford notes, Indian warriors became, at least until the Terror changed the Romantic poets' views on the French Revolution, a representation of the kind of martial manhood required by those British men who would fight against tyranny (24–25). Thus, judgments of these descriptions as purely negative miss the point that Romantic "demons" could be figured as revolutionaries fighting for justice and liberty. David Armitage describes Milton's work as alluding to the brutal colonization of "a new world" by Satan ("Literature and Empire" 120), an interpretation that highlights Milton's reservations about colonization and the bloody conflicts it provoked. Richardson's depiction of the "new" world as similar to Milton's Hell conveyed his own mixed attitude both to colonization and to rebellion. Richardson's Jacobite family had rebelled against British authority in 1715 and 1745. Despite the family's fervent Loyalism in Canada, these histories of rebellion affected his perspective on colonial politics.

JUXTAPOSITION AND ANALOGY

Richardson's terrifying descriptions of Indian warriors in battle are juxtaposed with more detailed portraits of individuals, such as Pontiac, who closely resembles De Haldimar both in his haughty demeanour and strategic abilities, and Oucanasta, described as "that kind woman" (*W* 257). And Oucanasta's brother is described by one of the British sailors on Lake Erie this way: "That 'ere Ingian's one of us!" (330). Nor are the British always depicted as honourable. The troops sent out to recover what they think is Frederick de Haldimar's body signal with a white flag, which indicates surrender or the wish for parley.[4] However, in this case it is used to lure the Indians out of hiding and as a pre-arranged signal to deploy the guns, which blow many Indians to pieces. This violation of the convention of the white flag was (and is) a war crime. After that, the Indians look at Frederick, still held in their camp, "with an expression that seemed to say a separate torture should avenge the death of each of their fallen comrades" (276). Their savagery is motivated by the savagery of the British.

Later, when Pontiac uses the white flag to approach the fort, the officers remark that he must have learned this "civilized" method from a European (185). They know from Frederick, who has escaped, of Pontiac's scheme to stage a lacrosse game as a celebration of peace. This game is intended as a ruse to allow the warriors to storm the fort. This knowledge leaves the reader (or the military reader, at least) wondering whether the British use of the white flag should be seen as a war crime or not—an ethical quandary that Richardson does not resolve. However, unlike the British, the Indians do not break the truce gained with the white flag, although they do use the parley as part of a larger stratagem. During this parley the governor catches Pontiac offering him "the pipe of war and not the pipe of peace" to confirm their agreement (204). De Haldimar diplomatically responds as if this is a mistake and suggests that Pontiac and his men return later with the proper pipe. However, the point is made that Pontiac could not have smoked the peace pipe and then gone on to pursue war, unlike the British violation of the white flag, since the Ottawa view a pledge made with the peace pipe as sacred (189).

Richardson's use of telling juxtaposition continues in the description of an exciting hand-to-hand battle outside the doomed Fort Michilimackinac, in which an Indian is described as a "fiendish murderer" (317), while an English soldier who has just "cleft asunder" the skull of another Indian looks on, horrified. Such closely juxtaposed representations of the bloody fighting on both sides undercut any blanket impression that the British are always in the right. Richardson deals with the carnage in a welter of parodic exaggeration. The question is whether these depictions consolidate readers into voyeurs, smugly assured of their superior civility, or whether they inspire them to realize the absurdity of such brutality and reflect on its causes, rather than simply to cheer for the heroic British soldiers. Richardson can be condemned for his choice to exaggerate commonplace tropes of savagery, to drive them into the realm of parodic excess rather than to avoid them, but given their routine appearance in descriptions of Indians, his choice might be seen as a strategy born of desperation. Readers expected such tropes: scalping, torture, cannibalism, and compliant dusky maidens were the staples of any treatment of North American colonial history. Rather than avoiding these tropes, Richardson works to undercut the assumption that went with them: that Indigenous people were savage Others.

SCALPING

Scalping was depicted in the British press as particularly savage, despite the European practice of decapitating criminals and enemies and displaying their heads on stakes or bodies on gibbets. Public hanging continued in Britain and Canada until the mid-nineteenth century (Strange).[5] De Haldimar proposes to display Wacousta's corpse on the fort's flagpole. Although some have argued that scalping was a European introduction, James Axtell convincingly reviews archaeological, linguistic, and archival evidence to the contrary. However, he notes that the practice was quickly adopted by European leaders, who offered bounties for the scalps of Indigenous people first in 1637 and for European scalps first in 1688. Daniel N. Paul's *We Were Not the Savages* details the history of the British practice of offering large bounties for scalps in Acadia and elsewhere, sometimes including those of women and children (112–29; see also Potter 70).

It is the British Wacousta who takes the first scalp in the novel (30). Richardson, in his account of the reported scalping of Tecumseh by Americans in the notes to his long poem of the same name, remarks, "If the Indians have sometimes treated the Americans with cruelty, they, at least, were not Christians; and as for simple scalping, it has been a custom with the natives from time immemorial—the scalp being considered merely as a warlike trophy" (*Tecumseh* 113–14; see Benn 83–84). In *The Canadian Brothers*, the comment that "the top knot or scalping tuft, which to a true warrior is indispensable" describes its function as a challenge to the daring opponent (70). In the dinner party scene, General Brock says, "I do not (*entre nous*) see, in the mere act of scalping, half the horrors found usually attached to the practice" (1: 93). D'Egville comments that the Kentucky backwoodsmen also scalp, a claim that the American Montgomerie dodges by arguing they are a "separate race": "Half horse, half alligator, as they are pleased to term themselves, their roving mode of life and wild pursuits, are little removed from those of Indians" (1: 94). At this point, the gentlemen decide that since the war is being fought mainly by Kentuckyans and Indians, one group of savages exchanging scalps with another "can prove but an indifferent source of national umbrage" (1: 94). Here Richardson counters a discourse that ascribed all savagery to the Indians by ascribing it also to Americans, a common Loyalist move. Similarly, his long poem *Tecumseh* states that the Americans flayed Tecumseh's body to make souvenir razor strops (113–14).[6] Such descriptions held Canadians apart from savagery and have proved a consistent strain in the discourse of Canadian tolerance and civility with respect to Indigenous people. But it did make the point that Euro-Americans could be savage too.

TORURE

In the dining room conversation in *The Canadian Brothers*, General Brock points out that Indians no longer burn or torture captives, noting that "Indian cruelty does not exceed that which is practiced even at this day in Europe," pointing to Spain and the practices of the guerrillas in the Peninsular War (1: 93–94).[7] Indeed, the most vivid descriptions of torture in *Wacousta* are the products of British imaginations. While Wacousta is briefly in their hands, the officers of the fort consider how he might best be punished for killing their beloved fellow officer Charles de Haldimar:

> One was for impaling him alive, and setting him up to rot on the platform above the gate. Another for blowing him from the muzzle of a 24-pounder, into the centre of the first band of Indians that approached the fort.... A third was of opinion he ought to be chained to the top of the flag-staff, as a target, to be shot at with arrows only, contriving never to touch a mortal part. A fourth would have had him tied over the sharp spikes that constituted the chevaux-de-frize garnishing the sides of the drawbridge. Each devised some new death—proposed some new torture; but all were of opinion, that simply to be shot, or even to be hanged, was too merciful a punishment for the wretch who had so wantonly and inhumanly butchered the kind-hearted, gentle-mannered officer.... (508)

Like Wacousta, they don't get the chance to enact their revenge, and it is Oucanasta's brother who finally kills him. However, their thirst for torture appears to be quite as strong as that of the Indians, who soon after are depicted running their captives through the gauntlet outside the fort (534).

Torture cannot be assumed to have the same meaning in all cultures. For Christian martyrs it is a route to sainthood, and for other Christians, mortification of the flesh has long been an admired and institutionalized practice. For the Huron, Georges E. Sioui says, torture was a way to end war because it "imposed respect and restraint" on warriors engaged in the fighting (54–55). Carl Benn, in his *Iroquois in the War of 1812*, notes that

> Whatever the reasons for war, aboriginal people often framed their motivation within a convention of avenging deaths suffered by their community through one of several methods: killing and scalping members of the enemy community, capturing people for adoption into the tribe, or capturing and torturing them. Avenging a death appeased a dead person's lust for revenge and enabled him or her to find a haven in the next world. (53)

Nor were prisoners routinely tortured, as often stated. In fact, the Potawatomi and some of the Huron fighting in Pontiac's War made peace with the British after some British captives were tortured to death, and the leaders of the Chippewa, the Erie, and the Delaware are reported to have criticized Pontiac for this episode (Potter 24). Of course, the tropes of torture and the "Indian massacre" appeal because they produce innocent and heroic early settler forebears. For example, the killing of Brébeuf and seven companions in 1649 and the defeat and killing of Dollard des Ormeaux and his men in 1660, both by the Iroquois, have long provided irresistible fodder for nationalist writers in both Quebec and English Canada. That many Iroquois were stalwart allies of the British during the American Revolution and the War of 1812 did not, apparently, impair these long memories.[8]

CANNIBALISM

Burke accused Indians of "even devouring their captives." The belief in Indigenous cannibalism began with the arrival of Columbus in the Caribbean. In a letter to Ferdinand and Isabella of Spain, he mentions the island of Carib, whose people "are regarded in all the islands as very ferocious, [and] who eat human flesh" (qtd. in Hulme and Whitehead 15). The rest is discourse: the name of these purportedly ferocious man-eaters became the name for the whole region, and the term "anthropophagy" was joined by

FIG. 3   *America*, by Theodore Galle, after a painting by Johannes Stradanus (Jan van der Straet), ca. 1580. Print collection, Miriam and Ira D. Wallace Division of Art, Prints, and Photographs. New York Public Library, Astor, Lenox, and Tilden Foundations.

"cannibalism," which now is the common word for the practice.[9] This shift implied that cannibalism was—like scalping—a practice solely of the Other in the Americas, in Africa, or on the fringes of civilized life.[10] Sixteenth-century representations of America included cannibal scenes, notably Jean van der Straet's drawing of Amerigo Vespucci (ca. 1575), which was widely circulated in the engraving by Theodor Galle. In the foreground of Van der Straet's image, a fully clothed Vespucci meets a recumbent, naked female, the allegorical "America" ripe for the taking by the "civilized" (see Montrose). In the background, Indians are roasting human body parts. Michel de Montaigne's "Of Cannibals" (1580, trans. 1603) is already playing with a long-standing discourse as he criticizes the European torture of living heretics as more barbarous than the eating of dead enemies that supposedly prevails in the New World:

> I conceive that there is more barbarity in eating a man alive, than when he
> is dead; in tearing a body limb from limb by racks and torments, that is yet
> in perfect sense; in roasting it by degrees; in causing it to be bitten and wor-

ried by dogs and swine (as we have not only read, but lately seen, not among
inveterate and mortal enemies, but among neighbours and fellow citizens,
and which is worse, under color of piety and religion), than to roast and eat
him after he is dead.

Jonathan Swift's "A Modest Proposal" picked up the trope in 1729, when
English colonial oppression meant that Irish babies were starving to death.
Swift's deadpan narrator argues logically that since they will die anyway,
as will many of their parents, why not fatten and butcher them for food?
At least this way their brief lives will have some economic benefit. Swift's
satiric excess is intended to force readers to think critically about mainstream attitudes and practices. His point still stands: colonizers have systematically starved, killed, tortured, raped, and enslaved men, women, and
children, justifying this cruelty with loaded labels like "cannibal," "savage,"
"primitive," and "terrorist" that assert moral superiority over evil Others,
characterized as other-than-human.

Nonetheless, Montaigne's argument simply flips the binary: "they" are
cannibals, who eat people who are already dead; "we" Europeans (who
are not cannibals) are even more barbaric when we torture living heretics
to death. Nonetheless, the identification as cannibal still works to mark
off Indigenous people and other non-Europeans from whites. William
Arens, in *The Man-Eating Myth* (1979), comments that "[t]he existence of
man-eating peoples just beyond the pale of civilization is a common ethnographic suggestion" (165). He notes the tendency of explorers and ethnographers to uncritically record such stories as fact rather than opinion.
However, his argument that *no* cultures had institutionalized practices that
could conceivably fall into the category "cannibalism" led to much debate in
anthropological circles. Marshall Sahlins produces considerable evidence
for such practices in areas where Arens argues it did not exist. However,
Sahlin's triumphant reinscription of the "fact" of cannibalism fails to deal
with Arens's point about how such labels work to define others as barbaric.

Margaret E. Owens dates European preoccupation with cannibalism to
the proclamation of Pope Innocent III in 1215 that the consecrated wine and
host were the actual blood and body of Christ. She suggests that "to manage their the anxiety about adopting a doctrine that verged on cannibalism,
European Christians phobically projected" the threat on to others (155),
including the Jews (see also Van der Horst), "witches" (see also Levack),
and the peoples of the New World. Others, notably Gananath Obeyesekere,
have argued that the "phobic projection" was reinforced by the unfortu-

nately common need during the era of exploration and discovery for British sailors, explorers, and sometimes settlers to engage in cannibalism to survive (see Stromberg).[11]

Debates over the empirical "reality" of cannibalism should not be conducted without noting that this word carries with it a discourse formed over hundreds of years (since Herodotus, at least), during which millions of words were produced condemning "anthropophagy" and then "cannibalism" as a barbaric practice of the uncivilized Other. Yet Indigenous people have as many taboos against eating humans as do Europeans, as exemplified by the horror of the Wendigo (Johnston, *Manitous* 247), the anti-cannibal Hamatsa rituals (Raibmon 24), and the stories about D'sonoqua, a female ogre who, like the witch in "Hansel and Gretel," eats children. Patrick Moore recounts the horrified reaction of some Kaska people in the Yukon to the discovery that a starving Hudson Bay trader had eaten his partner in 1850.

The binary distinction between discourse and reality explains the impasse that Obeyesekere and Sahlins came to: the former was talking about the power of the discourse and the label (as was Arens), the latter about an "empirical" fact that he saw as independent of rather than constructed by "cannibal discourse." The essentializing social category "cannibal" bears an immense moral charge. Consider a similarly charged category, "sodomite," that has also been used to justify incredible cruelty to the people assigned to it. Socially constructed categories can sponsor very real physical violence. That the designation of a particular group as cannibal was then used to justify practices that were even more barbaric than cannibalism is Montaigne's point. Killing or enslaving *cannibals* did not need justification, since they were a priori not human. Similarly, words like "savage," "massacre," and "scalping" drag with them the whole discourse that marks Indigenous people as inherently and collectively primitive and violent.

Richardson first joins the discourse of cannibalism in the notes to his long poem *Tecumseh* (1828), where he remarks on the "propensity for human food" of the Menomonie: "And wild Minoumini of flaming eyes / who feeds on human flesh" (2: 93–94). In a note, he recounts strolling into their camp with a companion to find them cooking "their untempting meal":

At the surface of the boiling water appeared an offensive scum and each warrior had his own particular portion attached to a small string ... they stated with evident satisfaction that it was an American, and extended their invitation to the Author and his companion, who to conceal their loathing, while declining the honor, were prudent enough to dress their countenances in a forced smile, which ill accorded with their feelings. (71–72)

Desmond Pacey sees this passage as evidence of Richardson's "penchant for the sensational" and continues, "That the Indians may have been joking seems never to have occurred to Richardson: he was never distinguished by his sense of humour" ("Colonial Romantic" 1: 26–27). Certainly, this passage is hard to read and hard to know how to read, but joking must have been a tempting response to the European assumption that all Indigenous people were savage cannibals. However, Pacey doesn't consider that Richardson might be passing along a joke first made at the expense of a two gullible Canadian boys. Something about his picture of the "warriors," each holding his own "small" string attached to his "particular" portion rings false. Is Richardson trying to put his readers into the same uneasy position in which he found himself, half-doubting and half-fearing, required to force the smile intended to hide a complete inability to read a possibly dangerous stranger's tone? Whatever the facts, such "eyewitness" reports sold books by picking up on a dominant narrative that put readers on the side of civility. The "cannibal" passage in Richardson's late novel *Wau-nan-gee; Or, the Massacre at Chicago* that Monkman rightly singles out for criticism revels in hyperbolic excess.[12] However, Richardson uses the trope of cannibalism in *The Canadian Brothers* in ways that work to refute Burke's "atrocity discourse" aimed at Indians: the only character described as a cannibal is a white man.

In this novel, Captain Jackson of the American Army is escorting his prisoner Gerald Grantham, the elder of the Canadian brothers, to headquarters. On the way, they discover Wacousta's American son, Desborough, squatting in a deserted hovel and demand food and lodging from him. He boasts of living on "human flesh," which he describes as "quite as sweet as a bit of smok'd venison" (2: 382). Here Desborough, of course, may well be lying to save the little food he has for himself. When Jackson inquires further, Desborough says, "'[T]hat's off an Ingin's arm'—'Oh an Ingin's only, is it?' returned the Aid-de-Camp, whose apprehension began rapidly to subside, now that he had obtained the conviction that it was not the flesh of a white man" (2: 382). Later Jackson refers to it as "nigger's flesh" (2: 385). Since Desborough's barbarity has already been established, the racism of the American officer becomes the issue. Richardson here condemns what he sees as widespread and casual racism in the United States against both Black and Indian by likening it to cannibalism.

As with cannibalism, racism is imputed to those "just beyond the pale of civilization"—in this case, white Americans of all classes. Here, however, Richardson himself teeters into racism by figuring them as cannibals. The negativity of the trope of the Black and Indian cannibal remains no less vital if it is shifted to white Americans, since those who hate them because they are "cannibals" become doubly racist. The romantic plot of *The Canadian Brothers* coalesces around a scene where Matilda Montgomerie is surprised by her lover and fiancé, Colonel Forrester, "hanging on the neck of another" (2: 416). She is embracing her father, Jeremy Desborough, who has disguised himself as a Black man to visit her; her lover, however, accuses her of "vile intercourse with a slave" (2: 418).[13] Here Richardson uses blackface to mark the American Desborough as the source both of Matilda's ruin and her contamination of Gerald, since she seduces him into her plot to murder Forrester, who has rejected both her explanations and her hand in marriage. Richardson uses the strong racial bar between white and Black to strengthen the distinction between white American and white Canadian without questioning the logic that figured miscegenation as unnatural, or, as Matilda puts it, "the most diabolical suspicion that ever haunted the breast of man," a "debasing imputation" (2: 417) that arouses Gerald's sympathy for her rather than any moral disquiet about the negative depiction of Blacks. In this scene, as Phanuel Antwi argues, "blackness becomes a mask that Richardson collapses onto Desborough's treacherous face" (44). And thus, the hatred of the American Desborough cannot be disentangled from the hatred of Black people, collapsing the distinction that Richardson wishes to make between Americans and Canadians.

Richardson is contaminated himself by the powerful tropes he uses here to argue that racism was something that Canadians, like Gerald, should abhor as they would cannibalism. Loyalist Canadians had to work hard to distinguish themselves from Americans after the Revolution. They did so by arguing that Britishness represented "a unique achievement of equality and liberty," a "truer civility" than that of the "disloyal" United States (Coleman, *White Civility* 20). In Canada the trope of the savage was reworked to "blacken" white Americans, as opposed to the tolerant and order-loving Loyalists to the north. Richardson's racialization of white British-descended Americans here reveals the link between nationalism and the exclusion of Others deemed to be innately inferior, an inferiority anchored in the human body as biological. Richardson intuited that the desire to belong to a nation characterized by an impossible moral purity invariably invited moral disaster; the intuition explains the dreadful fate of the Canadian brothers.

WOMEN, SEXUALITY, AND THE AGENCY OF THE OTHER

Richardson's account destabilizes a variety of dominant assumptions about gender and sexuality, many of them anchored by the assumed innocence and purity of women—or at least, women of the "higher" classes—a position they can maintain only if they remain submissive, stripped of any agency. Indian women are depicted as independent and resourceful; European women, however high-minded and attractive, as unable to cope unprotected. Although Ellen Halloway displays enough gumption to disguise herself as a drummer boy so that she can plead with the governor to pardon her husband, she goes mad with grief when her pleas fall on deaf ears. Madeleine, Frederick's fiancée, attempts to warn her father as the attack on Fort Michilimackinac begins, but paralyzed by fear, she acts far too late. She then succumbs to despairing helplessness, surviving only because Oucanasta rescues her (*W* 361–65). Frederick's far from intrepid sister, Clara, is the epitome of the fainting, weeping, clinging, sentimental heroine, who is handed from man to man like a package (324). All she can do for herself is assert her honour and plead for mercy. The man who rescues her at the fort is killed as he passes her to another; finally, she makes it possible for Wacousta to escape because she comes too close to him while imploring him to have mercy on her brother Charles; he grabs her and uses her as a human shield so he can escape. Just before he is killed, he throws her, perhaps already dead from fright, off "Bloody Bridge." Their demonstrations of the behaviour appropriate for the well-brought-up sentimental heroine lurch into parody, since Richardson had grown up in a world where even upper-class women faced serious physical and mental challenges (as did his grandmother in the siege of Detroit).

Further, the use of rape to control women and to necessitate male protection is not part of Indigenous warfare or daily life as Richardson depicts it. Clara de Haldimar has been taught to fear the worst of Indians, "something worse even than death" (312), but, in fact, Wacousta is the only serious threat to her honour (435–36). Indeed, he does assault Ellen Halloway, who conceives Jeremy Desborough; her son carries her curse on the De Haldimars to the next generation.

Oucanasta is made of sterner stuff than Ellen, Clara, and Madeleine. She intervenes frequently to help the British, motivated by her love for Frederick, but also by her dislike of the boastful Wacousta. She can be seen as just another Pocahontas, totally smitten by a white man; her recognition that she cannot be Frederick's wife, as just another warning against miscegenation. This reading certainly goes with the dominant discourse and is how

E. Pauline Johnson read her. In "A Strong Race Opinion: On the Indian Girl in Modern Fiction," Johnson comments that

> Captain Richardson, in that inimitable novel, 'Wacousta' ... has his Indian heroine madly in love with young de Haldimar, a passion which it goes without saying that he does not reciprocate, but which he plays upon to the extent of making her a traitor to Pontiac inasmuch as she betrays one of the cleverest intrigues of war known in the history of America.... In addition to this de Haldimar makes a cat's paw of the girl, using her as a means of communication between his fiancee and himself, and so the excellent author permits his Indian girl to get herself despised by her own nation and disliked by the reader. Unnecessary to state, that as usual the gallant white man marries his fair lady, whom the poor red girl had assisted him to recover. (*Collected Poems* 179–80)

This feminist interpretation gives a little too much agency to Frederick, in that he doesn't know about Pontiac's scheme to take the fort until Oucanasta leads him into the forest to spy on the planning session. True, he does kiss her, but only once ...

The depiction of their chaste relationship can also be read as a tribute to Oucanasta's honour and agency. She knows that he is engaged to Madeleine, and so realizes that any sexual relationship between them would be secondary (*W* 260). There is no concealment in this novel of the commonplace affairs between soldiers and Indigenous women or between officers and the wives of the men (268, 300). When Oucanasta reveals her love to Frederick, he is at first simply annoyed, until he realizes that she might be able to rescue Madeleine. This realization leads to a clumsy and almost funny interaction as his grateful kiss leads to her slipping and breaking a branch and to his recapture (259–60). The common knowledge of relationships between the men of the garrison and the local women makes it possible for Frederick to convince Wacousta that he has been outside the fort pursuing a sexual intrigue, rather than spying (270). Oucanasta's loyalty is also motivated by more than the white man's inherent sex appeal (Frederick saves her from drowning [258–59, 361]). In Johnson's amused account of the typical plot involving lovelorn Indian maidens, the spurned Oucanasta should, in fact, paddle out to the middle of the river, sing her death song, and drown herself. In spite of this trope, however, she survives to be thanked with gifts. She and her brother remain in the picture at the end as friends of Madeleine and Frederick and teachers of their children (542–43). Oucanasta's brother has a long-standing quarrel with Wacousta (246) that explains why he kills him: he does not act out of automatic loyalty to the British. In other words, although these two characters do play instrumental and subordinate roles, their characterization is more complex than most readings make them. Indeed, L. Chris Fox argues that the replacement of Clara as the object of Madeleine's affection by Oucanasta challenges "the patriarchal structures of … old-world society … based on male homosociality" by replacing the Clara-Frederick-Madeleine triangle with the Oucanasta-Frederick-Madeleine triangle: "The novel's outcome seems to emphasize the importance of creating a community that includes strong female and native influences" (24). This point supports the idea that Richardson is writing against the "American" policy to exterminate Indigenous people by making them essential to the structure of Canadian society.

Interestingly, the exploits of Oucanasta and her brother reveal that the Indians and the French have far more mobility and agency than the British, usually pinned down in their fort, and when outside it, highly visible in their uniforms and highly audible in their boots. Frederick cannot manage without help from them and from François, the host of the inn outside the fort. Although Oucanasta has been represented as one of the novel's victims (Jones), in fact, she can be seen as its mastermind. She sets the plot in motion by appearing at the fort at midnight to guide Frederick to eavesdrop on Pontiac. In a funny scene that has attracted a lot of attention from critics, she convinces him to discard his noisy boots and wear her moccasins. For Frederick, at first the idea is "too un-European," but Oucanasta, "not to be outdone in politeness," takes off her moccasins and makes him feel her "naked sole" with its "ragged excrescences and raspy callosities"—at which point a "wonderful revolution came over his feelings" and he silently obeys her (W 241). Although the revolution in his feelings is not further described, it seems that his notion of men as physically superior to women has been shaken. Far from needing a gallant white rescuer, she is his equal in politeness and his superior in knowledge and in survival skills.

CONCILIATION AND THE MIDDLE GROUND

Frederick can, in fact, be seen as one of those "mediocre" heroes that Georg Lukács argues were essential for Scott's literary success:

> Scott always chooses as his principal figures such as may, through character and fortune, enter into human contact with both camps. The appropriate fortunes of such a mediocre hero, who sides passionately with neither of the

warring camps in the great crisis of his times, can bring readers "humanly close to the important representatives of both sides." (37)

Cooper's Natty Bumppo, for Lukács, represents the "world-historical tragedy" of North American colonization, of those "early colonizers who emigrated from England in order to preserve their freedom, but themselves destroy this freedom by their own deeds in America" (72). Richardson refuses both of the positions Wacousta and De Haldimar represent—roughly "going Native" where "Native" means the stereotype—or colonial domination. His solution, which amounts to continuing the practices of the middle ground that were in place during his childhood, could work only if relationships of mutual respect such as those that Frederick and Madeleine forge with Oucanasta and her brother were continued.

Faced with the difference between his life in the middle ground as a young man and the Canada that he found on his return twenty-three years later, Richardson had to account for the change. The idyllic picture of a peaceful and egalitarian nation that features at the end of *Wacousta* does not persist into the sequel. The conciliation that he remarks on at the beginning of *The Canadian Brothers* dissolves by the end of the novel with the deaths of Brock and Tecumseh—and of course his nostalgic picture of 1812 is strongly coloured by the reality of 1840. A Canadian nationalist, however despairing of the future, he chose to blame the Americans.[14]

THE THEFT OF INDIAN LAND

In *The Canadian Brothers* the issue of land theft is treated explicitly, rather than metaphorically as in *Wacousta*, perhaps because Richardson was aware that Indian removals had been proposed in Canada just before his return. The Bond Head Treaty of 1836, named after the lieutenant-governor of Upper Canada between 1835 and 1837, Sir Francis Bond Head, set aside Manitoulin Island as a hunting ground to which he proposed to remove all Indigenous people (see Surtees). This plan to move them from good farming land to rocky islands farther north was not fully carried out because Bond Head was replaced as lieutenant-governor after the rebellion of 1837.

In the dinner table scene, Richardson has the American Major Montgomerie admit that "our Government must to a certain extent plead guilty" to breaking treaties (CB 1: 77). Montgomerie then quickly turns to the excuse of "superabundant population" (1: 78). He also points out that "in almost all the contracts entered into by our Government, large sums have been given for the lands ceded by the latter" (1: 77–78). Asked how a similar takeover would work in Europe if Spain invaded Portugal, he replies by noting they are "civilized powers" of "the same rank" (1: 78). Clearly the speakers are well aware of the law of nations. But those deemed "inferior" cannot appeal to this law, at least not from Montgomerie's perspective. He points out that the "negro is from infancy and long custom, doomed to slavery, wherefore should the copper coloured Indian be more free?" (1: 78). He invokes Locke by pointing out that if the Indians are "incapable of benefitting by the advantages of the soil they inherit, they should learn to yield it with a good grace to those who can. Their wants are few, and interminable woods yet remain to them, in which their hunting pursuits may be indulged without a fear of interruption" (1: 79). Brock comments that he does not doubt the "*expediency* of ... measures" that take land by force, but wonders if might, in fact, should make right (1: 79; italics added). D'Egville adds that Tecumseh is struggling "for his country's liberty," a word that makes Indigenous war analogous to the Americans' similar struggle in the War of Independence. Here in a few paragraphs Montgomerie presents many of the arguments that were used to justify depriving Indigenous peoples of lands in Canada as well as the United States. Significantly, the Canadian leaders here—one of them a certified Loyalist hero, Sir Isaac Brock—work to refute these arguments.

This novel, given its focus on the iniquities of the Americans, certainly gave Canadians a chance to congratulate themselves on their superior treatment of Indigenous people during the War of 1812. In the introduction to *Wacousta*, the narrator points out that "conciliation" has meant that both the French and the Indians had become loyal supporters of the British in the years following the handover from France (11–12). And in fact, this loyalty can in part be attributed to the Royal Proclamation of 1763 and the Quebec Act of 1794, both of which achieved their purpose in securing the territory that became Canada by providing some recognition to the rights and cultures of those who preceded the British. The 1772 Somerset decision, which declared that slavery was illegal on British soil, explains the allegiance of Black Loyalists. John Graves Simcoe, appointed lieutenant-governor of Upper Canada, passed the Act against Slavery in 1793, which prevented slaves from being brought there.[15] Even though the Somerset decision was not extended to the colonies until 1833, British Canada was a more promising location for Black people than the United States at the time (Colley 234–35). Tellingly, however, such legal protections did not necessarily lead to diminished racism; many of the Black Americans who moved to Canada to escape enslavement returned to the United States after the American constitution was amended to outlaw slavery in 1865 (Winks 289).

Nonetheless, the attempt of the British to balance off powers in North America disaffected white British-descended Americans, who saw themselves as also British, and therefore superior to and deserving of better treatment than people of Indigenous, African, or French ancestry. Nor did these laws succeed in discouraging the exploitation and exclusion by British-descended white settler Canadians of the peoples they were intended to conciliate, something that subsequent history has made perfectly clear.

READING TONE IN RICHARDSON'S GOTHIC

Following Foucault, Dina Al-Kassim notes that "the conventions of resistant expression ... are allied to power and in fact represent it" (4). This point explains how Richardson could be seen as producing the powerful "fictive identity" of the "Loyalist brother" for settler Canadians out of the story of Henry Grantham, who kills his own brother by mistake and then is killed by the American, Desborough (Coleman, *White Civility* 46). Canadian fears of Americans continue; our supposedly characteristic mild-mannered tolerance often stops with them. As Foucault suggests, any attempt to conclusively finish off the nation also strengthens it. Readings of texts select evidence that aligns with powerful ideologies; resistance is rarely clear, even to the resistor.

For Foucault, struggle "takes the form of haphazard and murky speech at the margins of accepted intelligibility" (Al-Kassim 2). For him, "resistance is immanent to power and ... excess or unintelligibility exposes the presence of a norm, its contours and its authority" (Al-Kassim 3). Richardson's struggle with the dominant discourse of "the Indian" did not achieve intelligibility then, and may not even now. Al-Kassim quotes Theodor Adorno on those "inassimilable elements" in writing, "that have escaped the dialectic": "[I]t is in the nature of the defeated to appear, in their impotence, irrelevant, eccentric, derisory" (5). Richardson's own writing often evokes these responses in his critics; his biography is titled *The Canadian Don Quixote*. MacLulich calls him a "pathological case" of colonial inferiority. Desmond Pacey comments in a pair of articles in the newly founded journal *Canadian Literature*, "He was undoubtedly the most colourful figure in our colonial literature, and as certainly the most obnoxious. Excitable, belligerent, haughty, and quick to take offence, his life was a succession of quarrels, controversies, and duels" (1: 20). He further accuses Richardson of "tactless pugnacity" (2: 47), naïveté (1: 48), immodesty (2: 49), impulsivity (2: 50), grandiosity (for even *attempting* to write the *War of 1812* [2: 51]), angling for preferment (2: 51), "belligerence," "troublesomeness" (2: 52), "effrontery" (2: 53), and "haughti-ness" (1: 29). In Pacey's first article, Richardson is criticized for displaying one of his "life-long habits" of "relying on personal influence for advance-ment," in this case, the advancement being a chance to risk his life in the War of 1812 at the age of fifteen, and of later "pulling strings" to be posted to the West Indies, where he nearly died of yellow fever (1: 23). Although Richard-son gives motivations other than financial for many of his projects (even Pacey refers to his "martial ardour" [1: 23]), such disparaging remarks recur in later critics, who take the posture of the judge, not only of his writing, but also of his person, moving themselves above the struggles that they could not know about except by reading his own tonally uncertain accounts.

Al-Kassim notes that moments of "ranting appeal ... can only manifest themselves through abjection" (7). She argues that "the rant is not itself a genre ... but a telling and poignant symptom of a failed strategy of self-invention" (15). Even Richardson's most successful novel failed to achieve his goal of improving settler–Indigenous relations. Nor did his project of self-invention through copious writing over a long publishing career achieve success: in Canada he found little uptake either from his preferred audience or in his social life. The rant resembles the curse and the prophecy, all genres of the powerless. Richardson's main satisfaction must have been in exposing, if only in his writing, those who failed to treat Indigenous peo-ple honourably. Unfortunately, this satisfaction came at the cost of social suicide, a paradoxical result for someone who has been accused of vulgar social climbing and brazen attempts to find patrons. Richardson represents this social suicide particularly through the autobiographical references in *The Canadian Brothers*, where Henry and Gerald Grantham are modelled on himself and his brother Robert, who died in 1819 of "wounds received at the Battle of Frenchtown" (Stephens xxxii).

Just before Richardson left Canada for the United States, he wrote of his difficulties in finding an audience:

> As this is the last time I shall ever allude to the humiliating subject, I can-not deny to myself the gratification of the expression of a hope, that should a more refined and cultivated taste ever be introduced into the matter-of-fact country in which I have derived my being, its people will decline to do me the honour of placing me in the list of their "Authors." (*Eight* 94–95)

Disavowing any interest in becoming the Father of Canadian Literature (Hurley 3), he compares publishing in Canada to publishing in "Kamtschatka" (*W* 587), figuratively pushing his birthplace into a remote and nearly uninhabitable corner of the globe. If he cannot situate himself and his country permanently on the moral high ground, he prefers no ground at all. Henry's unburied bones were prophetic of his own fate, since he is said to have died of starvation in New York; he was buried in an unmarked grave (Beasley, *Canadian Don Quixote* 196).

Perhaps the reactions he received from both critics and readers in Canada reflect the recognition of someone who is "telling truth to power" (Foucault's *parrhesia*). One can certainly characterize many reactions as resisting his attempt to establish a more equitable relationship with Indigenous people. To move toward such a relationship risked revealing that Canadian sovereignty is based on land theft. Richardson's novels not only *describe* the power of a curse, they also can be seen as *laying* one on those who settled Canada, suggesting that if settlers did not treat Indigenous people well, they would become heartless exterminators like the Americans, and Canada would disappear as a distinctive nation. To "read beyond" this disappearance requires conciliation before reconciliation is possible. As both De Haldimar and D'Egville believed, the survival of Canada requires it.

Chapter Four

"We Have to Walk on the Ground": Constitutive Rhetoric in the Courtroom Addresses of Louis Riel (1844–1885)

During his trial for high treason in 1885, Louis Riel (1844–1885) stated, "God cannot create a tribe without locating it. We are not birds. We have to walk on the ground ..." (*Collected Writings* [CW] 3: 547). This image points to his life's mission: securing land for the people of the North-West. And in this brief passage he is doing more yet: with the collective pronouns he is speaking them into being as a social body, a nation created by God. This type of statement is what Maurice Charland calls "constitutive rhetoric" ("Constitutive Rhetoric" 134), rhetoric that performs sovereignty. If we set aside the notion of innate identity that Riel invokes by calling on divine origins, we can still argue that identities and their related claims to land and power are formed out of and with social discourse. In other words, identity is a "rhetorical effect" (133).[1] The two addresses Riel made to the court, the first to the jury and the second after the judge had sentenced him to death, together make up his land claim for the people of the North-West. Many contemporary listeners found his appeal eloquent and moving, but then and since it has often been judged to be incoherent. This chapter aims to move it closer to coherence in hopes that it will be read for the legitimacy of its argument, rather than for evidence that Riel was a saint, a madman, or a fraud.

Our first instinct as listeners or readers is to attempt to find coherence in even the most fragmentary or refractory language. As M.A.K. Halliday and Ruqaiya Hasan point out, a hearer or a reader invokes

> two kinds of evidence, the external and the internal: he [*sic*] uses not only linguistic clues but also situational ones. Linguistically he responds to special features which bind the passage together, the patterns of connection, independent of structure, that we are referring to as cohesion. Situationally, he

FIG. 4   Louis Riel addresses the court. Library and Archives Canada MIKAN 3192595.

takes into account all he knows of the environment, what is going on, what part the language is playing, and who are involved. (20)

Texts hold together internally through linguistic cohesion and are found coherent by audiences through their connections to situation and general knowledge: who is speaking, who listening, where, for what purpose, and about what. As Mona Baker puts it,

> We could perhaps say that texts are neither coherent nor incoherent by themselves, that whether a text coheres or not depends on the ability of the reader to make sense of it by relating it to what s/he already knows or to a familiar world, whether this world is real or fictional. A text which coheres for one reader may therefore not cohere for another. (221)

Riel worked hard to make his two addresses both cohesive and coherent, but ultimately faced incomprehension because his vision did not fit with the dominant views of land ownership, governance, race, or religion. His standpoint entailed a sincere respect for linguistic, ethnic, and religious difference, a standpoint that ran counter to the homogenizing drive of a burgeoning Anglo-Canadian nationalism.

Riel constituted himself in terms of his God-given mission to alleviate the suffering and deprivation of Indigenous people, "half-breeds," and whites in the North-West.[2] He also asserted his "right ... as co-proprietor with the Indians," that is, his right as a Métis to what is now called Aboriginal land title (cw 3: 547).[3] Speaking extemporaneously in a hostile setting, Riel struggled not only to make himself into a legitimate public voice for a people, but also to construct an audience that would hear him. He is speaking a new nation out of a complex web of discourse: as he put it, "I am more than ordinary ... I have been called on to do something which, at least in the North-West, nobody has done yet" (3: 541).

Even Riel's strong Roman Catholic beliefs did not enforce a rigid adherence to static doctrine or fixed hierarchy.[4] His political goals meant that he was able to creatively reconfigure these and many other social conventions to work out a practical plan for the future of "his" people. Facing execution, he predicted that more than his spirit would live: "I have writings, and after my death I hope that my spirit will bring practical results" (3: 525). The two addresses he made to the court can be read as constitutive rhetoric, as cohesive, and also, despite some opinions to the contrary, as coherent. It may be that not all his work is amenable to the same approach: much of it was private spiritual reflection; letters to family, friends, and allies; or writing aimed at audiences who agreed with him. These addresses, however, were aimed at a skeptical, perhaps even hostile audience and forced him to condense his lifetime's political work into a performance of only a few hours. They will emerge into coherence only if the collective beliefs of Canadians shift toward the acknowledgement of Indigenous rights and title. Kevin Bruyneel argues, in fact, that Riel marks the limits of Canadian sovereignty itself, which explains why he lives on in Canadian discourse, a liminal marker akin to Fred Wah's hyphen (728).

COHERENCE AND TEXTUALIZATION

Riel's speeches, apparently, were not always short or well formed. One of his first public speeches is described this way: "He came with a list of 12 points, and his discussion was long and 'somewhat irregular.' As was typical of Riel's public speeches, he tended to ramble" (Bumsted 28). Of his hour-long first address to the court, however, the Montreal *Daily Star* noted that "[h]is hearers were spell-bound, and well they might [be], as each concluding assertion with terrible earnestness was uttered with the force and effect of a trumpet blast. That every soul in the court was impressed is not untrue, and many ladies were moved to tears" (CW 3: 547n). Some of those present at the trial found the second address hard to follow, as reported in the same newspaper: "Assuming a dignified position, Riel immediately began a two hours address, which if in places incoherent, was nevertheless eloquent" (CW 3: 560n1). However, Charles Fitzpatrick, one of Louis Riel's lawyers, speaking fifty years later, called it an "amazing bit of oratory," and another, François Lemieux, said it was "delivered in perfect English and ... [was] most sensational" (qtd. in Davidson 199). However, psychiatrist C.K. Clarke writes of the transcripts in 1905, "What more insane productions could we find anywhere than his addresses to the jury, before and after the verdict?" (18). Desmond Morton, in the introduction to *The Queen v. Louis Riel* (1965), remarks of the first address, "It was not an ordered speech. There were no notes and little evidence of a plan, but there was eloquence and pathos combined as the big, powerfully built man struggled simultaneously to plead his sanity and the wrongs of his people" (xix–xx). Of the second address, Morton remarks, "He was more in control of himself than on the previous day, and his arguments flowed more coherently" (xx). Thomas Flanagan remarks on the "rather poor organization" of the first address (CW 3: 538n1). He adds, "The two long speeches he made at his trial seem to have been largely extemporaneous. We have a draft of only a small part of the first one. This may explain why they were rather rambling and seemed almost incoherent to the uninitiated listener" (CW 3: xliii). Michael Dorland and Maurice Charland say that the second address lacks "clear rhetorical structure" (189). Dorland and Charland spend one sentence listing the unrelated topics he touched on; none of the other critics back up their claim.

Incoherence can, of course, be seen as the mark not only of the visionary patriot, but also of the liar or the madman. Nonetheless, as Dr. Daniel Clark, brought in to testify at the trial on Riel's mental state, pointed out, "There are men who have held very remarkable views with respect to religion and who have been always declared to be insane until they gathered together great numbers of followers and became leaders of a new sect, then they became great prophets and great men" (qtd. in Morton 272). Sincerity and insanity, like coherence, are defined by reception and context.[5]

What constitutes narrative coherence is based on cultural convention, which also varies depending on genre and the dominant discourses of the context of creation and of successive receptions. Most humanities disciplines are engaged with producing and reading texts so as to enhance their coherence, as are many institutionalized rhetorical practices, such as the Sunday sermon in Christian churches. English literature students are taught to move from *Beowulf* to bill bissett, making sense of texts from oral epic to avant-garde poem with very different generic conventions of coherence. Similarly, different cultural conventions around interpretation offer different strategies to hearers and readers. John Borrows explains that Anishinaabe philosophical and narrative traditions give "greater scope ... for readers to use their agency by drawing their own conclusions about meanings hidden in the text" (*Drawing* xiv). Thus, as a text shifts out of one context and into another, in this case from the original spoken words of the trial, into the newspapers and trial transcripts, and then into versions with a variety of textual frames and annotation, readers are provided with or independently mobilize a range of ways to make sense of them.[6]

To read transcribed speech is always to lose the original context; the speaker's voice, accent, posture, and gestures; the reactions of the audience; the setting; the soundscape. To remind us of this inevitable shift, Susan Gingell calls such speech "textualized orature" (286). And print textualization also adds new meanings, however subtle, in the use of headings; sentence or paragraph breaks; standard spelling and "silent" corrections (which obliterate non-standard pronunciation and grammar); annotations; inserted images; and the like. The standard textualization of these addresses is Flanagan's edition in volume three of Riel's *Collected Writings*. Flanagan drew on three versions for his edition: *The Queen vs. Louis Riel: Epitome of Parliamentary Documents in Connection with the North-West Rebellion* (Ottawa: MacLean, Roger, 1886) and *The Queen vs. Louis Riel* (Ottawa: Queen's Printer, 1886), which vary slightly from each other; and "a rough typed version, apparently made from the [missing] shorthand transcript of the trial" discovered in 1980 (*CW* 3: 537n). Flanagan chose the *Epitome* version as his copy-text because "it had been more thoroughly edited" than the Queen's Printer version "so that it reads more coherently," and because Morton chose it for his reprint of the trial transcript in 1965.[7] Flanagan himself did not do much to improve readability: "[O]nly differences of wording which affect meaning are included in the textual notes" (3: 537n1). He did not add such aids to reading as paragraph breaks, quotation marks, or parentheses, although often they would be helpful.[8] Presumably they were not inserted in the *Epitome* version because of the rush to get the sensational trial transcripts quickly to the public. These addresses have complex ties to historical events, to other documents, to each other, and to the trial transcript, which is not included in the *Collected Writings*. When the text's coherence wavers—that is, when the reader cannot glean enough information to make sense of it—the difficulty can usually be traced to Riel's desire to respond to the disparate issues brought up in court.

Taking these texts out of the context of the trial, then, endangers their coherence at one level, but also may connect them in illuminating ways with other texts. Despite his comments on their coherence, Flanagan does say that they are "of unique importance" because "they summarize his career as Riel himself saw it, both as political leader and religious prophet" (xlvii). They are well suited for introducing readers to complex issues of Métis and Canadian history. Another justification for reading these two addresses as a single free-standing and coherent text is that Riel was using them to explain his political actions and his prophetic mission for the whole period from 1869 to 1885.

POSTCOLONIAL COHERENCE

In *Beyond Narrative Coherence*, Matti Hyvärinen, Lars-Christer Hydén, Marja Saarenheimo, and Maria Tamboukou ask important questions that are easily applied to the situation of Riel and the Métis, if not to everyone in the North-West:

> What happens to the desire for textual coherence when place and location as material coherences *par excellence* melt into fluid spatialities, forced displacement and diasporic subjectivities? How can coherence be sustained in narrative texts produced as effects of discourses of colonization? How can "the coherent self" be located across different national territories, ethnic locations and multicultural places when narratives of return cannot be imagined, let alone expressed or inscribed, when there is no material place of origin or beginning? (7)

In fact, Riel did not meet common expectations of coherence in his speech, his beliefs, his behaviour, or his identifications. Aged fourteen, he was sent to Montreal to be educated for the priesthood at the Sulpician seminary at the Collège de Montréal, founded in 1767. He was expected to become one of the first Métis priests (his sister Sara became the first Métis Grey Nun). He left at twenty, upset by his father's death, and after attending the Grey Nuns' School briefly and erratically and working as a law clerk in Montreal, he spent around two years in the United States before returning home to Red River. During this time, he certainly learned about tensions between the English and French in Canada, and about the recent American Civil War and related debates about slavery and civil rights. Speaking French, English, Cree, Latin, and likely Michif,[9] he had ties to cultures that were divided by language and often by religion, culture, politics, and much else.

It is hardly surprising that his views did not always accord with the dominant discourses of the day.

Before moving to the specifics of his addresses, some background is needed to explain his presence in the prisoner's box in Regina for five days in July 1885 and to set his words into the contemporary critical conversation. For those in court who were unfamiliar with the detailed history he references, some of which dated to the first resistance in 1869, likely only one "fact" survived: the idea that Louis Riel had murdered Thomas Scott, an Orangeman who had been arrested, tried, and executed by Riel's interim government in Manitoba. Riel's case subsequently became extremely polarized, with Protestant Ontario seeking to avenge an Orangeman[10] and French Canada claiming Riel as a martyr for the French language and the Roman Catholic faith.

The first Riel Resistance took place during the transfer of the North-West from the Hudson's Bay Company (HBC) to Canada, which was finalized in 1870. Even Prime Minister John A. Macdonald agreed that the government Riel formed in 1869 was legal, in that the land transfer had not yet taken place, and neither the HBC nor Canada was in a position to maintain the rule of law (Gwyn 113). However, Macdonald resisted arranging a promised amnesty for Riel and other leaders: if he granted the amnesty, he would lose votes in Ontario; if he refused it, he would lose them in Quebec. The amnesty materialized only in 1875 under the Liberal government of Alexander Mackenzie. Under the agreement made between Riel's provisional government and Ottawa, Métis received rights to land in the form of "scrip." However, because their leaders were not granted the promised amnesty, the Métis faced a new settler government unwilling to protect their rights or safety. Many sold their scrip to the speculators who followed the officials distributing it and moved to what is now northern Saskatchewan. In 1884, facing economic recession and continuing government neglect, the Métis delegated Gabriel Dumont to convince Riel to return. When fighting broke out, the new railway was used to bring twelve thousand troops to Saskatchewan; after several successes, the vastly outnumbered Métis were defeated at Batoche. Not surprisingly, many Canadian historians and authors have taken Macdonald's railway project as national storyline, one that tied the country together as a modern capitalist nation-state using the latest technology.[11]

FIG. 5   A sitting of the Half-Breed Commission at Devil's Lake, near Sandy Lake Reserve, NWT, 1900. Saskatchewan Archives Board S-B9750.

THE RHETORICAL AND LEGAL SITUATION OF THE TRIAL

The rhetorical situation was extremely fraught because of the nature of the charge and the constraints of the courtroom. Riel was forced to use his scarce time to counter the claim of the prosecution that he was not only a rebel, but also an imposter who put his desire for money before the cause. He also faced his own defence team's argument that he could not be hanged because he was insane. Either he could go along with his defence and refrain from speaking, which might have saved his life but certainly would have discredited his mission, or argue he was sane, defend his cause and his sincerity, and risk hanging. He chose the second route.

The recurrent debates over Riel are a symptom of a continuing struggle over meaning, marking unfinished national business around Indigenous claims for land and sovereignty. In its current state of play the discussion is mainly nationalist in its framing—Métis, Québécois, and Anglo-Canadians have all at some point claimed Riel as their own. He, however, situated himself as speaking for everyone in the North-West, although the Manitoba Act provided special land rights only for the "families of the half-breed residents" and, contrary to his idea of "co-proprietorship" with the Indigenous people, these land rights are provided in a section headed "Towards the Extinguishment of the Indian Title" (sec. 31). Those residents, presumably white, or at least deemed to be outside the categories of "Indian" or "half-breed," and "in peaceable possession of tracts of land at the time of the transfer to Canada, in those parts of the Province in which the Indian Title has not been extinguished," were retroactively granted "the right of pre-emption of the same."[12] In other words, although he envisioned a nation of the North-West, he was deemed to speak only for the English and French "half-breeds."

And perhaps rightly, since the Cree do not connect themselves with Riel. They were incorrectly alleged to have joined Riel en masse in violation of their treaties and unfairly judged as disloyal (see Stonechild and Waiser; see also Tremaudan 184–87). In retrospect, it seems clear that Big Bear / Mistahimaskwa and Poundmaker / Pitikwahanapiwiyin, although convicted of treason-felony, did not support Riel or intend to violate the treaties they had reluctantly agreed to.[13] The struggle even descends to the party level, since Flanagan, a Conservative, continues to defend John A. Macdonald's actions. Although Glen Campbell and Flanagan have analyzed some of Riel's poems (mostly in French and collected in volume four of his *Collected Writings*), scarcely anyone has attended to the literary and rhetorical qualities of his writing and orature. Yet dozens of books and articles by historians, legal scholars, and political scientists about Riel fill the shelves (volume five of the *Collected Writings* is a bibliography; much more has been published on Riel since 1985).

That said, cultural critics Albert Braz and Jennifer Reid have both published books on the many ways that Riel has been appropriated into Canadian national mythology (see also Gaudry). Riel's dramatic life story has attracted more attention than his political philosophy: Harry Somers wrote an acclaimed opera, *Riel*, for Canada's centennial, and Chester Brown's graphic biography, released in 2006, had sold fifty thousand copies by the end of 2010 ("Louis Riel [Comics]"). Of course, it is hard for a modern secular readership to come to terms with the words of a man who declared himself the Prophet of the New World (CW 3: 534) and who spent almost the whole period between 1876 and 1878 confined in insane asylums. Nonetheless, literary scholars frequently read poets deemed insane or claiming to be divinely inspired, including John Milton and William Blake, just to pick two of the most radical. Charges of insanity may discredit a political project or save someone from execution, but they do not disqualify speakers or writers from the canon.[14]

The charges, the venue, and the competence of the court, all examined in detail by the current chief justice of Canada, Beverley McLachlin, are relevant in analyzing Riel's addresses. Riel was charged under a statute dating from 1351 that accused him of "'being moved and seduced by the devil' and 'most wickedly, maliciously and traitorously' having levied and made war 'against our Lady the Queen'" (McLachlin 9; see also Goulet for a more detailed examination of the trial). McLachlin notes that "death was the only possible outcome upon conviction" (8). The charge of high treason was chosen by the justice minister and the prime minister because it suited their political needs: "[T]he record suggests that John A. Macdonald wanted Riel executed" (8).[15] This charge explains Riel's defence team's decision to argue for insanity: it was the only way to save him. They did not want him to speak in court because the jury then might decide he was sane. McLachlin continues: "[T]he government was politically motivated to paint the rebellion as the act of one evil man, rather than what it was: a Metis movement for recognition of their rights to land, language, and religion" (8).

Riel was the only participant charged with high treason. Other Métis were charged with treason-felony, a non-capital offence, as were Big Bear / Mistahimaskwa and Poundmaker / Pitikwahanapiwiyin, while the six Cree men who killed nine settlers at Frog Lake were charged with murder. These six and, two other Cree men who had been convicted earlier, were publicly hanged in the largest mass execution in Canadian history (Stonechild and Waiser 199–200, 225).[16] They were hanged just over a week after Riel, in front of their kin, brought in from the surrounding reserves and the Battleford Industrial School for Indians. Their names—Wandering Spirit, Round the Sky, Bad Arrow, Miserable Man, Iron Body, Little Bear, Itka, and Man without Blood—were promptly forgotten by mainstream Canada (Gwyn 476–78). The trials were held in Regina, where the territorial laws were "particularly harsh and outdated when compared with the English criminal law transplanted to Canada" (McLachlin 6).

In the courtroom, Riel was faced with the task of constructing an audience who could receive his words as coherent, a difficult task. He faced a jury of six, not twelve, all English-speaking men; in Manitoba, the jury would have contained at least six French-speakers, "much more his peers" (McLachlin 7). His several references to his difficulties with English highlight this problem, which was much more an issue with the Cree who were tried after him.[17] It is possible to see traces of difficulty in a few places, as when he calls himself a "decent prophet" instead of a true one (CW 3: 532), or says it "sored" his heart to leave for exile in the United States (3: 550–51).

Dorland and Charland explain how Riel was reduced to a position where he could not perform power, even with God at his back. What can be said in a courtroom is very different from what Riel might have been able to say in Parliament: "[T]he case of 'Riel' can find an idiom in Parliament, but there, Riel will not speak. He and the half-breeds will be spoken for by members who do not represent them …" (187). Riel had won a seat in the House of Commons three times in 1873 and 1874,[18] but with a reward out for his arrest in Ontario and no amnesty, despite promises from Macdonald, aptly nicknamed "Old Tomorrow," he could not take his seat.

At the end of his second address, he asked "that a commission be appointed by the proper authorities," including "the English [i.e., British] authorities" (CW 3: 565), to show that his provisional government in Red River had been a legitimate one. Macdonald had, in the end, implicitly accepted this argument by agreeing to grant Riel amnesty and funds (see Gwyn 150–52, 198). Further, clemency had been granted to Ambroise Lépine, sentenced to death for presiding over Scott's trial. Riel states, "[A]s I am tried for my career, I wish my career should be tried, not the last part of it" (CW 3: 558–59). In some ways, his addresses were aimed, not at the court, but at this hypothetical commission before which he hoped to live to speak. He was also speaking for posterity: "I will perhaps one day be acknowledged as more than a leader of the half-breeds, and if I am I will have an opportunity of being acknowledged as a leader of good in this great country" (3: 533). His belief in parliamentary democracy is telling: as someone who ran for office successfully three times, he saw himself not only as a Canadian citizen, but also as a Canadian leader who could represent everyone in his constituency. He also saw himself as Métis, without contradiction, although his vision of Canada and Macdonald's were diametrically opposed.

THE ADDRESSES: THE CONSTITUTIONAL ARGUMENT

Although he did not have time to summarize his entire constitutional argument, the addresses convey the skeleton of his case that he was not a traitor.[19] He argued that the elected provisional government set up by the Métis in Red River as a British colony was legitimate: "[T]hey were recognized as a body tribal … a social body with which the Canadian government treated" (CW 3: 542). He always called the Manitoba Act a treaty to emphasize that it was negotiated between nations (3: 549, 3: 542n). He further cites Macdonald as recognizing his status "as a governor" (3: 544).[20] Thus, Scott was executed by a legitimate government, and Riel was not a murderer (3: 559).[21] He notes that the Canadian government had neither consulted with the people (3: 542) nor responded to their petitions (3: 535) before some Canadian officials started arriving as "invaders" (3: 542). (Canada had sent surveyors before the land transfer from the Hudson's Bay Company was completed.) Riel thus was the founder of Manitoba in 1870 (3: 530) because, as president of the provisional government, he had presided over the negotiations with Canada for the territory's entry into Confederation. However, despite the success of his government in keeping order in Red River, Canada had quickly broken the provisions of the Manitoba Act (3: 549; see also Friesen 90; Weinstein 13; Pritchett). He had been repeatedly promised an amnesty, but this came only in 1875, and under its terms he could not represent his people in Parliament. As a result the Métis were systematically "disorganized" (*CW* 3: 549), and many sold the scrip that entitled them to land for far less than its value and moved west (3: 551).[22] Required to leave Canada for five years by the amnesty, he then became an American citizen (he comments, sardonically, "It is a wonder I did not take and go to Mexico" [3: 548]). Canada owed him money for his work as governor (3: 536), as well as for the forfeiture of his land claim (3: 551).

The prosecution frequently refers to the sum of $35,000, which they figured as a blackmail payment that Riel was attempting to extort from the government in return for laying down arms. Flanagan devotes a chapter of *Riel and the Rebellion* to the issue entitled "Blackmail or Indemnity": he concludes that "Riel's desire for money was an integral part of the sequence of causes that led to the Rebellion" (130). Richard Gwyn remarks, "Riel had never concealed from the Metis his personal financial claims, and none of them ever accused him of false motives" (440). In the addresses Riel figures the money as compensation to support him and his family because he had left his land and his career as an elected politician behind when he went into exile (see Gwyn 440).[23] Other government leaders were paid for their work, and Riel argued for the same right.

Riel refuses to see a difference between the situation in 1869 and in 1885: "[T]he troubles of the North-West in 1885 are the continuation of the troubles in 1869 ..." (*CW* 3: 542). This refusal, of course, is a refusal to admit that the transfer of the North-West from the Hudson's Bay Company to Canada made any difference to the legitimacy of his leadership. Canada had ignored the people of the North-West before 1870 and continued to neglect them, as in 1885 he returned to find starvation and only a "sham" government (3: 535). The government formed in 1885 "would have been constitutional ... if ... we had not been attacked" (3: 529). In other words, they were attacked first by the police and acted in self-defence (see also Morton 113; Canada, "The Battle at Duck Lake").[24] So he maintains that Canada was not the legitimate government, as it did not govern, and that the Métis nation and its supporters were legitimately defending themselves against invasion.

Riel pulls the threads of this argument together in a quick summary in his second address, ironically taking the position of the Canadian government: "We have made a treaty with him, we do not fulfill it; we promise him amnesty; he is outlawed; we take his country and he has no room even to sleep. He comes to our help. He governs the country during two months and the reward is that he is a bandit. He comes to the help of the Government with 250 men and the reward is $5000 for his head" (CW 3: 552).[25] In sum, Riel and the Métis had been treated unjustly in the aftermath of the first resistance,[26] and this injustice continued. He repeats words in this brief summary that make cohesive ties through repetition in both addresses: treaty, amnesty, bandit, and reward.

THE PARADOX OF TREASON

Producing this constitutional argument was only one of his rhetorical tasks; in order to establish the legitimacy of this argument, which he had authored along with others in a series of petitions, proclamations, and letters since 1869, he had to argue against the defence of insanity put up by his lawyers. It is relatively simple to count bodies and weapons, whereas the "fact" of sanity is particularly difficult to prove, as the inconclusive testimony of the asylum doctors showed. As the Crown counsel pointed out, if Riel was insane, then so were his followers: "Is there any escape from the one inevitable conclusion that either the prisoner at the bar was perfectly sane, or that all the half-breed population of Saskatchewan were insane?" (Morton 328). Riel knew that he could not simply deny the insanity imputed to him by his own counsel; rather, he must *perform* sanity. He argued that "an insane man cannot withhold his insanity" (CW 3: 532). In performing sanity, or constituting himself and his cause as sane, he was successful, although debate continues over whether the government was guilty of what one commentator called the "judicial murder" of an insane man (Clarke 25). Riel made use of the connection between sanity and responsibility to argue that, in fact, it was not he but the government that was insane.

One of the paradoxes of power is that the powerful often have it both ways, while others find themselves damned if they do, damned if they don't. Riel demonstrates in both speeches a clear awareness of the paradoxes of his situation and heightens them for effect. *Paradox* (from Greek, "contrary to opinion") is a rhetorical figure that employs an apparent contradiction to expose a truth (Burton). Kimberly Roppolo writes that paradox is valued in Indigenous rhetoric because it poses listeners with a problem they must work out for themselves (307–8). Riel opens his first speech by saying that when he returned to the North-West, he found "the Indians suffering, the half-breeds eating the rotten pork of the Hudson's Bay Company and getting sick and weak every day"; even whites were "deprived of their public liberties" (CW 3: 524). Close to the end, framing this address, he says of the Canadian government that "the British government has defined such government as this which rules the North-West Territories as irresponsible government, which plainly means there is no responsibility, and by all the science which was shown here yesterday [by the doctors], you are compelled to admit that if there is no responsibility, it is insane" (3: 535). Thus, he and his followers were restoring sanity to an insane territory.

If he is insane, he says, then the jury should acquit him. If he is sane, then he has been acting "in self-defence" against the attack of an insane and irresponsible government (3: 536) and they should acquit him. At this point, he is putting the government into the same bind into which it had put him: "[M]y accuser, being irresponsible and consequently insane, cannot but have acted wrong, and if high treason there is it must be on its side and not on my part" (3: 536). The judge here interrupts: "Are you done?" (3: 536). Although Riel is using wit here, it is deadly serious wit. What does a government owe its people? Is it treason to rebel against a distant government that deliberately fails to govern, even in a time of recession and famine?[27] When does so-called treason or madness actually work to protect hard-won principles of freedom and democracy against corruption?[28]

Neither the judge nor the prosecution would allow evidence that spoke of the government's failure to answer the many grievances of those in the North-West. Father Alexis André, asked about the "constitutional agitation" of the "English and French Half-breeds" before Riel's return, notes that the only response to their petitions to the federal government was "an evasive answer saying they would take the question into consideration" (Morton 228). The Crown counsel at this point said, "I must object to this class of questions being introduced. My learned friends have opened a case of treason, justified only by the insanity of the prisoner; they are now seeking to justify armed rebellion for the redress of these grievances." The judge commented that this line of argument "would be trying the government" (229), which was exactly what Riel wanted. Riel was also pointing to another paradox of treason: the Crown is both plaintiff and prosecutor. As the defence pointed out in their objections to the size of the jury and the venue, "the Crown is a party to the suit and therefore special provision is made [in England] for the protection of the individual as against the Crown" (13). No such special provision protected Riel.

In Riel's case, the appeal went to the court of the Queen's Bench, in Manitoba, which upheld the decision. The Privy Council in Britain declined to review the case. When the Quebec ministers in Macdonald's cabinet asked for another medical review, the report went to the cabinet, chaired by Macdonald himself, with predictable results. Indeed, Macdonald falsified the response of the one doctor who did find Riel insane, something Flanagan describes as a "discreditable episode" (*Louis "David" Riel* 182). Once again, a case regarding Indigenous land rights ended in a way that seriously damaged the honour of the Crown. All of these cases are governed by the same paradox: even if the government has broken the law, it still runs the trial. The judge, Hugh Richardson, was "a stipendiary magistrate serving only at the pleasure of the government" and he was the one who chose the names of the thirty-six prospective jurors (Groarke 218n).

One of Riel's defence team, Charles Fitzpatrick, also pointed to the paradoxical nature of treason in his closing speech. He begins with a disclaimer, "I know it is not right to preach treason, and it is no part of my duty to do it," but he nonetheless continues:

> I say, gentlemen, look at the page of history of our country, look at the pages of the history of England and tell me if there are in all of those bright annals any of those that shine brighter than those written by Cromwell at the time of the revolution? Tell me, gentlemen, if the liberties which Britons enjoy today were bought too dearly, even with the life blood of a king. I say they were not. (qtd. in Morton 288)

The paradox of Riel's ongoing loyalty to the British Crown and to British principles of justice was mentioned in court: his council toasted the queen in 1885 (qtd. in Morton 68, 157). This can be contrasted to his attitude to Canada, which he called "our sister colony in the East" (*cw* 3: 548). In his address he notes that in 1871, he and his men were asked by both Colonel Irvine of the Mounted Police and Lieutenant-Governor Archibald to assist in repelling a Fenian raid on Manitoba from the United States. He notes the paradox: "[A] rebel had a chance to be loyal then" (3: 552; see Pritchett). Almost at the end of the second address, he notes yet another paradox. At first he was happy that the jury had pronounced him guilty because it proved he was sane, but then he realized that he might now be seen simply as an imposter exploiting the Métis, rather than as a sincere leader: "Now, I am judged a sane man, the cause of my guilt is that I am an imposter, that would be a consequence" and says that he wishes to be examined by a commission of doctors to decide his sincerity: "[I]f I have been astray, I have been astray not as an imposter, but according to my conscience" (CW 3: 560). In its opening address, the prosecution had agreed that he had only pretended to be inspired by God to delude his followers, describing the rebels as "poor dupes" because "it was not so much rights of the half-breeds he was seeking as the power and benefit of Louis Riel, and money that Louis Riel wanted to extract from the Government" (qtd. in Morton 74).

One of the jurors, Edwin J. Brooks, interviewed around four decades later, also commented on the paradoxes of the trial:

> We were asked to declare the man insane. He seemed to us no more insane than any of the others who addressed us and they were the ablest of men in all Canada and he was more interesting and effective than some of them. We could not declare him insane. We were in a dilemma. We were in sympathy with the Metis, knowing they had good cause for what they did. We often remarked that we would like to have the Minister of the Interior in the prisoner's box, charged with inciting the Metis by gross neglect and indifference, but we could not pass judgement on the Minister of the Interior and we had to give our finding on Riel according to the evidence.... What could we, the juryman do to help him out? That was the concern of all of us. There was no dissention or division of any kind. The only thing we could do was to add a clause to the verdict recommending mercy. We knew it was not much, but it was not an empty formal expression and it revealed the serious desire of everyone on the jury. We (the jury) tried Louis Riel for treason, but he was hanged for the murder of Thomas Scott. (qtd. in Davidson 200)

Of course, this is commentary given in hindsight and mediated through the reporter, but it is telling that one of the closest witnesses to the trial was prepared to state his support for Riel so clearly.

RESISTING THE DOMINANT DISCOURSE

Just as the government forges the law, the dominant society forms the dominant discourse. Riel was well aware of these constraints, remarking "how it is difficult for a small population, as the half-breed population, to have their voices heard" (CW 3: 544). Thus to read Riel's speech properly requires consideration of the rules of interaction, how "the imperative of coherence works to legitimize certain narratives while excluding or marginalizing others from the narrative canon" (Hyvärinen et al. 7). The elite would have found Riel's ideas traitorous or insane because he resisted the dominant view of Canada. A widely accepted racializing discourse did not see Métis or Indian men as competent to speak in the public arena as equals with "civilized" white men. J.M. Bumsted points out, "[F]rom the Canadian perspective, the resident 'half castes' (as Prime Minister Macdonald preferred to call them), did not really count as potential citizens, and the delay [in responding to petitions] was to permit further European settlement." He quotes a letter written by Macdonald in 1869: "In another year the present residents will be altogether swamped by the influx of strangers who will go in with the idea of being peaceful and industrious settlers" (21). Democracy could wait until the majority would vote for Macdonald. However, the support of minority rights is a true test of democracy. As Riel points out, the Canadian government "by its greatness ... had no greater rights than the rights of the small, because the rights is the same for everyone, and when they began by treating the leaders of the small community as bandits, as outlaws, leaving them without protection, they disorganized that community" (cw 3: 549). The problem of defending minority rights against governments elected by the majority is a serious one, highlighted by what happened in the North-West. Unlike Quebec francophones, Indigenous people do not constitute an electoral force and their territorial base is widely scattered; they have had to rely on the courts to defend their rights.

RACIAL LOGIC

Evidence of the pervasiveness of the racializing discourses of the time is that Riel himself writes with and within them; he explains why the provisions of the Manitoba Act left public lands within the control of the federal government: "[A]s the half-breed people were the majority of Manitoba, as at their stage of civilization they were not supposed to be able to administer their lands, we [the provisional government] thought that at that time it was a reasonable concession to let them go, not because we were willing to let them go, but because it seemed impracticable to have the administration of their lands" (cw 3: 544). Later he points out that the benefits of civilization would raise the value of the land in Manitoba that was to go to the Métis and the Indians: "[C]ivilization has the means of improving life that Indians or half-breeds have not" (3: 548). This view had a long history: "Locke seemed to have shared the view of many Europeans that the comforts which the Europeans could provide, and teach the Indians how to provide for themselves, would easily compensate them for their loss of the traditional, and wasted, hunting grounds" (Pagden 45). Like everyone who spoke in the courtroom, Riel put the British at the top of the hierarchy of civilization, followed by the Métis, and then the Indigenous people.

This effective discourse has a long and continuing force. In *Metis Legacy* (2000), Leah Dorion and Darren Préfontaine provide a review of the literature on Riel (26–28), noting that in 1936 George F.G. Stanley figured the Riel Resistance as a clash between "civilized and primitive peoples" in *The Birth of Western Canada* (26). This book was a successor to earlier historians' accounts that saw those of mixed ancestry as primitive "savages" or worse, beginning with Francis Parkman (1823–1893) and Lionel Groulx (1878–1967) and running through Stanley, Morton, Donald Creighton, and finally Flanagan. Flanagan wrote in 1986 that "the myth of Riel's insanity is made to order for the contemporary liberal who does not want to face some of history's sterner truths: that civilization expands into the territory of more primitive peoples ..." ("Crazy" 117). For Flanagan, any disparity between Indigenous people and other Canadians is the result of history's "truths"; his vision of history as progress—the march of civilization—is the justification for colonization. This vision supports might-makes-right history, a vision that is strongly contested, and not just by liberals, because this view constitutes the harm done to Indigenous people and other minorities as justified: the necessary collateral damage of progress. However, it is rather telling that "civilization," despite its supposed truth and inevitability, so frequently seems to require the brutal suppression of those whose rights are supposedly guaranteed by (civilized) law.

Despite Riel's apparent acceptance of the civ/sav distinction (LaRocque 35), he drew a line to protect the sovereignty of the North-West: "[W]hen they [the British-descended settlers] have crowded their country because they have no room to stay any more at home, it does not give them the right to come and take the share of all tribes beside them" (CW 3: 547). His respect for British civilization was strong: "I believe that the English constitution is an institution which has been perfected for the nations of the world ..." (3: 555). He mentions English "fairness" and belief in "fair-play" twice (3: 526, 3: 527). However, he did not want the North-West to be populated solely by those of "Anglo-Saxon" descent: "When we gave the lands in Manitoba for one-seventh ... in giving it to the Canadian Government it does not mean that we gave it with all the respect that I have for the English population, the Anglo-Saxon race, we did not give it only for the Anglo-Saxon race" (3: 555). He wanted the North-West to be governed by British constitutional principles, but not settled solely by British settlers. He wanted them, "the people who have no country, [to] understand that we have a country here which we have ceded on conditions" (3: 545). Riel said other things as well: "Yes, you are the pioneers of civilization, the whites are the pioneers of civilization, but they bring among the Indians demoralization" (3: 530). Further, he asserts his desire for "co-proprietorship" (3: 545) of the land with the Indians, and also acknowledges his "Indian blood" (3: 557).

Understandably, Stonechild and Waiser quote his opinions on the Cree and Blackfoot with some bitterness:

> Riel regarded Indians as a simple, primitive people, who should be made to work "as Pharoah had made the Jews work." He also assumed that the Métis, because of their mixed-blood parentage, could help solve the so-called Indian problem—in his words, "show them how to earn their living" by exercising a positive, uplifting influence on them. "The crees are the most civilized Indians of the Canadian northwest because they have been ... in constant communications with the halfbreed," he wrote.... "The blackfeet and the bloods are nothing but savages." (77)

Still, although the trial offered Riel many opportunities to pick up on the discourse of the savage cited here, he did not do so in court. The idea that Riel might have brought on "the calamity of an Indian war with all its attendant horrors" (Morton 74) was constantly kept in play by the prosecution. In response, the idea that "the half-breed" was all that kept the Indians from killing prisoners or otherwise running amok was repeatedly raised by the defence: "You have found the half-breed always stood between the Indians and his fellow white man" (289). Witnesses were asked repeatedly whether they had seen any Indians with the Métis (100, 130, 144, 193). The newspaper coverage of the second resistance was filled with the rhetoric of the "anti-Indian sublime, a rhetoric that allowed the most amazing and spectacular predictions of Indian depravity" (Silver xix–xx).[29] This rhetoric was hardly deflated by the revelation of what actually happened. For example, the murders of nine men, including the Indian agent and two priests, at Frog Lake are usually referred to as a "massacre" and framed as part of a general Cree "uprising." However, after intervening, Big Bear / Mistahimaskwa took charge of the seventy or so settlers that some young men of his band had taken captive. Two white women in the group, Theresa Delaney and Theresa Gowanlock, whose husbands had been murdered, were assumed by eastern newspapers to have been "outraged" and then murdered, which supported soaring patriotic calls for revenge. They reappeared two months later, alive and well treated (Carter, Introduction). Nonetheless, this rhetoric of Indian depravity supported not only the convictions of the Cree leaders and the naming of particular bands as treasonous, but also the ongoing harsh treatment of all Plains peoples (Carter, Introduction xxxvii–xxxviii). One can see how Riel's speech was constrained, then, not only by the situation of the trial, but also by larger discourses. Some, such as the discourses of civilization, liberty, responsible government, and the law of nations, he used to buttress his case. However, he did not use the rhetoric of the anti-Indian sublime in his addresses to the court.

MOTHER COUNTRY AND THE BIRTH OF A NATION

One discourse that Riel does pick up and even turns into an extended metaphor is the common one of the mother country (see McClintock). In his first address, he makes the point that he is as helpless before the court "as I was helpless on the knees of my mother the day of my birth" (CW 3: 524). In this passage he appeals to the court as a vulnerable newborn, dependent on them for life as he once was on his mother. He notes that the North-West "is also my mother." He conflates in this set of relationships his own mother, the court constituted in the North-West, and the North-West itself: he appeals to the court to save his life as a mother would save her helpless child. These are not the identifications we might expect from a rebel leader. However, treason is often figured as analogous to attempting to kill one's parent, and since Victoria was on the throne, the maternal images become even more appropriate. The logic is that he could not possibly hurt her, vulnerable as he is. Although the Roman Catholic iconography of Mary with the infant Jesus on her knees, an image that pre-figures the Pietà, could have been evoked here, Riel never follows through on the issue of martyrdom or the imitation of Christ. He makes it clear that as a prophet he was aiming at "practical results" (3: 531). ("Practical" is a key word in these two texts, occurring eleven times.) His goal was to work for his people as a live politician rather than as the martyr he became for many after his hanging.

His main difficulty is that his "mother country is sick and confined in a certain way," that is, a mother who is vulnerable, attempting to bear and raise a living child. As his real mother needed help "to take care of me during her sickness," so does his mother country (3: 524). Here his survival and that of the North-West are related, a theme he continues when he argues that the delayed amnesty kept him from leading his people by taking his seat in the House of Commons. He turns around the image of the treasonous rebel trying to kill his mother; here it is a mother, figured as the court constituted by his mother country, that has the power to kill him but cannot possibly do so, "because a mother is always a mother, and even if I have my faults if she can see I am true, she will be full of love for me" (3: 524). He also depicts himself and the people he hoped to unite as deprived of a healthy mother country that could responsibly care for them.[30] Implicitly, the Canadian government that should have supported Manitoba as a mother country, a nation, has instead demonstrated irresponsible, even callous, neglect.

Like their mother country, her children are sick and deprived. Because of the near extinction of the buffalo, the bad weather that hindered the Indians who had taken treaty and started to farm from getting a crop, and an economic recession, many in the North-West were dependent on food rations (see Daschuk).[31] Even the whites were suffering, as they were "deprived of responsible government, I saw that they were deprived of their public liberties" (CW 3: 524). "Although a half-breed," he remembers that "the greatest part of my heart and blood was white, and I have directed my attention to help the Indians, to help the half-breeds and to help the whites to the best of my ability" (3: 524–25). Out of his threefold identity, he constitutes himself as a true son of the North-West, a legitimate agent to petition the Canadian government, the supposedly responsible authority, for help. This expansive vision certainly ran counter to the inferior "half" identity allotted him by the dominant discourse.

After some digression on claims he was egotistical, on "foreign policy," and on his papers, he comes back to the main topic: "No one can say that the North-West was not suffering last year" (3: 526). The next section is united by the sixfold repetition of the word "mission." He mentions the word, not "to play the role of insane before the grand jury so as to have the verdict of acquittal," but to speak to his work "to get free institutions for Manitoba" (3: 526). He then points out that his mission was interrupted, as he "was banished for five years" (3: 526). Despite his efforts, "I am forgotten as if I was dead." Here is another image of abjection, like his self-representation as a helpless newborn before the court. Faced with this social death, he "became what doctors believed to be insane" (3: 527) and received comfort from his bishop, who counselled him, "Be ye blessed by God and man and take patience in your evils" (3: 527). From this point variants of the word "bless" and "benediction" occur twenty times in two pages (3: 527–28). God is behind his mission, proved by his survival even "when bullets marked my hat" (3: 527) and "when bullets went as thick as mosquitoes in the hot days of summer" (3: 528). These blessings were a "guarantee that I was not wrong when by circumstances I was taken away from my adopted land [the United States] to my native land" to help the Métis (3: 527). Since much of his constitution of the Métis as a nation is based on their acceptance of him as a prophet, this self-construction is central to the addresses.

PRACTICAL PROPHET OF THE NEW WORLD AND LAND DISTRIBUTION

"Hunted as an elk" (CW 3: 541), unable to take his seat, with a warrant out for his arrest in Ontario and a price on his head, Riel's personal and national project was in tatters after 1870. In December 1875, Riel had mystical experiences that he saw as the beginning of his mission; however, his friends and family saw them as insanity, and by March he was in an asylum (Flanagan, *Louis "David" Riel* 63). He began to identify himself as a prophet, priest, bishop, and even pope (74). Flanagan relates these beliefs to those of the Quebec ultramontanes, many of whom supported Riel. They believed that Quebec had a special mission from God to convert the Indigenous peoples so as to produce a Catholic nation in the North-West (47). Riel easily transferred this idea to the Métis, a new nation born of New France, just as Quebec had been born of Old France (89–90). Here Riel was also working with the biblical discourse of Israel as a "small people" destined for world importance at the heart of a new religion: "Do you know, these people of mine are just as were the children of Israel, a persecuted race deprived of their heritage. But I will wrest justice for them from the tyrant. I will be unto them a second David" (qtd. in Flanagan, *Louis "David" Riel* 126). Riel used the staple analogies of Roman Catholic biblical interpretation that had for centuries been making a set of disparate religious texts into a coherent narrative to work out a new coherent narrative for the North-West and Canada. To mark his new conviction, he took on the name David for himself.

He explains that he had split from Rome, "inasmuch as it is the cause of division between Catholics and Protestants" (CW 3: 531): ultimately, as a practical prophet, he wanted "his children's children … [to] shake hands with the Protestants of the new world in a friendly manner. I do not wish the evils of Europe to be continued … [even if] it is the work of hundreds of years" (3: 531). Therefore his land distribution would go beyond the Indigenous peoples and the Métis to invite immigrants from the United States, including the Italians, the Irish, the Bavarians, the Poles, and the Belgians. He also includes the Protestant Scandinavians, so as "to show that we are not fanatics, that we are not partisans, that we do not wish only for the

Catholic, but that we have a consideration for those who are not Catholics" (3: 545). He includes the Jews, as well, although only if they convert (3: 545). The Métis were promised territory amounting to approximately one-seventh of the territory first designated as Manitoba (the size of Manitoba was substantially increased in 1881; the province did not reach its current size until 1912).[32] Riel first planned to divide the land equally into sevenths, but as he notes, he invites more nationalities than seven. Gwynn says that Riel envisioned a "distinct society" for the Métis, "a sort of self-governing reserve, one comparable to, but with greater autonomy than, the reserves of the Indians" (438). Riel further proposed that "the Indians and the half-breeds of the east [should] ... have a revenue equivalent to about one-seventh" (cw 3: 545). What he does, finally, is erect the notion of sharing the land in the North-West and British Columbia into a "principle" that would extend across Canada to include Indians and Métis, as well as ethnically diverse groups of settlers (3: 545). This vision certainly would have been seen as crazy by Macdonald, with his vision of white supremacy for British settlers.

INDIGENOUS DISCOURSES

Clearly, Riel's vision was ahead of its time. As what he called a practical prophet, or what William M. Ramsay calls a "modern prophet" or an "activist prophet" (2), he could be seen as attempting to perform this vision into existence. What often causes difficulty in the speech of visionaries, prophets, and activists is that they are arguing for a future barely conceivable in the terms of their current time and place, and as a result, they cannot achieve the support required to constitute a social reality.

Flanagan argues that Riel was a "typical Catholic millenarian," and also the leader of a "nativistic resistance movement in the colonial world" (*Louis "David" Riel* 197). Although most such movements (he lists, among others, the Ghost Dance, Rastafarianism, the Cargo Cult) are syncretic, he argues that Riel's teachings were almost completely Christian. However, I argue that they also reveal ways of thinking and being derived from Indigenous Plains traditions, the traditions in which Riel grew up. Kerry Sloan says that his views reflect "Catholic teachings as well as Nehiyaw (Cree) and Anishnibek (Ojibway/Saulteaux) religious philosophies" (168). She sees his vision of people from many ethnicities living in peace as deriving from the history of Haudenosaunee and Anishnabek confederacies.

Certainly, to construct a following, he would need to connect with Métis beliefs, which were based not only on Roman Catholicism, but also on Indigenous traditions. Cultural flexibility and creativity was what had ensured Métis survival; indeed, Michael Barnholden sees it as central to the character of Gabriel Dumont, Riel's adjutant general (13). Leaders had to earn their position, both in the Métis tradition of the annual election of a government for the hunt (Weinstein 3) and the Plains tradition of earned leadership that did not coerce followers (Haggerty).[33] Although one witness at the trial suggested that he had been coerced by Riel (Morton 238–39), leadership of a large number of armed, mounted, and independent-minded followers required charisma and ability. Riel says, "I did not wish to force my views, because in Batoche to the half-breeds that followed me I used the word, *carte blanche*" (CW 3: 531). He defends himself as a "decent prophet," rather than "a prophet who would all the time have a stick in his hand, and threatening, a prophet of evil" (3: 532). The egalitarianism of the *Exovede*, "out of the flock," a Latin word coined by Riel to describe his relationship to his followers, is just one example of his idea of good leadership. Riel says, "I prefer to be called one of the flock, equal to the rest" (3: 534). The principles of egalitarianism and independence found in the small self-governing hunting nations on the plains formed his political theory.

Reid, in her *Louis Riel and the Creation of Modern Canada: Mythic Discourse and the Postcolonial State* (2008), makes some of the argument for his deployment of Indigenous principles without explicitly recognizing them as such. She summarizes several of his remarks to show the "value he placed on expressions of respect" (192). She quotes Riel: "The people of the North-West were justified in taking up arms against the Dominion ... because 'they' [the Canadians] respect no right" (192).[34] I cannot argue that Indigenous people have a lock on respect. Nonetheless, the notion of respect carries stronger obligations in Indigenous society than in mainstream discourse, where it often simply means displaying good manners. Respect in Indigenous society requires that one refrain from even the appearance of telling others what they should think or do because that implies that they cannot think for themselves.[35] This attitude of respect extends from governance to pedagogy to rhetoric and covers not only adults, but children and the living world. And Riel used the word far more than anyone else at the trial. Of thirty instances of the word in the transcript, sixteen were either in his addresses or quotations of his speech by others; fourteen were not—but all fourteen appeared in set phrases such as "with respect to." For Riel, respect is a rhetorical and philosophical touchstone. Charland analyzes this stance, which might seem obsequious to a modern audience, as deriving from the traditional genre of the petition to the powerful, particularly under the monarchy, that works "to establish a familial relation of mutual obligation" ("Louis Riel's *Ethos*" 273). To argue that Riel's deployment of respect derives from Indigenous notions does not disqualify this point: in fact, they can be seen as working together.

Indeed, in his opening prayer, Riel asks God to bless all participants, including the prosecutors "because they have done, I am sure, what they thought was their duty" (*CW* 3: 524). He also gets a laugh near the end of his first address when he thanks the jury: "I do respect you, although you are only half a jury." He says to the judge, "[B]ecause you appointed these men, do not believe that I disrespect you. It is not by your own choice, you were authorized by those above you.... [Y]ou have acted according to your duty, and while it is, in our view, against the guarantees of liberty, I trust the Providence of God will bring out good of what you have done conscientiously" (3: 535). Here he is working within a paradigm that requires the respectful acknowledgement of all participants, even in a courtroom where prosecution and defence face off to produce oppositional arguments that will lead to a clear verdict of guilt or innocence.

Ron Scollon and Suzanne B.K. Scollon give a picture of the worldview of Athabaskans (like Riel's Chipweyan great-grandmother), which they label "bush consciousness": "Whereas the modern consciousness focuses on the outcome of the argument, someone wins and someone acquiesces, the bush consciousness focuses on the process of argumentation and seeks a consensus throughout" (186). They quote others who see this worldview as extending across the north to include many different groups, including the Cree, and quote one expert: "The individual is bound by few taboos and coerced by no authority" (200). Deanna Reder similarly argues that *kisteanemétowin*, "respect between people," was "more important than epistemological differences" for the Cree ("âcimisowin" 147). In the Western tradition, this stance may seem weak, even unethical or deceptive. Reder analyzes what appear to be contradictions in the autobiographical "Old Keyam," written by Poundmaker's great-nephew Edward Ahenekew, an Anglican priest. She quotes a discussion between him and his wife concerning a conference on Indian education, where they agree with different speakers. Old Keyam says,

> The Chief who spoke in opposition was another fine speaker—a credit to us all. Now I am not naming these Chiefs on purpose. It is not that I have forgotten their names.... I would not slight any of those who represented our people at that conference. We can be proud of them. It is not easy to take the stand that some of them did, and to speak boldly. (147–48)

Here, he sees the voicing of diverse standpoints aimed at finding a consensus as a more important value than achieving it.

Taiaiake Alfred argues that Indigenous theorization contains "an imperative of respect that makes homogenization unnecessary. Native people respect others to the degree that they demonstrate respect. There is no need, as in the Western tradition, to create political or legal uniformity to guarantee respect. There is no imperial, totalizing or assimilative impulse" (*Peace* 140). Similarly, Neal McLeod notes that "Cree narrative memory is ongoing, and is sustained by relationships, respect, and responsibility" (18), and of course all these words are interconnected. The phrase "all my relations"—which means far more than respect for one's own human relatives—is intended to remind everyone of the importance of *all* the relations engaged in between humans and the entire social and ecological web of kinship, including "all the animate and inanimate forms that can be seen or imagined" (King, Introduction ix). This way of regarding the universe is far different from the dialectics and categorization typical of Western intellectual discourse. However, this attitude of respect does not mean that Riel could not be clear about his opinions—he too spoke boldly: "[I]f at times I have been strong against my true friends and fathers, the reverend priests of the Saskatchewan, it is because my convictions are strong. There have been witnesses to show that after great passion I could come back to the great respect I have for them" (CW 3: 530). In another place he asks of the jury, "Am I insulting?" and replies, "No, I do not insult. You don't mean to insult me when you declare me guilty; you act according to your convictions, I do also according to mine. I speak true" (3: 558). Leaders were expected to speak and act according to their convictions and their duty, while maintaining respect for others. Riel was, I would argue, working with a broader range of epistemological traditions than those he learned in church or at school.

Flanagan frequently comments on places where Riel appears to be concealing his most radical ideas or tempering his words to his audience. He sums up this line of interpretation: "Thus Riel learned from the fiasco of his first attempt to be a religious founder that a prophet cannot succeed without a willing audience. He ultimately demonstrated the ability to speak in religion, as he already had done in politics, not only to speak but to make himself heard, to lead by offering his followers a message they could accept" (*Louis "David" Riel* 104). If all that Riel wanted was to stay in power, to delude his followers, as the prosecution suggested, to offer his followers "a message they could accept" might be seen as compromising his real principles. However, if we regard Riel less as an individual and more as part of a collective trying to produce a constitutive and consensual narrative out of the available discourses, it would seem strange that he and the Métis would not draw on their Indigenous intellectual heritage. And one can see Riel working in these two addresses to try to construct a receptive audience, both literally, in asking for a commission to replace a trial court, and also in the pragmatics of his speech. He enlarges the potential audience for his words, moving from remarks directed at those in the courtroom to hypothetical future listeners: "If I can't do it in my life I leave the ideas to be fulfilled in the future" (CW 3: 557). One can see him working in the present, in an extemporaneous speech, to make connections that will foster the emergence of a new polity. That his people became the landless "Road Allowance People" (Campbell) living in what Howard Adams called a "prison of grass" did not prevent this vision from living on in their lives, stories, and activism.

MOVING FORWARD

Riel's difficulty in achieving coherence has been connected to the difficulties Canadians have found in producing a coherent national narrative. This is the gist of the first chapter of Harold Cardinal's *The Rebirth of Canada's Indians* (1977), where he argues that traditional Indigenous people know what they mean when they say they are Canadians, which is that they need to maintain "a balanced relationship to the land" (11). He continues, here speaking of the Cree in particular, "I do not know if the white man's understanding and definition of the word is as precise as ours when he identifies himself as a Canadian" (10). As Dorland and Charland put it, mainstream "Canada has often been described as marked by an ironic sensibility, because it is aware that it lacks a grand narrative to provide a strong and unambiguous sense of its identity, purpose or destiny" (214). Riel's story, they argue, despite the frequency with which his image has been appropriated, cannot provide that narrative: "No heroic narrative, either of victim or victory, can be told that links the North-West, Riel, and Canadian justice through a happy process of identification." They argue that revisiting this case requires an identification with some kind of failure: "of meaning, of law, of reason, of justice" (190). They argue that this failure rests in "the loss of the monarch from the Canadian rhetorical and constitutional landscape.... Under Canadian Confederation the Crown remained, but no longer as the incorporation of the realm, but as an abstract principle of legality" (306–7). Here they are arguing, as has the Supreme Court of Canada, for the consistent maintenance of the honour of the Crown. I agree that

Riel's fate starkly outlines the failure of the dominant story of a tolerant Canada and an honourable Crown. However, they do not make it clear how the monarch's reappearance in "the Canadian rhetorical and constitutional landscape" as something more than an abstraction would accord Canadians a "happy process of identification." Still, Dorland and Charland's concern to find a single story that will lead to such an outcome is commonplace. Sometimes it is simply asserted, as in the first line of John Ralston Saul's *A Fair Country: Telling Truths about Canada*: "We are a metis civilization" (3). This statement counts as self-constituting rhetoric, but it seems to claim more for mainstream Canadians than they can or would wish to articulate for themselves at present.

Reid suggests that Canada lacks "a coherent historical narrative" because we "cannot even agree on its primary defining events. The Conquest of Quebec cannot satisfy Anglophones' need for a foundational moment in their state, just as the Confederation of 1867 will never provide a focus for Quebec nationalists; and, obviously, neither event signals the beginning of modernity for Aboriginal peoples in Canada" (245). Reid suggests that Riel was countering an overarching nationalist narrative with another one that she labels postcolonial, a vision of Canada that refused notions of homogeneity based on religion or ethnicity, calling on Riel's vision as a "a model for a potential alternative to the nation-state (which, when all is said and done, is a political configuration quite unsuited to the postcolonial period)" (247). Reid's belief in the need for "a firm understanding of a shared identity" different from that provided by nationalism is problematic to the extent that it relies on fixity (suggested in words like "firm" and "model"). Fixed narratives are the exception rather than the rule in oral tradition. Truth emerges for each teller and each hearer as that teller works in a new situation to adjust the story to produce a truth relevant to the audience and to current needs. Thomas King would also warn against the label "postcolonial" because it ties too closely to colonialism and nationalism ("Godzilla vs. Postcolonial"). Further, with Judith Butler, I would argue that identification is as much the problem as the solution, and would ask with her, "[W]hat political possibilities are the consequence of a radical critique of the categories of identity?" (*Gender Trouble* xxix). To counter such single-minded viewpoints based on the assumption that we need a shared national identity, we perhaps instead should try to become what Daniel Coleman might call "epistemological cross-talkers," and to question basic assumptions, as J. Edward Chamberlin does when he suggests replacing underlying Crown title to Canada with Aboriginal title (*If This Is Your Land* 229).

Thus Reid's suggestion that Riel can provide Canada with a new narrative and a new postcolonial identity is an appropriation that demonstrates her admiration for him, but that may lead to the recurrence of old problems. For example, colonial law first legislated an overarching identity, "Indian," out of a group of disparate nations, and then proceeded to fragment this category as the state saw fit. All identity categories both exclude and rely on what they exclude for their definition. Indeed, even my focus on coherence in this chapter can be seen as a version of homogenizing discourses such as that of nationalism. Riel's narrative will resist coherence to the extent that his world is not mine—and it is not mine. In his terms, however, I should still respect it and him, for speaking boldly. Here I also follow Chamberlin, who suggests that academics should "interrupt our stories so that they don't incarcerate us" (*If This Is Your Land* 239).

If we accept that Canadians need a new self-constituting narrative, clearly it cannot be constructed as if there were only one single worldview or epistemology in Canada. Chamberlin points out in *If This Is Your Land, Where Are Your Stories? Finding Common Ground* that stories carry contradictory truths and that we need many such stories, in his view, not just one. Further, as Ian Angus notes, the "rules of interaction" must also be considered: "Aboriginal speech, for example, has been present in Canada since its inception but the Canadian nation-state has never ceded it an equal right to construct the rules of interaction. Speech that is barred from touching the rules of interaction becomes a 'minority' speech precisely through this bar" (892; see also Charland, "Louis Riel's *Ethos*" 271). Big Bear was making this point when he said that what he most feared was "the rope to be about my neck" (Stonechild and Waiser 25). However, Governor Morris, at Fort Pitt to negotiate a treaty, was given the wrong translation, and thought Big Bear feared "hanging" rather than being led as by a leash or harness. He reassured Big Bear that all were equal under the law (Stonechild and Waiser 25–26; Harring 252). This law was precisely the problem as far as Big Bear was concerned, a point Sidney L. Harring highlights with his title, *White Man's Law*.

What if the law itself needs rethinking? A series of Supreme Court of Canada decisions have slowly been reworking Canadian law to speak to the mistakes and deliberate injustices of colonial rule. However, decisions driven by minority activism and hard-raised legal fees, decisions taken only by one arm of government, are not enough. If Canada as a nation is to truly shift, more than one national narrative must co-exist and permeate law and other broader discourses. One such narrative, as Quebec sovereignists have so persistently made clear, is not enough. And in fact, these narratives may no longer be best described *as* national (here I do agree with Reid). John Borrows has called for a new recognition of what he calls "multi-juridicalism" (*Canada's* 282). This recognition would require bringing the many Indigenous legal traditions into conversation with Canadian law in a way that will not simply subjugate them to it. Situating Riel's words in a context where they "make sense" requires contemporary readers to become the audience he did not have in the courtroom. Imagining how oppositional minority discourses might make sense, however apparently incoherent, requires serious and respectful political effort. The easy way out is to label them as authored by frauds, madmen, or criminals. Only after an effort has been made to respect their authors can real disagreement become public and real consensus-making begin.

"We Indians Own These Lands": Performance, Authenticity, Disidentification, and E. Pauline Johnson / Tekahionwake (1861–1913)

The impossible question that haunts Johnson's career (and that even got to her on occasion) might be posed this way: "Pauline Johnson: Was she really Mohawk?" The definition of identity, like the diagnosis of insanity, is never fixed, but depends on social relations and social context. Attempting to answer this "simple" question moves the discussion away from her writing and performances to focus it on her biography and markers of legitimacy such as her blood quantum or her ability to speak Mohawk. The assumption is that *if* we could only get clear whether she was Mohawk or not, *then* we could assess the value of her poetry and ideas. Greg Sarris decries this strategy, calling it "nail down the Indian in order to nail down the text" (128; see also Warrior xix). Indeed, since critics disagree completely on how Mohawk she "really" was, the debate could be seen as a case study in how identity politics can operate as "a politics of distraction" (G.H. Smith). However, Johnson fronted identity in her performances, where she typically appeared in both buckskins and evening dress, using the mainstream obsession with authenticity to propel her career. Her itinerant life reveals her complex relationship to the land where she was born and grew up, the Six Nations Indian Reserve near Brantford, Ontario, a relationship that can be articulated only by considering her gender and her personal history.

In their aptly titled biographical study, *Paddling Her Own Canoe*, Veronica Strong-Boag and Carole Gerson describe her as someone "who both upheld and transgressed cultural codes" (102). She was "always highly mediated," not only by her own self-representations, but also by the representations of her biographers and critics, then and now (102). The complexities of the case do not deter anyone. All her critics, myself included, obsess over her identity, however pathological this obsession may be. Her contemporaries' answers to the impossible question range from "hardly at all" to "absolutely."

Horatio Hale, the Harvard-educated anthropologist who worked with her father and grandfather, describes her as "a well-bred and accomplished young Canadian lady with a dash of Indian blood" (4). Ernest Thompson Seton, the writer responsible for the "Indian" influences on the Boy Scouts of America, describes her as "the ideal type of her race." Contemporary Mohawk critics also disagree, with Rick Monture seeing "her Canadian identity superseding her Iroquois identity" ("Beneath" 130) and Beth Brant asserting that "Canada may attempt to claim her as theirs, but Johnson belonged to only one Nation, the Mohawk Nation" (175). This wide disparity of opinion shows how fixed conceptions of identity beleaguer all those seen as speaking for a minority group. Under patriarchal Canadian law, because her father was Mohawk, she was a Status Indian, a ward of the federal government. However, Mohawk clan membership comes from the maternal line: her mother was English. The uncomfortable but productive position in which she found herself has been theorized by Gayatri Spivak as that of the "native informant," who, unlike the subaltern, could speak—although the reception of this speech was usually, as Spivak puts it, "foreclosed" (*Critique* 4).[1] She, as Spivak puts it, had "the certified half-caste's limited access to the norm" (168). This limitation is marked by the usual interpretation of her life and writing through frameworks that stress identity.

Johnson herself found the obsession with authenticity ridiculous: "How can one be consistent until the world ceases to change with the changing days? It always amuses me when some very clever critic undertakes to tell you exactly what kind of person you are 'under the skin'" (qtd. in Strong-Boag and Gerson 9). Johnson consistently asserted that she was Mohawk and wrote and indefatigably performed works that dramatized the dispossession of Indigenous peoples. Her claim to authenticity gave her a platform and an audience and she made the most of it. Her goals, stated in a letter to a friend in 1890, are quite clear: "I have a double motive in all my strivings—one is to upset the Indian Extermination and the noneducation theory—in fact to stand by my blood and my race" (qtd. in Strong-Boag and Gerson xvi). These words, written before her performing career was even thought of, might be understood as a mission statement.

One way to understand the ways she worked to engage her audiences with her political message is to read her performances through the notion of "disidentification." As theorized by Michel Pêcheux and elaborated by José Esteban Muñoz, disidentification is neither assimilative nor oppositional, but rather works to reformulate the world "*through* the performance of politics" (xiv):

Disidentification is a third mode of dealing with dominant ideology, one that neither opts to assimilate within such a structure nor strictly opposes it; rather, disidentification is a strategy that works on and against dominant ideology.... [It] is a strategy that tries to transform a cultural logic from within, always laboring to enact permanent structural change while at the same time valuing the importance of local or everyday struggles of resistance. (Muñoz 11–12)

An acclaimed poet whose work was quickly integrated into the canon (Shrive; Strong-Boag and Gerson 124–31),[2] Johnson also became a celebrity performer (York 43–46). She put on around two thousand performances between 1892 and 1909 in Canada, the United States, and Britain, sometimes alone, but generally with a partner, first Owen Smily and then Walter McRaye. Except for Quebec, she performed in Canada from the east coast to the west at every railway stop where an audience could be gathered and, on occasion, even beyond the rail lines. She also appeared at Toronto's Massey Hall, Harvard University, and London's Steinway Hall, and in the homes of many wealthy patrons and important Canadian officials (Keller 148, 209; McRaye 66). She and other accomplished Indigenous people of the day demonstrated that Indigenous people could succeed—even excel— by the standards of white society. Their success, in fact, threatened the primary rationalization for Canadian colonization, which was that Indigenous people lacked civilization and required white educators, missionaries, and Indian agents to help them achieve it.[3]

Her reception was mediated by long-established discourses. One of the ways non-Indigenous people vanished the Indians was simply by not seeing them if they did not dress and act in the ways the stereotype suggested that they should. Her performances invoked and complicated a variety of classed, gendered, sexualized, and racializing stereotypes about women, "Indians," and Indigenous women. Because she often began with "Indian" subject matter and dress and moved to "European" evening costume and poetry (Strong-Boag and Gerson 106), critics have argued that her mainstream audience simply read her act as modelling a narrative of progress from tradition to civilization. In this story, the (vanishing) Indian leaves a primitive identity behind and moves into a new one (white, but not quite) through assimilation into modernity (Monture, "Beneath" 123). This narrative of transformation was repeated over and over again in the photographs of children brought into residential school, first photographed with their long hair and Indigenous dress on entry, and then later, with hair shorn, wearing European clothes and often in school settings, as if by magic "civilized." Carole Gerson argues that "her performing sequence effectively contained the potential disruptiveness of her native material" (*Canadian Women in Print* 184). However, Nellie McClung recounts a performance where Johnson appeared first in evening dress, which somewhat undermines the force of this view. Perhaps worse, however, she may well have been read by some as proclaiming both "sides" of a conflicted and doomed "halfbreed" identity riven by the difference between savagery and civilization. The offspring of supposedly "pure" races were often described as innately unhealthy, tragic, or tormented. For example, the title character of Duncan Campbell Scott's poem "The Half-breed Girl" (1913) is, as D.M.R. Bentley puts it, "so conflicted as to render her little short of insane and suicidal" ("Shadows" 758). Such contending interpretations of Johnson's performances can easily be found, reflecting the jarring effects of disidentification. She exploited her ability to vanish and reappear before the audience's very eyes.

Her "Wild West" buckskins both authenticated her identity and drew audiences. Indian dress both risked the word "squaw" and openly defied it at a time when, as Jean Barman puts it, "Aboriginal women became sexualized as prostitutes" ("Taming" 243; see Carter, *Importance* 9). However, her evening dress resisted the negative sexualization of Indigenous women. It also made the point that she was in no need of civilization. She also distinguished herself from another group of women often seen as morally dubious, actresses, who performed the words of others, because her publicity material emphasized that she wrote all her own poetry. As Lorraine York points out, Johnson worked extremely hard to keep her career going at both the popular level (which provided her with an independent income) *and* the elite level (which maintained her class status). Aware of the dangers of being seen as too closely aligned with a popular market, Johnson used the money from her performing career[4] "to have her first book of poems published by a prestigious British press. Thus she used the fruits of her labour in the field of large-scale production to ensure herself a coveted space in the field of restricted production" (York 36). She used her cultural capital strategically.

Her audiences, at least in the west of Canada, were a heterogeneous mix who likely read her performances into their own disparate perspectives; McRaye notes that on their tour in British Columbia to Barkerville in 1901, for example, they played to "ranchers, miners, Indians, half-breeds [*sic*], and farmers" (75). The reactions of these audiences certainly would

FIG. 6   E. Pauline Johnson / Tekahionwake.
Vancouver Public Library, VPL 9429.

differ from those in eastern Canada, the United States, or Britain; unfortunately, no memory of Indigenous audience responses has been recovered. McRaye describes the partners as the first "Crusaders for Canadian literature" (160–61).[5] However, Johnson's self-descriptions as a performer always emphasized that she was Mohawk. Strong-Boag and Gerson note the many ways she described herself in print and letters: "Mohawk Indian Poet-Reciter," "The Iroquois Indian Poet-Entertainer," and "The Mohawk Author-Entertainer" (105). In contrast, she was often described by reviewers as a poetess ("Canadian, Indian, Mohawk, or Iroquois"), dramatic reciter, elocutionist, and even comedienne (Strong-Boag and Gerson 106). Whatever the motives of her audiences, she was on stage to proclaim herself as first a Mohawk and then a Canadian, a claim that she refused to see as contradictory (see Viehmann 263). Despite the occasional self-doubt and discouragement expressed in her letters, Johnson consistently brought a charming, witty, and vigorous persona to a variety of stages, impressive and ramshackle, private and public.

My argument is that she was performing her ability as a Mohawk woman to move into modern elite Canadian society while remaining Indigenous. She performed during a time of profound and rapid shift in settler–Indigenous relations. Her performing career began in 1892, only seven years after the second Riel Resistance, and ended in 1909. Duncan Campbell Scott, her fellow poet, became the senior administrator in Indian Affairs the year of her death; he quickly moved to further enforce and amplify the provisions of the Indian Act.[6] By increasing the control of Indian agents over reserve populations and sending more and more children to abusive residential schools,[7] he made it ever less likely that "ordinary Canadians" would encounter accomplished Indigenous people like Johnson in their daily lives. In fact, he ensured that few Indigenous people would get the education or opportunities to write and travel freely that had fostered her ability to make a living. Residential schools were not intended to produce competitors for "white" jobs, let alone confident cultural leaders and literary celebrities like her. Despite the dangers of a narrow focus on biography and identity, reading Johnson's work depends on understanding her unusual social position.

Johnson could easily have "passed" as an upper-middle-class white woman, given her appearance, her excellent if unconventional education, her father's and grandparents' status in both Mohawk and settler society, and her mother's ferocious insistence on decorum. Further, she was brought up in the traditions of Six Nations, where women played vital political roles; she was a witness to the highest levels of public ceremony. The seat on the Six Nations Confederacy Council held by her father, George Johnson, was controlled by his mother, Helen Martin Johnson, a powerful clan mother.[8] Pauline grew up in a home that welcomed those from the highest levels of Indigenous, British, and Canadian society and where the politics of the day were constantly discussed. However, when her father died in 1884, the Six Nations Confederacy Council, backed up by the Indian superintendent, refused to give her mother a widow's pension (Strong-Boag and Gerson 48). The family moved out of Chiefswood, the family home (now a National Historic Site), and apparently none of them lived on the reserve after that.

Johnson's refusal to pass as white was based on more than family feeling, although her stories reveal her admiration for her father and his parents. In fact, part of her failure to fit neatly into the categories allotted to her by mainstream society came from her Mohawk upbringing, in that their alliance with the British explained the presence of the Six Nations in Canada. The Johnson family's Loyalism[9] underpinned her identification as both a Mohawk and a Canadian. Since Canadians were described until 1946 as British subjects (Canada, Citizenship and Immigration), her patriotism featured considerable slippage between loyalty to Canada and to the British Crown (see Berger). As her poem "Canadian Born" puts it, "[W]e were born in Canada beneath the British flag" (Johnson, *Collected* 125). When she was born, Confederation was still a work in progress, as were policies concerning citizenship and Indigenous people.[10]

In retrospect, Mohawk Loyalism can be seen as a mistaken trust in the honour of the Crown. Around two thousand of the Six Nations people adopted this allegiance by moving north from their traditional territories in what became upstate New York in 1783 at the end of the American Revolutionary War. They received land to compensate for that lost in the Treaty of Versailles, some situated on the Bay of Quinte and some along the Grand River. In the War of 1812 they fought to regain their lost territory in the United States to no avail: the Treaty of Ghent also ignored their claims.[11] Johnson's stance of difference and equality was derived from this history, and it allowed her to oppose many of the stereotypes of inferiority that her own performances risked evoking. Without the cultural capital of her privileged upbringing in both Mohawk and white ways, she would never had been able to write canonical poetry or move confidently in the highest mainstream social circles. Nonetheless, to assume that therefore she was *really* white or that she must have aspired to *be* white is rather like imposing on her the stereotype of the abject Indian maiden, helplessly in love with an indifferent white man.

Homi Bhabha argues that the stereotype is colonialism's "major discursive strategy," seeing it as "a form of knowledge and identification that vacillates between what is always 'in place,' already known, and something that must be anxiously repeated ... as if the essential duplicity of the Asiatic or the bestial sexual licence of the African [or the savagery of the Native American] that needs no proof, can never really, in discourse, be proved" (66). This "anxious repetition" speaks to the idea that identity, although seen as something essential, something people are born with and continue to "have," must be repeatedly performed to retain its effectiveness. Johnson's white audience members anxiously attended performances expecting displays of the "savage" or the "Indian princess" to reassure themselves about their own claim to virtue, civilization, and territory. Their need provided Johnson with an audience before which she could work to reconfigure these stereotypes. Diana Taylor asserts that "we learn and transmit knowledge through embodied action, through cultural agency, and by making choices.

Performance, for me, functions as an episteme, a way of knowing, not simply an object of analysis" (xvi). Johnson's performance signalled an episteme other than the dominant.

Yet her career was highly contingent; given her upbringing and cultural capital, Johnson, like many other women of part-Indigenous parentage during that time, was expected to marry, if possible, "up" into whiteness. Her resolutely pro-marriage biographer, Betty Keller, saw her refusal "to downplay her Indian ancestry" as ruining her chances to capture a white suitor, since "[t]he matrons of Brantford found her utterly charming, but none was anxious to accept a half-breed [sic] daughter-in-law no matter what her other qualifications were" (54). An attractive woman, she received proposals from both white and Indigenous men (Strong-Boag and Gerson 67; Gray 96). Her only known brush with marriage was an engagement to Charles R.L. Drayton, a member of an upper-class immigrant British family, whose father taught law at Osgoode Hall and whose older brother, Henry Lumley Drayton, became minister of finance in 1919. She consented to marry Charles Drayton in January 1898, when she was thirty-six and he twenty-five. He eventually asked her to release him from the engagement (which she repeatedly announced in the press along with notices of her continuing performances), presumably after pressure from his father (Keller 134–35). By this time she had been touring for six years and had been well received in London, where her first book, *The White Wampum*, was published by the well-known publisher John Lane. At this point, it would have been difficult for her to recede into married whiteness as Mrs. Charles R.L. Drayton.

It is no surprise that her writing casts a spotlight on the ways in which the marriage market intersected with racialization and, even more important, with land. Controlling Indigenous people entailed imposing the European model of patriarchy, which treated women as the property of their father or husband, without any control over the property they brought into the marriage or the children they bore (Chambers). "Unattached" (implicitly sexually "loose") women embodied a threat to this system.

Lasting unions between European men and Indigenous women had been common only a generation or so earlier, during the Hudson's Bay Company's rule, as these connections served to facilitate trade (Van Kirk, *Many Tender Ties*). Indeed, such relationships have produced at least two nations, the Red River Métis and the Labrador Métis (also Inuit-Métis, or NunatuKavut). Johnson's boys' story "The Shaganappi" turns on the discovery that Lady Bennington, the mother of the most popular boy in the school, is "a half-breed" (*Collected* 282). In this same story the governor general is introduced to another boy, Fire-flint Larocque, who is also described as a "half-breed." The governor general responds, "I certainly do not like that term 'half-breed.' Most of the people of the continent of America are of mixed nationality—how few are pure English or Scotch or Irish—or indeed of any particular race? Yet the white people of mixed nations are never called half-breeds. Why not?" (263). Examples of elite marriages like that of the fictional Benningtons would have been well known to Johnson. James Douglas, governor of the Colony of Vancouver Island (1851–1864) and later also of British Columbia (1858–1864), married Amelia Connolly, the daughter of a white fur trader and Miyo Nipiy, a Cree woman (Van Kirk, "Tracing" 152). Isabella Sophia Hardisty, daughter of the chief trader of the Hudson's Bay Company in Labrador, married Donald Alexander Smith, later to become Lord Strathcona. He is the man in the top hat hammering the last spike in the famous photograph of the completion of the transcontinental railway in 1885. Hardisty's father was English and her mother of Native and Scottish parentage. However, although Strathcona was one of the richest men in Canada (he donated $7.5 million to a variety of causes, including a women's college at McGill University), he suffered from gossip all his life about his wife's ancestry and her earlier marriage by Indigenous rites (called *à la façon du pays*, or country marriage). He also worried about the legitimacy of their children and whether they could inherit his estate (Gwyn 115–16; Carter, *Importance* 34–35; Reford).[12] Even though Isabella was presented to King Edward VII and Queen Alexandra in 1903, wealth and status can do only so much to resist racist and sexist social mores entrenched in law. Lord and Lady Strathcona became Johnson's patrons in 1906 when she visited England, where Lord Strathcona was the Canadian high commissioner. Like her governor general in "The Shaganappi," Johnson was quite able to see through the fiction that Indigenous people were innately inferior to whites and that "mixed-race" people like herself were anomalous at best and at worst evidence of a failure of civilized control.

Such marriages began to be discouraged as scandalous rather than tolerated as pragmatic when land controlled by the Hudson's Bay Company was transferred to Canada and as white settlement reinforced racist attitudes in the new nation.[13] Johnson's parents' marriage, unusual in that it was between an Indigenous man and an English woman, was a subject for gossip when the wedding took place. (The woman-as-property metaphor prevalent at the time would figure the property in this case as moving the "wrong" way, that is, out of white patriarchal control.) In fact, the union was

FIG. 7 Donald Alexander Smith driving the last spike of the Canadian Pacific Railway. Library and Archives Canada, MIKAN 3194527.

opposed by both families (see Johnson, "My Mother").[14] It was still occasioning comment in the local papers on Emily Johnson's death; in the obituaries, readers were reminded of the general "astonishment" that had greeted the news of her "unusual" marriage (Keller 137). By the time Johnson was an adult, the social climate had become even more racist. That she refused all proposals but one for a physically arduous and financially precarious life on the stage attested to her desire for independence in a world where marriage to a white man implied female submission and risked obliterating her identification as Mohawk. Although marriage to an Iroquois man might have resolved some of Johnson's difficulties, she did not choose this route either.[15]

Not surprisingly, Johnson used representations of marriage to convey ideas about equality, mutual respect, and happiness that by analogy could extend to nations within Canada. Rauna Kuokkanen argues that Johnson's fictionalized account of her parents' happy marriage, "My Mother," works in the same way as Latin American "foundational fictions." She states that "[i]n 'My Mother,' love that crosses races, bloodlines, nations and discrimination becomes an allegory for politics of inclusive nationalism" (65).

Kuokkanen notes that in Canada, this allegory faced stronger social opposition than in Latin America, and that this story and others that represented such happy marriages were more concerned with "expressing the distinctiveness and uniqueness of a particular nation in order to resist the assimilation into the white society" (68). Johnson's account of her parents' marriage was aimed at those who supported the segregation of so-called races. Indeed, she herself exemplified the success of a "mixed" marriage.

Johnson, such are the joys of performance, played a wife many times on stage, notably in her poems "Ojistoh" and "A Cry from an Indian Wife," but also in a short play that she made out of a story, "A Red Girl's Reasoning." This story won a prize in the *Dominion Magazine*'s short story contest in 1892, and Johnson began using it in her performances as early as September that year. She rewrote it "as a playlet for herself and Smily, and they used it as the grand finale to their show" (Keller 70). This story makes the social difficulties faced by the second generation of "mixed" marriages crystal clear. But it also shows how these prejudices connect to the theft of Indigenous land.

In the story, Christy, the daughter of a Christian "Indian" woman and "old Jimmy Robertson," a Hudson Bay trader on the prairies, marries Charlie McDonald, who has been working for the Department of Agriculture. Christy is "all the rage in the provincial capital that winter" (Johnson, *Collected* 191). However, when she publicly reveals that her parents were not married by a priest or a magistrate, but by "Indian rites" (193), Charlie is humiliated. He, who "has always thought so much of honourable birth" (194), chastises her for disgracing herself and her parents: "[Y]ou have literally declared to the whole city that your father and mother were never married, and you are the child of—what shall we call it—love? certainly not legality" (196). Christy responds, "[D]o you mean to tell me that because there was no priest and no magistrate, my mother was not married? Do you mean to say that all my forefathers, for hundreds of years back, have been illegally born? If so you blacken my ancestry beyond—beyond—beyond all reason" (196). Charlie's response is that now, in more "civilized" times, her father should have married her mother "properly" when the priest arrived. Christy recounts her mother's response when the priest made this suggestion: "You go away. *I* do not ask that *your* people be remarried. Talk not so to me" (196). Charlie responds, "Your father was a fool not to insist upon the law, and so was the priest" (196). She replies, "Law? My people have no priest and my nation cringes not to law." Charlie talks of the "miserable scandal" that will spread, making it impossible for her to be presented in

Ottawa to the governor general: "I'll be pointed to as a romantic fool, and you as worse; I can't understand why your father didn't tell me before we were married; I at least would have warned you to never mention it" (197). Christy's response is that there was no time before they were married because "we are not married." She continues:

> Why should I recognize the rites of your nation when you do not acknowledge the rites of mine? According to your own words, my parents should have gone through your church ceremony as well as through an Indian contract; according to my words, we should go through an Indian contract as well as through a church marriage. If their union is illegal, so is ours. If you think my father is living in dishonour with my mother, my people will think I am living in dishonour with you. How do I know when another nation will come and conquer you as you white men conquered us? And they will have another marriage rite to perform, and they will tell us another truth, that you are not my husband, that you are but disgracing and dishonouring me, that you are keeping me here, not as your wife but as your—your *squaw*. (197–98)

She makes her point. The British recognized only British law; its imposition was a form of conquest. This conquest rendered all that went before savage, lawless, and sexually profane. Why should Indigenous peoples honour British laws, if the British do not honour theirs? The only possible explanation is that Indigenous people have been coerced: might has been made right. Another striking point of this speech is its acknowledgement of the existence of different epistemologies and multiple truths. Pierre Bourdieu's analysis of the performative force of law is prefigured here by someone who knew that different systems of law co-existed in Canada, despite the mainstream belief that there was and could be only one law. The audiences at Johnson's performances were being presented with a challenge to their ways of knowing the world, however difficult it is to know now to what extent any of them engaged with this challenge.

Christy's reasoned argument that Indigenous law was equal to British law—inconceivable to white settlers like Charlie—derived from Johnson's own Mohawk upbringing. She regarded the Iroquois as a sovereign nation: they had been British military allies and they were still largely in control of their traditional government. Significantly, Christy is depicted as wearing a red cloak like the one that Johnson wore over her buckskins, symbolizing their connection. When the play ended the performance, Johnson would have worn it over her evening dress as she performed Christy (Christy and Charlie are at a high-society ball when she makes her revelation). This piece of red broadcloth was a highly symbolic object for Johnson, as Prince Arthur, Duke of Connaught and Strathern, Victoria's third son,[16] had knelt on it to be adopted into the Mohawk in 1868, a ceremony in which her father played a central role (Keller 27–28, 263, 272). That she wore it during both halves of the performance served to unite them, as well as to symbolize her loyalty as a Mohawk to the British Crown.

After the quarrel, during which Christy throws away her wedding ring, she decamps in the night, ending up in Ontario. That she saw such an act as possible may again be connected to the ease with which either party could end a marriage both in Plains and Mohawk custom (Carter, *Importance* 10; US Department of the Interior). Her final word to the remorseful Charlie, when he finally locates her, is this: "[N]either church nor law nor even—and the voice softened—nor even love, can make a slave of a red girl" (Johnson, *Collected* 201). The word "slave" resonates, as did "squaw." If Britons "never, never, never shall be slaves," as the patriotic song "Rule Britannia" puts it, neither shall the Mohawk. Christy symbolizes the Indigenous nations, bound to the British by Christian belief, law, and even love, but adamantly proclaiming the equality of their own laws and customs. Christy clearly still loves Charlie, but refuses to return to him. And it does not occur to him to suggest that they marry in a ceremony acceptable to her and her people.

Christy's insistence on equality can be connected to the message of the famous Two-Row Wampum, an agreement made between the Five Nations and the Dutch in 1613 and considered to be the basis of all subsequent agreements with European migrants. It consists of two rows of purple beads, symbolizing the newcomers and the Haudenosaunee, each holding to their own path or remaining in their own canoe or ship. Three rows of white beads between these two purple lines are said to represent the principles of "peace, friendship, and mutual respect." These rows both separate and bind together the two peoples (Akwesasne). Johnson would have known the message of this most famous wampum belt, since her grandfather, John "Smoke" Johnson, was a wampum reader.

Johnson wrote "A Red Girl's Reasoning" years before she met Drayton: that he broke the engagement proved her prescient. As she grew up, she would have become well aware of the tensions that would make it difficult or impossible for her to marry, or—once married—to fit herself to the expectations of any husband, white or Indigenous. In the end, Johnson did not choose the "obvious" solution to the quandary posed by her socially ascribed identity, a compromise in marriage.[17] She was able to forge a career: a choice that was available to her because of her unusual family, privileged upbringing, and personal talent. Nonetheless, although she did better than Christy, her life was always financially precarious; she did not achieve the life of upper-middle-class comfort that her father was able to provide her mother.[18]

Johnson's public performances of this story articulated how individual choice and agency were constrained by both written and unwritten rules regulating the marriage market. Christy and Charlie clearly loved each other; racist attitudes, social snobbery, and Charlie's inability to understand Christy's position parted them. However, they remained married under Canadian law. The regulation of marriage in turn regulates the ownership and inheritance of property. Before 1832 in Upper Canada under the law of coverture, all women's property became their husbands' on marriage; subsequent changes to the law improved matters only slightly (see Chambers). A Status Indian woman who married a non-Status man incurred even more serious losses. As Beth Piatote puts it, "[T]he Indian Act sought to transfer property, cultural and legal rights from indigenous polities under the rubric of consent and love" (18). Piatote argues that by marrying Charlie, Christie has perforce consented to a kind of suicide, in that under the Indian Act, Indigenous women who "married out" lost their Status and they and their children were severed from the community (18). Until the law was amended in 1985 by Bill C-31, non-Indigenous women who married Status men were given Status, as were their children. Thus, laws around marriage led to women who knew little or nothing of Indigenous culture or language moving into the reserve community while Indigenous women who "married out" had to leave, forced to raise their children in isolation from their culture and their extended family. This legal sorting of bodies into separate locations worked to weaken Indigenous cultures, languages, and communities. Christy may declare that she and Charlie are not married, but under Canadian law, her claim to the land and culture that her mother refused to give up by marrying "properly" has been legally extinguished. Further, Christy's decision to leave Charlie and her refusal to return to him force her into a life of poverty as a seamstress off the reserve.[19] As a result of the Indian Act, more Aboriginal women have moved to cities than have Aboriginal men, who could stay on the reserve no matter who they married. The Indian Act therefore consolidated Indigenous men's power on reserves, shifting them toward a patriarchal model more like that of the dominant society (Miriam McNab). Over time, the law has also worked to dispossess Indigenous people and to free the federal government from any obligation to them. In a chapter titled "Regulating Native Identity by Gender," Bonita Lawrence notes that "[e]specially in Haudenosaunee society, female-led clans held the collective land base for all of the nations of the confederacy. Removing women, then, was key to privatizing the land base" (*Real Indians* 47).[20] Once Johnson's performing career began, she returned to Brantford mainly to visit her mother and sister Eva. Although she and her siblings shared the rent from Chiefswood, it's not clear whether she ever revisited her childhood home. Nonetheless, Johnson worked to transform the patriarchal system from within, not only by becoming a powerful woman and by performing powerful women, but also by arguing that Indigenous lands had been stolen.

The logic of "A Red Girl's Reasoning," as we shall see, is the logic of several of Johnson's other works. In poems where Indigenous people speak, the powerful voice is often that of a woman, just as women spoke powerfully in Iroquois councils. "Ojistoh" is set during the wars between the Huron and the Iroquois in the seventeenth century. Ojistoh describes herself as "the wife / of him whose name breathes bravery and life / And courage to the tribe that calls him chief" (Johnson, *Collected* 114). Although this move to "wife" may suggest to mainstream listeners that Ojistoh is subordinate to her husband, his name is never specified: Ojistoh calls him "my ... Mohawk" or "the Mohawk." A revengeful Huron chief carries her off on his galloping horse—an evocative image of the sexually wild and violent savage. Implicitly facing rape, Ojistoh seduces the Huron into unbinding her and then stabs him with his own knife, riding back to her husband on her captor's horse. In no need of rescue, she ends up in control of the symbols of sexual power: the knife, the horse, the husband.[21] Enacting the story of Ojistoh risked evoking racist or sexist responses that would affect her directly, as well as the Mohawk or Indigenous people more generally (Monture, "Beneath" 124). Part of the power of Johnson's performances, both everyday and on stage, however, was found in the way she kept all imputations of savagery and sexual looseness at bay. So Johnson here works with entangled and sensational discourses while firmly recuperating Ojistoh's— and, by implication, her own—sexual purity at the end of the poem: "My hands all wet, stained with a life's red dye / But pure my soul, pure as those stars on high. / 'My Mohawk's pure white star, Ojistoh, still am I'" (*Collected* 116). The poem also evokes the fantasy of achieving a pure Mohawk identity, albeit one located in a romantic past, by declaring loyalty to the Mohawk as a people as much as to a husband. The poem deploys a series of enmeshed distinctions and desires, drawing on and complicating the dominant discourses of identity, gender, sexuality, ethnicity, and racialization. This is what Muñoz calls the work of disidentification.

Johnson uses established discourses and sentimental tropes not only to arouse conventional emotions but also to deploy affect, which relies on social relationships for its bodily effects. Arising out of the attempt to think not just about minds, but about embodied minds with unconscious desires and physical sensations, affect theory focuses attention on "those intensities that pass body to body (human, nonhuman, part-body, and otherwise)" (Seigworth and Gregg 1). Affect theory has an affinity with performance, which deploys human bodies in conjunction with costumes, movement, sound, light, music, and symbolic objects (for example, Johnson's costume, with its scalps, bear-claw necklace, wampum, red cloak, and, of course, the knife) to make complex meanings: "Because affect arises out of muddy, unmediated relatedness and not in some dialectical reconciliation of cleanly oppositional elements or primary units, it makes easy compartmentalisms give way to thresholds and tensions, blends and blurs" (4). Affect thus evokes human connections that are denied by categories such as "civilized" and "savage."

"WE INDIANS OWN THESE LANDS"

In two other poems Johnson frequently recited, "A Cry from an Indian Wife" (*Collected Poems* 14–15) and "The Cattle Thief" (*Collected Poems* 97–99), women directly decry the injustices of colonization. "A Cry from an Indian Wife" deploys ricocheting twists of logic to evoke powerful emotions and affects, leading to the forthright declaration: "By right, by birth, we Indians own these lands." Certainly this declaration was mediated, as Johnson performs a Cree wife speaking during the Riel Resistance of 1885. In fact, the poem was first published in *The Week* in June 1885, "between the surrender of Poundmaker (May 26) and the surrender of Big Bear (July 2)" (Gerson, "The Most" 100).[22] The role of "Indian wife" provided Johnson with a way to articulate a larger theme of Indigenous dispossession. The speaker shifts her position several times. First, she encourages her husband to fight against the British soldiers: "Go; rise and strike, no matter what the cost." Then she immediately changes her mind: "Yet stay, revolt not at the Union Jack." She continues, "They but forget we Indians owned the land" and suggests, as did Christy to Charlie, that imagining themselves as vulnerable to conquest could provide settlers with a clearer perspective:

> They never think how they would feel today,
> If some great nation came from far away,

Wrestling their country from their hapless braves,
Giving them what they gave us—but wars and graves.

This thought moves the wife to once more spur her husband to war, as she lapses into self-pity ("Who pities my poor love and agony?"). She then extends this pity to the whole nation, imagining the priests who pray for the white soldiers, while no one "prays for our poor nation lying low." Once again she urges him on, only to think of the women who would be as devastated as she by the deaths of their white sons, brothers, and husbands: "[H]ow her white face quivers thus to think / How *your* tomahawk his life's best blood will drink."[23] She shifts again when she realizes that the white woman "never thinks of my wild aching breast, / Nor prays for your dark face and eagle crest"—again she urges him on to war: "Go forth and win the glories of the war." Then come the last four lines:

Go forth, nor bend to greed of white men's hands,
By right, by birth, we Indians own these lands.
Though starved, crushed, plundered, lies our nation low ...
Perhaps the white man's God has willed it so.

Here, like Christy, the wife points to how might makes right—the meaning of "right" defined, of course, by Western law and religion—although it should not. The last line turns to God's will, which anchored so many colonial discourses. The effect, particularly if we imagine the ringing tones of "by right, by birth" moving to a quiet delivery after "low"—is pathos. The Indians have been defeated not only by men, but also by an alien divine power. This final line, with its tone of quiet resignation, may have removed any ethical quandary from the minds of the white members of the audience, already conditioned to see their possession of Canada as providential. Still, such a resounding declaration of Indigenous rights was rare at the time in any context. Even with its force constrained by circumstances, it might well have, in Paulette Regan's terms, "unsettled the settlers." At least one audience member who fought against Riel is said to have regretted it to Johnson after a performance (Keller 60). Part of the poem's rhetorical force, in fact, lies in the wife's vacillation between militance against white conquest and empathy for the young white soldiers and the women who love them. Again Johnson uses marriage and the maternal in rather subversive ways.

Johnson revised the poem to enhance its effect between its first publication in *The Week* in 1885 and its publication in *The White Wampum* in

1895 (Gerson, "Postcolonialism" 432–33). The first version did not include the last four lines quoted above, but went from "win the glories of the war" to these lines:

> O! heart o'erfraught—O! nation lying low—
> God, and fair Canada have willed it so.

Rather than relying on ambiguity of the word "fair," as Gerson suggests she did in the first version ("Postcolonialism" 433), in her revision Johnson made perfectly clear points about Indian land rights, unjust treatment, and a foreign God. This "white man's God" stands in for the epistemological difference and intercultural incomprehension that led to the collapse of Christy's marriage. Both in poetic and political terms, the revision was a great improvement.

A forthright woman speaker also features in "The Cattle Thief" (*Collected Poems* 97–99). This poem begins with desperate riders, "their British blood aflame," pursuing a Cree man who has killed some of their cattle. The audience, implicitly British, is brought along in a rush of loyal feeling but then the poem abruptly requires them to disavow it. The Cree comes out to face the riders "unarmed"; they shoot him and "rush like a pack of demons on the body," which they propose to cut up to leave for the wolves. Then his daughter appears and stands them off "with a courage beyond belief": she says, "If you mean to touch that body, you must cut your way through *me*" and indignantly continues "in the language of the Cree":

> What have you left to us of land, what have you left of game,
> What have you brought but evil, and curses since you came?
> How have you paid us for our game? how paid us for our land?
> By a *book*, to save our souls from the sins *you* brought in your other
>   hand …
> When *you* pay for the land you live in, *we'll* pay for the meat we eat.
>
> (*Collected* 99)

We are hearing the words that the murderers cannot understand. The poem inverts long-standing tropes of Indians as demons, and as Strong-Boag and Gerson point out, as another twist, the Cree chief is compared to a lion, a symbol of Britain (206). Further, the poem points out that he was driven to his "crime" by starvation. That injustice is voiced in Johnson's work by women rather than men makes another point: Indigenous women have suffered more from colonization than Indigenous men. If Indigenous title to land came from the mother, the imposition of patriarchy empowered Indigenous men at the expense of women. One can see Johnson's assumption of her great-grandfather's Mohawk name, Tekahionwake, as appropriating male power, countering both her exclusion from Mohawk society and the expectation that she would take on an unrelated man's name in marriage.

DISCOUNTED IDENTIFICATIONS

As I pointed out above, Johnson faced and still faces a problem common among those of "mixed" ancestry: her identifications were and are discounted. Because authenticity is an impossible ideal, none are authentic enough to suit either those with "stronger" claims or those Marilyn Dumont calls "the white judges" (11). Johnson was wholly conscious of the problem. McRaye recounts a story she told about herself and an American woman on a ocean liner back from England. The American, complaining about the deficiencies of the Old Country, remarks:

> "[W]hen I asked for ice water they looked at me as if I was a North American savage." Johnson deflated this diatribe by remarking, "That's nothing, that's exactly the way they looked at me." This gave the lady pause, but she rallied and said, "Excuse me Miss Johnson, but was your father a real Indian?" "Yes," answered Pauline, and as she told it, "I foolishly asked the woman why?" "Well," she says "excuse me again, but you don't look the least bit like it." Pauline came back quickly with "And was your father a white man?" The woman answered, "Well yes, of course he was." "Well," said Pauline, "I'm equally surprised." (162–63)

This tiny interchange shows how packed with hostile implication social discourse can be, especially "polite" conversation between strangers.[24] (Notice how the woman prefaces her inexcusably nosy questions with the politeness marker "excuse me.") This example of small talk shows, in fact, how ideological discourses are produced in everyday conversations, which are revealed as tiny struggles for social dominance. It is apparently all right—even commonplace—for a white woman to check out the authenticity of someone presumed to be a member of a minority. However, it is unusual, even rude, to question the authenticity of a "superior" white person. The American woman is startled to have a version of same question she has asked come right back at her, while the quickness of Johnson's reply indicates that she's been asked such questions before (and foolishly once again tries to derail them). The transaction also reveals Johnson's wit in playing on the sense of "white" in the expression "that's white of you," where white means "honorable or square-dealing" ("White"). This anecdote shows her giving as good as she got. McClung remembers Johnson telling a different version of this story that featured a supercilious countess with a lorgnette (33). In Canada, either version would have evoked amusement, but perhaps Johnson told the one about the countess in the United States and the one about the American in London. Regardless of whether this conversation even happened, the story reveals the bumpy social terrain that Johnson had to travel. And although records of the comic anecdotes that Johnson told in her performances are scanty, this was the sort of patter that held her more formal poetic recitations together and earned her the title of comedienne. Clearly comic patter about such "small" talk serves to reveal and undercut serious social prejudices.

In this anecdote, the white woman is able to cast doubts on Johnson's authenticity while simultaneously "complimenting" her by suggesting that she doesn't *look* like "a North American savage," even if she is one. This implies that given a choice, everyone would prefer to be white. Johnson, as her side of the conversation makes clear, was proud of her ancestry. In fact, at least once she expressed the desire to look more "like an Indian." "Looking like one" may be no picnic when it evokes racist reactions, but at least makes the performance of identity less arduous, less anxious.[25] In letter to Arthur Henry (Harry) O'Brien in 1894, she wrote, "We are getting into Indian country now. Every town is full of splendid complexioned Ojibwas, whose copper colouring makes me ashamed of my washed-out Mohawk skin, thinned with European blood, I look yellow and 'Chinesey' beside these Indians" (qtd. in Keller 113). She sees herself as looking Chinese rather than white in this comparison, aligning herself with a group constructed as even more distant from "proper" Canadianness than Indigenous people. Johnson certainly deployed such commonplace hierarchies, for example by putting the "pagan" Six Nations at the pinnacle of Indigenous nations and "heathen" nations such as the Delaware further down on the chain of value (*Collected* 218). In an interview copied from a London paper, she reportedly said, "I am an Iroquois, and of course I think the Iroquois are the best Indians in civilization and birth, just as you English think you are better than the Turks" (qtd. in "Fate of the Red Man"). Here again she figures the Iroquois and the British as equals.

Most postcolonial critics still tie identity to ancestry, despite our disavowal of the related notions of biological race and racial hierarchy. But one can see that even ancestry for Johnson was full of pitfalls: which ancestors? Discourses of purity usually trump those of mixedness. John Borrows asserts, "Nothing in blood or descent alone makes an Aboriginal person substantially different from any other person" (*Recovering* 153). Nonetheless, descent remains at the base of the claim for social justice, because it is on the basis of descent that social and legal discrimination occurs ("was your father a real Indian?").

However, huge problems remain in moving on from "blood or descent *alone*." What is it that is *added* to descent that consolidates one's identity as authentic—one that *works* in the social contexts that an individual wishes to enter as an equal? What happens when this claim combines descent with self-assertion, as when Johnson took the name Tekahionwake? How can or should identity best be authorized—by ancestry; by self-assertion; by the community collectively acting to determine membership; by the federal government, with its complex web of ever-changing legal definitions; or by some combination of some or all of these? Or, as Butler and others argue, does the fractious history of identity politics reveal such categories as a divisive trap? Johnson's example reveals that there is no simple answer to these questions. However, that she chose to perform her mixed identity on the stage might lead us to consider the extent to which people perform their identities, which might explain why posture, dress, manners, conversational style, and personal taste are so crucial to how one is welcomed (or not) into particular locations. Sovereignty requires a kind of collective performance, and this performance is one that the Six Nations have expertly practised for many generations.

The Haudenosaunee have always rejected the Canadian government's claim to legislate their identity and continue to do so (Alfred *Peace, Wasasé*; Catapano; Leitner; *Mitchell v. Minister of National Revenue*). Their treaties were made with the British Crown, not Canada. They still issue their own passports. (Levi General / Deskaheh used one to travel to speak before the League of Nations in Geneva; Monture, *We Share* 231n.) Even after their hope of getting land back south of the border was dashed after the War of 1812, they have continued to assert a special relation to the Canadian state. It was only in 1924, over a decade after Johnson's death, that Duncan Campbell Scott forcibly abolished the traditional Haudenosaunee government in which George Johnson had played a prominent role. And Johnson herself was only occasionally constrained by her Indian Status.[26] What this Status meant to her is not clear, but it must have been quite different from what it came to mean to those born later. However, like Christy, she would have lost it if she had married a non-Status man.

Johnson clearly did not receive an uncomplicated endorsement of her identifications by the Six Nations community. Monture helpfully situates Johnson's family within the political conflicts on the reserve, and notes that "a curious tension often emerges in her writing, particularly within her articulation of the 'Iroquois nation,' a conception that was at odds with what most Iroquois people would have agreed with then and would agree with now" ("Beneath" 119). Her "distance from the Six Nations Reserve resulted in a rather hollow activism when it came to addressing Iroquois issues of the day" (138). Monture notes that a "pattern of placing the Iroquois firmly within a Canadian geography, even though they had emigrated to Canada only a hundred years before, is something that Johnson referred to again and again, and it indicates her larger 'project' of attempting to incorporate the Iroquois into a national, and physical, space" (123). Certainly Johnson appeared to be more concerned with having her identity as Mohawk accepted off the reserve than on it, and she often situates herself (or is situated) as a pan-Indigenous spokesperson when she recites poems featuring Cree women speakers. Monture sees her as assimilating the Iroquois into the Canadian nation and as stereotyping them in ways typical of non-Native poets, most ironically, Duncan Campbell Scott: "By casting Iroquois figures as heroic individuals in a precontact setting, Johnson effectively romanticizes the past and perpetuates themes of sexuality, violence and death among Iroquois society in the process, themes that, interestingly, also resonate in Scott's 'Indian poems' written during the same period" (125). In reading her this way, Monture resists her claims to be Mohawk, not on the grounds of her ancestry, but in terms of the difference he sees between her poetic politics and Iroquois beliefs and politics past and present ("what most Iroquois would have agreed with then and would agree with now"). More recently, he comments on her characterization of the Iroquois as patriotic: "Obviously, her views differed from those of the large majority of people at Grand River, who did not view themselves as being under the authority of the Canadian government" (*We Share* 83).

Taiaiake Alfred, a major Kanien'kehá:ka political theorist, argues "that what makes an individual 'indigenous' is his or her situation within a community" (*Peace* xvi). Perhaps because of his focus on Kahnawake (older spelling, Caughnawaga), the village south of Montreal founded in 1718 (Alfred, Heeding 40), no member of the Johnson family appears in the indexes of any of his three books. However, he recently tweeted that "Six Nations Chiefs Recover 1812 Belt Sold Off for Personal Profit to American by Poet Pauline Johnson in 1800s." Johnson's use of wampum belts in her performances and as part of her costume requires more analysis than there is space for in a tweet. But certainly her sale of wampum belts and other artifacts reveals her distance from both tradition and her home community.

Rick Hill, the chairman of the Six Nations Legacy Consortium, states of the belt in question that "Pauline Johnson didn't have the right to bargain [the Claus or Pledge of the Crown belt] away—the belt is a communal property." He sees its safe return just before the anniversary of the War of 1812 as providential (qtd. in ["Two Hundred"]). A display at Chiefswood I viewed in May 2013 noted that "[t]he wampum belts of the Six Nations were under the stewardship of John Buck, Sr., Onondaga chief and wampum keeper. After he died his heirs began to sell them—between 1893 and 1905 E. Pauline Johnson acquired four, including the Claus [Pledge of the Crown] Belt" (Chiefswood). Few would now argue that these belts were private property, although she must have convinced herself of it.[27] Michelle A. Hamilton describes the complex politics behind the Johnson family's collection, display, and sale of wampum, masks, and other objects (134–42).[28] In acquiring and then selling the Claus belt and other similar objects, Johnson transformed symbolic goods owned collectively by the Haudenosaunee into private commodities owned by a white collector. Their subsequent display in a museum transformed them again into the property of the mainstream public, and their return to Six Nations restored them to their former community, but with a new history. The reading of the Claus belt provided by Chief John Buck in 1897 was "that the government would never force the Indians to change their customs" (Six Nations Legacy Consortium). Johnson's display of such belts in the context of her poetic assertions about the equality of Indigenous rights and customs kept that meaning alive. She used the money she received from selling them to finance two trips to England, where she reiterated the connections between the Crown and the Indigenous people. Joe Capilano and his delegation were in the same place for the same purpose when she met him there in 1906. Clearly, however, she was not authorized by anyone but herself to undertake these ventures in which she formed alliances with particular symbolic objects to enhance the rhetorical force of her performances.

Monture and Alfred both react to what they see as her overarching loyalty to both Canada and the Crown, loyalty that is most plainly proclaimed in her poem "Canadian Born," the first and title poem of her collection *Canadian Born*: "[W]e, the men of Canada, can face the world and brag / That we were born in Canada beneath the British flag" (Johnson, *Collected* 125–26). Nonetheless, she included Indigenous people in this category in the inscription to the collection: "White Race and Red are one if they are but Canadian born." Gerson and Strong-Boag argue that this inscription "makes explicit her vision of an egalitarian nation" (xix; see also 178–79). However, even in their exemplary edited collection of her work the inscription does not appear with the poem; without it, "Canadian Born" is likely to be read into a settler-nationalist story. Johnson's assumption of an easy Iroquois or wider Indigenous loyalty to Canada and Britain is far from easy nowadays. It was difficult even then: her brother Beverly "relinquished his family's traditional support for the Conservative party when John A. Macdonald's government brutally suppressed the starving prairie tribes during the Northwest Rebellions of 1885" (Strong-Boag and Gerson 52). Now, over the hundred years of colonization since her death, political loyalties have become more fraught. And political loyalties matter in evaluating authenticity because it is allocated through political debate, even when people assert that "facts" like blood quantum or ancestry or Status should be what determine it.

Kristina Fagan argues that literary criticism generally avoids moving into these politics: "Literary scholars ... have tended to stay away from specific Political (with a big P) topics within Native literature, such as land ownership, law and governance. They tend instead to focus on small-p politics—that is, on power relations—and on large-scale issues such as colonization, sexism, and so forth" ("Tewatatha:wi" 3). By separating literature and culture from "big-P" politics, critics may sidestep the material or personal consequences that might result from the logical extension of their arguments. Reading Indigenous literatures via Indigenous nationalism, a theoretical approach now seen as central to the criticism of Indigenous literature, Fagan argues, ensures that these big-P political issues come back into play.

Fagan then reads Alfred's *Peace, Power, and Righteousness: An Indigenous Manifesto* (1999) as political literature. This book, she argues, works rhetorically through his self-situation in the context of tradition, of traditional genres such as the Condolence Ritual, and of thoughtful conversation with other Iroquois people. He enacts in print the traditional way of achieving consensus through public oratory and community deliberation. Fagan's notion of "how Aboriginal literature functions as a speech act" (14) connects both to Alfred's subtitle (the manifesto as a call to action) and to his promotion of traditional orature. Nonetheless, she also notes that Alfred's work has been criticized as unduly focused on leaders and notes that "his arguments often seem overly simplistic: Aboriginal people are presented as either traditional nationalists or assimilated sellouts. For most Aboriginal people, I would suggest, the issue is not so black and white" (14). Certainly, Alfred's tweet situates Johnson as a sellout.

Like Monture with Johnson, Fagan measures Alfred's arguments against the beliefs of the community: "Alfred himself admits that his views are different from those of 95 percent of Aboriginal people in Canada" (15). She quotes Joyce Green to the effect that Alfred does not address "the syncretic nature of cultures ... and the many contingent choices individuals make in their cultural selections (14–15), and thus argues that his views have the potential to become "oppressive fundamentalist formulations" (15). The restriction of authenticity to those who agree with the majority of the community or the nation forces dissenting individuals to the margins or excludes them altogether: ironically, this is where Alfred admits that he is located. The survival of Haudenosaunee difference, Alfred eloquently points out, requires the maintenance of a worldview that is demonstrably tied to tradition. However, Alfred sees this tradition as in need of interpretation not by elders and traditional teachers, who no longer have "solid, well-defined traditional roles"; instead, he argues "contemporary scholars, writers, and artists must take on the responsibility of translating these traditions and providing the guidance to make those traditions part of the contemporary reality" (Alfred qtd. in Monture, "Beneath" 137). One could argue that Johnson took this path over a hundred years before Alfred recommended it. Like him, she uses her identification as Mohawk to make political claims independently of the Haudenosaunee political structure.

Certainly Alfred's position remains Mohawk just as Johnson's does, whether or not any other Mohawk person agrees with it, because they have Mohawk ancestry, they identify as Mohawk, and they ground their work in Mohawk traditions. But clearly there is a difference between marginalizing those who do not agree with the dominant community narrative and respecting individuals who draw their own conclusions. One works by excluding those who disagree from the community and from authenticity; the other keeps them inside the community, admittedly at the cost of constant debate to maintain a functional consensus. This debate is the cost of admitting diversity of whatever kind into any community, from the Haudenosaunee to Canada to much larger polities. The name "Six Nations" and, before 1722, "Five Nations," indicates Haudenosaunee priority in and success at taking this cost into account.

As Strong-Boag and Gerson and Monture point out, Mohawk and other Indigenous women have seen Johnson as an inspiration. Writers and performers Frances Nickawa (Cree), Rita Joe (Mi'kmaw), Bernice Loft Winslow / Dawendine (Mohawk), Lee Maracle (Sto:lo), and Joan Crate (Métis) all have taken her as an example (Gerson and Strong-Boag, Introduction xxxvii). Beth Brant commented in 1994, "It is time ... to recognize Johnson for the revolutionary she was" (qtd. in Gerson and Strong-Boag, Introduction xxxvii). And it is not only Indigenous women who have found her inspiring. Rebecca Margolis notes that Johnson's work inspired two Yiddish-speaking Jewish immigrant critics, H. Caiserman and B.G. Sack, for whom "Johnson's Native heritage was a model for resistance to assimilation into Canada's dominant culture" (169). Their hopes for linguistic and cultural accommodation in the 1920s disappeared in a rising tide of anti-Semitism, however. Jewish immigration was cut off in the 1930s, condemning many would-be immigrants to death in Europe. Obviously, the reception and influence of Johnson's work over time should have some bearing on how it and she are judged.

This brings us to one more influential opinion on the nature and impact of Johnson's performances and writings. Daniel Francis writes in *The Imaginary Indian* (1992):

> Celebrity Indians did not challenge the values of mainstream Canadian society. Pauline Johnson was an outspoken patriot who wished to see Native and non-Native merge in a common nationality.... Celebrity Indians were hailed as spokespeople for their race, but they delivered a message that mainstream Canadian society was prepared to hear. If they had not, if they had tried to convey an overtly political message for instance, they would not have received a platform at all. The dominant society set the agenda and the terms of the discussion. At the same time when Pauline Johnson and Grey Owl attracted so much public acclaim, Native leaders who were attempting to achieve political gains for their people were meeting a blank wall of indifference. (142–43)

Francis's binaristic model is both purist and depressing: one can challenge the mainstream with an "overtly political message" and fail, or take up the agenda set by the mainstream and fail that way too, because one's message is by definition evacuated of any challenge. He clearly sees the former option as more virtuous.[29] Further, he sees Johnson as an assimilationist for wishing to "merge Native and non-Native." Her project was clearly not that simple, as "A Red Girl's Reasoning" and "A Pagan in St. Paul's Cathedral"—to pick just two works that reject this option—make clear. Absent from his analysis is any notion of the syncretism and contingency mentioned by Joyce Green. Given Francis's perspective, the success of his own *The Imaginary Indian* (eighteen thousand copies sold in seven printings since 1992) should cause him to wonder whether he is simply "delivering the message that mainstream Canadian society [is] prepared to hear" (Shyla). Cari M. Carpenter has argued against such approaches to Johnson, suggesting that "instead of trying to fix her into a rather narrow assimilated/nonassimilated divide, we should concentrate on her tactics of survivance, to borrow Gerald Vizenor's terms" (57). To see Johnson's work as disidentification or survivance resists the limitations of binaries such as traditionalist/sellout, political activist/celebrity, and political/apolitical.

Judith Butler sees "identity as a *practice*." For Butler, the performance of identity is judged as intelligible based on its conformity to "a rule-bound discourse that inserts itself in the pervasive and mundane signifying acts of linguistic life" (*Gender Trouble* 184). If identity is (per)formed out of a variety of historically shifting social discourses, then "it is only within the practice of repetitive signifying that a subversion of identity becomes possible" (185). For Butler, performance is not the same as performativity: "performativity [is] *that aspect of discourse that has the capacity to produce what it names*" (Interview; Butler's italics). She argues that this effect "always happens through a certain kind of repetition and recitation" (Interview). Usually, acts that carry the power of the performative are those that are socially legitimated: some examples are baptisms, marriages, the naming of a ship. One has to be authorized by some community in order for these actions to be effective. Christy's parents' marriage was legitimated by Indian custom, for example, but the power of that community to stabilize a performative declined as colonial regulation increased. For Johnson, ironically, the white audience authorized her performance of Mohawk identity at least to the degree that it matched the stereotype of the Indian princess. That authorization gave her room to transform her performance into a performative over the course of her career. The "break" in her performance between "Indian" and white was both a reassurance (she was actually *not* a wild savage) *and* an enactment of a Mohawk woman asserting equality (even superiority) despite the everyday racism of Canadian society. That she had the equivalent of a state funeral after her death in Vancouver, with Indigenous and settler mourners lining the streets, confirms that her identifications had a performative impact there, however transient. Johnson's life and works have continued to prove "good to think with" in testing nationalist, feminist, and Mohawk perspectives on identity. Her case reveals the complex and often conflicting interplay over time between individual, national, and state ascriptions of what constitutes an Indigenous identity in Canada. One thing that becomes clear in reading her life and works is that identity is a complex mix of family, education, upbringing, gender, class, racialization, experience, and opinion, all of which affect how particular individuals are received into different communities during their lifetimes and beyond. Despite her ancestry, Johnson had trouble finding a role for herself in the Mohawk community. She used her literary and oratorical talents to consolidate that identity in a wider forum. Another famous performer in buckskins, Archibald Belaney, although English by birth, used many of the same performative moves in becoming Grey Owl.

Chapter Six

"They Taught Me Much": Imposture, Animism, Ecosystem, and Archibald Belaney / Grey Owl (1888-1938)

Archibald Belaney lived most of his life as a self-described "half-breed" trapper, packer, and guide in northern Ontario and Quebec. Late in life, as Grey Owl, he published four bestselling books—*The Men of the Last Frontier* (1931), *Pilgrims of the Wild* (1935), *Sajo and the Beaver People* (1935), and *Tales of an Empty Cabin* (1936)—and undertook, in full Plains Indian regalia, two extremely successful international lecture tours promoting conservation.[1] Son of the black sheep of a middle-class English family and his "child-bride," Belaney was raised with the utmost propriety by his grandmother and aunts (D.B. Smith 11). He resisted his aunt Ada's control by "playing Indian," based on his reading of James Fenimore Cooper and Ernest Thompson Seton. He even attended one of Buffalo Bill's Wild West shows. At seventeen he arrived in Canada to put his dreams into practice. His imposture was revealed to the public the day after his death at the age of fifty.

As writer and speaker, Belaney's main political point was that Indigenous lands were being ravaged and that the solution was to pay Indigenous people to be the stewards they had always been. However, his message has been foreclosed by his lack of authenticity. Indignant, dismissive, or snide reactions are common: for example, James Polk describes him as a "colourful northern screw-up" and "faux Indian wreck" (12). Unlike many who "played Indian" (P. Deloria), however, he had long-standing and close personal and political relationships with many Indigenous people; to discredit his ideas is to risk discrediting theirs.

A trapper for over twenty years, he reacted not only against the taking of the land, but also against the near-complete destruction of the life that it supported through practices such as poorly regulated commercial trapping and clear-cut logging, practices that left the Ojibwa and Cree people starving. They had been able to manage until a combination of colonial land theft with new technologies such as the railroad, small marine engines, and bush planes "opened up" the hunting territory that one James Bay Cree hunter, Job Bearskin, called "our land, our garden" (qtd. in B. Richardson 121; see Brody for similar responses from hunters in British Columbia). Belaney, in living closely with Indigenous people and getting his living in the ways they typically did, can be seen struggling to move from a relationship with land, "Nature," and the "wilderness" framed by mainstream concepts toward something that approximated Indigenous teachings.

Soon after arriving in Canada, Belaney met John Egwuna and his family, who lived on Bear Island in Lake Temagami, Ontario. Belaney spent time with the family and trapped with them in the winter of 1909–10, working hard to learn Ojibway (D.B. Smith 41). He married Angele Egwuna, John Egwuna's niece, in August 1910. However, in fall 1911, he abandoned Angele and their daughter, Agnes, claiming he was needed in Biscostasing as a translator (44). He continued to work as a trapper, fire ranger, "riverman," and enlisted sniper until he made his decision to try to bring the beaver back from near extinction in 1928. During all this time, he was famous for keeping notes, writing even after a hard day portaging and paddling (52, 72). Belaney learned much from Anishinaabe people like the Egwunas and later, the Espaniels, particularly about what is called the ecosystem.

ECOSYSTEM / "ALL MY RELATIONS"

Scholars in many fields such as science studies, ecology, and eco-criticism have begun to rethink the nature/culture divide. Nature has been separated from human culture and named variously as wilderness, *terra nullius*, or frontier, and then, more recently, what was formerly separated as nature and culture has been renamed and retheorized as the "ecosystem," "naturecultures," "hybrids," and "assemblages" of objects and affects, among other terms (see also Seibt).[2] These retheorizations include humans and their beliefs, affects, emotions, discourses, and activities within the web of nature rather than installing them in a separate category.

Indigenous people, including scholars and artists, have made their claims to land based on traditional epistemologies that never separated nature and culture. For example, artist Lawrence Paul Yuxweluptun's words represent the land as animate biosystem inhabited equally by humans and other-than-humans: "How do you paint a land claim? ... I find myself coming back to the land. Is it necessary to butcher all of this land? The grizzly bear has not signed away his land, why on earth should I, or a fish or a bird? ... All the money in the bank cannot buy or magically bring back a dead biosystem" (878–79). In *Sacred Ecology* Fikret Berkes notes that "[i]n the Canadian North ... aboriginal peoples often refer to their 'knowledge of the land' rather than to ecological knowledge. Land to them, however, includes the living environment" (5; see also Hallowell). This perspective means that human beings are not in charge: "animals control the hunt" (Berkes 98). Hunters have social obligations to "the living environment [which] is a community of living beings that are supernatural as well as natural" (98). Another term for this living environment is "all my relations," an expression that makes it impossible to push "nature" away to be looked at and exploited as abstraction, inanimate object, or female monster, but which includes the speaker in a web of reciprocal respect and responsibility. In his literary anthology *All My Relations* (1990), Thomas King explains his title as a phrase that is "at first a reminder of who we are and of our relationship with both our family and our relatives [and] ... all human beings." He continues, "But the relationships that Native people see go further, the web of kinship extending to the animals, to the birds, to the fish, to the plants, to all the animate and inanimate forms that can be seen or imagined." This relationship entails a responsibility to live "our lives in a harmonious and moral manner" (ix). Of course, to live harmoniously and morally is a widespread human ideal, but not all cultures share an epistemology that entails egalitarian relationships with such an extensive array of material and spiritual beings.

Belaney admitted that he did not always live this way. The Espaniels once nearly threw him out of their camp when they discovered he was keeping dynamite for blowing up beaver lodges under his bed (D.B. Smith 72). Many of Grey Owl's tales deal with his own failed macho exploits; several ended with him being rescued by Indigenous families (see Chapin). He always respected those who taught him how to hunt: who "had turned me out, so they consider, a finished project" (*Men* 153). He admits, however, that "even today there are times when my failure to apply the lessons so painstakingly taught me, if known, would be the cause of much disappointment, and apt but terse comment ... in certain shadowy lodges" (153–54). This story reverses the usual great white hunter's tale where the guides recede into the background when they have done their job of keeping the hunter alive and positioning the game in front of his gun. Surviving to become such a guide, Belaney nonetheless often failed to respect the animals he depended upon. It was while hunting out of season that he was confronted by the mewling of two beaver kits he had condemned to death

FIG. 8 Archie Belaney and Anahareo
holding beaver kits, Abitibi, Quebec, 1927.
Archives of Ontario C273-1-0-41-14 S15547.

by trapping their mother. His wife, Anahareo, insisted on raising them and their beaverly charm did the rest.[3] He soon started his conservation work, which Anahareo inspired by suggesting he publish articles and give talks at tourist lodges. I argue not only that he "went Indian," but also, following Carrie Dawson, that he "went beaver," developing a profoundly queer set of relationships, where his beavers became his people and where Jelly Roll, the oldest female, became his "Queen" (*Tales* 244).[4]

Discussion of these relationships have been foreclosed in many ways, by labels such as "fraud," "imposter," and "faux Indian wreck," or stalled by applying the words "nostalgic," "anti-modern," "sentimental," and "anthropomorphic" to his thinking (Loo 111, 114). A man who moves beavers into his cabin, taking the roof off to film them, while thoughtfully building a separate cabin for his wife and their baby daughter, can easily be dismissed as a self-centred maniac. What he did (and did not) learn of Indigenous ways is still worth considering. His behaviour should not, however, be authenticated or justified by mapping it on to Indigenous relations with the animate world, since his was an idiosyncratic and partial internalization of already non-homogeneous Indigenous worldviews. As he says of beavers, "Indians become much attached to them as pets and refer to them as 'Little Indians'" (*Men* 235)—but, unlike him, Indigenous people did so while also continuing to trap and eat them. If he spoke to his mainstream audiences as "humanity's delegate back from Eden," as Donna Haraway might put it ("Promises of Monsters" 307), it was an Eden where many established hierarchies, both mainstream and Indigenous, had been scrambled, queered, and transformed.

ANIMACY AND ANIMISM

The relations that cross the constructed human/other-than-human divide are embedded in Algonquian languages like Ojibwe/Anishinaabemowin and Cree/nêhiyawêwin, because all nouns are marked for animacy. Inanimate nouns usually include man-made objects and features of the landscape. Animate nouns usually include not only people and spiritual beings, but also animals, trees, insects, and fish. Worth emphasizing is that "animate" does not mean "human," but rather that these languages have "a system that allows speakers to express what they think has a mind and what they think doesn't." What is marked as animate "can shift depending on whose beliefs you're representing" (Muehlbauer). Although it is difficult to know whether Belaney ever became fluent enough in Anishinaabemowin to internalize these differences (D.B. Smith 41), such grammatical categories can affect speakers' more general thinking (see Gentner and Goldin-Meadow). Mutsumi Yamamoto points out that "it is of significant interest to linguists to capture the extra-linguistic framework of the animacy concept, because, as it were, *this concept is a spell which strongly influences our mind* in the process of language use" (qtd. in Chen 9; Chen's italics). That many languages mark animacy in ways that ignore the human/other-than-human divide likely tells us something about how humans have been able to thrive in ecosystems that seem uninhabitable to modern city-dwellers. Belaney remarks on the animism of the men he learned from. He notes, for example, "Indians frequently address an animal they are about to kill in terms of apology for the act" (*Men* 179). Lovat Dickson comments that he always "spoke of Nature ... as though it were an animate thing, and had a voice that could speak, a heart that could feel, and a mind that could understand" (*Green Leaf* 11).

WHAT IS A FRAUD?

For some the revelation that Grey Owl was English automatically discredits his message, as in this review of the Hollywood feature film *Grey Owl* (1999), directed by Richard Attenborough: "Grey Owl being a fake soils the message and turns his speeches from valid to sideshow" (Gallagher).[5] Apparently only those in possession of a transparently authentic identity—like the one this BBC critic assumes for himself—can speak the truth. Another commentator argues that Grey Owl should be forgiven as "a great naturalist and a crusading animal-lover"—two heroic identities that apparently compensate for any fraud (qtd. in Dickson, *Green Leaf* 43). Another comment resists purism by setting the case into the foreboding context of the year Belaney died: "The case of Grey Owl reminds us a little of the new race phantasies which poison life in Germany. There it matters everything what a man's grandmother was, and less than nothing what his own achievements in life have been" (qtd. in Dickson, *Green Leaf* 39).

Despite such widespread fantasies of racial purity and authentic identity, Belaney's friends and acquaintances in the bush either knew he was English and indulged his pretense or took him at face value. Anahareo commented that he "'lived like' an Indian, 'identified with Indians,' and 'was an Indian'" (qtd. in Braz, "St. Archie" 208). She also remarked, "Had Archie known how seriously people were going to take his ancestry, this would have been the time to have clamped down on that 'full-blooded Indian' stuff. But how was he to know that the more he wrote, the more Indian he became in the eyes of the public?" (*Devil* 138). Her stance on identity was both respectful and relational: Belaney wouldn't have been seen as a fraud if the mainstream audience hadn't wanted an impossibly authentic Indian so badly. Belaney justified his performance during his two lecture tours as a rhetorical tactic, arguing that without it, no one would have paid attention to his message: "People expect it. It means a great deal more to them to see me in beads and feathers than if they merely saw a plain woodsman playing with a beaver. This is something they will remember. And brother, I *want* them to remember. That is part of my job!" (D.B. Smith 92).[6] One contemporary writer, Howard O'Hagan, interpreted Belaney's actions this way:

> An actor? Of course. Playing a part? He was living it. He *was* Grey Owl. No Indian would speak of "illimitable forests." He would take them for granted. Few white men would have the effrontery to say "us" in such a context. But the speaker was neither red nor white. He was Grey Owl, Archie Belaney's imaginary man. And not only had Archie created a character to suit the part.

He had even created a country. The term "Grey Owl country," a nebulous region of forest and stream in the Canadian hinterland, was already in common use. (119)[7]

Here O'Hagan describes disidentification: Grey Owl performs a persona "neither red nor white," an act that called both terms, and indeed the notion of a fixed identity itself, into question. Belaney was repudiating his Englishness with this persona derived not only from literature, but also from personal experience. And he was claiming rights to land on behalf of the community to which that persona belonged. To read him as a cultural appropriator and a white wannabe is to oversimplify. As a white male immigrant, he could have owned land. But this was not the relationship to land he valued. Instead he tried to communicate his vision to politicians and used what money he had to make films to convey his values to a wider public.

FROM FRAUD TO POETIC MYSTERY

Belaney's unusual life, which was characterized by self-making and re-making, is a trajectory that is most common (or at least most obvious) in those at odds with the social roles laid out for them. Such people actively seek out and produce cultural and social models for a way of being that enables them to feel fulfilled—or, at least, to survive. Dominant society often sees such behaviour as wasteful, deviant, excessive, dangerous, or even insane because it counters the idea that we are born with fixed identities and should move only into the social roles prescribed for us. For example, Belaney's cheerful, alcohol-fuelled introduction of a "war dance" to Biscostasing was apparently received with some skepticism by the local Anishinaabeg, as Armand Garnet Ruffo's poem *Grey Owl* describes it: "What's an Indian War Dance? None / of us Indian people have had one of those recently" (37). The local paper reported that the performance focused "on the wrongs that the whiteman had done to the Indian" (qtd. in Ruffo 37). Few Victoria Day celebrations in Canada in 1923 likely shared this focus. Here Belaney took a tired stereotype and used it strategically "*through* the performance of politics" (Muñoz xiv) to make his point, just as he did later in his public lectures.

Literary critics have been wary of Grey Owl's deviant performances. During the 1960s and 1970s, mainstream English-Canadian literature and criticism generally starred white settlers, compiling a story that overlooked colonization and racism and that stereotyped or ignored Indigenous people and later non-Indigenous arrivals, who were categorized as "immigrants," rather than "settlers." Activists from a variety of "minority" communities began to be heard criticizing this exclusionary narrative in the late 1980s. What came to be called the "appropriation of voice" debate was crystallized in Lenore Keeshig-Tobias's 1990 article in the Toronto *Globe and Mail*, "Stop Stealing Native Stories." In "The Magic of Others," she wrote:

> Well today it seems, there's a host of professionals dealing with the printed word (editors, publishers, producers, directors, writers, storytellers, journalists), all non-Native, who have taken over the work of the missionary and the Indian agent. They now know best how to present the Indian perspective, never dreaming, of course, it is basically their own perspective coloured with a few canoes, beads, beaver ponds and a buffalo or two—romantic clichés of how they see Native people. (174)

As result of this debate, those who worked in the fields of Indigenous or postcolonial literatures in the 1980s and 1990s tended to condemn white literary wannabes in general and Grey Owl in particular, if only to prove that they themselves were not colonizers, wannabes or voice appropriators.[8] The 1996 publication of Ruffo's long poem, *Grey Owl: The Mystery of Archie Belaney*, marked a shift in opinion. Ruffo clearly felt that Grey Owl had done more than dress up. Carrie Dawson remarks, "Where other historians have been evasive, dismissive, acerbic, or excessively distanced in their treatment of Grey Owl, Ruffo treats the dedicated animal rights activist—in all his manifestations—with sympathy and respect. For this reason, his biography stands out as original …" ("Never Cry Fraud"). One problem with dismissing Belaney as a fraud is that rejecting his self-identification suggests that the only valid foundations for identity are biological/genealogical ("race," ancestry) or state-accredited ("Status Indian," "Canadian citizen"). The label relies on the myth of a pure, empirically valid identity, a myth that the Indigenous people Belaney met did not appear to share. Ruffo's response to Belaney puts the person first. His decision to write the biography as a long poem speaks to the importance of story as a way to convey the past. Despite his extensive personal and archival research, he leaves Belaney's life as a mystery, rather than purporting to "unmask" him.

Jonathan Dewar begins his article on Ruffo's book with a childhood story: "Growing up, I knew two Indians, or rather, I knew two representations of Indians. One was my great-grandfather Alderic Groslouis, a full-blooded Huron-Wendat, who died shortly before I was born. The other was Grey Owl ..." (256). Dewar had trouble seeing his great-grandfather as authentic because "he was always wearing a three-piece suit in those photos. A wholly costumed Grey Owl, on the other hand, seemed truly unmistakably Indian, despite the fact that I knew he was not" (256). Dewar shows how the insistence on authenticity drains credibility not only from Belaney, the "English imposter," but also from his own great-grandfather, who worked as an advisor to Prime Minister Louis Saint-Laurent. Dewar notes, "[A]s a person of mixed-blood heritage, I have often turned to literature for answers as much as for entertainment" (257). Indigenous stories are told with the expectation of such personal reflection. They are aimed at the listener(s), who are expected to think about how the story applies specifically to them.[9] Engaging seriously with story can lead to personal and social transformation, as Lee Maracle points out: "As listener/reader you become the trickster, the architect of great social transformation at whatever level you choose" (Preface 13). Belaney might be seen as an example of a "naive" reader whose transformed life was a result of engaging seriously with his childhood reading.

IDENTIFYING WITH/AS IMPOSTER

As Dawson has aptly argued, "imposture suggests itself as a trope through which to interrogate the preoccupation with authenticity in settler cultures" ("Never Cry Fraud").[10] Dewar notes that many contemporary Indigenous people have to cope with feelings of inauthenticity, with not being "Indian enough" to fit the stereotypes that colonize the minds of everyone in Canada, Indigenous and non-Indigenous alike: "That feeling of not belonging or being an imposter is a real and valid emotion that contemporary Native writers deal with regularly, particularly with regard to the mixing of white and Native cultures and the issue of mixed cultural backgrounds" (270). As Sneja Gunew explains, "[I]n a move [Rey] Chow terms 'coercive mimeticism,' ethnics are pressured to represent themselves in ways that have already been choreographed through their stereotypical interpellation by the dominant culture, a first world hailing of third world difference" ("Between Auto/Biography and Theory" 368). This coercive mimeticism ensures that only stories and identities that accord with the dominant are authorized. Unable or unwilling to perform as required, those marked as other may internalize a feeling of inauthenticity. This feeling may convince them that it is too late to connect with their culture, because this connection is supposed to be and feel "natural." For example, Shirley Sterling's residential school novel, *My Name Is Seepeetza* (1992), began with a small assignment in a university creative writing class. She writes, "I have never thought of myself as a particularly traditional or spiritual Nlakapamux person. In fact I delayed writing in the First Nations voice for many years because I thought I was not raised traditionally enough" ("Seepeetza Revisited"). How many such important projects have been abandoned or never even considered because of such feelings?

Belaney can be seen as an escapist from the dominant discourses around pure identity, a "disidentifier." He was privileged in being able to fling himself into the stereotype because it did not apply to him; it had not bedevilled *his* childhood with racism. Indeed, he identified with the stereotype as an act of rebellion against Englishness. However, his life cannot be seen as pure wannabe appropriation, which in his case is usually implied to be the spectacularization of a false and stereotypical identity in return for fame and money, because between 1906 and 1929 or so, he had no idea that in the last few years of his life he would become a celebrity. Like the Indigenous people he knew, he faced a bleak future when trapping failed; unlike most of them, he was able to put his cultural capital toward solving the problem. Thus he can be seen as a model of someone who worked hard at learning what it meant to be Indigenous from close relationships with Indigenous people, who practised what he learned and, later, preached it as best he could. That cultural skills and viewpoints are learned, not innate, is something that the fiction of the "natural" and authentic identity overlooks: no one is born, as Basil H. Johnston would put it, "thinking Indian" (*Think Indian*).

Grey Owl recounts, for example, how the white trapper often learns Indigenous methods: "He overcomes his difficulties by skill and cunning, not by force, taking a leaf from the Indian's book ..." (*Men* 46). This stance is commonplace among Indigenous hunters; for example, the reaction of Koyukon people to the dynamiting of a river ice jam was to see it as an "arrogant use of physical force" against which the river would certainly retaliate (Berkes 114). Grey Owl further points out that along with the hunting techniques come the spiritual practices, however diluted:

Even at this late date, the arts of woodcraft are practiced as originally acquired from the Indian, whose highly specialized faculties his white contemporary has more or less successfully emulated. Having for neighbours men who carry drums to celebrate the Wabeno [shamanistic ceremonies] and who wear charms to ward off evil spirits, the white trapper has naturally imbibed some of their lesser superstitions. If he has bad luck, he is none too sure that he is not conjured by some enemy. He feels that there is no actual harm in cutting out the kneecaps from the hind legs of his beaver carcasses and burning them, or by placing a small portion of tobacco in the brain box of a bear he kills and hanging the skull on a tree. (*Men* 53)[11]

Although Grey Owl gives a clear picture of the petty irritations, miseries, and frustrations of the trapping life, not to mention its life-threatening dangers, he also describes the rewards that come with that life for the hunter:

As he passes the first fringe of the forest, ... he enters the enchanted world of which he is as much a part as the ancient trees, the eternal snows, and the dancing Northern Lights. The magic of the winter wilderness descends on him like a cloak, and the waiting hush that covers the face of Nature reaches out and engulfs him. (*Men* 55)

This enchantment, which he powerfully conveyed in his lectures, came from learning to live as part of nature, rather than striving to conquer it. That said, his style here owes much to the traditions of the Romantic sublime and thus often assumes the separation between the grubby urban "real world" of the white audience and Nature, the enchanted world of the noble Indian.

Nonetheless, much of his perspective on animate nature would have been denounced as "superstition" in churches and residential schools. The cultural revitalization needed to restore this epistemology requires a commitment to imagine and perform not only what has been destroyed but new things too. Belaney's example is encouraging: after all, if an erratic and alcoholic white man can learn to think this way, others can as well. Philip Kevin Paul's poem "Taking the Names Down from the Hill" makes a sly allusion to Belaney: "I began to dance, I danced / At least as foolishly as a Scotsman / gone Indian, naked in the woods!" (95). These lines resonate with Belaney's "war dance," with the cliché that white men can't dance, and with Belaney's lies that his father was a Scot (D.B. Smith 50). The word "naked" reflects the vulnerability of those who enact the new to constitute a continuing Indigenous sovereignty. In this poem, although the speaker's homeland is buried under "tons of concrete and vulgar electric houses" (P.K. Paul 92), he is finally able to leave mourning aside and understand that his ancestors have left him "the magic in everything" (93). He is able to take the names down from the hill and restore them: "*this is Saanich.*" The poem concludes, "I called it the *Dance of Forever,* / our newest tradition" (95).

To invent and foster new traditions is crucial to cultural survival; Belaney not only presided over the war dance in Biscostasing, but also praised the annual "Song of Hiawatha" performances in Desbarats, Ontario, which featured Anishinaabe performers, allowing them to connect with each other at a time when travelling off reserve was often restricted and traditional ceremonies prohibited (*Men* 240; see McNally). Clearly, for some contemporary Indigenous writers, taking Belaney seriously can counter debilitating notions of authentic identity to produce a vision of an Indigenous culture that is resilient in the face of change and able to incorporate the new.

Like Dewar, Ruffo grew up with Grey Owl's photograph, but also with the stories he heard about him from his grandmother and his great-uncle: "As a child I had a photograph beside my bed of Grey Owl and my great-uncle Jimmy drumming together in Biscostasing, northern Ontario, Grey Owl's 'home town'" (213). Belaney called Alex Espaniel, Jimmy Espaniel's father, "Dad." He trapped with the family for two winters in the 1920s (D.B. Smith 71–72, 176–77). The Espaniels had taken him in after the war, when he returned with a wounded foot and an out-of-control drinking problem. Ruffo quotes from one of Belaney's notebooks for 1937:

> Early days everything rip-tearing speed
> After meeting Alex Espaniel more calm and quiet,
> contentment, little intimate enjoyments,
> appreciating bush in its finest sense. (164)

Taking strangers' self-representations at face value is part of the imperative of hospitality of the Indigenous people Belaney encountered: "hospitality is almost a religion with the Indian" (*Tales* 12). Indeed, his own psychological and physical survival was indebted to this ethic. Unsurprisingly, then, Belaney not only looked at the world from the perspective of his excellent British education and proper middle-class upbringing, but also tried to include and credit what he had learned from the Anishinaabe people who made him family. He wrote to Dickson in advance of his first lecture tour, "Half-breed trapper I am, and far more closely identified with the Ojibway Indians than any other people. I want the Ojibways to get any credit that may accrue. I am their man. They taught me much" (qtd. in *Green Leaf* 71).

WHERE IS NATURE?

As Bruce Braun notes in *The Intemperate Rainforest: Nature, Culture, and Power on Canada's West Coast*, "Nature" has always been a site of tense ideological struggle:

It is perhaps First Nations who most directly bear the cost of the externalization of nature in BC, even as many others in the province derive great economic and personal benefit. This is in part because if nature is to be successfully constructed as primal, First Nations must either be erased entirely or collapsed into it. These sorts of cognitive failures have allowed many other people—the state, industry, environmentalists—to speak for the rainforest and its futures, while Natives have struggled to have their voices heard. (x)

What Braun calls nature's "externality" refers to the dominant view of nature as a separate realm outside humans and their culture. Sometimes Indigenous people are figured as part of Nature, marking them as other-than-human rather than human, a position reserved for civilized white men. Braun asks, "[W]hat might a radical, *postcolonial* environmentalism look like?" (x). He argues that this radicalization will require the relinquishment of the vision of a pure nature devoid of politics and a rethinking of the nature/culture divide. Three general positions mark debates around nature in Canada. Some argue for the preservation of a primal, pristine wilderness; some for "multiple use" (with the uses ranging from wilderness tourism to unfettered resource extraction); and some for Indigenous control (a position that could be combined with some multiple uses, but likely not all).[12] Presumably a *radical* postcolonial environmentalism would resist the *terra nullius* hallucination of a pristine landscape and make Indigenous perspectives—even sovereignty—central. Quoting Donna Haraway to the effect that "nature cannot pre-exist its construction," he argues that multiple constructions of nature co-exist in Canada within a web of power relations (108), pointing to the fragile relationships between the ecology movement in British Columbia and the Nuu-chah-nulth (62). He argues that the task of critical inquiry is to discover how and why different conceptions of nature come to matter.

Bruno Latour's take on it is like O'Hagan's: nature, in the Western sense, does not exist for traditional Indigenous people. He continues, "[N]o culture outside that of the West has used nature to organize political life. Traditional societies do not live in harmony with nature; they are unacquainted with it" (*Politics of Nature* 232). Sandra Harding, writing of differences between the global north and south, notes that "[n]ortherners, for example, have conceptualized the planet as the Judeo-Christian God's gift to his people, as a cornucopia of limitless abundance for human use ('Mother Earth'), as a mechanism of one kind or another, and, thanks to recent environmental movements, as a spaceship or lifeboat whose occupants and their 'ves-

sel' must be carefully managed. Each metaphor or model directs different enquiry projects" (*Sciences* 139). Belaney had difficulty reconciling his
vision of an external nature with the Indigenous web of relationships, but
his attempts to do so reward examination. To become a *serious* appropriator
of Indigenous epistemology takes time and effort.

Part of the glamour of indigenization for Belaney was, in fact, that it
situated him in an idealized natural world that included Native people,
their egalitarian social attitudes, and their traditional thought. Embracing
an Indigenous way of life insofar as he could manage it allowed him to feel
that he had truly abandoned the class-conscious England in which he was
raised.[13] This kept him going even though he quickly realized that bush life
was not as "picturesque and romantic" as in books. In a letter he wrote at the
age of twenty-three, he notes, "[I]t is not near as interesting as it seems, to
be eaten up day and night by black ants, flies, and mosquitoes, to get soaked
up with rain, or burnt up with heat, to draw your own toboggan on snow-
shoes and to sleep out in 60 or 70 degrees below zero" (qtd. in D.B. Smith
45). He wrote out of the contradictions that the constructed divide between
nature and culture imposed on a man who in many ways defied it by "going
Native" and beyond.[14] What was unusual about him was that he did not just
"play Indian" (P. Deloria), he "lived Indian" (Ruffo 135). Without a series of
contingent events (meeting Anahareo, the near extinction of the beaver, his
mother's connection with *Country Life*), he might well have died a trapper,
rather than a literary celebrity. However, it is safe to say that the Anishinaabeg he lived with did not see the world they lived in the way he did.

They did not hold the secular utilitarian view of nature dominant in
modernity, but lived in a reciprocal relationship with a land that was animate, storied, beautiful, and sacred. This view can be found to some degree
in Romantic poetry, where, for example, the breeze of Nature's inspiration
moving both outside and inside the poet's body becomes the muse (see
Midgley, *Science and Poetry*). But few Romantic poets would see other-
than-human beings as ancestors, relatives, spiritual guides, and teachers,
relationships that Indigenous stories take for granted. Harry Robinson
recounts how many Okanagan people receive spirit power from what mainstream readers would regard as non-humans, as the title of one story makes
clear: "You Think It's a Stump, But That's My Grandfather" (*Nature Power*).
As Jonathan Goldberg-Hiller and Noenoe K. Silva point out, "[F]rom the
perspective of many Kanaka Hawai'i, sharks are also ancestors, protectors,
transitional body forms" (433).

The obviousness of the dominant notion of the nature/culture divide is the result of centuries of discursive work. Although beavers, trees, and rivers are real, how humans perceive them has always been mediated. The idea that there is a pure nature "out there" that can be meaningfully known only by empirical science has certainly been brought into question by feminists and science studies scholars, as well as by Indigenous thinkers. Having experienced unwanted sexualization via this perspective, sometimes labelled the "male gaze," feminists have been unwilling to observe the world solely from the objective God's-eye view of universal rationality promoted by Enlightenment thinkers. Thus, many feminists and philosophers of gender now refuse to see "woman" as a universal category or pure identity. As Simone de Beauvoir so famously puts it, "[O]ne is not born, but rather becomes, woman" (283). Feminist theory emphasizes embodiment: all humans have material bodies that are subject to natural laws. These facts cannot be ignored. But these bodies are situated, regarded, valued, preserved, or harmed through social practices. Thus, Haraway's term "naturecultures" reflects her insistence that the world is co-produced by material and cultural forces (*Companion Species*). Similarly, Indigenous worldviews do not figure the material world as dead matter that can be inspected from the outside by objective observers who do not belong to it. Of course this is only a sketch: neither feminism, empirical science, nor Enlightenment philosophy are homogeneous categories that can be represented fairly without more space and nuance than I can give them here.

LITERARY LAND CLAIMS

Grey Owl's first published article ("The Passing of the Last Frontier," 1929) began by describing the logged-off and trapped-out regions of where he had lived for over twenty years as "the last battleground in the long drawn out bitter contest between civilization and the forces of nature" (qtd. in D.B. Smith xi). Here he inscribes nature and culture as a binary. Despite his grasp of some Indigenous ideas, in "The Trail of Two Sunsets," the final story in his first collection, *The Men of the Last Frontier*, he situates himself as someone who, with the guidance of the oldest of Indians, has glimpsed a pure and feminine nature:

Neganikabo, my mentor, my kindly instructor, my companion in untold hardship and nameless tribulation, has pulled back little by little the magic invisible veil of mystery from across the face of the forest, that I might learn its uttermost secrets, and had laid open before me the book of Nature for me to read, and in my bungling way I have profited by his lessons, but the half is not yet done. (263)

The vision of Nature as a book to be read removes it from the realm of those who live most closely with it, transforming it into something that only the literate and educated can understand. The vision of Nature as woman who may be unveiled only by an enlightened man is a commonplace of science, a commonplace that uses the long-consolidated binary dividing man and woman to situate the man who "knows" nature as dominant over a submissive female Other (Midgley, *Essential* 291–93).[15] Although in Mary Midgley's account this trope refers to the ways in which scientists have represented their work to themselves and others since Francis Bacon's *The New Atlantis* (1624), it is also typical of many self-indigenizing literary accounts. Such accounts flip the values ascribed to the binary by replacing Western science with traditional Indigenous wisdom as the source of true knowledge. This replacement story, however, still maintains both the nature/culture divide and the centrality of the Western narrator. The Western individual first figures as an apprentice, a protegé, receiving this wisdom as an inheritance voluntarily granted by a shaman or elder who then conveniently vanishes. This story avoids the issue of land theft altogether and helps explain the epistemological and political conflicts between wilderness advocates and Indigenous people. The advocates see the land as their inheritance to protect as it supposedly existed in the past of the imagined noble savage. Contemporary Indigenous people are seen as a threat to this pure wilderness when they do not wish to preserve land as wilderness or museum, but to keep it living and to keep living with it.[16]

At the end "The Trail of Two Sunsets," Grey Owl is unaccountably drawn to travel to a location where in the past he had met with "the simple kindly people of [his] adoption," but which now is filled only with graves (*Men* 278). After a night dreaming of "barbarous nights" dancing at a feast, he wakes to find Neganikabo's canoe coming into shore. The shaman says that "of all my people, you are the only one who remembers the way of our race" (280), and announces that when he had named Grey Owl, he had also made him a member of the Beaver Clan. The narrator realizes that "I might never set another beaver trap, should I choose to remain true to this society of the Dead" (281).[17] After more conversation, Grey Owl waits respectfully for the elder to speak again, but finally realizes that the old man has died. He buries him "in his old canoe, with his muzzle-loading gun, his old-fashioned axe, and his beaded pouch of relics" facing west (280). This scene is clearly far from factual and full of colonizing literary conventions.

The story of a white person who is instructed by a wise old Indian mentor is typical of several fictional narratives famously billed as true, for example, Carlos Castenada's twelve bestselling books on the purported teachings of a Yaqui Indian shaman called Don Juan (see Marshall) and Lynn Andrews's bestselling book based on the supposed teachings of a Cree shaman implausibly named Agnes Whistling Elk (see Hagan).[18] Most now agree that Don Juan and Agnes Whistling Elk are literary characters, animated by readers' desires to know an exotic Other in a way that consolidates their modern superiority, given that the Other does not have the ability to know modernity or be modern. Vine Deloria Jr. comments sarcastically on the long list of "morally correct writers who have fatefully become confidants of wise old Indians, have been forced to write books lest secrets be lost, and have become famous for their knowledge of Indians" (24). English-Canadian literary works often depict alienated white characters finding wholeness through contact with Indigenous people or symbolic objects (Fee, "Romantic Nationalism" 17). This contact indigenizes the central character and thus constitutes a land claim. One version of this trope is what I call a "totem transfer," where such a person inherits a creature symbolic of Indigenousness, such as the stallion in Robert Kroetsch's *The Studhorse Man* (1970) or the bear in Marian Engel's *Bear* (1976; "Romantic Nationalism" 21). Often, the works that depict these transactions veer between heavy irony and naturalization.

Dawson suggests that this veering is common in contemporary writing about the connections between white settler Canadians and Indigenous peoples. Margaret Atwood gave her 1991 Clarendon lecture on Grey Owl at Oxford wearing fringed leather, a tongue-in-cheek allusion to his performances (Dawson, "Never Cry Fraud"). Dawson remarks that "Atwood's repeated references to Grey Owl's 'adopted' identity naturalizes his claim to Native ancestry and consequently makes it difficult to sustain her own performance of white-into-Indian as ironic" ("Never Cry Fraud"). Part of the difficulty here is the binary that contrasts the notion of inborn authentic identity with that of identity as learned and performed. And troubling this binary is concern over cultural knowledge as part of the assertion of rights to land based on ancestry and peoplehood. Belaney may have learned much from the Anishinaabeg, but what he learned did not give him Indigenous ancestry or rights to land. A wannabe, I would say, is someone who wants to skip the hard stuff (culture, language, ethics, and politics) and go straight to claiming the identity, the land, and any and all associated benefits. Classifying everyone who works hard at learning from Indigenous people as a wannabe or a fraud, however, certainly stalls a necessary conversation.

Of course, it's easy to see Atwood's ironic or my critical stance as defensive moves that allow us to retain a grip on our privilege as unmarked Canadians. Dawson calls someone who makes this kind of move a "nativized informer—an individual who undertakes to naturalize his own national affiliation by informing on or 'unmasking' another individual whom he depicts as less 'authentic' than himself" ("Never Cry Fraud"). Belaney, thoroughly unmasked, becomes an excellent resource for self-authentication by more serious and stable Canadians. However, this move does not work if the notion of authentic identity is held to be a construct that badly needs rethinking. Defending essential identities produces a criticism that focuses on attacking others' arguments and authenticity so as to seize the moral high ground (and retain the real ground) as the authentic knower. This activity can easily take the place of dealing with a messy history of colonization. Taiaiake Alfred puts this point more trenchantly than Dawson: "The colonizers who refuse to acknowledge their privilege and inheritance of wrongs are practicing another form of selfishness and hypocrisy—they claim the right and privilege of indignation and the power to judge the cruder colonizers among them and attempt to use this rhetorical posture to release themselves of their own responsibility for the colonial enterprise ..." (Wasáse, 105). He says that change will come only when Canadians can relinquish not just their self-image as morally superior citizens of an exemplary nation, but also actual control over land and resources. This process has begun, albeit slowly, in the courts. But to institute a less combative, expensive, and grudging process will require the decolonization of the dominant discourse around land and identity, a discourse that has been produced over a long time by mainstream culture and the academic disciplines that study it. It is also worth noting (as mildly as possible) that seizing the moral high ground is a move that should be used with discretion, since it can buy emotional gratification at the expense of persuasion or productive conversation. The Indigenous value of respect that Riel so strongly adhered to is one way to avoid the frantic raids on the moral high ground that often characterize the field of Indigenous studies. In the scramble to avoid being seen as "wannabes," many forget that most of us, like Belaney, are living on other people's land and profiting from their resources. Rather than spending our time as "nativized informers," contending for an ever-shrinking patch of moral high ground while the ecosystem goes downhill and colonization continues, we need to consider what indigenizing our worldview might mean in respectful conversation with elders and others who know the land better than we do.

The fantasy of the totem transfer is appealing because it suggests that Indigenous people voluntarily and freely passed the land to newcomers once and for all. Unfortunately, these fantasies and representations can be developed and deployed in complete ignorance of Indigenous people or their political concerns. Keeshig-Tobias highlights how this ignorance leads to the recirculation of stereotypes: "Stories are much more than just the imagination, and Canadian writers might research circumstances and events, artifacts and history, but—why bother if it's fiction?" ("Magic of Others" 176). She ends her article in the Toronto *Globe*, "Stop Stealing Native Stories," with a challenge that she borrows from Maria Campbell: "If you want to write our stories, be prepared to live with us," and adds, "and not just for a few months" (A7). By the time he began writing, Belaney had certainly met that challenge, although he was still struggling with inherited frames for thinking about Indigenous issues.

Although "The Tale of Two Sunsets" is far more fiction than fact, the elder, Neganikabo, is thought to be a composite of two Anishinaabe elders, "Old" Dan Misabi and "Temagami Ned," or Ned White Bear.[19] Belaney also calls Ned White Bear "Both-Ends-of-the-Day." He was the great-uncle of Belaney's wife, Angele Egwuna (*Men* 258). Unlike Don Juan and Agnes Whistling Elk, or the fictional Indigenous characters in the novels by Kroetsch, Engel, and many others, Misabi and White Bear were people with whom Belaney had spent time. Nonetheless, Belaney uses his story to authenticate himself, rather than Anishinaabe people, as nature's true inheritor, a literary land claim typical of Canadian nationalist writing. Like the anthropologists and collectors who figured themselves as rescuing Indigenous culture from the "vanishing" Indigenous people who were deemed to be no longer able to take care of it themselves, Belaney ends his first book as the sole inheritor of Beaver Clan wisdom bearing an Anishinaabe name that he appears to have made up for himself.[20]

As Belaney paddled, portaged, and packed his way through northern Ontario and Quebec, it seems safe to say that those Anishinaabe and Cree men who paddled with him were not thinking about nature as a woman to be unveiled. Still, for Anishinaabeg the earth is a woman: Norval Morriseau writes, "The Ojibway believe the earth to be our mother, and that we are children of the earth" (15; see also Basil H. Johnston, *Manitous* 10–15). However, relations between mother and child, for example as Riel figures them in his address to the jury, are also very different from the highly exploit-

FIG. 9 Old Misabi and "Temagami Ned" White Bear, also known as "Both-Ends-of-the-Day," ca. 1910–1920. Archives of Ontario C273-1-0-43-11 S15142.

ative and violent sexual relations that play out in a colonized territory (see Barman, "Taming"; Andrea Smith). Notably, Belaney always argued against the commonplace that man should have dominion over nature (nor did he choose submissive women as partners, one might add):

> Man, that is civilized man, has commonly considered himself the lord of creation, and has been prone to assume that everything existing on this planet was put there for his special convenience, and that all animals (to say nothing of the so-called "subject" races of his own kind) were placed on the earth to be his servants. And this in spite of the fact that members of many of the "backward" races are often just as intelligent as he is, and that there are myr-

iad of creatures extant, any one of which could, on even terms, as man to man so to speak, trim him very effectively on less ground that he was born on. (*Tales* xii; Belaney's quotation marks).

Despite the admirable broad-mindedness of this passage, it must be said that Belaney made racist comments about non-British immigrants, particularly the eastern Europeans he called "Bohunks" (*Men* 211–13). Indeed, he was able to be both racist and homophobic in the same breath, as in a letter to a critic where he says he admires the United States, "but less the emasculate gigolo element we hear in the monkey band over the radio" (qtd. in Braz, "Modern Hiawatha" 61). Still, he eagerly welcomed learning from Indigenous political leaders when he got the chance.

Belaney encountered Cree leader John Tootoosis in Ottawa in 1936. Tootoosis was there to deliver a message from the League of Western Indians to the Indian Department (D.B. Smith 149). This meeting led to an invitation to attend the celebration of the sixtieth anniversary of the signing of Treaty 6 in Fort Carlton in August that year. Here the Cree adopted Lord Tweedsmuir, the governor general,[21] and "5000 visiting Cree, Assiniboine and Sioux Indians" camped and danced (160). Belaney was invited to speak to an audience of several hundred men. His biographer, Donald B. Smith, focuses on what he calls Belaney's "total self-delusion," his inability to dance, and the likely suspicions of those present about his identity (161–62; see also Historica Canada). However, Smith also says that Indian leaders realized "they needed public figures in the dominant society to speak on their behalf" (162). Further, like Jonathan Dewar, Philip Kevin Paul, and Armand Garnet Ruffo, they may well have recognized some of their dilemmas in his. Here is Tootoosis, speaking about the effects of residential school:[22]

> When an Indian comes out of these places, it is like being put between two walls in a room and left hanging in the middle. On one side are all the things he learned from his people and their way of life that was being wiped out, and on the other side are the white man's ways which he could never fully understand because he never had the right amount of education and could not be a part of it. There he is, hanging in the middle of two cultures, and he is not a white man and he is not an Indian. (qtd. in Troniak 3)

COMMUNITY-BASED NATURAL RESOURCE MANAGEMENT

Belaney reported to Tootoosis about Lord Tweedsmuir's visit to his cabin in September 1936. Indians, he argued to the governor general, should have a role in Canadian economic life, rather than being regarded as a drain on government resources, taking on

> work connected with the administering, protection, and proper control of our natural resources, particularly in relation to wild life, timber, and related issues; at these the Indian is expert, and his technical knowledge, accumulated during thousands of years of study and observation, could be of immense value in helping to save from destruction Canada's wilderness country and its inhabitants, which are, together, Canada's greatest asset, and are suffering great loss from the lack of proper knowledge displayed by many of those who are trying to handle them. (qtd. in D.B. Smith 164)

His use of the words "administering," "proper," "expert," "technical," and "study and observation" were chosen deliberately to counter stereotypes of Indians as superstitious, lazy, and primitive. He took this message of Indigenous stewardship to his audience with King George VI, Queen Elizabeth, Queen Mary, and Princesses Elizabeth and Margaret in 1937.

Belaney was proposing a model that has now achieved the status of an acronym: "community-based natural resource management" (CBNRM). As Annie Lowenhaupt Tsing points out in *Friction: An Ethnography of Global Connection*, this model is not a panacea. But despite what she calls its "situated dilemmas," it provides a framework and a narrative that has managed to unite diverse stakeholders, including nature lovers, middle-class students, and Indigenous peoples, to stave off resource extractive industries from exploiting Indigenous lands. The blockade that prevented the proposed expansion of the Red Squirrel Road through territory claimed by the Teme-Augama Anishnabai at the north end of Lake Temagami in 1988–1989 is a good example of results achieved with this model. Nonetheless, these forests where Belaney spent many years are, despite the protests, still under pressure from "development."

REAFFIRMING INALIENABLE AND PERPETUAL RIGHTS

Belaney is reported as saying that he had "two aims in life: one was to help his fellow Indian reach a position of respect and a means of livelihood in Canada; the other was to teach protection of this country's diminishing wildlife" (D.B. Smith 205). If it had been enacted, his proposal to the governor general and the king would have accomplished both aims. He was well aware of how the treaty process had failed. In his first book, he asserted,

> We must not fail to remember that we are still our brother's keeper, and having allowed this same brother to be robbed of his rights and very means of his existence (solemnly agreed by treaty to be inalienable and perpetual, where he was a self-supporting producer, a contributor to the wealth of the country and an unofficial game warden and conservationist whose knowledge of wildlife would have been invaluable) we must now support him. And this will be his downfall by the degrading "dole" system. (*Men* 187)

Here, along with the biblical resonances, is an affirmation of treaty rights, support for economic self-sufficiency rather than welfare, and respect for traditional knowledge (see also *Tales* 133).

In both places where Belaney spent his early days in Canada, treaty rights were an issue. Two of his first friends on Lake Temagami, Aleck Paul and Frank White Bear, had just signed a petition asking Ottawa for a reserve when he arrived (D.B. Smith 38). The band started to produce such petitions in 1877; almost a hundred and forty years later, disagreements over jurisdiction continue to block a resolution.[23] When the Temagami Forest Reserve was set up in 1901, the local Anishinaabeg were prevented from using it. In 1910, "Chief Francois Whitebear wrote to the Indian agent: 'We have to get permission from the chief fire ranger to cut even firewood'" (Bray and Thomson 148). The following year, hunting and fishing in the reserve were prohibited, and various areas where Anishinaabeg were living were flooded by hydroelectric dams (Theriault 84–85). Those who had cleared land and built on it had it taken away by incomers (26–27). In 1929, the province started charging the Bear Island band rent, a problem solved only when the federal government purchased the island from the province in 1943 for $3000 (Teme-Augama Anishnabai). One square mile was allocated as a reserve only in 1970, which the Temagami First Nation agreed to accept under protest (see Temagami First Nation website). In 1991, the Supreme Court ruled that the band members were covered by the 1850 Robinson-Huron Treaty, although no representative of theirs had signed it (McNab 40). The judgment was based on forged documentation originally produced by George Ironside Jr., the Indian agent at Manitowaning, who used monies he claimed to be passing on to the Temagami Anishinaabe people to pay his debts (48). David T. McNab notes, "Stealing monies was not an unusual practice in the Indian Department at that time" (35). And such bureaucratic obstruction was not exceptional, but, in fact, typical of the other places Belaney lived. As Smith points out, "Just after the war, in 1920, the Department of Indian Affairs had also refused to grant a reserve to the Indians at Bisco" (150). Belaney and Anahareo were married in Abitibi by Chief Nias Papaté, "on the trapping grounds of the Grand Lac Victoria and Lac Simon Indians ... who had never signed a treaty with the federal government" (79). Chief Papaté wrote to the Department of Indian Affairs to let them know that because of an influx of trappers using the recently constructed railway (which included Belaney and his friends, the "Bisco Bunch"), his people were starving (80). The west was no better when Belaney began to work for National Parks—his cabin at Lake Ajawaan was in Prince Albert National Park, Saskatchewan, where the Cree were forbidden to hunt after it was founded in 1927: "The Crees had hunted and trapped there for decades. Grey Owl felt strongly that the provincial and Canadian governments had behaved despicably ..." (150).[24] As Bonita Lawrence outlines in *Fractured Homeland*, her book about the struggle for land by the Algonquin people in the Ottawa River watershed, often the parks remained the only location where any animals survived because of the clear-cutting, dams, and other development outside them. Men caught hunting there to feed their families were criminalized, and often their children were taken away by social services.[25]

LEARNING FROM THE "LITTLE INDIANS"

Dawson's "The 'I' in Beaver" focuses on *Pilgrims of the Wild*, a book that condenses the events of the years between 1925 and 1934, when Belaney and Anahareo raised two pairs of beavers and Grey Owl became known through the articles he published in the British magazine *Country Life* and in *Canadian Forest and Outdoors*.[26] Dawson points out that although Belaney sees Indigenous people as part of nature, he also includes "those of other races who have lived for many years in the wilderness" (*Pilgrim* xiv). This point "allows Grey Owl to establish that he is indigenous without making any genealogical claims" (Dawson, "The 'I' in Beaver" 119). Dawson's article focuses on his relationship with animals, particularly the beaver; I want to extend her case that he used the beaver-as-metaphor to indigenize himself.

Many of the tales in *The Men of the Last Frontier* are descriptive rather than personal, perhaps because of Grey Owl's inability to find a clear narrative perspective. He writes that he plans to include some personal history in *Pilgrims of the Wild*, or, as he put it, "a few good healthy unequivocating 'I's' standing up on their hind legs" (185). Dawson argues that because he remarks so often on how his beavers stood up on their hind legs, "he is identifying his narrator with or as a beaver" ("The 'I' in Beaver" 120). His beavers lived in his cabins, sometimes getting in and out of their pond through a hole in the wall or floor. Dawson points to a passage where he says the beavers "invade" his quarters; he illustrates this sentiment by drawing a beaver standing in the doorway of the cabin over the caption "My Quarters Have Been Invaded." She comments, "[T]he caption can be simultaneously attributed to the beaver, the narrator, and the narrator-as-beaver" (121). In *Tales of an Empty Cabin*, he wrote that the beaver was "representative not only of all North American Wild Life, but of the wilderness itself" (206; see also *Pilgrims* 48). Dawson tracks the history of literary analogies between beavers and people. Not only do beavers stand up and chatter, make cries that sound like those of infant humans, and build homes with several rooms that they keep impeccably clean and dry, they re-engineer the landscape—or rather, the waterscape—to suit them.[27] Belaney's feeling that he, the beaver, the wilderness, and Indigenous people were all at risk, all vanishing along with "the last frontier," shows his identifications widening through the ecosystem, rather than focusing on his solo persona.

Dawson sees one problem in nature writing like Grey Owl's to be the difficulty it has in representing more than the relationship of one alienated individual with animals or the wider natural world ("The 'I' in Beaver" 123–24). As the title of his last book, *Tales of an Empty Cabin*, makes clear, he found life at Lake Ajawaan desperately lonely, as he longed not only for Anahareo, who had left him to go prospecting,[28] but also for the glory days of the Bisco Bunch and the rivermen whose exploits he memorialized in the two films he made in 1937. Part of the problem was that he was physically less and less able to withstand the rigours of such work. Further, he had been moved out of an ecosystem, however wrecked, into the artificial wilderness of a national park. He and his beavers and the other animals he tamed lived in isolation during the winter.[29] Dawson comments that his writing "produces an 'I' who lives in nature" but "has failed to produce a 'we' who live 'in relation' to nature" (124). Belaney's focus on reworking the dominant imaginary through writing, lecturing, filmmaking, and tourist promotion did isolate him from what might be seen as more practical projects, although he received up to seven hundred visitors in the summers he presided at Lake Ajawaan (D.B. Smith 159). His isolation from any community making practical change on the ground may partly explain Tina Loo's negative evaluation of his ideas about conservation. Her clarity about Grey

Owl and conservation has been "good to think with" here, in part because engaging with her argument reveals the sticking points of a much larger intellectual discourse.

ANTI-MODERN, SENTIMENTAL, ANTHROPOMORPHIC, AND NOSTALGIC

Loo thoroughly discusses Grey Owl's writing in *States of Nature: Conserving Canada's Wildlife in the Twentieth Century*, finally excluding his thinking from serious consideration in what is a very comprehensive and detailed historical study. *States of Nature* won the Canadian Historical Association's Sir John A. Macdonald Prize for the best scholarly book in Canadian history in 2007 and the Harold Adams Innis Prize for the best English-language book in the social sciences awarded by the Canadian Federation for the Humanities and Social Sciences in 2008. Without the careful work of Loo and historians like her, I could not have produced this book. Here I read her assessment of Grey Owl to highlight some blind spots that result from the clash between Western and Indigenous epistemologies. Loo favours approaches that put ecology over emotion (xix), thus defining ecology in a way that replicates the nature/culture divide and that prefers science to literature and other "emotional" ways of understanding the ecosystem. This move is a typical rather than an exceptional one for the social science disciplines, whose break with the humanities is marked by the word "science" in their name. Historians often ally their work with science because of its emphasis on evidence and facts, rather than seeing it (also) as a narrative discipline. Loo's book forecloses Grey Owl's message as "antimodern," "sentimental," "anthropomorphic," and "nostalgic" (113–14). His experience as a trapper and with Indigenous people does not count as a credential: "He was not an ecologist or even an amateur naturalist"—he was a "poet," a role that disqualifies his message (116).

Despite the care with which Loo reads Grey Owl, her interpretations of his work serve to stabilize an approach to wildlife management that includes Indigenous people only to a point, overlooking or discounting both their worldviews and their land rights. Her book concludes with a call to "embrace the political nature of conservation" so as to acknowledge "that conservation has and should serve human interests," part of her argument against those who see the wilderness as a space that should be kept free of human activity. She notes that attention to politics "would highlight the extent to which culture and nature are interconnected, and diminish the alienation that is the cause of so much environmental destruction" (214).

Despite this point, her account does not engage with Indigenous politics or Belaney's perspective.

One of Belaney's major goals was to use literature, lectures, films, and educational tourism to diminish the alienation of modern city dwellers from nature. However, he would resist the idea that conservation should "serve human interests" as too close to the idea that "Man" should have "dominion" over nature. Further, Loo's formulation of culture and nature as interconnected does not recognize that culture and nature did not begin as separate categories that later could be "interconnected," but rather have been constructed as separate from a particular cultural standpoint: ours. The Indigenous people Belaney lived with did not separate themselves from what we call nature.

Loo favours those who manage to produce a compromise between defining "wildlife as a thing (property) or a spirit (wildness)" (213). Putting Grey Owl into the same category as nature writers Charles G.D. Roberts, Ernest Thompson Seton, Jack Miner, Farley Mowat, and Bill Mason, she argues that they all removed animals from the web of human and ecological relationships by making them stand for an abstraction, wildness.[30] Although the following passage might at first seem to support her conclusion, in fact Grey Owl complicates this abstraction as he writes:

> In some intangible way they [the beavers] and their kind typified the principle that is inherent in all Nature. The animal supreme of the forest, they were the Wilderness personified, the Wild articulate, the Wild that was our home, and still lived embodied in the warp and woof of it. *Through them I had a new conception of Nature.* Although I had not hitherto given the matter much consideration, it was not inconceivable that every other creature was, according to its place and use, as well provided to fulfill its special purpose as they were, although perhaps not so obviously. (*Pilgrims* 203; italics added)

He might be seen here as isolating the essence of the wilderness in one exemplary animal, but then he says, "[T]hey lived embodied in the warp and woof of it." Further, he says that the beaver has taught him that all creatures might teach such lessons.[31] Basil H. Johnston argues that this is how Indigenous people understand the inter-relatedness of all life on earth: "By observing the relationship of plants, animals, and themselves to the Earth, the Anishinaubae people deduced that every eagle, bear, or blade of grass had its own place and time on Mother Earth and in the order of creation and the cosmos" (*Manitous* 15). This perspective can be seen as the reverse of abstraction.

Loo's criticism of Grey Owl's work as "nostalgic" is, again, part of a larger discourse that condemns longing for the past. Jennifer Ladino begins an article on the "official" nostalgia promoted by US national parks by noting that "nostalgia stands accused of being 'ersatz, vulgar, demeaning, misguided, inauthentic, sacrilegious, retrograde, reactionary, criminal, fraudulent, sinister, and morbid.'" Modernity, it seems, must keep everyone looking resolutely forward. Ladino shows how Grey Owl's contemporary, Dakota writer Zitkala-Ša (1876–1938), produced a counter-nostalgia by picking up on the widespread longing for a pure, even Edenic nature, and then showing how its "loss" took place and what the consequences were for Indigenous people. The National Parks vision entailed "the implicit separation of humans from nature, the reification of nature as distinct from everyday life, the assumption that the parks' attractions are democratically available, and the exclusion of native peoples' histories in the service of constructing a dominant narrative of American nature."[32] By living himself in a park as an Indigenous person, sometimes with Anahareo and their daughter, Belaney certainly troubled this view. Ladino remarks of Zitkala-Ša: "The natural home for which she is counter-nostalgic is most definitely inhabited, and any Edenic qualities it possesses stem from human interactions with their environment." Ladino argues, then, that for an Indigenous person to be "nostalgic"—homesick—runs counter to the dominant narrative of progress, which hustles us moderns impatiently toward an ever more developed civilization, implicitly urban.[33] Indigenous people have always been seen as unable to join this onward rush, because they are locked in the past, tied to uncivilized places, and inevitably vanishing (see Fabian and Bunzi). These interconnected tropes of civilization, progress, and modernity in part explain why Loo calls Grey Owl "anti-modern" (113). However, Indigenous nostalgia supports the return of homelands to Indigenous people, a radical political goal that they are still pursuing.

Loo also sees it as a failing that "[a]s the anthropomorphism that animated his characterizations of the beaver suggests, Grey Owl believed that the key to wildlife conservation was to see animals as human" (114). Belaney would respond this way: "I do not … ascribe human attributes to animals. If any of their qualities are found to closely approximate some of our own, it is because they have, unknown to us, always possessed them, and the fault lies in our not having discovered sooner that these characteristics were not exclusively human …" (*Pilgrims* xxi; see also Dawson, "The 'I' in Beaver" 120). In fact, Latour argues that those who decry anthropomorphism for warping objectivity are the most anthropocentric of all, because this view reserves agency to human beings alone, without considering how humans are dependent on relationships with both animate and inanimate beings:

> The accusation of anthropomorphism is so strong that it paralyzes all the efforts of many scientists in many fields—but especially biology—to go beyond the narrow constraints of what is believed to be "materialism" or "reductionism." It immediately gives a sort of New Age flavor to any such efforts, as if the default position were the idea of the inanimate and the bizarre innovations were the animate. ("Compositionist" 481)

Here we return to the Anishinaabe view of the world as animate. Beavers are fairly easy to see as actors and agents, but even those "objects" that might be seen as most inert, such as rocks and trees, are seen as living relatives. Anishinaabe elders taught that cutting down green trees should be avoided to save the trees from pain (D.B. Smith 41). Roger Spielmann gives an account of the rocks that heat the sweat lodge—called "grandfathers": "As the grandfathers were brought into the lodge, I began to see why the Anishinaabe language refers to rocks as 'living beings.' You could actually see their veins as they throbbed …" (159). Latour's point is less emotive: without networks of animals, objects, and people, human life could not continue.

Loo contrasts Belaney's work with a project that she sees as successful, initiated by James "Jimmy" Watt, a Hudson's Bay Company factor, with the Cree: "While the federal government was showcasing Grey Owl and his trained beavers to promote the cause of conservation, the HBC was assisting researchers from Elton's Oxford Bureau of Animal Population and implementing measures aimed at increasing the beaver 'crop' through the application of scientific knowledge" (9).[34] Although "ecological knowledge" should include cultural attitudes and human emotions as well as scientific study, Loo often contrasts Grey Owl's emotional and poetic approach with one she characterizes as practical, economically sound, and scientific.[35] Yet the proposals put forward by Belaney and Watt both supported a version of community-based resource management as the answer to restoring the ecosystem.

Watt, the factor at Rupert House (now Waskaganish, Quebec), founded in 1668 on James Bay, was appalled by the starvation that followed the near extinction of the beaver. In 1933, there were 162 beavers in the area that he and his Cree employees staked out as a beaver preserve; by 1943, 18,000 beavers were living there and 1800 beavers had been trapped by those Cree families selected by the company. The success of this experiment led to the company's taking it to other locations, where, as in the first project, Indigenous people were paid to carry out a census, and then, when numbers permitted, allocated rights to hunt according to need (Loo 108–9).[36] Loo figures Indigenous people as "partners" in conserving a resource that was "regulated to a great extent by the people who depended on it and used it." The result, "a locally sustainable community project," is said to satisfy all parties (120). Loo states that "the success of the preservation" was "ultimately due to the knowledge and cooperation of the Cree" (9). However, she does not consider that the Cree knowledge that enabled this success was not Western scientific knowledge.[37] As Berkes points out, "In Western science and its applications to fish and wildlife management, it is assumed that humans can control animal populations. In Cree worldview, by contrast, 'human management' of animals and environment is not possible" (99). Loo remarks that "Grey Owl argued that humans had to become Aboriginal in order to be conservationists" and to learn, like them, to "*respect* the plan of nature" (116; italics added). She does not agree with this proposition.

However, her perspective implies the opposite: that Aboriginal people have to become white in order to conserve wildlife, although it was white interventions that put it at risk in the first place. Frustratingly, she almost sees the problem with this idea when she quotes J.W. Anderson of the HBC on the cause of the destruction of the game: "[T]he old tribal laws [had] lost their effectiveness and the Indian gradually lost control of his tribal lands" (104). What neither she nor Anderson notes is that this "loss" was the result of colonial land theft and modernization. Indigenous people had a sustainable way of being in the world that could not withstand pressure from the deluge of inexperienced "railway trappers" and the depredations of logging companies. Because Indigenous starvation was overseen by the federal government and the extinction of wildlife by the provincial government, intervention was slow and ill-coordinated.[38] Licence fees and taxes were paid, but the money didn't return to the north or Indigenous people. Aleck Paul commented around the time that Belaney arrived at Bear Island, "If an Indian went to the old country and sold hunting licenses to the old country people for them to hunt on their own land, the white people would not stand for that. The Government sells our big game, our moose, for $50 license and we don't get any of it. The Government sells our fish and our islands and gets the money but we don't get any share" (qtd. in D.B. Smith 37–38). Like David Mackay speaking to the British Columbia land commissioners in 1888, Paul is not advocating a return to the past here, but for a share in control and profits.

The result was a "tragedy of the commons" in the north where every hunter—Indigenous or not—tended to kill every fur-bearing animal in sight, because if he didn't, the next hunter would (Loo 104–5). The loss of respect for other people and for animals was near total (Grey Owl, *Pilgrims* 50). Once the resource was gone (the silver, the fur, the trees), those who had profited departed, leaving the Indigenous people in polluted and devastated surroundings with no livelihood. Maud Watt, Jimmy Watt's wife, told of how malnutrition led to the deaths of all thirteen children in one Cree family, and ten of the twelve children in another (Loo 103).[39] Grey Owl describes such deaths poetically, nostalgically, and sentimentally, to be sure:

> And ever in my heart there was an aching loneliness for the simple kindly people, companions and mentors of my younger days, whose ways had become my ways and their gods my gods; a people now starving patiently, quietly, and hopelessly in their smoky lodges on the wind-swept, ravished barrens that Progress had decreed they should dwell in. I thought of the young children who died so pitifully, while the parents with stony faces kept vigil turn about to keep the flies away, till, like little beavers, they slipped silently and stoically away on the grey wings of dawn that carries so many souls into the Great Unknown. (*Pilgrims* 210)

Here and elsewhere, he evokes stereotypes of the stoical Indian. If we did not know how much he loved beavers, his comparison of these dying children to beaver kits could be seen as racist. Further, he uses words like "Progress" and "Civilization" as if they were forces outside human political control. However, Belaney did engage in politics at the highest levels he could access, not only talking to Lord Tweedsmuir and the Royal Family, but also petitioning Prime Minister Mackenzie King for funding to support his educational film projects.[40] Dickson paraphrases his message to King George: "He pleaded that the Indians should be returned to the Wilderness from which in so many cases they had been driven by the white man. He asked that they, and not white men, should be employed by the government as fire rangers and wardens, and as protectors of the wild life and forests of the country over which once they had dominion" (*Green Leaf* 22). This idea had been around since the mid-1840s; nothing was done about it (D.B. Smith 164; see also Feit).

Loo notes that Watt and the government were motivated in part by the need to reduce the "rising costs of Aboriginal welfare," a point that takes no account of the failure to honour or even enact treaties in ways that would have allowed Indigenous people to protect their lands so that welfare was not needed. This conversion of treaty rights into what Grey Owl calls the "degrading dole system" was one of the most effective moves of Duncan Campbell Scott's regime. This system not only rendered Indigenous people governable, but also demonstrated that they were averse to work. In this model, any money going to Indigenous people was praised as white generosity or resented as unearned. Racism proved a bar to Indigenous people and the non-British immigrants whom Grey Owl racialized as "Bohunks" to get jobs to replace hunting as a way of life. In areas where jobs were few in the first place, those Indigenous people who did get them were seen as taking them from their rightful (white) owners (see Lutz 159ff.); those who did not get them were seen as lazy. Nor was "welfare" widespread: only the most destitute and "deserving" were given any support during this period, despite the starvation that the Watts's efforts foregrounded.[41]

Loo does not turn the same critical gaze on government officials or the Hudson's Bay Company men that she focuses on Grey Owl. To ensure that its hunters could survive to the next season, the HBC sold goods on credit. Belaney paid back this "grubstake"—if he could—in furs (*Pilgrims* 76–78). The "company store" kept the price for fur low and the costs of commodities high; by this time the HBC had a monopoly (see *Men* 181). Watt certainly was charitable and enterprising; however, the profits that he and the company were "risking" were extracted from Indigenous labour and land in the first place. And protecting the Cree and the beaver meant that the company would benefit in the long run.

Loo's description of the Cree as "equal partners" rings of the "level playing field" of equality and justice for all that is the frequent recourse of those who see Canada as always having been a tolerant and fair country. At the time of the project, however, the Cree were destitute wards of the state without the vote. Even now, Harvey A. Feit notes that despite some recognition of Cree hunting territories in game management planning, "neither the national state governments nor the Cree hunters fully control lands, wildlife or peoples, nor can any one of them alone fully conserve game or forests. But their capacities are not equal, and the failures of the nation state governance to conserve lands, forests and wildlife since the 1970s are tragic" (282; see also Berkes 234).[42] Equal partnership remains an ideal, not a reality. And this ideal does not include the animals.

Loo is quite correct to point out that Belaney thought that all humans had to become Indigenous to become conservationists. He argued that to avoid the kind of devastation inflicted on the ecosystem that he saw over the twenty years he trapped in the north, all humans had to think like the Indigenous people who had lived there "since time immemorial." Many cling to the destructive epistemology of "mastery over nature" because it allows them to pretend they can control "Nature" from the outside, and indeed, that there is an "outside" they can inhabit. As Latour points out, this viewpoint not only underpins Western science but also anchors the fiction of the superiority of the West, since only the West is deemed (magically) to have science (*Modern* 105). In *We Have Never Been Modern*, he argues that "the modern" is a collective hallucination that constructs the West as different from and superior to the rest. Thus, those who feel that to "go Native" entails abandoning science are those who cannot accept that there might be more than one kind of science. To solve this problem, Latour advocates a kind of animism: reworking our epistemology (he calls it a constitution to emphasize that it is a human construct) to give all beings, including people, a seat in a (similarly constructed) Parliament (see Latour, *Politics of Nature*).

Harding, although appreciative of Latour's insights, argues in her *Sciences from Below* that the "we" in the title of *We Have Never Been Modern* refers to those elite white men who did not attain the state of modernity they aspired to. Women, Indigenous people, and other minoritized groups always knew that they were deemed incapable of becoming modern. Thus she concludes that "Latour has no sense of the difference which the absence or presence of women and other 'minorities' does and could make in the production of scientific [or other] knowledge" (45). Latour, she argues, is still constrained by the idea that identities are fixed, instead of seeing that they can be performative, bringing groups into existence "in a different way, namely 'for themselves,' as self-conscious collective agents of history and knowledge" (37). What he misses is that people might take on these identities, previously argued to be determined by biology, as "political projects ... chosen, not pre-given by nature or society" (38). Only these groups can invent the new concepts that make visible the phenomena that the dominant discourse has rendered invisible or failed to notice in the first place. By living as a hunter with Indigenous people for many years, Belaney was able—to some extent—to learn to think in ways that countered the dominant and to speak convincingly about these ways of thinking. Harding argues that society needs to include "differing interests about nature and social relations" and to "create pluricentric and democratic modes of getting on together" (40). To move to asserting common ground and equal representation too quickly will foreclose the emergence of new ideas and undermine the collective shift to new understandings.

Grey Owl's writing, like that of some of the other nature writers Loo examines, was always too popular to be canonized as literature, a bias that may shift with the advent of cultural studies and ecocriticism. A new edition of Anahareo's *Devil in Deerskins* makes her perspectives, perspectives that were so influential on him, available to readers and teachers. Their writing does meet the criteria for environmental literature set out in Lawrence Buell's *The Environmental Imagination* (1995), a work often cited as marking the beginning of a new field of literary study. They describe the other-than-human environment in a way that implies "human history is implicated in natural history"; makes it clear that "human interest is not the only legitimate interest"; holds humans accountable to the environment; and sees the environment as a process, rather than a static arrangement (Buell 7–8). Human alienation from the living world is at the heart of the environmental destruction that drove Grey Owl to take a public stage. His suggestion for re-enchanting this world was to promote ways that Indigenous people could continue to live in and maintain responsibility for the lands that had inspired their worldviews.

Chapter Seven

"They Never Even Sent Us a Letter": Harry Robinson (1900-1990) on Literacy and Land

The distinction between cultures with writing and those without has been called the "Great Divide." It has also been described as a "relic of academic colonialism," but it lingers on (Jack Goody qtd. in Finnegan, "Not by Words" 270; see Gingell and Roy). Like most colonial beliefs, this binary has led mainstream scholars to misrepresent, discount, or ignore Indigenous writing systems in North and South America (see Coe) and a great deal of historical Indigenous written cultural production as well. All Indigenous cultures were assumed to be "oral," because writing was definitive of civilization.[1] Therefore, Indigenous people who achieved literacy were, by definition, assimilated. Harry Robinson, a Syilx storyteller from the Okanagan territory on the Canadian side of the border, puts conflicts over literacy at the heart of an origin story. In the last section of this story, "Coyote Makes a Deal with the King of England," he connects the white man's theft of literacy to colonial land theft. He sees the acquisition of literacy by Indigenous people as closely connected to the return of their land.

ANTHROPOLOGY AND THE STORIES OF THE WISE OLD MEN
In the late nineteenth century, anthropologists sought stories that reflected a supposedly timeless period before Indigenous cultures were "contaminated" by settlement and modernity. Although the material collected by anthropologists is a huge resource, this emphasis on traditional authenticity meant they tended to overlook stories that dealt with contemporary life. Even Franz Boas, despite his support for Indigenous cultural traditions and social welfare, saw these cultures as threatened, rather than adapting. He hired several literate and multilingual Indigenous men to transcribe stories for him, paying by the page.[2] When one of these men, Henry Wellington Tate (ca. 1860-1914), wrote down stories in English first from his own

knowledge, and then translated them into Tsimshian, Boas protested; he wanted Tate to take down the stories the way "the wise old men" told them (qtd. in Maud, *Transmission* 18). Tate ignored this request. Since he himself was quite competent in both supposedly separate "realms," the oral and the literate, it is unlikely he would have found the notion of the Great Divide compelling. In *Transmission Difficulties: Franz Boas and Tsimshian Mythology*, Ralph Maud explains the lengths that Boas went to so that he could present these tales as initially told in Tsimshian and therefore as authentic. When Tate's language seemed too biblical, Boas changed it (46–47). Establishing the new discipline of anthropology, Boas wanted what could be published as data representative of *all* traditional Tsimshian culture (10),[3] not one Christian young man's written English version, however charming.[4] Anthropology tended to represent Indigenous cultures as past, static, and vanishing, and Indigenous people as hampered by their cultures in coming to terms with a modern world characterized by literacy. Stories that discussed contemporary history or made political claims were airbrushed, much as Edward S. Curtis doctored his photographs to remove signs of the modern from the images of the Indigenous people who posed for him ("Edward S. Curtis").

However, political and historical stories were being collected by the bureaucrats and commissioners tasked with dealing with the "Indian Problem" and the "Indian Land Question" in British Columbia. And it is these documents, of vital interest to every Indigenous person in the province, literate or not, that provide one useful context for the stories about literacy that Harry Robinson told to Wendy Wickwire. Robinson, who spent most of his life as a cattle rancher in the interior of British Columbia, learned stories from his grandmother and other elders. He met Wickwire, an ethnographer, in 1977, after he had been retired for five years. They taped hundreds of his stories. Robinson's goal was to reach a wide audience: "I like to tell anyone, white or Indian" (*Living* 89). *Write It on Your Heart*, the first collection of his stories, appeared in 1989, just before his death; two others have appeared since, *Nature Power* and *Living by Stories*.

Wickwire explains that she at first was not quite sure what to think of "Coyote Makes a Deal with the King of England,"[5] because it deals with historical events, people, and issues: "Because I had encountered so few references to whites and other postcontact details among the published 'myths/legends' I had surveyed, I bracketed this story as an anomaly" (Introd. *Living* 11). She put it in *Living by Stories*, the third collection to appear. However, it continues on from the origin story that begins *Write It on Your*

FIG. 10   Wendy Wickwire and Harry Robinson. Courtesy of Wendy Wickwire.

Heart, a story of how Indians and whites are divided by literacy when the first white man steals a paper that God has written for the Indian. Here, following Keith Thor Carlson, I also place "Coyote Makes a Deal" into the context of a particular historical event, the visit of a delegation of chiefs from British Columbia to King Edward VII in 1906 (Carlson, "Orality about Literacy"). Writing is central to "the deal" because in the story, Coyote conscripts the king of England to write a book of laws to regulate land ownership. Robinson was reflecting on the ways in which oral cultures differed from literate ones at the same time as the scholars associated with what has been called the "Toronto School of Communication," including Marshall McLuhan, were doing the same thing.[6] Contrasting Robinson's perspective with that of the Toronto School provides another important context for this story. Although Robinson connected literacy to theft, greed, and fraud, he saw how it could be useful in regulating land disputes between settlers and Indians. For the Toronto School, literacy was vital for the higher thinking that characterized civilization.

ORALITY, LITERACY, AND THE TORONTO SCHOOL

Walter Ong's influential and much reprinted *Orality and Literacy: The Technologizing of the Word* (1982) crystallizes the historical discourses that produced the binary in its title. Although Ong never studied or taught at the University of Toronto, his master's thesis was influenced by Toronto School ideas; it was supervised by McLuhan during the brief period he taught at St. Louis University. Ong went on to become a priest, received a doctorate from Harvard, and eventually became president of the Modern Language Association, the large organization representing academics who teach and study languages and literature at universities in North America. Ong handles orality in two moves, both congruent with Christian beliefs around conversion and with ideologies of progress and civilization. First, orality is seen as a necessary—and valuable—stage on the route to literacy: "[O]rality needs to produce and is destined to produce writing" (14). Without literacy, cultures are doomed to remain primitive, without any higher learning: "Literacy, as will be seen, is absolutely necessary for the development not only of science but also of history, philosophy, explicative understanding of literature and of any art, and indeed for the explanation of language (including oral speech) itself" (14). Second, literacy is figured as transformative; once achieved, there is no going back. The individual consciousness is irrevocably changed: "Oral cultures indeed produce powerful and beautiful oral performances of high artistic and human worth, which are *no longer even possible* once writing has taken possession of the psyche" (14; italics added). Writing is fetishized as a magical instrument of psychic and cultural conversion. Literacy is the only way to achieve full humanity: "[W]ithout writing, human consciousness cannot achieve its fuller potential" (14). Jacques Derrida tackles the colonizing effects of this binary in *Of Grammatology* (1967), but the divide continues to operate in many institutions, including the academy, where oral tradition is generally the province of anthropology rather than literature departments.

Since authentic Indigenous people were deemed to be "oral," anthropologists focused on collecting stories from the oldest and least literate storytellers (Boas's "wise old men"). The goal of anthropology was to produce texts that could be presented as unmarked by colonization or by the act of collection and translation, an ideal that tended to erase the roles of the ethnographers and those of the literate and multilingual Indigenous people they hired to work for them. Then seen as assistants, translators, or interpreters, now these men (and occasional women) are recognized as ethnologists in their own right (see Fee, "Rewriting").

LITERACY AS CONVERSION/ASSIMILATION

Literacy, like Christian conversion, was evidence of a radical cultural transformation, albeit a secular one: from primitive to civilized, ward to citizen. The Gradual Civilization Act of 1857 included provisions for the "enfranchisement" of Indian men over twenty-one who were, among other things, "able to speak, read and write either English or the French language readily and well" and "sufficiently advanced in the elementary branches of education" (Canada). What appeared to be the promise of equal treatment as citizens was firmly tied to the attainment of literacy. However, the word "gradual" reveals the expectation that Indigenous people had a long way to go before that equal treatment would be required. The narrative of progress was put to use: like colonies, Indigenous people could be continually represented as "belated"—making steady progress under white tutelage, but never quite managing to catch up. Status Indian men who "obtained a university education, or served in the armed forces ... could get immediate [land] title and enfranchisement without probation, because apparently the act of obtaining an education, or serving the church or the military, proved the ability and the desire to assimilate" (Brizinski 185). Enfranchised men could vote but lost their Indian Status, as did their wives and children. The land they were "given" was usually cut off from their reserve. Those who enfranchised were prevented from staying on the reserve and discouraged from contact with their extended families and community by the Indian agents, who remained in charge until 1969 (Satzewich). Unsurprisingly, few chose enfranchisement.[7] Given strong Indigenous kinship ties, higher education triggered heavy penalties for Status Indians. Those who chose this path did not necessarily abandon their people, however. For example, the Reverend Peter Kelly (Haida; 1885–1966), who completed a degree in theology and who was a strong advocate of assimilation, lobbied Ottawa for the fair allocation of land all his life (Van den Brink 253).[8]

Missionaries invariably linked Christian conversion with literacy; Jews, Christians, and Muslims are called "people of the book" for a reason. The Mi'kmaq, the Cree/nêhiyawêwak, the Ojibwa/Anishinaabeg, the Gwich'in, Inuit, and other Indigenous groups adopted writing systems introduced by missionaries with an ease and speed that belied the implications of the Gradual Civilization Act. They did not find this supposedly new and alien "technology" difficult. Indeed, scholars have recently proposed that some of the writing systems credited to missionaries might better be described as adaptations of existing Indigenous ones (Battiste; B.F. Edwards, *Paper Talk* xiii, 30–38). For example, Father Christian Leclerq noted the existence of Mi'kmaw hieroglyphics on his arrival in 1677. By the 1760s, literacy was widespread among the Mohawk (Goddard 24). Methodist missionary James Evans was inspired in the production of his famous Cree syllabary in 1840 in part by Sequoyah's Cherokee syllabary (Nichols 599). The Cree achieved near-universal literacy in this script (Bennett and Berry 90). In Labrador, "by 1862 most of the Inuit belonged to the Moravian Church and could read and write" (Petrone 105). The Cree syllabary was adapted for Inuktitut (Laugrand) and for use with Athabaskan languages in British Columbia in the 1880s (Moore, "Gwich'in Literacy"). Early missionaries also deployed various shorthand systems to provide orthographies for languages with very different sound systems from English or French. Father Le Jeune, working in Kamloops, British Columbia, introduced Duployan shorthand to Chinook Jargon speakers and in 1891 founded a newspaper, *Kamloops Wawa*, that was printed in this shorthand (Lynn Blake).[9] In many places, literacy spread quickly without the formal mediation of school or church (Bennett and Berry; Fagan, "Well Done"). Robinson learned to write as a young man from a friend, not at school, which he attended only briefly (Wickwire, Intro. *Write It* 12). Clearly, literacy did not require formal education, lead to the loss of one's storytelling ability, or irrevocably force one into modernity.

Despite intense efforts to produce writing systems to support conversion, when residential schooling showed success in destroying "primitive" Indigenous languages in the early twentieth century, these literacy systems were often abandoned, and government interest in promoting Indigenous literacy declined (B.F. Edwards, *Paper Talk* 29–30). The hopes of Indigenous people for education were high, but the residential schools were designed to turn out domestic servants, agricultural workers, and tradesmen. Many educated young Indigenous people could not get jobs because of widespread racism (Barman, *West* 172; see also Lutz).

Nineteenth-century Canadian educators of all religious backgrounds shared a consensus on the role of literacy (Graff 37). It was always to be inculcated within a system of Christian moral teaching to ready children for their preordained place in society either as contented and productive workers or, for an elite few, as professionals and leaders. Despite the insistence on the importance of literacy, any hope that it would lead to social advancement was in fact usually trumped by ethnicity, religion, gender, and class: "The majority of Irish Catholics were literate … but they stood lowest in wealth and occupation…. Women and blacks fared little better, regardless of literacy" (Graff 320). Similarly, the high rates of literacy achieved by

Indigenous peoples in the nineteenth century in their own languages did not lead to any advances toward control over their own affairs.

LANGUAGE AND LAND

For those like Harry Robinson who speak N'Syilxcen, a Salishan language, land and language are inextricable. Jeannette Armstrong says that the words meaning "our place on the land" and "our language" are the same: "We think of our language as the language of the land. This means that the land has taught us our language" ("Community" 37). Many Indigenous languages reflect a tight connection to particular landscapes not only in vocabulary, but also in grammar. For example, in English and other European languages, directions can be expressed without reference to particular landscapes (north is north anywhere on the globe), a result of the conventions of mapping and the use of the compass. However, hən'q̓əmin'əm, the Salishan language spoken by the Musqueam people living at the mouth of the Fraser River, indicates "direction of movement and location on land or water ... with words that refer to the shore and the flow of water" (Suttles 488). The words translated into English as "north" and "south" "actually refer to the two ends of the great inland sea that the Halkomelem language straddles, ... the northern end of the Strait of Georgia and ... Puget Sound" (Suttles 491). For those who came to Canada, however, the land was more abstract; it was generally seen as "new," and any cultural, emotional, and linguistic ties to land that prevailed in the Old World were cut, whether with regret or relief. Some have even argued that "settler" is just as inaccurate a term as "nomad," which was applied to Indigenous people to indicate that they lacked attachments to particular territories, so that the lands then could be claimed as "empty." During the "race for land" in Nisga'a territory in British Columbia, "not a square mile of arable land was left unstaked in the Aiyansh and neighbouring valleys or in any other place exhibiting the possibility of raising a potato" (Moeran 156). A newspaper report in 1965 comments that in 1917, New Aiyansh had about "50 white families, compared with five today" ("Ancient Printing Press"). Settlers rarely stayed on the lands they pre-empted for more than a generation or two, so they did not develop the knowledge of and attachments to these lands characteristic of Indigenous nations, attachments that permeated their language and stories.

INDIGENOUS DISCOURSES OF LAND AND LITERACY

Between James Cook's arrival at the place he named Nootka Sound in 1778 and the entry of British Columbia into Confederation in 1871, many First Nations there had little contact with whites, apart from surveyors, gold miners, and road construction crews. Missionaries began to arrive on the mainland only in the late 1850s. Well before Robinson was born, however, serious discussions were taking place in Indigenous communities across the province about the interconnections of literacy, writing, land, and settler discourses of legitimation around books, letters, documents, surveys, and maps. F.H. DuVernet, the Anglican archbishop of Caledonia between 1915 and 1924, described the cultural shift this way: "Degrading heathenism is now a thing of the past on the Upper Naas River, and the Indians on the whole are an intelligent and fine band of people, not yet perfect by any means but steadily progressing, enlightened by the Gospel of Christ" (qtd. in Moeran 221). Despite the implication that these "steadily progressing" Nisga'a people were progressing toward assimilation and modernity, in fact, they had an active land committee in place by 1913[10] and used their literacy and printing skills to promote their land claim. Paul Tennant documents one example:

> Founded in 1891 by the Anglican missionary J.B. McCullagh and called *Hagaga: The Indians' Own Newspaper*, it was initially published in the Nisga'a language by means of phonetic script. Later, a newspaper printing press was brought to Aiyansh by McCullagh and seven Nisga'a became competent typesetters. The paper began using English and seems to have been an important stimulus and means for the Nisga'a to learn to speak and write English. By the late 1890's the Nisga'a had taken over the newspaper "and made it a vehicle for organizing the Land Movement in the region.... to McCullagh's discomfort." Renamed the *North British Columbia News*, the publication appears to have had "fairly wide circulation among both Indians and Whites in the Nass region." (85)

Reading the report of one of the early commissions formed to inquire into complaints about land received from these Nisga'a and others shows the clash between the settler "claim by discovery" and the logic of Indigenous ownership. In 1887, Joseph Phrys Planta, acting for the new province of British Columbia, and Clement F. Cornwall, acting for Canada, were appointed to look into these complaints. Their report, *Papers Relating to the Commission Appointed to Enquire into the Condition of the Indians of the North-West Coast*, shows the clear failure of the government to properly establish a claim to the land, whether through discovery, conquest, treaty, law, or logic.[11] The Nisga'a Final Agreement, completed in 2000, is just one of many belated recognitions of this failure.[12] Pleased with displays of bunting, street lights, firefighting equipment, and brass bands that greeted them in the villages, the commissioners were not so pleased that those they met asserted "'Indian Title' to the whole country," requiring them to "combat and deny this" (British Columbia, *Condition of the Indians* 418).[13] Nor did those they spoke to generally welcome the idea of the Indian Act, or of Indian agents (419). Those who spoke to the commission were looking for resolution to the serious land disputes that arose once their traditional forms of governance had been disrupted or abolished by colonization,[14] disputes not only between white settlers and Indians, but also between different nations, and between groups within nations who adhered to different Christian sects.[15]

Many requests were made for "paper" that would prove ownership as well as for treaties. Family Bibles were produced as evidence of particular dates and events to do with land (428). In a hearing in Naas Harbour, Charlie Russ from Greenville (now Laxgalts'ap) noted that they wanted a "strong promise" on paper (432). Frederick Allen, from Kincolith (now Gingolx), remarked of some land, "[N]o one interferes now, but some white people might want it and we want to be able to say that it is ours and to have a paper to show" (427). Faced with such requests, the commissioners explained the British North America Act, which gave power to the provincial government to reserve lands for the Indians. Russ responds,

> [T]he words you have read to us we have never heard before in our lives. When they made the laws that you speak about, they had never been to see us…. Why they never even sent us a letter to tell us it was done. You see these chiefs present laugh. We cannot believe the words we have heard, that the land was not acknowledged to be ours. We took the Queen's flag and laws to honour them. We never thought that when we did that that she was taking the land away from us. (433)

A man called Neis Puck stood up and declared, "I am the oldest man here and I cannot sit still any longer and hear that this is not our father's land. Who is the chief that gave this land to the Queen? Give us his name, we have never heard it" (434). Their response highlights how Indigenous peoples must have felt across the country as colonization took hold: astonishment at what must have seemed to be bare-faced lying used to rationalize settler land claims (see Cardinal and Hildebrandt 58). How could this land on which they had always lived suddenly belong to someone else? One remarks, "We have heard of the Queen's kindness, but we have never seen it" (British Columbia, *Condition of the Indians* 443). One can understand their desire to actually visit the monarch so frequently invoked as the new owner to get matters cleared up. The idea that Coyote must have been involved in such a powerful transaction made sense to Robinson, as it must have to many of his listeners, since Coyote is the source of all major transformations in the Indigenous cultures of the British Columbia interior.

The next day, An Clamman explains what might have seemed like rudeness: "You saw us laughing yesterday ... because you opened the book and told us the land was the Queen's and not the Indians'.... No one ever does that, claiming property that belongs to other people. We nearly fainted when we heard the land was claimed by the Queen" (438). Richard Wilson, described as an Indian teacher, said, "Look across the bay here, we have seen it in the papers and have also heard about the 'land grabbers.' I suppose the land has been sold; we don't know anything about it. We haven't seen half a cent of the money we suppose it was sold for. It was our own land. It is the same with the land everywhere, which the white people have everywhere ..." (449). Significantly, he notes that even illiterate white men seem to flourish: "[T]here is a Frenchman—St. Armand—living near here; he can't read or write, and yet he buys the lands and we don't know what happens with the money" (449). Such settlers appeared to be doing very well, while Status Indians were generally blocked from pre-empting land after 1866 (Harris, *Making Space* 68).[16] Here is the reaction of people who had a working system of governance in place, confronted with an implacable and implausible new regime. The illiterate St. Armand flourishes, while they can only read about their land loss in the newspaper.

In just this one document, it becomes clear that Indigenous people—literate or not—were very familiar with the conventions of literacy, not to mention appropriate protocols in dealing with people of other nations. However, they still felt the need for an education in English. Frederick Allen of Kincolith remarks, "We can't all read and understand for ourselves, so we always depend on the explanation of our teacher" (British Columbia, *Condition of the Indians* 443). A. Leighton, described as "one of the principal Indians and who had worked in the saw mill for years," states, "There is something else we want to ask for from the Government. That is a government teacher to teach our children English ... [because] we want about our land made clear to us" (457). If they had known how schools for Indigenous children would operate, for the most part failing in the most basic duty of care or education, they might have thought again (see Castellano, Archibald, and DeGagne; Milloy). Even today, there is no level playing field in education: "elementary and high schools on reserves are funded by the federal government at rates 20 to 50 per cent below public school norms" set by the provinces ("Success" 78). Nonetheless, literacy in English proved to be one key that opened doors for activists to begin the long process of resolving the "Indian land question."

CHANGING VIEWS OF ORAL TRADITION IN COURT

Like First Nations across the country, those in British Columbia fought a determined battle to keep their land, although the mainstream has generally ignored the struggle except at times of crisis. Oral traditions, however, have always been imbued with relationships to land. The Supreme Court decision in *Delgamuukw v. British Columbia* (1997), a case started in 1984 by the Gitxan and Wet'suwet'en people in northern British Columbia, brought Aboriginal oral traditions into connection with Western notions of history and truth. Until the 1990s, British Columbia maintained that Indigenous land title had been extinguished by 1871; over a hundred years later, the Supreme Court of Canada in *Delgamuukw* "held that the Royal Proclamation of 1763 does indeed apply to British Columbia and that aboriginal title there was never extinguished" (Roth 150).[17] Nonetheless, as many critics have noted, the Supreme Court has laid out rules about how Aboriginal title is to be defined.

Most important from a literary perspective is that the decision said that oral narratives, used by the plaintiffs to make their claim, had to be taken into account in these and similar proceedings. Although the Supreme Court decision did not explain how to choose expert witnesses to interpret such testimony, it established its importance for the courts.[18] And courts were changing: in 2007, Justice Vickers of the British Columbia Supreme Court wrote, "[I]n order to truly hear the oral history and oral tradition evidence presented in these cases, courts must undergo their own process of decolonization" (*Tsilhqot'in Nation v. British Columbia* 36). Carlson argues that historians and political scientists must also "decolonize" their disciplines in his account of several "Salish stories of diplomacy" from southern British Columbia that deal with agreements with the Crown ("Aboriginal Diplomacy" 156). He notes that these stories cannot be documented as fact in Western terms, but they certainly do reveal the expectations around international relations held by the Indigenous people. The spoken words of various officials that they remembered often proved to be very different from what was put down in writing (see also Cardinal and Hildebrandt).

INDIGENOUS DIPLOMACY AND CONFLICT RESOLUTION

As Carlson notes in "Aboriginal Diplomacy: The Queen Comes to Canada, and Coyote Goes to London," several stories told by Robinson focus on questions of diplomacy, including "Coyote Makes a Deal with the King of England." Because the residential school policy to eradicate Indigenous languages had clearly succeeded,[19] Robinson decided to tell his stories in English rather than N'Syilxcen so that younger Okanagan/Syilx people and others could understand them (Wickwire, Intro. *Living* 29).[20] From a culture that regards reciprocity as a foundational value, he saw the solution to conflict in sharing of information, rather than in ignoring or hiding it. In his culture and that of many nations in the province, the tradition of feasting ("the potlatch") served many social purposes, but one was to resolve conflicts by bringing parties together to work out a resolution in public and to consolidate such agreements with gifts (see Wa and Uukw, 30–31; Mills 146, 153).[21]

As Wickwire points out, literacy, paper, and books are associated not with civilization for Robinson, but with fraud ("Stories" 464). Nonetheless, he turned to the production of written texts in English so as to resolve the conflict between white and Indigenous viewpoints by sharing his perspective as widely as he could. Although he regarded writing as a powerful tool, he did not see a shift toward literate practices as requiring an abandonment of his own cultural perspective. Indeed, as we will see, he connected the achievement of literacy to the resolution of land claims rather than to assimilation. For him, as for those who spoke to the commissioners, literacy and education were necessary not so they could attain the privileges of "civilization," but so they could get the land back.

Wickwire met Robinson when she was working on her doctoral dissertation; fifty years her elder, he worked with her to preserve his stories. Wickwire writes of how she at first had difficulty with the many non-traditional elements in his repertoire and with the idea that he might have been aiming his stories specifically at her and other non-Native people: "I reflected on how passionately he had told his stories about whites and how quickly I had dismissed these as anomalies" (Intro. *Living* 19). Just as his grandmother had taught him the stories, the childless Robinson could be seen as taking her on as an apprentice/grandchild who would facilitate the shift from speech to text so the stories could reach beyond the Okanagan/Syilx to a larger audience. At first, she scrupulously paid him for his time; he convinced her to enter into a different reciprocal relationship: stories for errands, transport, and companionship (Wickwire, Intro. *Nature* 9). He worked hard to establish a relationship with her that embodied and reflected the exchanges promoted by what Blanca Schorcht calls his "storied world" ("Storied" 23). He did not see their partnership as simply preserving the past, but as an intervention into a vital contemporary white–Indian conversation. He launched the project with his origin story about paper and book for a reason (Wickwire, "Stories" 483).

GOD MAKES FIVE MEN

Robinson's origin story[22] explicitly deals with ethnic difference: in a world covered by water, God creates five men out of the leaves of a wild rose bush. They represent five peoples: the Chinese, the Hindu, the Russian, the Indian, and the white. God starts with four leaves: "And there should be four," because four is the number Okanagan/Syilx people expect in stories, just as Euro-Canadians expect three bears, three billy goats, three blind mice, and the like (*Write It* 34n). However "one of them is doubled" so in one way it looks like one leaf, and in another it looks like two (34). The doubled leaf makes twin men, the younger the white and the older the Indian. Robinson's origin story is a version of a widely dispersed class of traditional origin stories called earth diver stories, although often the divers are animals (Wickwire, Intro. *Write It* 17; see also Wickwire, "Stories").[23] However, this story has obviously been adapted to explain post-contact relations. Further, the "God" referred to here behaves in some ways like the Christian God (Wickwire, Intro. *Write It* 17–20). Nonetheless, despite many qualities that would upset Boas, the story accounts for the peoples of the world from within a Syilx worldview.

Robinson connected land and God, as did the men on record in the various land commission reports: "The land is our own; God has given it to us to get our living from" (British Columbia, *Condition of the Indians* 447). Sometimes, this God is explicitly the Christian God: "Chief Herbert Wallace, a Methodist Tsimshian of Port Simpson, wrote in January 1889, 'We want the whole of the Tsimpshean peninsula. We were heathen people once; then we did not know anything about our land, but now we are being civilized we know this is our land from our knowledge of God'" (qtd. in Patterson 46). Such references to God are also common in the transcripts of the McKenna-McBride Commission (the Royal Commission on Indian

Affairs for the Province of British Columbia), which held hearings between 1913 and 1916 (Wickwire, "Stories" 469–70).

Often in earth diver stories, it is the last diver, the smallest and weakest, who finally succeeds, sometimes dying after surfacing with a little earth. Here, the fourth diver, the Indian, gets "a very little small grain" of earth under his fingernail (*Write It* 36). The earth grows from the tiny grain, and God throws the three older men, the Chinese, the Russian, and the Hindu, to their respective countries, each with his "paper." However, he has only one paper left to share between the twins. (The anomalous younger twin is already causing trouble!) God leaves the paper under a rock and goes away to think. The younger twin starts worrying that God will give the paper to the older brother, and that "he's going to be the boss," so he decides to hide it (44). This is the point at which whites steal literacy from Indians. When God returns and asks for it, the white man tells him the wind blew it away. God knows he is lying and banishes him across the ocean, but he lets him take the paper. God tells him that after a long time, he will come back, and then he should tell the older brother what's on the paper.[24] Robinson's origin story reveals that "it was God's original intention that Salish people be literate" (Carlson, "Orality" 48). Interestingly, just as in Cree, where "older brother" is a reference to Coyote (McLeod 14), this Indian proves also to be Coyote (*Write It* 52).

This story connects the loss of literacy to the unjust loss of land; after all, it was the Indian who recovered the little grain from which the earth grew. It also makes it clear why "the white man can tell a lie more than the Indian," because of that first lie to God (*Write It* 46). Robinson notes that whites built a road through the reserve in 1929 and said they would pay the Indians for it: "And when did they pay? / They never paid 'em yet. They never did pay" (46). He notes, "[T]his is a government man ... he was telling lie" (46). So right in the middle of a traditional earth diver origin story is a recent memory of land stolen by the government: this intrusion of the contemporary is only startling to those who see such stories as properly locked in the past. And Robinson adds that not only did the whites not pay for the road, they still haven't told the Indian everything that is on the paper (46). The only time whites seem to be forced to tell the truth is in court: "You kiss this bible to say the true" (46).

Several things make this story unusual. First, it is clearly post-contact, since the Okanagan would not have heard of or met any of the peoples it mentions before then.[25] That it is told as an origin story marks its importance. Most stories of this type use the number four as a base; this one shows the colonizer as a sort of graft (the joined leaf, a twin), an anomaly, perhaps, and certainly a continuing philosophical and political problem. In a culture where reciprocity is crucial, the theft of the paper and the continuing refusal to share its contents matter more than what might be written on it. Robinson says that it contains instructions "that'll tell you what you going to do / from the time you landed in there / till the end of the world" (41). Although this description makes the paper seem like a religious text, Robinson doesn't make this link. Only God and the white man know what's on the paper. This lack of knowledge on the part of the Indian is compensated for by a stronger ethic of sharing that the white man lacks.[26]

COYOTE VISITS THE KING

After his success at earth diving, Coyote has various exciting adventures, which culminate in a presumptuous and unsuccessful contest with God to move mountains around. As punishment for his arrogance, God exiles Coyote to a raft shrouded by fog. The whites begin to pester him, trying to get close enough to his raft to take his picture. They keep developing bigger and faster boats, but God keeps them at a distance.[27] Finally, God realizes that he needs Coyote, as things are not going well in the British Columbia interior. He sends an angel to hire Coyote to go to England to "talk to the king, / and you and the king going to make the law / [for] the white people and the Indian" (*Living* 67). Coyote sneaks into the palace, introduces himself as a fellow king, and tells the king that his "children" aren't behaving well: "They just go and claim the land / and they just do as they like / If my children tell them 'Here, this is mine' / then they will kill 'em" (70). When the king demurs, "[Y]our word, it sounds like war," Coyote asks him to look out the window, where God has produced a frightening scene filled with "nothing but Indians," all armed with spears. Coyote politely tells the king that it's up to him if he wants a war; the king reluctantly has to confess he isn't quite ready. Then Coyote says, "Once you say that we're not going to fight / we can make out a paper and sign" (73). Here is the notion of a peace treaty and a land settlement rolled into one.

At this point, Coyote suggests that finally he is ready for a photo op: another white technology enters the Indian world, but only with permission. Then Coyote gives some guidance about the law to the king and says, "When you finish, all the paper, that could be the Indian law, / You give 'em to my children. / Not right away, but a long time from now" (73–74). He proposes that reserves be surveyed and that these can never be taken away from the Indians, "[b]ut still the Indians, they got a right / on the outside of the reserve as well" (74). The king isn't really satisfied, but Coyote has the upper hand.

This treaty—dictated by Coyote, backed by God—is what prevents reserves from being sold, even in British Columbia, although "in another way, they always take a little" (75). Reserves, like all private property in Canada, are subject to expropriation for the public good. However, railways, roads, sewage outlets, dam spillways, and so forth, always seem more likely to go through reserves than private property, revealing that both the "public good" *and* "private property" belong to the majority. The Indians speaking to the commissioners in 1888 had heard that the Songhees reserve in Victoria had been cut back for a railway line (21–22). The commissioners reassured them. By 1911 the Songhees lands across the harbour from the Empress Hotel and the British Columbia legislature had been sold and the Songhees people moved off these lands altogether (Victoria Heritage Foundation; Barman "Race, Greed"; Mawani, "Legal Geographies").[28]

Then Coyote instructs the king to write the law in a book, and when it's done, to give it to his children, the Indians, who by then will be able to read it. But this king doesn't really want to write the law, and three other kings after him don't finish it either: "that's the four" (*Living* 76). This long delay in coming to terms with the issues certainly reflects the foot-dragging of both British and Canadian bureaucrats and politicians. The next in line to the throne is a woman. Although Robinson may not have been thinking about specific kings, there have been four successive kings named George. George I reigned from 1717 to 1727. His successors were George II (d. 1760), George III (d. 1820), George IV (d. 1830), and William IV (d. 1837), followed by Victoria (d. 1901). When the queen finds out that the book hasn't been written, "she decides to do it, / because it's supposed to be done" (78). Again, whether Robinson was thinking about Victoria or not, his queen shared Victoria's strong sense of duty. And the "book" might well be Robinson's version of a more widely held proposal. The Reverend McCullagh, the Anglican missionary to the Nisga'a, felt reserve lands were inadequate. He wrote of a hearing he attended: "The chiefs and others who were present vigorously advocated a repeal of the 'Indian Act,' substituting for it an imaginary statute which they called the 'King's Law,' by which they hoped to obtain a larger measure of tribal authority" (qtd. in Moeran 158). Rather than seeing this as an "imaginary" law, one might see it as a serious counterproposal that may have circulated around the province in various forms: after all, new laws and policies are always acts of the imagination, as are nations, those "imagined communities" (B. Anderson). Or perhaps they were referring to George III's Royal Proclamation of 1763 (Wickwire, "Driving" 37).

The queen not only takes up the task of writing the book, but also makes four copies, "good and thick" (*Living* 78). When the book is finally done, it "could be somewhere around 1850," in the middle of Victoria's reign and just as gold rushes on the mainland of what is now British Columbia were set to drastically change the social dynamic (79). Despite Robinson's gestures at dating, one might not want to read this story as factual history, but it certainly can be read as an allegory of political relationships. Vickers writes:

> Many of the oral histories and oral traditions I was privileged to hear ... were woven with history, legend, politics and moral obligations. This form of evidence is a marked departure from the court's usual fare and poses a challenge to the evaluation of the entire body of evidence. Courts generally receive and evaluate evidence in a positivist or scientific manner: a proposition or claim is either supported or refuted by factual evidence, with the aim of determining an objective truth. However, in cases such as this, the "truth" which lies at the heart of the oral history and oral tradition evidence can be much more elusive. (*Tsilhqot'in Nation v. British Columbia* 137)

As we will see, a lot of history is embedded in this story, although its purpose is not so much to fix dates and facts as to describe and comment on relationships.

STORIED HISTORY

Coyote's visit to the king prefigures an important visit by British Columbia chiefs to London to protest their treatment at the hands of the new government. Finally, British Columbia Indians could deal directly with the imperial power, rather talking to colonial bureaucrats. In 1904 Chief Louis Clexlixqen of the Shuswap (now the Secwepemc; see Thomson) and Chief Johnny Chillihitza of the Okanagan Nation went to London with Father Le Jeune of Kamloops. Ironically, they were en route to a conference on Indigenous literacy: in Rome, they had an audience with Pope Leo XIII. Joe Capilano, of Squamish, "learned of the 1904 journey to Rome through Le Jeune's Chinook-jargon-language newsletter, the *Kamloops Wawa*" (Carlson, *Power* 266; see Lang) and was inspired to organize a delegation to meet with King Edward VII to discuss land rights. Contemporary newspaper accounts record that the group was officially bid farewell by the mayor's delegate, who gave his address in Chinook Jargon ("Plaint of the Siwash").

FIG. 11   BC First Nations leaders seeing off the delegation to King Edward VII, 1906.
City of Vancouver Archives, AM54-S4 P41.1. Photo by J.S. Matthews.

With Basil David (Shuswap/Secwepemc) and Chief Charlie Isipaymilt of
Cowichan, Joe Capilano met first with the prime minister, Wilfrid Laurier,
in Ottawa, and went on to London and an audience with the king. Carlson
argues that in making this visit, "the delegation's aim was to draw attention
to the injustice of Canadian Indian policy in British Columbia as a whole,
and in so doing embarrass the Dominion government into applying the
rule of law in all of its provinces" (*Power* 267). Coyote certainly embar-
rassed the king.

Robinson explains the strange customs at court, where there is con-
sternation around the possibility of having a woman queen—"because the
woman is not allowed to be in the business like that" (*Living* 77). God finally
intervenes and suggests that they could make a mechanical bird that would
decide the issue by sitting on the chosen one's head three times in a room
full of both men and women "all mixed": this is how the queen is finally
chosen (77). This part of the story may owe something not only to Okanagan matrilineal traditions, but also to another oral story. According to the
Sto:lo, in the course of a dinner meeting in London during the visit in 1906,
the delegation translator, Simon Pierre, a young shaman from Katzie, "conjured a small bird and caused it to circle repeatedly less than a metre above
his head" (Carlson, *Power* 267). Robinson's story of the mechanical bird,
with its suggestion of technical expertise and random sampling, contrasts
nicely with the Katzie man's different conjuring of a live bird. Carlson notes
that subsequent Sto:lo stories about the visit see this demonstration of sha-

manic power as "in large part responsible for the delegation's success." The colonial version suggested that the delegates returned home awed by the grandeur of the capital and humbled into subordination (267). As Carlson points out, this delegation was extremely important for Indigenous history since it was the first time that "an Aboriginal leader presented himself as the spokesperson for the entire Indigenous population" of British Columbia, an act that marked the beginning of province-wide political organizing (269).

The way the non-literate Coyote guides the king on how to write his material resembles the way Robinson worked with Wickwire. Coyote sets outs out what the king should do—"just the points like"—and then says, "When I leave you … take your time and do the rest" (*Living* 73); Robinson writes to Wickwire: "I wrote the some of it or I mention on tape and you do the rest of the work. The stories is worked by Both of us you and I" (Wickwire, Intro. *Nature* 10). This analogy equates Robinson with Coyote, and Wickwire with the industrious queen. Perhaps this is why Robinson did not have any of those four kings do this important work—to honour his collaborator.

The next stage of the story introduces the notion of photographic evidence, however anachronistically (even given the roughness of Robinson's dating, the king took Coyote's picture well before the invention of photography). The queen keeps a copy of the book and sends her representative to put one in Ottawa, one in Winnipeg, and one in Victoria. Robinson says that the man who guided the British representative to Victoria was an Okanagan man, TOH-mah. The Englishman showed TOH-mah the book, and although TOH-mah couldn't read, he did recognize the frontispiece: a picture of Coyote. Robinson uses this photograph to authenticate the travels of the book and its link to Coyote. Carlson notes in "The Indians and the Crown" that photographs were used to document both the 1904 and 1906 delegations to London. Father Le Jeune returned with 120 stereopticon photographs of the first trip. The leaders of the second delegation returned with photographs of King Edward VII, using them to authenticate their words about the meeting. This use of a photograph as a form of "witnessing" can be seen as an adaptation of the continuing tradition of appointing honoured guests at a ceremony as witnesses who are then held responsible for remembering what went on (Wa and Uukw 39). This witnessing is just one way First Nations people in British Columbia ensure that important knowledge is passed along accurately, despite the mainstream belief that oral transmission is less trustworthy than writing.

Robinson goes on to state that the book did make it to Victoria, because he, Tommy Gregoire (an accomplished rodeo rider and subsequently an

FIG. 12 Cowichan Indians displaying a picture of
King Edward VII, 1913. Image H-03662 courtesy of the
Royal BC Museum, BC Archives.

Okanagan elder), and Andy Paull, an important Squamish politician, actually saw it there in the 1940s.[29] Again the story is grounded in personal experience and historical fact: almost certainly these three men did go to Victoria in search of information. Paull would have been getting ready to go to Ottawa for joint parliamentary committee hearings on the Indian Act held in 1946 by the new Liberal government (see Dunlop 221–22). However, when they found it, the book "was locked. It was padlocked." Although in the story, Robinson and Gregoire think Paull should read it, "he never said nothing. He never move" (*Living* 85). Robinson felt it should be opened, "because now all these Indians everywhere, they can read. / Just like white people. / It's only me because I didn't have enough school. So they should give 'em by now" (85). Once it might have been acceptable to keep the book only for those who could read—the whites—but no longer. The point is clear: despite having achieved literacy, as required by the discourse of civilization, Indigenous people are still not being treated as equals. The book containing Coyote's law is still padlocked.

Coyote had passed a magic word along to the king during their discussions. In land claims, "they got to say the right word. / If they don't, well they were beat" (85). Certainly those who spoke to the commissioners in 1888 received little satisfaction. The leaders who diligently testified before the McKenna-McBride Commission (1913–1916) clearly didn't say this magic word, because the commissioners recommended the removal of some land and its replacement with other, less valuable lands (Harris, *Making Space* 241–46). In 1927, discontent led to a parliamentary hearing in Ottawa. It was after this hearing that officials moved to revise the Indian Act, adding section 141, which prevented Indians from hiring lawyers to prosecute any legal claims (*Indigenous Foundations*). This section remained in force for twenty-four years, until 1951, another reason why it was easy for the government to "always take a little" of what reserve land remained.

PAPERS CONNECTED WITH THE INDIAN LAND QUESTION

Robinson was thinking of a real book; however, in the story it remains more symbolic than real. Robinson is using it to represent an entire worldview based on written documentation that largely replaced an earlier one based on oral contracts. Robinson correctly notes the bureaucratic habits of the whites: of the book he says, "They hiding 'em. / But they never throw 'em away. / They still keep 'em but they wouldn't show them to the Indian / unless the Indian say about and ask 'em about" (*Living* 85).[30]

Significantly, the joint committee hearings in 1927 became focused on a particular book: *Papers Connected with the Indian Land Question, 1850–1875* (British Columbia; see Tennant 106–7).[31] And Paull had been there to put forward the claims of the Allied Indian Tribes of British Columbia with Kelly, Basil David, who had been in the 1906 delegation to Ottawa and London, and Chillihitza, who had travelled to Europe in 1904. They were accompanied by the lawyer Arthur O'Meara (see Morley 104–17; Foster). Although several accounts suggest that O'Meara was not as cogent a speaker as Paull or Kelly, Indigenous people who wanted access to important government officials required white spokespeople and translators, usually missionaries or lawyers. The committee objected to O'Meara quoting from various authorities on the grounds that he was quoting inaccurately and had not tabled the documents. Paull intervened:

> There is a book that has been published many years ago, which contains all the dispatches in colonial days with the Imperial government. All of those dispatches are contained in that book and we have been trying all the time to get a copy of it. I have been to the Department and Dr. [Duncan Campbell]

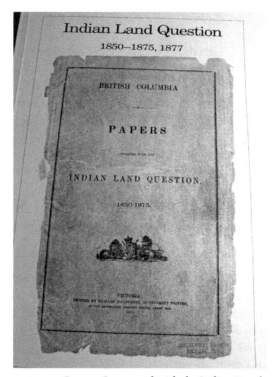

FIG. 13 *Papers Connected with the Indian Land Question, 1850–1875.* Photo Margery Fee.

> Scott could not let me have it. I have been to the Library and they have not
> got it there. I know that Commissioner Ditchburn has that book; and I would
> ask to have access to it. (qtd. in Tennant 107)

In fact, Tennant says that two copies were in the room, but the chair stated
that "the book ... belongs to the Indian Department, and they have only
one copy of it, and they cannot let it go" (107). Here is one source for the
notion of a book without enough copies, one that remained locked up,
despite its vital importance for land claims. Significantly, Robinson
declared of his own stories, "Is not to be Hidden. It is to be showed in all
Province in Canada and United States" (Wickwire, Intro. *Nature Power* 15).
Rather than padlocking books in libraries where only the authorized could
see them, his culture shared stories with those who should hear them.

Tennant describes the hearings as "quick and casual, displaying no
concern for reasoned explanation that could withstand serious scrutiny"

(109; see also Patterson 50). Although the committee paid no attention to their requests, the report did patronizingly note that "the evidence of Messrs. Kelly and Paull was given in idiomatic English, clearly and forcibly expressed, and both the matter of their evidence and the manner of presentation were highly acceptable to your Committee" (qtd. in B.F. Edwards, "I Have Lots of Help" 15). Similarly Alan Morley, in his biography of Kelly, praises Kelly and Paull, but remarks of the testimony of Chillihitza and David that the "exhibit of two illiterate chiefs who could not even speak English was pitiable, if not farcical" (112). The idea that it was shameful to be illiterate and unable to speak English obviously still prevailed as late as 1967, when Morley's book was published. No wonder leaders worked so hard to master these skills.

Unfortunately, the book does not contain a picture of Coyote (that would really confirm the argument that this is the book written by the queen!), although symbolic animals—the British lion and unicorn—do grace the front cover. Now online, it was first printed in 1875 by the government printer in Victoria. It was compiled by members of the Opposition as part of an inquiry (Tennant 47–49) and reprinted only in 1987. The field of land claims in Robinson's day was filled with documents that were hard to access or even imagine. Like Edgar Allan Poe's purloined letter, what was written in them is less important than the ways in which they were hidden because their contents, if revealed, could have profound consequences for the nation. This particular document begins with what came to be known as the Douglas Treaties, described in a heading as "conveyance of land to the Hudson's Bay Company by the Indians" (British Columbia, *Papers* 5), the last completed in 1854 (see Makmillen). It ends in a flurry of inconclusive back-and-forth letters in the 1870s about the acreage to be granted to Indians. This inability of the federal and provincial governments to agree typified all dealings with Aboriginal lands. As Hamar Foster, Heather Raven, and Jeremy Webber point out,

> Notwithstanding that BC law permitted settlers to pre-empt up to 320 acres and effectively denied Indians the right to pre-empt any land at all, the government insisted that ten acres per family was sufficient. Although by 1874 Ottawa had come down to twenty, the two sides then deadlocked over whether this figure should be restricted to reserves not yet confirmed. (18–19)

The "book" imagined by Robinson as outlined by Coyote and written down by one powerful author, the queen, in the form of a coherent and single "law," was a compilation mainly of letters between government officials, with a few enclosures of news reports and letters written to the government by concerned parties. It makes uneven reading, with its contrast between letters by bureaucrats, which are usually short, formulaic, and scant in emotion and detail, and those enclosures by members of the Aborigines Protection Society (see Heartfield) and missionaries, aggrieved white settlers, or news reports. The latter make dramatic predictions (usually of war or violence to come) and accusations (of cruelty, injustice, delay, and the like). The letters by bureaucrats are written with an eye to the record (what it must contain and what it must omit), with a sense of power (letters need to be answered, particularly those that make accusations, but once answered, their content can be ignored) and a sense of the distance between that power in law and on the ground. A proper survey seemed always to be too expensive (British Columbia, *Papers* 57, 77, 117, 123). Although a few individuals write many of the letters, sometimes officials change; Edward Bulwer-Lytton, secretary of state for the colonies, is away, so Lord Carnarvon takes his place to reply to one of Governor Douglas's letters.[32] During the period in question, the lands constituting British Columbia were transferred twice, from the Hudson's Bay Company to the Colonial Office (1851), and from the Colonial Office to the Dominion of Canada (1871) with an attendant delay in getting a new set of officials up to speed.

Robinson's idea that this compilation was a book, which he calls "The Black and the White" (*Living* 78), written by one person is like the notion of "the Bible" held by the religious or "the dictionary" by the literate. The Bible is clearly a historical compilation consisting of a variety of genres, including stories, letters, prophecies, songs, historical and genealogical accounts, sermons, brief biographical accounts, and laws. However, because it is seen as issuing from a single inspiration—it is God's Word—it is seen as a seamless whole without the textual failings of such compilations made for secular purposes. Similarly, dictionaries are put together by humans from limited and sometimes defective evidence, but once published, they magically move into a position of authoritative singularity: arguments about language are settled by reference to "the" dictionary, just as, despite its dozens of translations, "the" Bible is used to guide lives. Ordinary readers rarely question the origins, production, translation, or inconsistencies of such texts. Although this might seem naive, in fact, these books, written by ordinary men, do become more than an arbitrary compilation. Legal cases transform them into a powerful source of evidence, for example. This "magic" of writing explains the courts' difficulty in admitting oral tradition as trustworthy evidence.

Robinson's description of the writing of the book in London by the queen is a fiction, a fiction that contemporary readers can see through easily enough. But the historical letters are also clearly based on fiction as well, the fiction of British law. When I call the law that regulates our society a "fiction" I do not mean that I do not respect it or take it seriously. Quite the contrary. What I hope is becoming clear here is that this law has been flouted in British Columbia, as even a perfunctory reading of the *Papers* makes clear. Indigenous people repeatedly demonstrated that they were prepared to honour this law and negotiate with it as nations, provided these negotiations embodied a reciprocal "honour of the Crown."

HONOUR OF THE CROWN

Colonial officials consistently produced a constitutive fiction of the Crown, embodied in the form of a person, the queen, as if the power and justice of the monarch extended to the colonies without their mediation. Here Lord Carnarvon ends a letter (11 April 1859) to Governor Douglas: "It is to be hoped that by such ... means which your experience will enable you to devise, the Indians may in these, the most recent of the British settlements, be treated in a manner worthy [of] the beneficent rule of Our Gracious Sovereign" (British Columbia, *Papers* 18). For those who live in a constitutional monarchy, the Crown, backed by the Christian God, anchors the fiction that regulates justice, property, and governance. Robinson showed how his God and Coyote similarly anchored and regulated such relationships from an Okanagan perspective. When colonial officials in British Columbia failed—refused—to deal with land as required by the Royal Proclamation of 1763, they brought the honour of the Crown into disrepute, a disrepute that was signalled recently in the 2004 *Haida* Supreme Court decision, in which the justices felt obliged to state (again) that in land negotiations, "Sharp dealing is not permitted." Annoyingly, Indigenous people in British Columbia persist in pointing to this "sharp dealing" and the lack of a proper resolution to their land claims, although officials persistently try to stall or silence them.

Despite their diverse authors, these letters are marked, just as Robinson's story is, by a set of assumptions about proper behaviour, particularly with respect to land. Lord Carnarvon's remark about the queen's beneficence is quickly followed by "you will, I am persuaded, bear in mind the importance of exercising due care in laying out and defining the several reserves, so as to avoid checking at a future date the progress of the white colonies" (British Columbia, *Papers* 18). Clearly settlement, not beneficence, was the priority. The letters also reveal a distinct lack of "due care" in practice. The hasty way in which the land was parcelled out is in part excused by potential and actual conflict during repeated gold rushes. Since the local Indigenous people, and possibly an attached missionary, were the only ones who had any real knowledge of the lands that were being surveyed or of their customary uses, there was little possibility that it could be properly surveyed (a metaphor that implies that it could all be seen from above in a God's-eye view), prior to being parcelled out (another problematic metaphor, since much land was shared between families and larger groups—some now defined as nations—in complex ways; see Thom). Certainly this survey would be possible in some valleys and over some "prairies," but much of the land in question was mountainous and heavily timbered. Repeatedly, agents are requested to make a "rough sketch" (22, 32, 83, 84, 94, 95, 111) and to blaze trees and put up marker posts until it is possible to have a proper survey done. Stories of marker poles shifted and signage torn down recur (62). Maps were inaccurate (141). Nor can all the survey maps promised in these documents as evidence of reserve boundaries be located (51, 61). Some think that Joseph Trutch, who severely reduced land grants made under Douglas, had them destroyed; others argue that they were never actually made, "as Governor Douglas in the opinion of Reserve Commissioner G.M. Sproat, was 'negligent in the extreme' when it came to keeping records of reserve allotments" (Foster, qtd. in B.F. Edwards, "I Have Lots of Help" note 50). Yet these are the documents that are presented in court as fact, while Indigenous oral tradition is discounted.

That the book was "padlocked" in the 1940s certainly represents the state of affairs at that time, and, indeed, for decades to come. The archives, including this book, have nonetheless proven a fruitful resource since the 1973 Supreme Court of Canada decision in *Calder et al. v. Attorney-General of British Columbia* acknowledged the validity of Aboriginal title in areas not covered by treaties, that is, almost all of British Columbia.[33] However, the provincial government only moved to set up the British Columbia Treaty Commission in 1991, and only a few First Nations have completed a treaty under this process, although others are in process. (The Nisga'a Final Agreement of 2000 did not use this framework.) Gordon Campbell was still adamantly refusing to negotiate land claims when he came to power as premier in 2000; the government spent $9 million on a referendum in 2002 that was widely seen to be biased against treaty making (British Columbia Treaty Commission). Many feel the process as it stands is profoundly flawed, in part because the Crown is still not acting honourably. The central conflict of interest was pointed to in 1916 by Indian spokesmen "who asserted that the 'real position of the Government of Canada is not that of guardian protecting our rights, but that of an interested party … seeking to take away our rights'" (Barman, *West* 163–64). This foundational conflict of interest means that the Crown is hard pressed to act honourably.

Robinson clearly felt, however, that education and literacy would prove useful. The point of his story is not any secret meaning to be discovered and deciphered, a mode of interpretation admired in a text-oriented culture (as my interpretation itself demonstrates). Rather, he was interested in conveying ideas about proper behaviour. The younger twin consistently violates protocols on how family, interpersonal, and intercultural relationships should be conducted. Robinson insists that for a good relationship, everything on the paper must be shared freely. There should be no "secret words." His putting human relationships before written documents accords with that held by the Dene, Cree, Saulteaux, and Assiniboine treaty elders who spoke to the treaty commissioner in Saskatchewan in the late 1990s: "[T]heir focus was on the 'nature and character of the treaty relationship' as opposed to the contents of the written treaty texts created by the Crown" (Cardinal and Hildbrandt 25).

Despite the differences between the parties, the story leaves the possibility of reconciliation open. Finally, it shows how oral narrative can be used as a way of theorizing contemporary political relationships and land claims. Unlike Ong, Robinson was able to see orality and literacy as intersecting practices that were privileged and used differently by different cultures, rather than as starkly conflicting. Although Paull and Kelly did not achieve a solution to the land problem, that they were cogent speakers and literate in English meant that they could find a hearing in Victoria and Ottawa, even though no one was prepared to listen until 1946. For these men, it was entirely logical that they should use all their skills, however acquired, to regain land and sovereignty.

As Wickwire points out, anthropologists who worked in this region, such as Boas, Marius Barbeau, and Edward Sapir, preferred "authentic" stories, and "downplayed stories about current events, personal experiences, and nineteenth-century epidemics, explorers, technology and religious ideas" ("To See Ourselves" 3). Boas's most famous successor, Claude Lévi-Strauss, argued that the "savage mind" had the same structures as the "civilized" (*The Savage Mind*, 1962), but nonetheless, he was uninterested in those Indigenous groups that had script and in those aspects of their culture that could be seen as "contaminated" by modernity. Lévi-Strauss "appeals above all to the notion of primitive and scriptless societies" because the let-ter "promotes the lapse from grace" (Brotherston 41). Wickwire notes that Lévi-Strauss "had delineated world cultures as 'cold' (mythic natives who resist any form of change) or 'hot' (historical westerners who thrive on con-stant and irreversible change)," but, as she points out, "Robinson seemed just as comfortable telling historical narratives set in real time as so-called mythical narratives set in the deep past. If analyzed in Lévi-Straussian terms, then, his repertoire was actually more 'hot' than 'cold'" ("Stories" 454).[34] Schorcht argues of the binary between orality and literacy that "[t]hese kinds of attitudes toward traditional Native American stories perpetu-ate the notion that we are 'unfortunately' left with 'only' the written forms—inferior representations of a once-powerful reality. These attitudes also per-petuate nineteenth-century myths about Natives as part of 'dead and dying' cultures" (*Storied Voices* 26). Robinson agrees, pointing out that "nowadays, the SHA-ma [white] was trying to make the things all in one, / On his side, on his way" (qtd. in Schorcht, *Storied Voices* 46). In fact, oral storytelling is alive and well and must be heard, as the *Delgamuukw* decision makes clear.

The first book of Lévi-Strauss's famous four-volume *Mythologiques*, *The Raw and the Cooked* (1964), inspired Jacques Derrida to write *Of Gramma-tology* (1967), where he argues against such universalizing binaries. Instead, he argues that speech and writing share a vital quality, what he calls iter-ability, citationality, the trace (and also, confusingly, writing). Despite our desire to fix and limit the meaning of words, that they can be repeated and quoted in new contexts makes this desire impossible to fulfill. When mean-ings become stable, that stability should not be seen as a *natural* quality of words, but rather as the result of concerted social and institutional forces. These forces include education, which standardizes speech and writing, and laws, such as those that define which human bodies are to be designated Indian and which not. Derrida further questions what for many was an obvious difference between speech and writing: that writing was "deriva-tive" of speech and marked the entry of repressive political forces into "oral" cultures. He notes that "Rousseau and Lévi-Strauss are not for a moment to be challenged when they relate the power of writing to the exercise of violence," but points out that this violence should not be considered "as *derivative* with respect to a naturally innocent speech" (*Grammatology* 106). In fact, he argues, there is no speech or writing that is pure, proper, or natu-ral. Thus, Robinson is not morally superior simply because he works in the oral tradition, no more than documents are inherently superior to spoken words. Words must be judged, whatever their origin.

Although some take the "objectivity" of scientific language as a fact rather than an ideal, all language is interpreted through conventions, contexts, assumptions, and cultural frames. Derrida's argument that there is no single universal truth has often been accused of supporting radical relativism, where one can say anything at all, but Derrida disagrees. He believes that the notions of clear, universal, and fixed truth that he puts into question are stabilized by a confluence of beliefs, laws, histories, institutions, and political forces. In order to understand and either agree or disagree with these "truths" one must, in fact, submit to the pragmatics of the situation, "to the norms of the context that requires one to prove, to demonstrate, to proceed correctly, to conform to the rules of language and to a great number of other social, ethical, political-institutional rules, etc." (*Limited* 150–51). Humans create just or unjust societies through texts such as constitutions and laws as well as novels and poems: these are not graven on stone tablets handed down from above, nor are they dictated by Coyote to kings. These texts are the product of human minds: some gain the force of law. Nonetheless, those whom these laws dispossess and exclude are best placed to perceive and report on their deficiencies, since those who benefit often not only refuse to hear these reports but also *cannot* hear—in the sense of understand—them. Morley's contemptuous attitude toward Chillihitza and David is just one example of how the inability to hear is structured by broad discursive forces. These forces rendered their language gibberish and their actual presence in the halls of power an embarrassment.

In British Columbia, the confluence of a number of historical forces drove the "truth" of settler claims to land into conflict even with national and imperial beliefs that treaties must be properly made before settlement could take place (Harris, *Making Space* 91–92). One force was the speed of settlement and colonization powered by the steamboats that took settlers, soldiers, and anthropologists to remote coastal areas (those boats used to harass Coyote). In the absence of roads, crises involving coastal tribes, perceived or actual, were managed by sending gunboats (Gough). (Joseph Conrad's description of a French gunboat shelling the coast of Africa in 1890 could just as easily have applied to the coast of British Columbia decades earlier.) That the settlers were in the minority during the early years led to fear and fear-mongering; an 1866 editorial pointed out that if Indians could vote, some "ten thousand whites would have to contend at the polls with fifty thousand painted, whisky-drinking 'red skin' voters ... peradventure to sit in a legislature in which the savage element largely predominated" (qtd. in Foster 62). Later, the Canadian Pacific Railway caused a similar impact in the interior. In this newest colony, two worldviews collided quickly and starkly: white settler modernity faced off with Indigenous tradition. The settler truth that only they had the right to land and the vote became precarious as literate and articulate activists like Paull and Kelly countered this position not only with their own stable truth anchored in traditional culture, but also with arguments that resonated in settler culture, such as the ties between God, civilization, rights to land, and literacy that Robinson outlined in his stories. Indeed, the power of their arguments forced the Canadian government to use legal violence against them in the amendment of the Indian Act in 1927, which prevented any more such irritating debate until 1951. Frank Calder and the Nisga'a Nation were among the first to start the discussion up again with a case they took to court in 1967; the Supreme Court acknowledged in 1973 that pre-contact Aboriginal title existed, something the provincial government had until then denied (see Foster, Raven, and Webber). What is notable about Robinson's story is that while it anchors its case in Coyote as God's emissary and strongly criticizes white land grabbing and deception, it also connects the achievement of literacy by Indigenous people to a just resolution of land claims. White people are involved as close kin in the story from the beginning, and it is their bad behaviour and unwillingness to learn that produces the need for "The Black and the White," the law that will allow Indigenous people and whites to live together harmoniously as twins should.

(In)Conclusion, or Attawapiskat v. #Ottawapiskat

My people will sleep for one hundred years, but when they awake, it will be the artists who give them their spirit back.

Louis Riel (oral tradition), ca. 1885

Traditional stories leave conclusions for the listener to draw. Although this is not a traditional story, its force depends on its readers. Julie Cruikshank writes of what she called the storytelling event that "a good listener is expected to bring different life experiences to the story each time he or she hears it and to learn different things from it at each hearing." Storytellers are not "trying to spell out everything one needs to know," but to inspire "the listener to think about ordinary experience in new ways." She concludes that "[s]torytelling is possibly the oldest and most valued of the arts and encompasses a kind of truth that goes beyond the restricted frameworks of positivism, empiricism, and 'common sense'" (33–34). Stories bear the obligation not only to listen, but also to reflect. The truth of stories lies in what we make of them as much as in their content.

Storytellers of many Indigenous nations in Canada believe that their stories have the power to maintain their laws and cultures in the face of ongoing colonization and, indeed, to change mainstream society. Harry Robinson did not want his stories kept secret: he wanted them to change North America. The power of such stories is the power Thomas King celebrates in *The Truth about Stories*: "Just don't say in the years to come that you would have lived your life differently if only you had heard this story. You've heard it now" (167). Stories about land told by Indigenous people need to be brought to the attention of a public that rarely hears them.

Some do not see the power of story in the process of forming ideals, relationships, and cultures, or they would not position humanities subjects at universities as "add-ons" to the more serious and important work in social sciences, science, engineering, and medicine. Apparently they believe that students' perspectives are best formed by reading commission reports, policy documents, research papers, contracts, laws, business plans, instruction manuals, and the like. But none of these texts mean much without an underlying ethic. As Hubert Zapf, a cultural ecologist, argues, "[E]thics ... cannot be based on and derived from 'facts and fact-based theory' alone"; he continues, "[A]ny ethical stance involves intellectual, moral, and emotional decisions by the individual subject as a culturally embedded agent." Such decisions are "mediated and ultimately made possible by the communicative medium of language and of texts" and further, require a diverse set of "cultures of knowledge which are interdependent with but cannot be reduced to each other" (850). Stories not only preserve memory and form community, but also, as they are retold, envision and form the future. As L.M. Findlay remarks, the humanities are well designed for "reading justly and reading for justice" (43), although humanities scholars do not always read this way.

In fact, few people would seriously argue their ethical position came from reading a policy document or even the Ten Commandments. My childish ethical development was fuelled by repeated readings of *The Little Red Hen* ("'I'll do it myself,' said the Little Red Hen"), countless Little Golden books, Classic Comics, and works by Beatrix Potter, J.M. Barrie, E.E. Nesbit, Mark Twain, and Dr. Seuss, especially *Horton Hatches the Egg* ("I meant what I said and I said what I meant, / An elephant's faithful one hundred percent"). Oh, and Laura Ingalls Wilder (how to conquer the West), Rudyard Kipling (how to conquer the world), and Robert A. Heinlein (how to conquer the galaxy). I accumulated individualistic and colonizing attitudes as I voraciously read through my children's books and beyond. Fortunately, some of them bore titles declaring them to be for boys only, which somewhat buffered my dreams of total world domination. So did my realization that I was neither American nor British, and therefore unlikely to be at the centre of the excitement in New York or London. And fortunately, I learned much more from the ethical behaviour of those I grew up with and those I am still learning from.

Stories are not, in themselves, good. As my childhood reading list makes clear, stories may promote unethical behaviour. Stories always need interpretation and evaluation. Indeed, stories are now being investigated from scientific perspectives, which range from those of evolutionary psychology and its close relatives, sociobiology and "literary Darwinism," through to those philosophies that put process before object (or, if you like, Heraclitus before Plato), many of which use the word "ecology" in their self-descriptions.[1] Many agree that the Western intellectual tradition has spent too much time taking things apart and too little time putting them back together, too much time believing in facts, and too little time wondering how they relate to stories.

The powerful stories of imperialism, nationalism, and capitalist development are all alive and well as they intersect in Canada. Burke's stories about savages have been moderated only slightly over time: Indigenous protests are often represented much as he would have described them. The resistance at Oka/Kanehsatake in 1990 reveals how quickly the assertion of sovereign Indigenous control over a small graveyard can focus the attention of the armed powers of the state, not to mention the international media. This armed standoff[2] was followed by a more common Canadian response to conflict: the Royal Commission on Aboriginal Peoples (RCAP) was set up in 1991. Its four-thousand-page report, delivered in 1996, provided rich food for thought, but generated little government action.[3] Nor did this report end the frenzied nature of mainstream responses to any Indigenous assertion of sovereignty. In 1995, members of the Stoney Point First Nation occupied Camp Ipperwash in Ontario to protest the government's failure, after repeated promises, to return land expropriated through the War Measures Act in 1942. The resulting police action led to the killing by a police sniper of an unarmed man, Dudley George, and an inquiry that reported only in 2007 (Ontario). That same year, Secwepemc sun dancers were served eviction notices on a site near Gustafsen Lake, British Columbia, where they had been holding ceremonies. Sandra Lambertus's book, *Wartime Images, Peacetime Wounds*, begins, "The 1995 Gustafsen Lake standoff was the largest and most expensive Royal Canadian Mounted Police (RCMP) operation in Canadian history" (3). In 1999, the Supreme Court of Canada ruled that treaties made in 1752 and 1760–1761 gave Mi'kmaq fishermen the right to make a "moderate livelihood" (*R. v. Marshall*). This decision led to the destruction of fishing gear, violent clashes between Indigenous and non-Indigenous fishermen, and Mi'kmaq boats being nearly run over by those of the Department of Fisheries and Oceans. Alanis Obomsawin's film *Is the Crown at War with Us?* (2002) conveys the perspective of the Mi'kmaq fishermen from Burnt Church, New Brunswick. A protest in 2006 by the Six Nations over the development of land they claimed at Caledonia, Ontario, led to another crisis (sometimes called the Grand River dispute). Cameron Greensmith reports of the ensuing media coverage that "Indigenous peoples are overtly represented as 'violent,' 'dangerous,' 'uncontrollable,' 'criminal,' 'abnormal,' 'problems,' 'irrational,' and 'deviant'" (28). In such events, the media often depend solely on official news sources—government, police, or army—which makes it difficult to produce balanced reports. The anonymous comment lines beneath the online news stories about such events collect many ignorant or racist opinions that are derived from stories isolated from facts.[4] What happens after the frenzy dies down and the court cases and commission reports appear is reported on far less widely.

ATTAWAPISKAT COMES TO #OTTAWA(PISKAT)

By 2006, news and comment were travelling in new ways on the Web.[5] The history of Attawapiskat First Nation's attempt to publicize federal neglect of its obligations on the reserve reveals how the internet may mean wider and more interactive coverage but does not necessarily improve its accuracy or civility. In November 2011, Chief Theresa Spence appealed to the Canadian Red Cross to assist residents of the Attawapiskat First Nation, many living in inadequate, overcrowded, and unhealthy housing. The federal government is responsible for providing housing on reserves; residents take on mortgages or pay rent. Those writing in the comment lines often appeared to believe that the government simply "gives" houses to Indigenous people, while overlooking that they themselves also benefit from government-subsidized infrastructure, schools, hospitals, and even housing. In response to Spence's public appeal, the federal government imposed third-party management on the reserve, creating the impression that the problem was financial mismanagement rather than inadequate funding and bureaucratic delay. Spence commented, "I guess as First Nations, when we do ask for assistance and make a lot of noise, we get penalized for it" (qtd. in "Feds Aware"). The Attawapiskat First Nation appealed this imposition to the Federal Court, which reported in 2012 that "[d]espite the comments about management, the Respondent [Canada] has not produced evidence of mismanagement or incorrect spending" (*Attawapiskat First Nation v. Canada*). It also pointed out that a statement by the prime minister which gave the impression that $90 million had been provided for housing in fact referred to total federal funding over five years and therefore "could not have related exclusively to the funds made available for housing repair or reconstruction."

In winter 2013, the housing crisis still unresolved, Spence carried out a six-week hunger strike on Victoria Island, near Ottawa. Her action led to even more widespread accusations of mismanagement aimed at the reserve council, although the decision of the Federal Court was openly accessible on the Web, as were the Attawapiskat financial records. Christie Blatchford, a *National Post* columnist, called Spence's hunger strike "an act of intimidation if not of terrorism" and stated that Aboriginal culture is likely so "irreparably damaged" that the nation-to-nation talks Spence was asking for would be unrealistic. Tolerant ordinary Canadians were once again seriously inconvenienced by ungrateful, dishonest, and potentially violent Indigenous people. This discourse supports the notion that the land and its resources rightfully belong to Locke's "Industrious and Rational" landowners.

Nonetheless, the internet delivers an array of resources for those interested in finding fairer and more factual stories, including those produced by Indigenous bloggers (see Vowel); these resources do make it possible to investigate and report on the biases of the mainstream media more quickly than in the past. For example, the #Ottawapiskat hashtag turned comments about mismanagement at Attawapiskat against the government of Stephen Harper, at this point mired in a scandal over expense claims by senators and other accounting problems: "Could AADNC [Aboriginal Affairs and Northern Development Canada] recommend a third-party manager? Canada can't account for $3.1 billion in anti-terror funding" (Daniel Rueck 30 April 2013). The turn to humour on Twitter, often featuring Chief Harper in a feather headdress, cheered up the discussion.

Spence's common-law partner and band co-manager was charged with fraud and theft in March 2014 (Attawapiskat First Nation).[6] Although the outcome of these charges is still unknown, it might push readers back to binary thinking: Harper is right and good and Spence is wrong and bad. Both Harper and Spence head governments, one big, one small, and have responsibilities to do their duty. But if Harper fails, few conclude that everything he has done is wrong or find all Canadians to blame because of his actions. If Spence fails somehow it brings all Indigenous leaders into disrepute, those who voted for her take heat, and once more the stereotypes are confirmed. In a recent story in *Maclean's*, "Out of Sight, Out of Mind: Canada Has a Race Crisis Worse than America's," Scott Gilmore points out the problems with such all-or-nothing blame games. On seven measures expressed as a percentage of the national average (unemployment, median income, incarceration, homicide, infant mortality, life expectancy, and school dropout), Indigenous people in Canada do worse than Black people in the United States. He then asks, "Who do we blame?" and lists an array of possibilities, including the Canadian justice system and the band administrators at Attawapiskat. He concludes that the problem cannot rest with any individual, group, or institution, but says it ultimately rests on mainstream Canadians' long history of believing "our own hype about inclusion" (25). As John Richardson realized, Canadian identity has been constructed on our supposed moral superiority to the Americans, particularly in dealings with Indigenous people. Looking too closely at the truth of this claim risks undermining that identity, its claim to civility, and its related claim to land.

This sanctioned ignorance explains why appeals to justice made by political figures like Spence seem to produce as much backlash as progress. This reaction certainly does not mean that such appeals should be abandoned. However, less direct and more empathetic interventions made by humour, wit, and artistic production can also help change the mainstream discourse while forming and focusing Indigenous standpoints.[7] The period just before Oka/Kanehsatake marked an outpouring of creativity by Indigenous people. Issues that no one had mentioned in public, or that, if mentioned, had quickly been forgotten, suddenly were made both public and memorable in literature and other artistic production. Beatrice Culleton Mosionier's bestselling story of the treatment of Native foster children during the "scoop-up," *In Search of April Raintree* (1983);[8] Jeannette Armstrong's account of 1970s activism in *Slash* (1985); Tomson Highway's *The Rez Sisters* (1988); and Basil Johnston's memoir, *Indian School Days* (1988),[9] all described suppressed histories. Indigenous-made documentaries, such as Obomsawin's *Kanehsatake: 270 Years of Resistance* (1993), became another powerful way to explain Indigenous communities and their ethos.[10] Works like these make it more likely that Canada's colonial history will be acknowledged as a matter of widespread concern.

Nonetheless, as Kristina Fagan has pointed out, literary criticism often neglects the "big-P" political issues. Renée Hulan notes the general difficulties with focusing on culture rather than politics: "In a plural society, cultural differences can always be tolerated and assimilated without conceding much power, while political differences cannot" (18). Once again an institutionalized binary makes it difficult for the mainstream to understand Indigenous perspectives. Politics is serious, culture is not. When Indigenous people are deemed to be "political" instead of "colourful," they are defined as troublemakers, traitors, or terrorists. However, it is the mainstream that divides culture from politics in the first place. The widespread Indigenous belief that the world is a web of relationships and responsibilities allows Indigenous people to see through and beyond such distinctions.

Even Supreme Court decisions, despite their performative power, cover very little of the territory that law does for many Indigenous people. Wanda McCaslin describes the meaning of law for the Plains Cree: "Law is a whole way of life. Through countless means, our traditions teach us how to be respectful of others and mindful of how our actions affect them" (qtd. in Lawrence, *Fractured* 28). This conception of law explains why many Indigenous people live where they do, despite the presumed attractions and relative luxury of the city. Here, an elder from Attawapiskat, David Tookate, speaks:

> We were given the sacredness of the land. We must take good care of it, as our future generations will depend on it. As well, we were given that gift and that responsibility by Kitche Mando and we must respect this gift and the life Kitche Mando has given us. They say that the federal government owns this land. They say that we only have "surface rights," and the government owns the rest. The White man stands on the graveyard of our ancestors who are underground. They were here first. This is a fact. And what they say about it is not true. It was not the federal government that gave us life. Life was given by the Kitche Mando. When there is a discussion on land claims, this is Indian land. (qtd. in Hookimaw-Witt 136)

Here again are revealed some of the differences between Indigenous and Canadian concepts, in this case of law. And Tookate's concern for "future generations" is typical; if Indigenous cultures are to survive, knowledge holders must always send the story forward.[11]

POLITICS, LAW, AND CIVIL DISOBEDIENCE

Thomas King's novel *Green Grass, Running Water* (1993) criticizes Henry Thoreau's model of individual civil disobedience because it does not ensure that the story is transmitted from one generation to the next. Eli Stands Alone, a retired English professor, occupies his mother's house in the spillway of a new dam to prevent it from becoming operational. Unimpressed by his performance as a lone male hero, his sister nags him to fulfill his neglected obligations to counsel his hapless nephew and attend the Sun Dance. Even though Spence did not act alone, she was depicted as isolated from her people: a politician in the worst sense. Mainstream accounts of her protest resembled those deployed by the prosecution in Riel's trial: her followers were dupes and she was interested only in money. This stance allows commentators to claim sympathy with the ill-housed people of Attawapiskat while simultaneously rejecting Spence's attempt to bring their plight to public attention. In March 2013, just after she ended her hunger strike, around 270 youth marched from northern Quebec to Ottawa to focus attention on reserve poverty; the prime minister, welcoming two pandas arriving in Toronto as part of a trade deal with China, could not see them ("Cree Youth"). A year later, cheered on by Spence, another group is walking the 1400 kilometres from Attawapiskat to Ottawa in mid-winter ("Attawapiskat Walkers"). Clearly, the Attawapiskat First Nation hasn't given up. Whether any prime minister ever agrees to see these walkers or not, such events bring Indigenous communities across the north together and inspire youth to organize more such actions that combine personal effort with community solidarity.

In late 2012 and 2013, the grassroots movement Idle No More used social media to bring Indigenous people and all manner of others together to dance, drum, and sing. This movement figures the relationship to land as "taking back our role as caretakers and stewards" (Eriel Deranger, qtd. on the Idle No More home page, 2013). Working the stereotype of the dancing and singing Indian, this popular action sidesteps other forms of negotiation, often either high-level and bureaucratic or street-level and violent. Lively Indigenous people briefly emerge out of the urban streets where they live and work to join with others who support them. They choose to vanish before established political leaders can co-opt them or state control can evict them. These events connect to a long tradition of guerrilla theatre and performance art characterized by the presence of living human bodies.[12] Such performances of a performative, like those of E. Pauline Johnson and Grey Owl, move audiences and collect supporters. Certainly these Idle No More dancers perform the survival and the politics of both Indigenous bodies *and* cultures in the location perhaps most representative of modern civilization, the major urban intersection. This is Indigenous territory too.

MODES OF RECONCILIATION

The affective work of cultural display can focus mainstream attention directly on the land only if supported by other interventions. We have seen how easy it has been to veer off from that difficult topic. At some levels, for example, the prime minister's apology on 11 June 2008 for the abuses of the Indian residential school system and the subsequent processes of compensation and memorialization can be seen as—however important and necessary—such a deflection. From 2003 to 2005, the government piloted an alternative dispute resolution model for dealing with abuses. This model was rejected by Chief Robert Joseph of the Residential School Survivors' Society and others as inadequate. It focused on a limited range of physical harm, rather than recognizing the broader damages of colonization: "pain and suffering—loss of language and culture, loss of family and childhood, loss of self-esteem, depression, addictions and suicide" (Joseph qtd. in Regan 127). The subsequent Indian Residential School Settlement Agreement was agreed upon by legal counsel for former students, the churches, the Assembly of First Nations, other Aboriginal organizations, and the Government of Canada as a better way to deal with the largest class-action suit in Canadian history (Regan 6–7). Given the likelihood of an otherwise long, expensive, and painful legal process, this agreement was probably the best that could be done to compensate the survivors. The Indian Residential School Truth and Reconciliation Commission (TRC), founded as part of the settlement, has a "mandate to make a public and permanent record of the legacy of the schools, in conjunction with the earmarking of a significant portion of the settlement fund for healing and commemoration programs" (qtd. in *Baxter v. Canada* [Attorney General]). However, the emphasis on the schools can make it appear that this enforced "education" is the only part of its past that Canada needs to grapple with and that the apology has ended colonization in Canada. Stephen Harper demonstrated remarkable amnesia to the G20 conference just over a year after the apology when he announced that Canada has "no history of colonization" (qtd. in Ljunggren).

Paradoxically, the TRC has had to take the Canadian government to court to fulfill the mandate handed down by that same government. A court hearing was necessary to obtain records of criminal proceedings against some teachers and employees of the notoriously brutal St. Anne's Indian Residential School (1904–1976) in Fort Albany, Ontario. This was the school attended by Attawapiskat children until it closed (see *Fontaine v. Canada* [Attorney General] 2014). In *Baxter v. Canada*, Justice Winkler noted "the potential for conflict for Canada between its proposed role as administrator and its role as a continuing litigant"—and imposed as a solution that the courts "will be the final authority" (para. 39). These cases once again reveal the colonial paradox of Canadian administrative and legal control over Indigenous people. One part of the state is tasked with helping them but faces another part that hinders any such move.

The TRC brings Indigenous residential school survivors together to tell their stories to sympathetic witnesses, often members of the same churches who were responsible for the neglect and cruelty at the schools. This process aims to heal the sufferer and educate (even absolve) the listener, and one cannot deny its potential to do this. But it is hard not to see this process as the state protecting itself and the churches as much as helping the survivors, their families, and communities (Regan 121). The TRC has transformed bad publicity into good, and perhaps this process is the only way to overcome the darkness of the past in what is still a chilly climate for Indigenous peoples. The decision of many survivors to speak at the TRC should be respected and honoured. However, this process is represented in TRC material as a gift to those who previously could not speak: "Those that lived, attended and worked at the schools will finally be given a voice through the statement gathering process" ("Statement Gathering"). This model of "giving a voice" represents these survivors as rescued subalterns, although most Indigenous leaders and elders attended these schools and nonetheless speak with strong voices both inside and outside their communities.[13] Perhaps the process should be figured as one that helps mainstream Canadians to learn to listen, but even this formulation reveals a paradox.

In this wording and in the TRC process itself, the possession of a voice depends on mainstream listeners, given that the goal is reconciliation. The process is very similar to confession, the Roman Catholic sacrament of penance and reconciliation. This sacrament foregrounds the sinful speaker reconciling with God by confessing to a powerful and superior priest. For Roman Catholics and other believers, Indigenous and non-Indigenous alike, this promise of reconciliation has power. However, the TRC similarly foregrounds Indigenous speakers in ways that situate the listeners—or at least the non-Indigenous ones—as representatives (whether they like it or not) of a sympathetic, superior, powerful Canada. Notably, the relational identities required by reconciliation also flip easily from this model (witness as empathetic listener) to the witness figured as self-abasing and repentant former evil colonizer in need of forgiveness. "Look at how good we are for giving you a voice" flips into "look at how bad we were for allowing you to be abused (but please forgive us now we've apologized)." And actual perpetrators are nowhere to be found in this process. Insofar as the witnesses stand in for the perpetrators, they can be seen as shielding them from public scrutiny and just punishment.

The civ/sav binary still has power to lock white settlers and Indigenous people together in ways that privilege the figure of the white Canadian. Reconciliation has the potential to keep the binary alive within the epistemological framework of a settler state and a white national imaginary. Perhaps inevitably, the TRC entails bringing identified Aboriginal individuals into visibility before unnamed white witnesses performing an act of recognition. Kelly Oliver (reading Fanon) notes, "Insofar as the demand for recognition is created by the colonial situation in which the recognition of humanity is denied to the colonized, the demand for recognition itself becomes a symptom of the pathology of colonization" (6). Charles Taylor's well-known essay "The Politics of Recognition" (1992) reviews many of the issues around the idea of recognition. However, his argument is grounded in Anglo-Canada and European philosophical debate, and his focus on French Quebec and on "multiculturalism" leaves aside many of the questions of Indigenous land ownership traced above.

The representation of Indigenous people as being "*given* a voice" is part of a model centred on majority white settler society. This generous act might seem like a good response to the long history in mainstream society of "vanishing" the Indian. However, this form of recognition is pathological because it assumes the centrality of white settlers to the process. This assumption underlies the time-worn narrative of white settler Canadians graciously civilizing the Indigenous people by taking away their land, resources, and children to be cultivated, developed, and civilized and then taking up the burden of benevolently extending a welcome to "their" country to later arrivals, constituted as less worthy "immigrants." As Glen S. Coulthard points out, such a politics "promises to reproduce the very configurations of colonial power that Indigenous people's demands for recognition have historically sought to transcend" (437). That is, Indigenous people will be recognized by superiors who control the law and the land and therefore who have the power to say, "We will give you this much of land." Or, Indigenous people will be forced to forgive self-abasing "former" colonizers who *still* retain the power to say, "We will give you this much of land." What is needed instead, he argues, is a "critically self-affirmative and self-transformative process of desubjectification" that leads to freedom, rather than dependence on recognition by another (456). This desubjectification is important for Indigenous and non-Indigenous people alike. Offering to recognize Indigenous people (or expecting forgiveness and recognition from them) is simply to run around the same old colonizing discursive tracks.

However, those Indigenous people who participated in working out the TRC process did hope for good results. For those whose abusers told them that no one would believe them if they spoke out, the process was a validation. Vicki Crowchild, a participant, commented, "A lot of people got healed just by telling their story" (qtd. in Perkel A3). Along with those survivors and witnesses who voluntarily engaged in the process were honorary witnesses, who were appointed for each hearing: "Witnesses are asked to store and care for the history they witness and most importantly, to share it with their own people when they return home" ("Honorary Witness"). One of them, Shelagh Rogers, a CBC journalist, comments that the schoolchildren "were taught that they were inferior, that they were uncivilized, that they were savages." And, she continues, "As the TRC Chair, Murray Sinclair points out, while they were being taught that, so were non-Aboriginal kids in public schools. Whole communities have suffered. Indeed, we have lost much and suffered 'a hole in our soul' as a country" ("Reflections").

Paulette Regan recounts her experience of listening to survivors tell their stories (171–72, 193–96; see also McKegney). She had spent time preparing herself for this meeting, which took place on Gitxan territory. As part of the process, the Gitxan asked her and other non-Gitxan government and church representatives to act as hosts at an "apology feast" to welcome the residential school survivors back into the community, finally "home" from school (193). This duty placed the non-Gitxan hosts in a "diplomatic, political and legal environment that was foreign to them, one where business was conducted in a language they did not understand and legitimated with unfamiliar storytelling, ceremonies and rituals" (201). Regan notes the irony that members of the culture that had banned the potlatch were now hosting one. The inexperienced hosts were in need of constant advice so that they could carry out their duties properly (201). However, she notes that this feast did not end the matter (196): decolonization and reconciliation are long processes, and forgiveness cannot be forced. Nor can the conversation around land ever be neatly concluded, despite government insistence on the need for "stability" that will enable continuing economic "development." The prior claims of Indigenous people cannot be extinguished: they will always have been here first no matter how often the late-arriving colonizers represent themselves as both "above" and "ahead" of them (see Povinelli).

DECOLONIZING CANADIAN LITERARY STUDIES

Moving the principle of respect into academic research and writing entails rethinking some of their typical qualities. "All my relations" requires connections to be made among researchers from different disciplines, and between researchers and other stakeholders, particularly those routinely neglected in the past, including animals, plants, rivers, lands, and ecosystems used in research. Interdisciplinarity should also characterize researchers' own individual thinking. Further, the principle of respect means that accusations or even implications of insincerity, ignorance, arrogance, carelessness, or immorality should no longer characterize debate. Such tactics do not incline anyone to change or rethink their position, but to hit back. Sterling calls the academy an "adversarial arena" ("Seepeetza Revisited). Sterling's *My Name Is Seepeetza* (1992) is a fictionalized account of her life in the Kamloops Indian Residential School (1893–1977), which she attended from age six through high school. The format—a fictionalized diary written by a girl in residential school—immerses readers in a story told by a naive child narrator and leaves readers free to take in what they are able to take in. Sterling's child self did not accuse; in fact, she felt responsible for all her supposed crimes. As an adult, Sterling worked hard to change the system that had oppressed her by earning a doctorate in education. Sterling says, however, that her "researcher voice"

> has been labelled the "white basher" on two occasions to date, and two of my articles were abandoned as a result. Ironically, it is this voice which comes closest to being guided by Western thinking. What does this tell us about writing which is weighted in analysis and logic and sound argument I wonder? Is it a way of welcoming researchers into an adversarial arena? ("Seepeetza Revisited")

Many Indigenous intellectuals use stories—often funny stories—to convey their truths, a practice that allows them to avoid the lack of respect embedded in the conventions and genres of academic writing. For example, academic writing often constructs a small group of specialists as its audience, avoids expressions of humility or uncertainty, and conceals the author's own position and experience while criticizing others to the last detail. And it avoids humour like the plague, tending toward the pompous and the pedantic (sorry!). As with the move of the "nativizing informant" that Carrie Dawson describes, such writing often slights or "unmasks" the arguments of others solely to legitimate its own, rather than attempting to begin productive conversations that might lead to something new. Certainly this is the tradition I have been trained in, and although I have worked to mitigate its worst excesses here, I am sure that they often remain unmitigated.

The decolonization of Canadian literature will require a new genre of academic writing, one that signals its acknowledgement not only of emerging from Indigenous land, but also of learning from Indigenous storied thinking. Already, we find such a new genre emerging, which might be called "story theory," or "story criticism" in works like Lee Maracle's "Yin

Chin," Thomas King's "Godzilla vs. Postcolonial," Basil Johnston's "Is That All There Is? Tribal Literature," and, more recently, Eden Robinson's *The Sasquatch at Home* and Warren Cariou's "Dances with Rigoureau." Both Jonathan Dewar's essay on Grey Owl and Armand Garnet Ruffo's long auto/biographical poem, discussed earlier, fit this category. Borrows's *Drawing Out Law: A Spirit's Guide* similarly foregrounds story not just as a traditional cultural artifact, but as a contemporary way of writing and thinking. Nor should literary scholars assume that "story" means the same thing in Indigenous cultures as it does in its dominant usage. Oral story carried all wisdom and knowledge from generation to generation in Indigenous cultures; this project is continuing, despite the damage caused by residential schooling. Story is being retheorized and the land restored.

MAKING NEW MISTAKES

In King's *Green Grass, Running Water*, the four old Indians keep coming back to fix the world, making mistakes, and starting over. And Coyote always gets in there too, doing a little singing, a little dancing, a little unexpected transforming with the usual unintended consequences. Humans always make mistakes and need to start the story over again with the help of their audiences. To counter discourses of extinguishment, disappearance, and extermination, whether literary or legal, conversations about the land should be kept alive in the traditions of Indigenous thinking (and horticulture), through judicious use and mindful attention (Deur and Turner). Many on the west coast take the "culturally modified tree" as a metaphor for this approach. Indigenous weavers take cedar bark only from part of the trunk, so the tree will go on living. Often such living trees bear the marks of planks taken for houses or of sections cut out for canoes. Bob Beal comments on the use of the metaphor of the tree to describe treaties:

> The pine tree was a frequent metaphor during the treaty process between the British and the Indian nations of the east in the 18th century. It represented the beauty and complexity of life. By linking the idea of treaties to a tree, the Indians were often making the point that for them a treaty relationship was not a static thing (as it tended to be for the British) but something that needed constant nourishment to survive and thrive. (125)[14]

Indeed, some have argued that all Canadians should begin to think of themselves as "treaty people," taking on both the rights and the responsibilities required to keep both the treaties and the land living (Epp).[15]

Duncan Campbell Scott, who came to have a great deal of administrative power over Status Indians, did not believe that the men he negotiated with were capable of understanding the terms of the treaty: "What could they grasp of the pronouncement on the Indian tenure which had been delivered by the law lords of the Crown?" (qtd. in Titley 74). Scott brought the honour of the Crown into disrepute by negotiating in bad faith, and he was not alone.[16] His attitude toward treaties has persisted in both the government and mainstream society. Few but Indigenous people took them seriously (see Cardinal and Hildebrandt). To characterize those who signed them as naive primitives, as Scott did, rationalized his own lies as well as the collective attitude that treaty promises were not really serious. To allow one part of the law to be disregarded, however, puts the entire legal system into disrepute.

Indigenous people knew that the Crown anchored the law—a law that they, in making treaties, agreed to obey. Sterling comments, "Seepeetza, age twelve, in the 1950's and 60's had no idea of the larger issues. She knew that more than anything in the world she wanted to go home, and that it would not be possible. She knew her dad didn't like the residential school either but he respected the law. He believed in the value of an education" ("Seepeetza Revisited"). When the servants of the Crown act without honour, the law is revealed as a fiction in need of constant narrative repair. Big Bear's problem with the law was that it was only white, imported from another cultural location and imposed on starving and outnumbered peoples with very different laws.[17] This imposed law, as Borrows has so eloquently made clear, needs to be "drawn out" in new ways if Canada is to continue to work as the just society that those who voted for Pierre Trudeau *and* those who voted for Harold Cardinal wanted it to be. If underlying title to the land of Canada is secured by the Crown, as are all laws, the Crown is a symbol. It is difficult to convey the power of this symbol in any other way than by calling it sacred collective ideal. This quality, I think, explains why Robinson's law, "The Black and the White," is written into an origin story. Something so sacred must have been in place from the beginning. God's law should have led to harmonious and just relations: that it did not was the result of the white man's theft and lies. That the law had the potential to be restored by God, Coyote, and successive monarchs in a new form for literate people was just as it should be. However, this restoration required contact and discussion at the highest level and, as Robinson pointed out, justice was not achieved at the end of the story. Because not all the land has been secured by treaty, and because the Crown has not been honourably served in the past, Canada is not a just society, despite the power of the ideal.

LEARNING TO SHARE?

Finally, the land. Traditional societies have developed ways to manage disputes through a wide array of diplomatic and ceremonial practices, practices that Regan suggests might provide useful models for decolonization. Traditionally, on the west coast, to enter someone else's territory requires permission and acknowledgement. In *Eagle Down Is Our Law*, Antonia Mills recounts a story told to her by Chief Gisdaywa about a Wet'suwet'en hunter following a bear he had wounded. When it crossed into someone else's territory, he yelled to the people there, "Bear coming down. If you kill it you can get the meat but I get the hide" (144–45). This hunter knew the rules but also expected to be able to negotiate a deal. Traditional practices have shown themselves to be flexible. However, Hookimaw-Witt notes how major were the differences between those making the treaties and the people who agreed to them:

> Whereas both province and dominion were making treaty for the sole purpose of extinguishing land title of the Aboriginal people, the Indians made treaty to keep the land and their way of life. These two positions, being so completely opposite, would have required lengthy negotiations in order to be resolved. However, lengthy negotiations did not occur, at least not with the Indian nations. (155)

Part of the problem is the common "all-or-nothing" representation of landholding, where individual freehold ownership is the model. Any future negotiation will require reconciling the idea of Lockean land ownership based on surveys, maps, and title deeds with Indigenous concepts. For example, Brian Thom points out in "The Paradox of Boundaries in Coast Salish Territories" that "[t]he cartographic practice of representing indigenous territories as discrete, mutually exclusive units contrasts sharply with indigenous discourse, which frames the notion of territory within a pervasive ideology of sharing" (179). The issue is how to share land, not only between Indigenous nations and newcomers, but also with the animals, the plants, the rivers: with all those beings and relationships that make up the living land. As Hookimaw-Witt suggests, lengthy negotiations remain if we are to find good ways to do this. Canadian literary studies, by continuing to move away from narrowly nationalist histories and perspectives to those that better articulate the multiple dilemmas of colonization, has a role to play in this process. As Marie Annharte Baker says, "we don't have to keep on blindly repeating the folly of 'settler lit' or 'settler lit(ter)'" (48).

Notes

1 The qualifier "Romantic" designates a period between 1770 and 1832 or so, during which this literary theory was developed. The ideas about national literature deployed by Canadian critics like Dewart and Lighthall can be traced back to German philosophers and critics such as Johann Gottfried Herder (1744–1803) and Friedrich von Schlegel (1772–1829), whose ideas entered English Romanticism and American Transcendentalism through the critical mediation of Samuel Taylor Coleridge. Katie Trumpener calls this form of literary nationalism "bardic" because the bard was deemed by Romantics to have formed the nation by singing the oral epics of the past (xxii). Benedict Anderson argues that newspapers and other products of print capitalism, such as maps, formed Romantic nationalism itself. Romantic nationalism has had a long afterlife, however, particularly in settler colonies, and still frames the study of national literatures.

2 Although I use "Mohawk," the term Johnson used for herself, Taiaiake Alfred says this is an anglicized Algonkian word meaning "cannibal monster"—he uses instead "Kanien'kehaka," meaning People of the Flint (*Peace* xxv). I sometimes use "Indian" when it was the dominant term in the period I am discussing and also to refer to the stereotype. Generally, I use "Indigenous" or "Native" to refer to actual people, historical or contemporary. If I mean Status Indian as defined in the Indian Act (1876) or Aboriginal as defined in the Constitution Act (1982), I use these legal terms. If possible, I use nation-specific terms for individuals and peoples.

3 Lighthall's ventriloquizing of settler desires through an "Indian" speaker was quite typical and continued in full force until what was called "the appropriation

of voice" debate gripped Canada in the 1990s (see Gagnon). This debate slowed the practice somewhat.

4 The history of the Writers Union of Canada is exemplary. It was founded in 1973 by a group of Canadian nationalist writers, including Margaret Atwood, Pierre Berton, Timothy Findley, and Farley Mowat. The union established the Racial Minority Writers Committee in 1990, which promptly began a struggle to have "minority" writers fairly represented on grant and prize juries so as to get equal access to publication. Mainstream responses, including those of their fellow union members, sometimes framed those on the committee as supporting censorship and even as deploying reverse racism (Fee, "Trickster" 64–65).

5 That is, they are represented as already dead or dying and therefore beyond help, cure, or justice. Achille Mbembe calls this biopolitical discourse "necropolitics" because it treats some living humans as already dead. The neglect by the police, state, and mainstream press of the many cases of missing and murdered Indigenous women is evidence of the power of this discourse. See Razack on the case of Pamela George and Manitoba *Report* for the case of Helen Betty Osborne, both marked by police and mainstream indifference and inaction.

6 The history of Indigenous relationships to the French, and later, to francophone Quebec, is covered here only fleetingly (but see Sioui; Thérien; White). The west was colonized from Ontario, which explains western critics' response to Frye and Atwood. For example, in 1974 Frank Davey, a British Columbian, condemned "superficial nationalism" and the "illusory identity of Canada as the 'honest broker' and peacekeeper for world society" (15). Eli Mandel, born into a Jewish family in Saskatchewan, also struggled with Romantic nationalism in several important critical works published in the 1970s.

7 For more on and by these early Canadian critics and others, see Ballstadt, *Search for English-Canadian Literature* and Lecker, *Keepers of the Code*. The attitudes expressed in the *Royal Commission on National Development in the Arts, Letters and Sciences 1949–1951* (Ottawa: Edmond Cloutier, 1951) are essentially Romantic nationalist.

8 Szeman distinguishes between Frye and Atwood, arguing that Frye, like George Grant, did not feel a Canadian literature could develop in the face of a "global modernity" (178). Certainly, Frye felt that a national literature had to develop out of an authentic oral mythology. However, his otherwise inexplicable promotion of the work of E.J. Pratt shows that he retained some nationalist hope. Epic poems were, after all, the basis for other national literatures, and Pratt was writing them for Canada, even though they were not, as the model required, oral in origin. The pieces collected in *The Bush Garden* were originally published between 1943 and 1968—Frye's main focus during this time was on his two

most important books, *Fearful Symmetry: A Study of William Blake* (1947), and *Anatomy of Criticism* (1957). In the latter book his main focus was on theorizing literary criticism as a self-contained discipline with a focus on "the centre of literary experience itself" (*Bush Garden* 216). In his view, in 1965, no Canadian literary work was among "the genuine classics of literature" (215). His belief that literary criticism should focus on the canonized classics was widely criticized as producing a disciplinary bubble that excluded literature from discourse and removed it from any political investment.

9 Jonathan Bordo has written several important articles on the function of the trope of wilderness, which he characterizes as "a highly productive site for the very invention of modernity itself" (227).

10 See Sherrill Grace's *Canada and the Idea of North* for an overview of the ways this idea has been used across a variety of creative arts. Renée Hulan, in *Northern Experience and the Myths of Canadian Culture*, tackles the topic skeptically: "I do not wish to defend the claim that literary representation of the north articulates a northern character that all Canadians share. This definition is severely limited because it rests on the specious notion of national consciousness" (27).

11 See Benedict Anderson on different conceptions of maps contrasted with "European-style maps" that "worked on the basis of a totalizing classification" (173); see Brody on Indigenous mapping.

12 As of 2006, over half of those identifying as Aboriginal now live in cities, mainly in Toronto, Winnipeg, Edmonton, Calgary, and Vancouver (Canada, Statistics Canada, "An Increasingly Urban Population"). For reasons I discuss below, they are disproportionately women with children. This shift should not be taken as obliterating their Indigenousness or claims to land.

13 Indigenous people were felled by introduced diseases to which they had no immunity, their susceptibility often increased by loss of access to traditional food, most notably the buffalo. They have also been "vanished" by being segregated on reserves and in residential schools, or forced by poverty and racism to live in slums on the margins of towns and cities.

14 Maurice Charland's "Constitutive Rhetoric: The Case of the *Peuple Québécois*" explains the power of the self-naming of French speakers in Quebec as "Québécois."

15 When I use the term "racialization," I reserve it for those negatively racialized by the dominant society. That said, Scottish and English settlers were racialized positively, as members of the "civilized" or "white" races. However, this racialization was until recently, at least, invisible and taken for granted; those who pass for white are often oblivious to their privilege in possessing what Denise Ferreira da Silva calls a transparent subjectivity. This subjectivity, theorized by

Hegel as culminating in post-Enlightenment Europe, represented "interiority" as "the private holding man has always occupied in western thought" (Silva xxxix).

16 Here Scott deploys the shock value of the racist slang expression "coolie" to seize the moral and poetic high ground from Pratt. Chinese boys and men were paid much less than European workers and did the most dangerous work.

17 *Standing Up with Ga̱'a̱x̱sta'las: Jane Constance Cook and the Politics of Memory, Church, and Custom*, by Leslie A. Robertson and the Kwagu'l Gix̱sa̱m Clan of Alert Bay, BC (Vancouver: U of British Columbia P, 2012), is just one example of work that details the complicated politics of Indigenous motivations to become Christian and to move away from some of the old ways, often while remaining strong activists for their people.

18 My use of "standpoint" here is a reference to feminist standpoint theory; see Harding, *Feminist Standpoint*. For a summary and critique, see Elizabeth Anderson.

19 Lee Maracle's "Yin Chin" (1990) and SKY Lee's *Disappearing Moon Café* (1990) are important early companion pieces, as is the conversation between Linda Griffiths and Maria Campbell in *The Book of Jessica* (1989) and the Telling It Collective's *Telling It: Women and Language across Cultures* (1990), where Jeannette Armstrong and Lee Maracle speak about the difficulties of connecting with white women in particular. For an important and controversial recent collaboration, see Lawrence and Dua.

20 Many scholars of story have regrounded story in Indigenous nations and expertise; see Archibald; Chamberlin; Cruikshank, *Social Life of Stories*; Keeshig-Tobias; Maracle; Maud; McLeod; B. Miller; Moore "Poking Fun"; Palmer; Reder; Schorcht; Scollon and Scollon; Wickwire; Womack. Obviously, to do this is to reassert the authority of Indigenous nations with respect to their own languages and cultures.

21 Not all stories are made available for interpretation by outsiders in this way, as Lenore Keeshig-Tobias makes clear.

22 Many others are at work on this task; see, for some recent examples, *Shifting the Ground of Canadian Literary Studies*, ed. Smaro Kamboureli and Robert Zacharias (Waterloo: Wilfrid Laurier UP, 2012); *Narratives of Citizenship: Indigenous and Diasporic Peoples Unsettle the Nation-state*, ed. Aloys N.M Fleischmann, Nancy van Styvendale, and Cody McCarroll (Edmonton: U of Alberta P, 2011); and *Cultural Grammars of Nation, Diaspora and Indigeneity in Canada*, ed. Christine Kim, Sophie McCall, and Melina Baum Singer (Waterloo: Wilfrid Laurier UP, 2012).

23 For a related argument focused on visual art, see Charlotte Townsend-Gault.

24 Palmer quotes Vi Hilbert, a respected Upper Skagit (Coast Salish) elder: "'This is part of our discipline. Respect [the speaker] even if it kills you. *Even if they have nothing to say.*' Respect, then, includes a discriminating attention, whether to the habits of a deer or the motives of a speaker" (19).

NOTES TO CHAPTER ONE

1 *R. v. Guerin* (1984) and *R. v. Sparrow* (1990) are two of the most important cases to come out of Musqueam, leading to landmark Supreme Court of Canada decisions that declared Aboriginal title a *sui generis* right, argued the federal government had a fiduciary duty to act in the best interests of the Aboriginal people, and supported the right to fish and to engage in other traditional practices (*Indigenous Foundations*). In a motion passed on 24 June 2014, Vancouver City Council acknowledged that "underlying all other truths spoken during the Year of Reconciliation is the truth that the modern city of Vancouver was founded on the traditional territories of the Musqueam, Squamish and Tsleil-Waututh First Nations and that these territories were never ceded through treaty, war or surrender" (Vancouver).

2 Pierre Trudeau's White Paper of 1969 proposed to abolish the Indian Act, defining "Indians" out of existence (Canada, Aboriginal Affairs and Northern Development). This would have made Status Indians "equal" while abolishing treaty promises and leaving Indigenous people mired in the poverty resulting from the abuse of residential schools, land theft, economic underdevelopment, and racism. The failure of this move, followed by the Supreme Court decision in *Calder et al. v. Attorney-General of British Columbia* (1973) acknowledging that the existence of Aboriginal title pre-dated the Royal Proclamation of 1763, meant governments began to take land claims seriously, although British Columbia stalled until 1992, when it set up the BC Treaty Commission. In March 2015, Premier Christy Clark halted treaty negotiations by refusing to appoint a treaty commissioner (Cassidy).

3 Tony Antoine's move may have made Cardinal wince, because the point of the protests for most Status Indian people was to keep the Act at least to the extent that it anchored their treaty claims. Few treaties were negotiated in British Columbia, which explains why Antoine had no investment in the Indian Act; however, in tearing it up, he certainly wasn't signalling agreement with Trudeau!

4 This point, although news to me, was not original with Antoine. David Mackay and other Indigenous men made the same point in 1888 (British Columbia, *Condition of the Indians*; see discussion in Chapter 7). Johnny David (Maxlaxlex), a Wet'suwet'en elder who testified in *Delgamuukw v. British Columbia*, says much the same thing in 1986: "You can see throughout our territory all the

stumps and the white people have pocketed millions and millions of dollars. All the money that has been taken off our territory, we want that back, and we want our territory back to the way they were" (16). The year before Antoine and I spoke, the annual conference at Glendon College had featured Quebec sovereignists. Imagine the shock to my emergent white settler nationalism of meeting René Lévesque in my first year of university and Tony Antoine in my second.

5 The government describes this document as "aspirational" and "non-legally binding" (Canada, Aboriginal Affairs and Northern Development, "United Nations Declaration"). So it appears that Canada signed merely to lower the political heat.

6 Victoria Freeman's *Distant Relations: How My Ancestors Colonized North America* is the account of someone who began her research believing her ancestors had arrived recently and had little or nothing to do with the colonization of Indigenous people.

7 "In 2017 the life expectancy for the total Canadian population is projected to be 79 years for men and 83 years for women. Among the Aboriginal population the Inuit have the lowest projected life expectancy in 2017, of 64 years for men and 73 years for women. The Métis and First Nations populations have similar life expectancies, at 73–74 years for men and 78–80 years for women. Life expectancy projections show an average increase of one to two years from the life expectancy that was recorded for the Aboriginal population in 2001" (Canada, Statistics Canada).

8 George Manuel's conceptualization of the "fourth world" in 1974 derived from the fact that unlike those nation-states characterized as "third world," Indigenous nations were still under the colonial rule of states dominated by non-Indigenous people.

9 See Barman, "Race, Greed and Something More" and "Erasing Indigenous Indigeneity in Vancouver" for a history of early land negotiations in Victoria and Vancouver, and the Papaschase First Nation website for the history of the people displaced from Edmonton in 1888.

10 Section 141 of the Indian Act was instituted in 1927 and repealed in 1951. See Venne.

11 Scholars disagree on whether section 35 of the Constitution Act is an acknowledgement of or a limitation on Indigenous land rights, as made clear by the papers in *Box of Treasures or Empty Box: Twenty Years of Section 35* (Walkem and Bruce).

12 That said, although the Supreme Court may be ahead of most Canadians, it can also be characterized as fighting a rearguard action against Indigenous sovereignty (see Alfred, *Wasáse* 136–38; Coulthard 45; Culhane 367–69; Lawrence,

Fractured 54–82). Grace Woo at her most hopeful says, "[T]he Supreme Court should be able to decolonize its thinking further without any revision of existing constitutional instruments" (229).

13 Cole Harris's "How Did Colonialism Dispossess?" points out that writing about texts can easily obscure the "experienced materiality of colonialism" (167), noting the role of physical violence in taking land.

14 Matthew Arnold, elected professor of poetry at Oxford in 1857, exemplified this transition away from religion in his *Culture and Anarchy* (1869), which promoted the civilizing effect of literacy and literature on the restless masses.

15 Scholars of science and technology point out that science is produced by human beings working within social discourses and, thus, its claim to truth is invariably mediated.

16 "Squatting" is a form of adverse possession. For a broad overview of the history of colonial claims to land, see Weaver. Tracey Lindberg provides a useful history of British and Canadian treaties and other claims to land in Canada.

17 As Douglas Deur and Nancy Turner point out, the belief that Indigenous people were hunter-gatherers who did not cultivate the land led incomers to the Pacific Northwest (and other locations in the Americas) to overlook the ways that Indigenous peoples modified the landscape to feed themselves without plows, fences, or land title offices.

18 For more on *Delgamuukw v. British Columbia* see Cruikshank, Culhane, Daly, David, Mary Hurley, Mills.

19 George Washington, who received thousands of acres through this proclamation, wrote to a business associate, "I can never look upon that proclamation in any other light (but I say this between ourselves) than as a temporary expedient to quiet the minds of the Indians" (qtd. in Wright 223). The "Proclamation line" the British drew between Indigenous hunting grounds and settler territory did not hold for long, and indeed caused much of the colonial resentment that led to the American Revolution.

20 These islands were subsequently flooded by the construction of the Trent-Severn Waterway, which began in 1833. After making a claim in 1988, the Hiawatha, Curve Lake, and Mississauga of Scugog Island First Nations were compensated in 2012 for the loss of their ability to harvest the wild rice on these lands with an award of $71 million (Steel). In *Fractured Homeland*, Bonita Lawrence recounts how Mary Buckshot brought wild rice from Rice Lake to Mud Lake in 1880, and tells of the subsequent "rice war" when the Ontario government decided to "open up" wild rice harvesting to commercial interests (139–43).

21 British Columbia also refused to negotiate treaties between 1871 and 1992, although the province did join the negotiations between Canada and the Nisga'a, begun in 1976, in 1990.

22 Derrida discusses the issues around "all or nothing" thinking promoted by binary oppositions (*Limited Inc.* 116). He insists that philosophy depends on demarcating such categories rigorously; he argues that when he and others attempt to "deconstruct the concept of concept otherwise" they must justify this move (117–18). What Derrida calls iterability (or writing, *différance*, mark, supplement, hymen, *pharmakon*, etc.) "is an ideal concept, to be sure, but also the concept that marks the essential and ideal limit of all pure idealization, the ideal concept of the limit of conceptualization, and not the concept of nonideality (since it is also the concept of the possibility of ideality)" (119). In his view, established concepts cannot be abandoned or transcended without rigorous discussion, a challenge Silva takes up with respect to the concept of race, a discussion which is often shortcut by remarks such as "biological race does not exist." Such remarks give biology too much credit for dissolving the long-standing ideas that ground both everyday and scientific racism.

23 Roman Catholic Irish were far less likely to rise than others, despite the exception embodied by Thomas D'Arcy McGee, a poet, critic, and Father of Confederation, and the first and only victim of assassination at the federal level in Canada.

24 Until the Métis were included in the Constitution Act of 1982, their claims to nationhood and Indigenousness were self-generated. Subsequently, *R. v. Powley* has clarified this identity, which can be seen both as a victory and as a loss of sovereignty, since the decision came from the Canadian state.

25 Goldie made amends by joining with Daniel David Moses to produce *The Anthology of Native Canadian Writing* (1992), which became the primary teaching anthology in the field; it is now in a fourth edition (2013) edited by Moses, Goldie, and Armand Ruffo.

26 Because of this disciplinary history, anthropologists have been grappling with issues around colonization and representation much longer and more effectively than have literary studies scholars. See Clifford and Marcus.

NOTES TO CHAPTER TWO

1 As Claude Allouez wrote in the Jesuit Relations of 1672–1673, "[T]he name 'Savage' gives rise to so very disparaging an idea of those who bear it, that many people in Europe have thought that it is impossible to make true Christians of them" (qtd. in Goddard 195). I have read more than once that the French *sauvage*, which can be translated as "wild" as in "wild strawberries," was not pejora-

tive as applied to Indigenous people in the early period, at least, but Allouez's remark counters this idea.

2 Clarence M. Burton states that Richardson's maternal grandmother was an Ottawa woman (qtd. in Quaife 12), but provides as evidence only the fact that Askin manumitted a female slave called Monette or Manette around the time his first three children were born. When Askin married Madeleine Barthe, these children were still young. However, both Pacey (1: 21) and Beasley ("Richardson, John") state Richardson's Ottawa ancestry as a fact. If it was (and it could have been), Richardson never mentioned it, either because it was kept from him or because he did not wish to make it public. That his grandmother might have been his grandfather's slave certainly could have qualified as a "family secret." As his portrait shows, he wished to be remembered as a successful British military officer.

3 Richardson lost his job with this Tory newspaper when he began to support Lord Durham's plans for responsible government in Canada (Beasley, *Canadian Don Quixote* 109–10).

4 The image of an Indian warrior and a British official shaking hands appears on treaty medals handed out after 1872.

5 Richardson spells Pontiac, Ponteac; I use the common modern spelling of this leader's name.

6 He attended such a ceremony at Walpole Island in 1848; see his "Trip."

7 The British general Proctor retreated before the battle in which Richardson was taken prisoner and Tecumseh killed, for which Proctor was court-martialled. In a famous speech, Tecumseh attempted to convince Proctor to stand and fight. See Richardson's history, *War of 1812,* for more.

8 Frye situated Canadian literature on the terrain of the gothic. However, Jennifer Andrews notes that despite Margot Northey's *The Haunted Wilderness: The Gothic and Grotesque in Canadian Fiction* (1976), which argued the importance of the gothic for Canadian literary studies, "few scholars in the 1980s and 90s used this concept," and those who did stuck to a limited set of novels (208). However, recently, critics have begun to refocus on the gothic (J.D. Edwards; Northey; Sugars; Sugars and Turcotte; Turcotte). And contemporary Indigenous writers have turned to it as well, for example, Eden Robinson in *Monkey Beach* (2000; see Andrews; Castricano).

9 Grant wrote in 1965, "This lament mourns the end of Canada as a sovereign state" (2); here he does not recognize any earlier loss of Indigenous sovereignty. Dennis Lee converts this lament into a way forward (43–54).

10 To be fair, he does go on to mention the extermination of the Beothuk in Newfoundland.

11 Burke's political speeches had much to do with this; he characterized the crowds who participated in the capture of Marie Antoinette as "resembling a procession of American savages, entering into Onondaga, after some of their murders called victories, and leading into hovels hung round with scalps …" (qtd. in Gibbons 84).

12 *Wacousta!* was first produced in 1976; Reaney went on to produce a play based on *The Canadian Brothers* the following year (Ross 15).

13 De Haldimar, a remarkably un-British name, alludes to Sir Frederick Haldimand (1718–1791), a Swiss German who served in the British army in North America during the Seven Years' War and the American War of Independence. He awarded land in Canada to some members of the Six Nations displaced by the latter war (Sutherland, Tousignant, and Dionne-Tousignant). The historical commander of Fort Detroit was Henry Gladwin. The siege was relieved by British forces, including those led by Robert Rogers, whose play about the Indian leader, *Ponteach* (1766), is strongly critical of the British treatment of Indigenous people in North America (see Potter).

14 Although I agree that the passage in *Wau-nan-gee* that Monkman quotes does sensationalize the Indian-as-cannibal, in the next chapter, I argue that Richardson's earlier accounts of massacres and cannibalism are more complex.

15 See Stoehr (181–82) for a similar opinion on the historical Pontiac's motives. Despite the pragmatism of Pontiac's response, Native peoples of this region did not categorize economic, social, political, and family concerns as separate. A trader like Alexander Henry the Elder might regard himself as a civilian non-combatant at his peril, for example. His adoption saved him. When leaders addressed Europeans as "father" or "brother," these terms carried with them a dense network of obligations that Europeans frequently did not understand or uphold. Notably, Richardson did regard Pontiac as less noble than Tecumseh, noting that "his practice was to offer terms of surrender, which never were kept in the honorable spirit in which the far more noble and generous Tecumseh always acted with his enemies" (Preface, *W*). For Richardson, honour remains key in any relationship.

16 This figure is very like what Michael Hurley calls "break boundaries," where dualities "are paradoxically subverted even as they are inscribed" (6). One can also see its connection to "disidentification," which I use as a way of understanding E. Pauline Johnson's performances.

17 Monkman's position on John Richardson's representation of Indians may have changed by 1992 when he and Douglas Daymond produced an edition of Richardson's long poem *Tecumseh*: "Against reductive either/or formulations, Richardson's poem insistently argues for a both/and construction yoking sav-

agery and civilization, martial progress and passive fortitude, without attempting to impose facile reconciliations" (Daymond and Monkman, Introduction, *Tecumseh* xxv).

18 I analyze similar uses of costumed performance by E. Pauline Johnson / Tekahionwake and Grey Owl / Archibald Belaney in later chapters.

19 See *Sinking Neptune*, by the Radical Dramaturgy Unit, Optative Theatrical Laboratories, 2006, a production aimed at exposing the racism of Lescarbot's masque on the occasion of its 400th anniversary.

20 One of Walter Scott's inspirations was his acquaintance, John Norton / Teyoninhokarawan, whom John Richardson knew as one of his grandfather's fur traders (Beasley, *Canadian Don Quixote* 11). Later, Norton led Mohawk forces in the War of 1812. Norton is said to have translated "The Lady of the Lake" into Mohawk (Fulford 9). Beasley argues that Norton was the model for Wacousta (*Canadian Don Quixote* 11); Klinck disagrees ("John Norton" 21).

21 Actually, Morton is Cornish, a Celtic nationality: Celts were differentiated from Anglo-Saxons in many representations as imaginative rather than practical; this distinction might underlie his volatile behaviour, so unlike that of the stolid Anglo-Saxon (436). Matthew Arnold uses these distinctions in *The Study of Celtic Literature* (1867).

22 Jean Barman recounts a similar process in "Erasing of Indigeneity in Vancouver," where the Coast Salish people living in Stanley Park were evicted, and the park decorated with totem poles from northern nations.

23 Duffy also says that Richardson undercuts this case "by lodging it within the context of the speaker's attempt to deceive his audience" (*World* 35). However, during this scene the governor also lies repeatedly.

24 He is infamous for his desire to infect Indigenous people with smallpox (Gill).

25 The Covenant Chain is derived from the Two Row Wampum or Guswentah that recorded the Haudenosaunee (then Five Nations) treaty with the Dutch (see Willig).

26 Klinck suggests that D'Egville is modelled on Askin, who knew and admired Tecumseh (Introduction ix). His attitudes also resemble those of Sir William Johnson, in charge of the meeting to introduce the Royal Proclamation. (Sir William was E. Pauline Johnson's great-grandfather's godfather, which explains the family's English last name.)

NOTES TO CHAPTER THREE

1 Phanuel Antwi notes that Richardson also collapses history in his depiction of Sambo, a Black character in both novels: "[W]hen Richardson refers to Sambo as a 'black servant,' he is mythmaking: he is simultaneously layering two or

more temporal periods to attempt to retroactively fix a history of Canada as free from black Atlantic slavery" (67). That is, Richardson is reading the Act against Slavery, passed in Upper Canada in 1793, back onto 1763 in order to free Canada from the imputations of slavery that he ascribes solely to Americans.

2 That said, his support of Durham likely reveals that he agreed the *Patriotes* were motivated by ethnic nationalism rather than a desire for responsible government. Durham categorizes French Canadians as "a people with no literature and no history" who needed to assimilate with the more progressive Anglo-Canadians (qtd. in "Durham Report"). E. Pauline Johnson's loyalty to both Canada and Britain was derived from the same Loyalist discourse as was Richardson's and has also led to similar confusion in those who would like her to be Mohawk or Canadian or British, not realizing that they are (like Richardson) reading national boundaries back in time. For her, overlapping loyalties were possible.

3 Richardson was educated in part by reading in his grandfather's extensive library (see Widder), a practice he clearly continued, given the wide-ranging political, literary, and historical interests revealed in his writing.

4 "Persons carrying or waving a white flag are not to be fired upon, nor are they allowed to open fire.... The improper use of a white flag is forbidden by the rules of war and constitutes a war crime of perfidy" ("White Flag," *Wikipedia*).

5 Riel's hanging was witnessed by the jury and reporters; the eight Indigenous men hanged shortly afterwards were hanged in public to discipline the Indigenous spectators, some of whom were transported to the hanging as witnesses (see page 98).

6 John Norton also recounts the same story, albeit in a more matter-of-fact way: "[T]hey barbarously skinned the Body of the gallant Techuthi," adding that although he did not see it himself, "This has been asserted by so many, that Force of Testimony compels its acceptance, notwithstanding its atrocity'" (243). Later, during his trip to Walpole Island, Richardson hears that the flaying did not occur, although an American is said to have cut a piece out of his (tattooed?) thigh to prove that he was dead ("Trip" 15).

7 Richardson fought in the First Carlist War in Spain, where torture and mass executions were common. Eventually, after much controversy, he was promoted to the rank of major and given an honorary knighthood.

8 Archibald Lampman's "At the Long Sault" is about des Ormeaux; see Patrice Groulx, *Pièges de la mémoire: Dollard des Ormeaux, les Amerindiens, et nous*, 1998, for writings in French about him. E.J. Pratt's long poem *Brébeuf and His Brethren* (1940) clearly influenced Frye's remarks about the Haudenosaunee. The theme has also been picked up by Indigenous authors Daniel David Moses in *Brébeuf's Ghost* (2000) and Joseph Boyden in *The Orenda* (2013). See Bruce

Trigger's *Natives and Newcomers: Canada's "Heroic Age" Reconsidered* (1985) for an overview of how historical narratives of this period deployed stereotypes, and Huron-Wendat historian George E. Sioui's account of the same period, *For an Amerindian Autohistory* (1992).

9 For the Spanish, the label justified enslaving instead of converting Indians (Basil A. Reid 97). Google N-Gram Viewer shows that "cannibalism" was ahead of "anthropophagy" in 1800 and surged ahead after that.

10 White men wearing solar topis roped back to back in the cooking pot of an overweight African chief with a bone through his nose was a staple image in the cartoons in the *New Yorker* magazines that I "read" before I could read.

11 In fact, Europeans themselves engaged in what has been called medical cannibalism or "corpse medicine" until the late eighteenth century, drinking the fresh blood of executed criminals and consuming the powder made from ground-up Egyptian mummies and, sometimes, more recently deceased bodies (see Sugg). The court case *R. v. Dudley and Stevens* (1884) dealt with the issue of survival cannibalism among British sailors; drawing lots to choose who would die so the others could live had long been practised as a "custom of the sea."

12 Although the passage is definitely excessive, it was written after he had left Canada in despair of ever making a living there. He may have justified the passage to himself as pandering to the depraved tastes of American readers.

13 Phanuel Antwi analyzes this scene at length in terms of the performative power of blackface minstrelsy (41–51).

14 Richardson had certainly plotted out *The Canadian Brothers* before he left England (Stephens), but what he found on his return apparently did not change its trajectory.

15 The Act against Slavery (1793) prevented the importation of slaves to Upper Canada. However, those slaves already there were not freed and their children were to remain slaves until they reached the age of twenty-five. In 1819, because many Black soldiers fought against the United States in the War of 1812, the attorney general of Upper Canada, John Beverley Robinson, declared that "residence in Canada"—that is, Upper Canada—made Blacks free (Historica Canada).

NOTES TO CHAPTER FOUR

1 Judith Butler would call constitutive rhetoric performative.

2 At the time he spoke, "half-breed" was the common English term for those of mixed Indigenous and British (usually Scottish) ancestry living in the North-West, while Métis was used only for those of French ancestry, who were usually Roman Catholic. Now, "half-breed" is widely seen as pejorative, although Maria

Campbell titled her 1973 autobiography *Halfbreed*. "Métis" is now used both for this group and for those of French and Indigenous ancestry. Riel himself discusses these terms; see "Last" 200. Since the 1982 Constitution Act, Métis has also been a legal designation. See *R. v. Powley* (2003).

3 He is even more forthright in his "Last Memoir": "What did the Government do? It laid its hands on the land of the Metis as if it were its own. By this one act it showed its plan to defraud them of their future. It even placed their present condition in jeopardy. For not only did it take the land from under their feet, it even took away their right to use it" (205).

4 Daniel Coleman's "Epistemological Crosstalk" notes the dangers of ignoring spiritual cosmologies such as Riel's.

5 Richard Gwyn comments, "A distinctive religion for the Métis would make them a distinctive people, in the same way that Judaism, for which he had immense respect, defined the Jews.... [I]f insane, [his spiritual vision] was politically and operationally rational" (410–11).

6 See Anderson and Robertson for an overview of the reception of the Riel Resistance in contemporary newspapers.

7 The Queen's Printer version is online at Peel's Prairie Provinces, University of Alberta Library.

8 *Riel's Defence: Perspectives on His Speeches*, edited by Hans V. Hansen, begins with Hanson's re-edition of the speeches to convey their meaning better in print, particularly by adding paragraphing to the second address. This collection is of more relevance to my chapter than I have been able to indicate, since it appeared after the manuscript had been submitted to the press: although the collection's authors have contrasting opinions, as a whole the collection gives a good picture of the rhetorical stakes of the trial speeches.

9 For more on Michif, see Bakker.

10 The Orange Order, a Protestant fraternal order founded in Ireland in 1795, had branches in Upper Canada as early as 1812. It was dominant in Toronto municipal politics from 1845 until 1954, when the Jewish Nathan Phillips became mayor.

11 Ironically, Jennifer Reid attributes much of the power of this storyline to the work of John Murray Gibbon, the British publicist hired by the Canadian Pacific Railway (CPR) in 1907 (67–68). E.J. Pratt's *Towards the Last Spike* (1952) turns this history into a nation-building epic poem.

12 The federal government retained rights to "all ungranted or waste lands" in the province (Canada, Manitoba Act, sec. 30)—a provision that did not apply to those provinces that joined Confederation earlier, and one that provided no compensation to Indigenous nations for the land outside treaties described

as "ungranted or waste" (see Canada, Dominion Lands Act, repealed in 1950). This exclusion contributed to the Prairie provinces going bankrupt in the depression.

13 See Canada, "First Nations Involvement in the 1885 Resistance."

14 Nonetheless, both men's literary reputations and lives were affected by their political views. Another interesting example, recounted in Paul Foot's *Red Shelley* (1980), is how Shelley was "rewritten" by the literary establishment to obscure his radicalism.

15 In a letter written to the governor general on 3 September 1885, Macdonald opined that rushing the execution to forestall a Privy Council review might look bad (qtd. in Charlebois 230). Clearly, he had considered this action. In the end the Privy Council declined to review the case.

16 Macdonald was heavily involved behind the scenes in all the trials; the trials of the Cree were a complete travesty of justice (Stonechild and Waiser 198; Harring 247–50). Thomas Scott's trial had been no better: it was held in French, which he did not understand, and allowed him no counsel or chance to question witnesses. His execution was bungled (Gwyn 127–28). It is widely said that Riel's worst mistake was executing Scott, and Macdonald's worst mistake was executing Riel. However, Macdonald did not pay for his mistake with his life or his reputation (at least in mainstream Canada).

17 When they were read the charge of treason-felony in Cree which accused them of "knocking off the Queen's bonnet and stabbing her in the behind with a sword," they were understandably taken aback (Stonechild and Waiser 200; Harring 240). According to North-West Mounted Policeman F.W. Spicer, Big Bear said in Blackfoot, "I don't want her hat and didn't know she had one" (qtd. in Wiebe and Beal 175).

18 He gave up his nomination in Provencher for Sir George-Étienne Cartier in September 1872 in hopes of Cartier's support for an amnesty, but Cartier died in May 1873. Riel won the by-election in October 1873. However, the government resigned after the Pacific Scandal broke (see note 28 below; "Pacific Scandal"). He won again in February 1874, but was expelled in April that year. He ran in the by-election to fill the seat and won again in September 1874. In February 1875 he was given an amnesty, which exiled him for five years and permanently banned him from taking political office.

19 These arguments have been summarized elsewhere, from a variety of perspectives, from Howard Adams to Jennifer Reid to Flanagan.

20 Here Flanagan notes that he cannot find anything that Macdonald said to this effect but that Cartier (Macdonald's minister of militia and defence) had said in May 1870 that Riel "should continue to maintain order and govern the country

as he has done up to the present moment" (cw 3: 561n). Manitoba entered Confederation on 15 July 1870.

21 Although Scott's name occurs rarely in the trial transcript, when Riel asks rhetorically, "Was Riel a murderer of Thomas Scott, when Thomas Scott was executed"(cw 3: 558), someone in the courtroom says, "You did [murder him]" (3: 562n). He replies, "If told by law it would not be said," that is, because his provisional government was legitimate.

22 See Flanagan, *Riel and the Rebellion*; Sprague; and Chartrand for different positions on the fairness of the scrip distribution, and Milne for an overview.

23 Apparently, he planned to use some of the funds to buy a printing press to produce a newspaper supporting the Métis (Flanagan, *Riel and the Rebellion* 116, 126; Jennifer Reid 222).

24 The North-West Mounted Police was founded in 1873. It was a paramilitary force formed with the specific goal of preventing any further impediment to settlement. In the first battle of the second resistance, the police attacked the Riel resistors, who had begun a parley under a white flag (see Canada, "Battle of Duck Lake"). As Sidney L. Harring remarks, "Wars are not usually the subject of legal history, but Canadian authorities insisted, for political reasons, on treating the rebellion as an internal act of treason" (245), leaving "the question of how and when the Indian nations were incorporated into Canada unraised and unanswered" (246).

25 Fenians from the United States occupied a customs post and a Hudson's Bay Company post in 1871 in the belief that these were in Canada; they were in fact south of the recently surveyed border. As requested by Lieutenant-Governor Archibald, in a demonstration of loyalty, Riel and his men captured the leader and turned him over to the US authorities (Pritchett). Edward Blake, leader of the Liberal Opposition in Ottawa, put up the reward for Riel to embarrass Macdonald and to keep Riel from taking his seat.

26 Depending on whose perspective one chooses, these armed encounters are a "rebellion" (the most common word), a "civil war" (Adams 46), or a "resistance." Dorion and Préfontaine use the last term by analogy with the French Resistance in World War II (26n). Riel called it "self-defence" (cw 3: 554). See Pritchett for an account of Anglo settler violence against Métis in Manitoba after Riel and other leaders had left, fearing arrest.

27 See Daschuk; Lux; and Stonechild and Waiser for detailed accounts of starvation among the Indians, who held begging dances during the trial.

28 Macdonald's government had to resign in 1873 as a result of what was called the Pacific Scandal. His party had accepted donations of $360,000 from Sir Hugh

Allen's Canadian Pacific Railway Company in return for a contract to build the transcontinental railway ("Pacific Scandal").

29 In the House of Commons, Macdonald blamed the resistance on savage instincts "in these half-breeds, enticed by white men, the savage instinct was awakened; the desire of plunder—aye, and perhaps the desire of scalping—the savage idea of a warlike glory … was aroused in them … forgetting all that the Government, the white people and the Parliament of Canada had been doing for them, in trying to rescue them from barbarity; forgetting that we had given them reserves" (House of Commons Debates 6 July 1885, 3119, qtd. in Williams).

30 This use of family metaphors is a telling feature of much Indigenous discourse, connecting to the discourse of kinship that Daniel Heath Justice theorizes as "kinship criticism"—it relates to peoplehood and decolonization in a way that asserts sovereignty as relationship-building (this is what treaties are—the assertion of a relationship by sovereign peoples).

31 In order to force Indigenous people into self sufficiency, Macdonald argued, it was necessary to be "rigid, even stingy, in the distribution of food and require absolute proof of starvation before distributing it" (House of Commons Debates, 3 May 1880, 1941–1942, qtd. in Williams).

32 Riel notes that the Métis should get more territory as a result of the 1881 change, equal to one-seventh of the new configuration (CW 3: 544).

33 For the Sarcee/Tsuu T'ina, Dumont's mother's people, see Edward S. Curtis 18: 102.

34 Here is Johnny David (Maxlaxlex), giving evidence a hundred years later in the *Delgaamukw* case: "[T]he people, the white people, had no respect for the Indian people. The Indian people would chase them off their land, and they would go and get their law and they would throw our people in jail" (24). Richard Daly's description of the difficulties of reconciling alternative worldviews and legal traditions within the oppositional structures of the *Delgaamukw* courtroom is instructive, as in his account of a high-ranking matriarch: "[H]ere on this witness bench she is not accorded the smallest scrap of respect. Any old lawyer can interrupt her words whenever he or she likes. The judge does the same" (8).

35 Attesting to the longevity of this attitude, Georges E. Sioui quotes Father Joseph Le Caron, who in 1626 wrote, "The general opinion [of Amerindians] is that one must not contradict any one, but leave each one to having his own thinking. There is, here, no hope of suffering martyrdom: the Savages do not put Christians to death for matters of religion; they leave every one to his belief" (qtd. 55; see also 103).

NOTES TO CHAPTER FIVE

1 One point of Spivak's much-debated and much-revised article "Can the Subaltern Speak?" is that when subalterns speak, those in power do not listen; if the powerful do hear, they misunderstand (see, for the most recent version, *Critique* 269–311).

2 Johnson's poetry was driven from the canon, along with that of other "sentimental" women poets, by later modernist critics (Strong-Boag and Gerson 126–30). This widespead anti-feminist move explains the long trough between first-wave and second-wave feminism. See also Bennett.

3 One notable example was her father's contemporary, Oronhyatekha, who had an illustrious career despite being trained as a shoemaker at the Anglican-run Mohawk Institute (Comeau-Vasilopoulos; Nicks). He was educated at the Wesleyan Academy, Kenyon College, and Oxford University and then attended the Toronto School of Medicine, qualifying as a medical doctor in 1866.

4 She also was supported by donors in Brantford (Gray 170) and sold valuable Iroquois artifacts that had belonged to her family or that she had purchased.

5 He was known for his performances of the dialect poems of William Henry Drummond, whose renditions of the broken English of the French-Canadian habitant consolidated their status in English Canada as colourful peasants (see M.J. Edwards).

6 They were on the same program in Toronto that began Johnson's performing career in 1892 (Gray 140) and she dined at his home once, although Mrs. Scott did not agree to let her wear buckskins to the table (Gray 147; see also Strong-Boag and Gerson 118–21).

7 Several of Johnson's works directly criticized these schools, including "As It Was in the Beginning" (Gerson and Strong-Boag 205–12), "Little Wolf-Willow" (Johnson, *Shaganappi*), and a poem, "His Sister's Son" (Gerson and Strong-Boag 123), of which only a fragment survives.

8 E. Pauline Johnson's great-grandmother Katherine Roulston (Evelyn H.C. Johnson spells it this way, 8; Keller and most other sources spell her name as Rolleston). She was captured from a Dutch settlement near Philadelphia as a young teenager; her adoption made her a powerful clan mother (Keller 8). Keller writes of Roulston's daughter, Johnson's grandmother, "Although her mother was a white woman, Helen Martin spoke not a word of English and even denied her white ancestry" (10). Despite Keller's somewhat miffed reaction, it's entirely possible that the explanation lies in Martin's Iroquois concept of adoption.

9 Lord Dorchester, governor of Quebec in 1789, declared "that it was his wish to put the mark of Honour upon the Families who had adhered to the Unity of the

Empires" and allowed those who "joined the Royal Standard before the Treaty of Separation in the year 1783" and their descendants to put the initials "U.E." after their names (Mackenzie). There were Black as well as "feathered" Loyalists, and associations of those with Loyalist ancestry still flourish across Canada (see the United Empire Loyalists Association of Canada web page).

10   Status Indian men who could meet the property requirements were able to vote until 1896, when the Laurier government adopted the principle of basing the right to vote in federal elections on the provincial voters' lists (Williams, ch. 4). Sara Jeannette Duncan's novel, *The Imperialist* (1904), describes how questions about the vote from "Moneida," that is Six Nations Grand River, contributed to the disqualification of the results of a vote that her hero had won, and his replacement as the candidate in the rerun.

11   The current reserve is only 5 percent of the original grant, which cut a swath through what is now a densely populated area of southern Ontario; the history of its reduction is complex. Much of it was leased or sold to provide funds for the Iroquois, but few leases were paid and large sums from land sales were either stolen by corrupt officials or allocated to other government purposes such as the Grand River Navigation Company, McGill University, and the Welland Canal (Monture, "Teionkwakhashion" 137). What money was paid out was rigidly controlled by bureaucrats (Catapano 263). See also Six Nations Lands and Resources; Coleman, *White Civility* 227–29.

12   It is easy to forget what a social stigma "illegitimacy" was, although such distinctions were only finally removed by the Constitution Act, 1982.

13   In Euro-American society, until recently women were exchanged between men—fathers and husbands—to consolidate political and economic relationships (Rubin). White elites saw no profit in consolidating intercultural relationships through marriage after the end of the fur trade. Indigenous people were to be transformed into a separate subject people. Although Indigenous marriage customs varied considerably across Canada (see Carter, *Importance*), the ease of divorce was a widespread feature. On Six Nations marriage and divorce customs in the nineteenth century, one document notes that "the Indian divorce, separation, or putting away has been a matter of choice, not necessarily mutual, but at the will of the dissatisfied party. The chiefs have sanctioned it and practiced it" (US Department of the Interior 483).

14   For George Johnson's mother's side of the family, the marriage was seen as disastrous because his children would not be Mohawk (see Johnson, "My Mother" 39–40). See Lawrence on the impact of the birth of such "clanless" individuals in Six Nations (*Real Indians* 51).

15 Linda Revie argues on the basis of her many intense relationships with women that she may have been lesbian; see also Gray (361–62).

16 The Duke of Connaught and Strathern (1850–1942) was the third son of Queen Victoria. He was governor general of Canada from 1911 to 1916. He visited Johnson shortly before her death, sitting at her bedside on a chair covered with this same cloak.

17 Keller argues that she manoeuvred Drayton into proposing, taking advantage of his youth. But if true, it shows that Johnson was able to choose, even at an age when she would have been seen as too old to marry. And she certainly could have charmed someone else into marriage, if she had wanted to.

18 A. LaVonne Brown Ruoff, writing of Johnson's career, quotes Nina Baym: "[O]nly middle-class women had sufficient education to know how to write books, and only those who needed money attempted it" (19). For poems that Canadian schoolchildren memorized in droves, Johnson received a few dollars (Keller 55). She was frequently desperately in debt and was supported through her long last illness from breast cancer by friends who helped her collect her previously published work into books (*Legends of Vancouver* appeared first in 1911, *Flint and Feather* in 1912; *The Moccasin Maker* and *The Shaganappi* were published posthumously in 1913).

19 Indigenous divorcées or widows did not get their Status back; marriage might not be for life, but the loss of Status was permanent.

20 Recent attempts (Bill C-31, 1985) to restore Status to these women and their descendants because this provision of the Indian Act contravened the gender equality provisions of the Constitution Act have left this group still less privileged with respect to Status than those who never lost it, including the non-Indigenous wives of Status men who married before 1985 (Lawrence, *Real Indians* 65–66). The "different" Status accorded by Bill C-31 does not pass securely to one's descendants; it can disappear if one's children and grandchildren "marry out" (that is, marry non-Status people, whether Indigenous or not). The notion of "blood quantum," in most other contemporary contexts decried as grounded in discredited notions of biological race, comes into play at this point, but only for those in this category. As Lawrence points out, white women who "married in" were granted Status, as were their children, and thus the requirement to prove one's "blood" is aimed only at those with Indigenous ancestry who are without this legally secured identity.

21 The knife that Johnson used in performance is now at the Museum of Vancouver. It was her grandfather's. Evelyn Johnson recalls that he strapped it on every morning "to the very day of his death" (10). Pauline Johnson supported her identity and stage presence through what Bruno Latour would call alliances

with things, objects with a strong symbolic aura and also personal "sentimental value." Evelyn Johnson's *Memoirs* reveals the strong importance Evelyn placed on conserving such objects, both for her family and the Mohawk (see Hamilton).

22 The poem drew on the widespread idea that there had been an "Indian war" on the prairies, although the organized resistance was a Métis resistance. Few Indigenous men joined Riel, despite the public view that Indigenous peoples on the plains were all equally guilty of rebelling against the Crown (see Stonechild and Waiser). Big Bear tried to prevent the killing of nine settler men at Frog Lake by Wandering Spirit and others from his band and protected their wives and children from harm afterwards (Carter, Introduction). The incident (of course routinely referred to as a massacre) began with the refusal of the Indian agent to distribute food; Johnson's poems "The Cattle Thief" and "Silhouette" both spoke of starvation on the plains (see Daschuk; Lux).

23 Tomahawks had long been obsolete. Johnson's anachronism draws on the same longstanding stereotypes that were deployed in the popular press during the Resistance. "Tomahawk" evokes "scalping" and the whole complex of negative stereotypes of the Indian as innately bloodthirsty. Such words held a double-edged aura of authenticity.

24 Foucault talks about such exchanges in terms of "micro-power": "The general juridical form that guaranteed a system of rights that were egalitarian in principle was supported by these tiny, everyday, physical mechanisms, by all those systems of micro-power that are essentially non-egalitarian and asymmetrical ..." (*Discipline and Punish* 222). Scollon and Scollon argue that the difficulty of engaging strangers in conversation without accidentally insulting them explains the resistance of those Indigenous people with what they call "bush consciousness" to small talk. Their response is a respectful silence, which is often interpreted as stupidity, sullenness, or hostility by chattier people (177–209).

25 Riel tells this story: "Very polite and amiable people, may sometimes say to a Métis, 'You don't look at all like a Métis. You surely can't have much Indian blood. Why, you could pass anywhere for pure white.' The Métis, a trifle disconcerted by the tone of these remarks, would like to lay claim to both sides of his origin" ("Last Memoir" 200). These conversations set up a hierarchy that leaves "minority" interlocutors speechless, at least if they wish to remain civil. Drew Hayden Taylor's story "Pretty Like a White Boy" recounts his similar difficulties with not looking "Indian" enough. He has published three collections of essays with the subtitle "Funny, you don't look like one," another phrase repeatedly used to reject the self-identifications of those seen as belonging to "minorities." See also Lee Schweninger, "'Back When I Used to Be Indian': Native American

Authenticity and Postcolonial Discourse" and Thomas King, "You're Not the Indian I Had in Mind" for more on how the distance between stereotypical expectations and complex individuality is negotiated.

26 She did have to get permission from Clifford Sifton, then minister of the interior in charge of Indian Affairs, "to raise $500 against her future share of the Chiefs-wood rent" (Strong-Boag and Gerson 97). Typically, she wrote to him directly to get it.

27 She asked Ernest Thomson Seton to recommend a buyer for one of her wampum belts in August 1905, stating that the going rate for them was $1600, although she was prepared to accept less. He sent her a loan and referred her to a collector, possibly George Gustav Heye (Gray 307–8). The proceeds likely supported her trip to England in 1906, during which she met Joe Capilano. Karen Dearlove, former curator at Chiefswood, says that Johnson acquired four belts; three are still unlocated (personal communication). Heye's collection eventually ended up at the Smithsonian Institution. Eleven of the belts sold by Buck's children were recovered by Six Nations from the Museum of the American Indian in 1988 (K. Coody Cooper). See also Fenton; Strong-Boag and Gerson 41; Willmott.

28 Sasha Kovacs has been tracking Johnson's wampum belts by examining their appearance and disappearance in her publicity photographs.

29 In part, I assume, because Native leaders have community input while celebrities are deemed to be isolated. However, as we have seen, Indigenous women were increasingly excluded from community input, and even from the community itself.

NOTES TO CHAPTER SIX

1 In 1935–36, Grey Owl spoke to over five hundred thousand people (Billinghurst 101). In fall 1937, he toured the United Kingdom, and then did a three-month lecture tour of eastern Canada and the United States, finally appearing before over three thousand in Toronto's Massey Hall (129–34). *The Men of the Last Frontier* sold over fifty thousand copies (D.B. Smith 115); *Pilgrims of the Wild* sold thirty-five thousand copies in three months, and *Sajo and the Beaver People* was also a bestseller (121, 123).

2 For sources of these terms, see the following: "ecosystem" (OED3), "naturecultures" (Haraway, *Companion Species Manifesto*), "hybrids" (Latour, *We Have Never Been Modern*), and "assemblages" of objects and affects (Deleuze and Guattari, *Anti-Oedipus*). Arguably this "new" vision comes from those working with traditional Indigenous people not just in Canada but worldwide (see Berkes; Deur and Turner; Tsing; Terralingua).

3 Her birth name was Gertrude Bernard; Belaney named her Anahareo after one of her Mohawk ancestors (D.B. Smith 81; see Gleeson; McCall, Afterword).

4 The National Parks Board paid him for all this; he worked for them from 1931 until his death in 1938. He put his pay into his cultural work and his community. Anahareo says he put $40,000 into the two silent movies he made (176); his publisher, Macmillan, funded *Men against the Snow*, but he self-funded *The Trail—Men against the River*, hiring Antoine Commanda, Jimmy Espaniel's brother-in-law, as a canoeist, and other old friends to help (D.B. Smith 174–75).

5 Attenborough, best known for the film *Gandhi*, and his brother David were profoundly influenced by hearing Grey Owl speak in 1936; Richard Attenborough made a feature film about Grey Owl in 1999, and David Attenborough became "the world's pre-eminent natural history journalist" (Duff and Stoneley).

6 He knew that wearing feathers was equivalent to wearing unearned honours, but he clearly could not resist it.

7 O'Hagan worked as a horse packer with Indigenous men on the trails near Jasper in between terms as a law student at McGill. He used these experiences to write stories for men's magazines, as well as a novel, *Tay John,* whose title character bears the nickname of an Iroquois-Métis man, Pierre Bostonais, also remembered in the place names Tête Jaune Cache and Yellowhead Pass (Akrigg and Akrigg 265).

8 See, for example, M.T. Kelly's negative response to Grey Owl (Atwood, *Strange* 56). Albert Braz usefully canvasses such critical opinions in his three articles on Grey Owl.

9 Telling stories made it possible to convey advice in ways that were not didactic or coercive. Listeners respected the teller by paying attention and thinking about how the story pertained to them.

10 Sneja Gunew has analyzed similar debates in Australia around imposters and authenticity; see her "Culture, Gender and the Author-Function: 'Wongar's *Walg*,'" and "Performing Ethnicity: The Demidenko Show and Its Gratifying Pathologies."

11 Morriseau writes that "[t]he beaver was considered sacred by the Ojibway, who, because of its meat and fur, regarded it as the source of life. No Ojibway will ever throw beaver bones to a dog.... The first beaver of the year that is caught by the Ojibway is always eaten in a manner that is considered sacred" (21).

12 Even if one discounts the idea that such control would entail traditional respect for nature, local control by definition tends to be respectful to the degree that those dependent on a nearby resource are far more likely to work to sustain it and to protect other parts of the ecosystem from the "collateral damage" of resource extraction, such as pollution of the land, water, and air. Big corpora-

tions have been known to take government subsidies, deplete resources, and then depart or go bankrupt without keeping their promises to hire locals or remediate the ecosystem.

13 It also brought him closer to his absconded father. As a boy, he had fantasized that his father was living on a ranch in Mexico with the Indians (D.B. Smith 14–15).

14 Braz quotes Gerry Potts, former chief of the Temagami First Nation (Bear Island), as saying that although white people approve of the assimilation of Aboriginal people into mainstream culture, they find it troubling that anyone would assimilate into Anishinaabe culture ("White Indian").

15 Louis Ernest Barrias's statue *Nature Revealing Herself to Science* (1899) is in the Centre Pompidou, Paris. The famous Canadian neurologist Wilder Penfield had a copy made by Adolphe Galli for the lobby of the Montreal Neurological Institute. One might see this symbolic striptease as a way to inspire young men to take up the hard and boring work of science. The feminization of Nature and the masculinization of the disciplines charged with its study is neither accidental nor natural, but built on Western gender relations.

16 When Indigenous people propose economic activities that go beyond traditional subsistence, they are often viewed as "contaminated" by capitalism. They are seen as authentic only if cut off from the modern economy that is available to whites.

17 Here the explanation for his decision to stop trapping beavers is quite different from the one he gives in his next book, *Pilgrims of the Wild*, where it is Anahareo's intervention that converts him (28–30, 46–47). He continued to support sustainable trapping, despite his personal decision (D.B. Smith 205).

18 Castenada received a BA (1962) and a PhD (1973) from the University of California at Los Angeles for writing some of this material. Andrews has written many books that follow this pattern; she also runs expensive workshops where she conducts ceremonies that she represents as Indigenous.

19 Donald B. Smith 39–40; Dickson, *Wilderness Man* 73–74. Theriault calls him David Missabie and recounts some of his life history (20–25).

20 John Egwuna gave him the nickname "Little Owl" because he paid attention to everyone and everything around him (D.B. Smith 41).

21 Lord Tweedsmuir wrote novels as John Buchan, famous for *Thirty-Nine Steps* (1915), which Alfred Hitchcock made into a feature film in 1935, and for subsequent novels featuring the very heroic and very British Richard Hannay. As a child, I read them all, many more than once.

22 He attended Thunderchild Indian Residential School in Delmas, Saskatchewan, founded in 1901 and closed in 1948.

23 The Temagami Wilderness Society, which was a major player in the blockade, is still active under the name Earthroots. In 2002, a tentative settlement was reached on land and compensation for the Temagami Anishinaabe people, but I can find no record of whether this compensation has actually been paid. See David T. McNab on problems with the treaties.

24 His story "The Sage of Pelican Lake" recounts the hospitality he was given by a Cree-Métis family while hunting for food outside the park himself (*Tales* 54–71).

25 Maria Campbell recounts how when she was a little girl, two Mounties offered her a chocolate bar to show them where her father kept his meat: he went to the penitentiary for six months for hunting in Prince Albert National Park (*Halfbreed* 54).

26 Many of these formed the basis of his first book, *The Men of the Last Frontier* (1931). National Parks made five silent films about him and his beavers ("Films on Grey Owl"). Two of these films, *The Beaver People* and *The Beaver Family*, can be watched online at the NFB. He went on his first lecture tour to the United Kingdom in October 1935, taking his films with him. One can imagine the impact of the impossibly photogenic couple, Grey Owl and Anahareo, with their cute beavers. Both could emerge from tent or shack looking amazing, as the many photographs of them reveal. They separated in September 1936.

27 Beavers are also an example of what is called a keystone species, a species that has an effect on biodiversity out of proportion to its numbers. Further, they preserve water: see Hood and Bayley.

28 Anahareo fled his obsessive writing when she could: "I was going to be stuck with a zombie all winter" (144). The beavers were less considerate of Belaney's need for peace: "As a tribe … they step heavily, pound violently, haul, push and heave vigorously, and are fanatically determined in the carrying out of any project they have decided … to complete. Hence the noise, which is unspeakable, indescribable, and unsupportable" (*Pilgrims* 306).

29 His cabin is still not accessible by car (D.B. Smith 217).

30 Her inclusion of nature writers in her study is to be lauded, but her ultimate discounting of their perspective serves to privilege history as a way of knowing. Of course, in complaining about this move, I can be seen as simply promoting my own discipline instead. Interdisciplinarity and community partnerships, however, are required if we are to avoid the many blind spots that result from the academy's forging of knowledge silos and hierarchies of expertise.

31 His story "The Tree" (*Tales* 117–42) puts a tree at the centre of such a web of relations.

32 Jean Barman's account in *Stanley Park's Secret* of how Chinese men and Indigenous and mixed-race families were cleared out of Stanley Park as "squatters"

despite their presence there prior to its founding replicates some of the events that Ladino discusses.

33 "Civilization," def. 3d: "the comfort and convenience of modern life, as found in towns and cities; populated or urban areas in general" (OED3).

34 Wildlife management was the purview of the provinces; Grey Owl was hired to work in a national park, with his tame beavers acting as a tourist draw. I think he would have approved of Watt's initiative, had he known of it.

35 Bruce Erickson argues that in his talks, films, and park activities, Grey Owl promoted wilderness as "an experience that could be bought and consumed by the public" (150). This focus, Erickson argues, helped inaugurate a discourse that he calls "recreational nationalism," one that features wilderness canoeing as central to forming the national imaginary as white. Given Grey Owl's resistance to identifying as white, I disagree, although obviously Grey Owl's life can be read in many ways. For another take on canoeing, see Dean.

36 Madeline Katt Theriault recounts how she and her husband did something similar, but that they could not maintain their beaver preserve. The only way they could keep the rights to trap in one location was to trap there every year; when her husband became too sick to trap, the beavers they had "farmed" were taken by others (94). This plan resembles what Anahareo and Belaney had thought of doing in Quebec. Their plan failed when a friend trapped all the beavers they were conserving, thinking he was helping them out (Anahareo 104).

37 The James Bay Cree, with whom Watt was working and about whom Berkes writes, share many beliefs about relationships with other-than-humans with the Anishinaabeg, and indeed, with Indigenous peoples across the continent.

38 Belaney and Anahareo moved to Quebec because of a ban on trapping beavers in Ontario for anyone without Indian Status between 1928 and 1937; by the time they moved to the west, there was a ban in Quebec (see Feit).

39 As a result of their success with their beaver conservation project, Jimmy Watt was named Amisk ogemow (Beaver Chief) by the Cree, and Maud became "the Angel of Hudson's Bay" for selling the idea to the government of the day (Hudson Bay Company).

40 He lived in King's constituency (D.B. Smith 154–55). And King did not fund him, nor did any discernable results come out of his discussions with either the king or the governor general.

41 Madeline Katt Theriault, born on Bear Island in 1908, lost her husband to tuberculosis in 1940. During the three years he was unable to work, they received twenty dollars a month for their family of four: "This was called a ration from Indian Affairs. Well, it wasn't enough" (97). She prepared furs for trappers,

knitted socks, and sold the furniture to make ends meet, as well as appearing in Indigenous dress at sportsmen's shows in the United States.

42 Shepard Krech III writes about the Watt project in his chapter on the beaver in *The Ecological Indian*. He notes that "[t]he old way of management amounted to control imposed by government agencies alone, usually uninfluenced by indigenous opinion" and sees the James Bay and Northern Quebec Agreement concluded in 1975 as the first to embody new principles of co-management (208). He writes in favour of the latter agreement, even though he believes that Indigenous people have no greater insight into the ecosystem and no better claim to land than anyone else.

NOTES TO CHAPTER SEVEN

1 See Boone and Mignolo; Brotherston; and Coe for how the writing systems of Central and South America were discounted. Western theories of writing consistently regarded the phonetic alphabet as superior to all other systems. See Robert K. Logan, *The Alphabet Effect: A Media Ecology Understanding of the Making of Western Civilization* (Cresskill, NJ: Hampton, 2004), a book derived from his collaboration with McLuhan which views the phonetic alphabet as a hallmark of civilization. Roy Harris's *Rethinking Writing* (rev. ed. London: Continuum, 2005) debunks this idea.

2 See Fee, "Rewriting." See also Maud, *Guide*, for more on these and other collectors.

3 Sex was airbrushed out too, or translated into Latin and put into endnotes (Wickwire, Introd. *Living* 8; Maud, *Transmission* 40–41). Wickwire's introduction to *Living by Stories* outlines this issue in more detail.

4 Some of Tate's original written stories have been published as *The Porcupine Hunter and Other Stories*, edited by Maud.

5 Part 1, "Beginnings: The Age of the Animal People" in *Write It on Your Heart* contains nine sections; I discuss "The First People," "Earth Diver," and "Twins, White and Indian." After the last story in this section, "Coyote Challenges God," Coyote is banished to a raft for his arrogance. "Coyote Makes a Deal with the King of England" (*Living by Stories*) begins when God lets Coyote off the raft to act as his diplomat to the British court. I realize that to speak as if there is a fixed order to these stories is a relic of "book thinking."

6 The Toronto School of Communication is not a formal institution, but a label used to describe the related concerns of many scholars; most of them, including Harold Innis, Eric A. Havelock, Marshall McLuhan, Edward Snow Carpenter, and Northrop Frye, were at some point based at the University of Toronto. See Grosswiler.

7 Only 102 men enfranchised voluntarily between 1876 and 1918; when enfranchisement was made compulsory for a brief period, it was protested (Brizinski 185).
8 Although Kelly did not bestow a Haida name on his son, the name is now held
   by his grandson: "Cle-alls is a chief's name. After I earned my doctorate, our
   clan's matriarchs named me at a potlatch. My grandfather, Dr. Peter Kelly, was
   Cle-alls before me, and the first Dr. Kelly" (Tracy and Cle-alls). The Rev. Peter
   Kelly is well remembered in Haida Gwai'i.
9 Chinook Jargon was a trade language or "pidgin" spoken widely along the coast
   from northern California to Alaska (see Lang).
10 For a group photo, see *BC Studies* 120 (1998/99): 36.
11 Cole Harris notes that the federal government disallowed the British Columbia
   Land Act of 1874 because it ignored the Royal Proclamation of 1763 (*Making
   Space* 91–92).
12 This agreement transferred control of around two thousand square kilometres
   of Crown land to the Nisga'a. See British Columbia, "Nisga'a Final Agreement,"
   2013.
13 Christopher F. Roth argues that the Supreme Court decision in *Delgamuukw*
   (1997) means that most of the land in British Columbia has never left Indigenous ownership.
14 British governance was challenged by gold rushes that brought hordes of miners
   of various nationalities into the region, notably in 1858 in the Fraser Canyon and
   in the 1860s in the Cariboo.
15 Although missionaries are often regarded from our contemporary perspective
   as complicit with government, in fact, this Commission was instructed not
   to use them as translators. They were seen as advocates for the Indians and as
   troublemakers who put ideas into Indian heads about land (see Foster, "We are
   not"). See also Heartfield.
16 A letter in *Papers Connected with the Indian Land Question* dated 1862 records
   that a Squamish man, Snat Stroutan, is asking to buy land "just like a white man
   would" (British Columbia 23). R.C. Moody, the writer, reassures the Colonial
   Office that "[t]he lot selected by him is at some distance from the town, so that
   it cannot prove an annoyance, and the man proposes to actually live thereon."
   He calls this "an interesting turning point in the history of the Indians of British
   Columbia." The purchase was allowed. Stroutan appears elsewhere in the *Papers*
   (74–75, 77–78). "Charley" is permitted to buy a piece of land near Sooke Harbour in 1870 (84). A long letter states that "pre-emption is but a nominal right to
   the Indian for whom it was not intended" (147).
17 The idea that the refusal of the province to enact treaties violated the Royal
   Proclamation of 1763 was not new; Arthur O'Meara, a minister and lawyer who

acted for the Allied Tribes of British Columbia in 1927 parliamentary hearings used this idea as the basis of his life's work on behalf of the British Columbia nations (see Mary Haig-Brown).

18 Elders might testify but be subject to interpretation by an expert witness. Further, those anthropologists most familiar with particular nations could be seen as "too close" to the nation to be objective (Culhane 366; see also Bruce Miller; Ray).

19 All the Indigenous languages of British Columbia are now critically endangered (Shaw).

20 His English has the charm found in other such productions, for example, the stories of two Yoruba men, Daniel Olorunfemi Fagunwa (1903–1963) and Amos Tutuola (1920–1997), which filter oral stories through learner English. Like Robinson, both these men were master storytellers in cultures overtaken by British colonialism. Tutuola's *The Palm-Wine Drinkard* was canonized by its publication by T.S. Eliot at Faber in 1952; both men were designated as literary ancestors by Wole Soyinka, winner of the Nobel Prize for Literature in 1986 (390). Thomas King's collection *One Good Story, That One* can be seen as a similar homage to Robinson (King, "Godzilla" 186–87).

21 The government banned the potlatch, the Sun Dance, and other traditional ceremonies from 1885 to 1951.

22 Carlson analyzes a somewhat different version of this story than the one published in *Write It* and discussed here ("Aboriginal Diplomacy" 170n7). I thank Wendy Wickwire for sending me a digitized oral version of another part of this story.

23 Rick Monture, in *We Share Our Matters* (3–5), tells a Haudenosaunee version of this story, which also features a good and a bad twin. Perhaps Robinson heard this story from one of the many Iroquois who moved west with the fur trade.

24 Other stories were circulating about literacy among the Okanagan. Bert Allison, an Okanagan Similkameen chief, told James Teit a story called "Coyote and the Paper" where Coyote lost a paper that God gave him: "If Coyote had not lost it, the Indians would now know writing, and the whites would not have had the opportunity to obtain written language" (Wickwire, Intro. *Living* 24).

25 Significant South Asian immigration into the interior of British Columbia began in 1904, consisting primarily of Sikh men from the Punjab who worked as loggers ("History," Canadian Sikh Heritage.ca). The Chinese, who arrived in numbers with the 1858 gold rush and then were recruited to complete the CPR, were a large percentage of the population when Robinson was a young man. Russian Doukhobors began settling in southern British Columbia on Okanagan traditional territory in 1908; by 1912, eight thousand had moved there.

26 Many of Robinson's stories focus on this ethic; for example, in one story a boy takes a stick to poke a chipmunk out from under a stump. The chipmunk transforms into a boy and says, "You think you're going to make a fun out of me," but "We both boy / So, it's better to be friends" (*Nature Power* 29). The chipmunk/boy and his grandfather, the stump under which he was hiding, give the boy the power not to be harmed by bullets. See Thom for the ways in which land was shared.

27 This theme of white curiosity, scientific development, and lack of respect for others is found in other works. Photographers try to get pictures of the Sun Dance in Thomas King's *Green Grass, Running Water*. In Eden Robinson's *Monkey Beach*, a little Haisla boy—influenced by the popular media—wants to take a picture of the sasquatch so he can sell it and get rich. One also thinks of the many anthropologists and photographers, including Edward S. Curtis and Harlan I. Smith (see Roy, *These Mysterious People*), who focused their lenses on sacred ceremonies. In Robinson's story, God prevents this intrusion.

28 Other urban nations, like Musqueam, were somewhat more fortunate. *Guerin v. the Queen* (1984) hinged on a large part of the Musqueam reserve that the Indian agent leased in 1958 to a golf club at less than market rates, concealing the details from the band (Reynolds). See Roy's "A History of the Site" for the dispossession of those living on desirable land—Kitsilano Point—in Vancouver (see also *Indigenous Foundations* for more on this land). Ironically, the surrounding neighbourhood is named after the chief who lived there, Kitsilano. The Squamish Nation recently received land and money as compensation.

29 Wickwire says that in another version Robinson attributed the discovery of the book to Edward Bent, of Shulus, near Merritt ("Driving" 34; see Carlson, "Orality" 50). Paull was an interpreter for the McKenna-McBride Commission. He worked in a law firm for several years, but if he had taken a law degree, he would have lost his Indian Status (Patterson 48; see also Dunlop).

30 The archives in the former Canadian Museum of Civilization, since December 2013 the Canadian Museum of History, were closed to the public in May 2013 (Slaney). The Harper government has also reduced access to Library and Archives Canada, limited the LAC mandate, and closed or privatized several government libraries. Padlocking is afoot (Turk).

31 Carlson, in his detailed analysis of a version of this story, connects Robinson's book to these collected papers ("Aboriginal Diplomacy" 167).

32 Earlier the chief trader at Fort Vancouver for the HBC, Douglas was Governor of Vancouver Island (1851–1864), and of the Colony of British Columbia (1858–1864). Bulwer-Lytton was a famous poet, playwright, and novelist. Lord Carnarvon is most famous for his involvement in the discovery of Tutankhamun's tomb in Egypt in 1922.

33 As well as the area covered by the Douglas Treaties on Vancouver Island (see Makmillen), Treaty 8 (1899) extends into northern British Columba.

34 This hot/cold distinction is also found in McLuhan, who was influenced by Lévi-Strauss (see James M. Curtis).

NOTES TO (IN)CONCLUSION

1 Gregory Bateson's *Steps toward an Ecology of Mind* (1972) is a central work. See also Seibt.

2 One police officer was killed by a shooter, who could not be identified. The inquest that determined this also stated that the attack on the protestors was unnecessary as there was no public danger. The province spent $108 million on this operation ("Report").

3 Regan notes that some of the statements in the RCAP report consolidated the myth of a beneficent Canada, for example: "The Canada that takes a proud place in the family of nations was made possible by the treaties. Our defining national characteristics are tolerance, pluralism and democracy. Were it not for the treaties, these defining myths might not have taken hold here" (qtd. 107). However, the RCAP report also contains important testimony, including some of the first public testimony about abuse in Indian residential schools. Notably, many Indigenous researchers and writers were involved in producing the document and many Indigenous people testified before its committees.

4 Both Gawker.com and the *New York Times* have moved to allow readers to vote to promote or demote comments, which leads to a more civil result (Konnikova). Some Canadian news outlets use this technique combined with a system that allows readers to report abuse as defined by rules for posting comments sometimes described as "community guidelines" (*Globe and Mail*) or "Community Code of Conduct" (*Toronto Star*).

5 Twitter, founded 2006; Tumblr founded 2007; Buzzfeed, 2006; the news aggregation website Huffington Post, founded 2005; Truthdig, founded 2005.

6 "On March 26, 2014, the Council of the Attawapiskat First Nation was informed by the Nishnawbe-Aski Police Service that the First Nation's former co-manager, Clayton Kennedy, had been charged with one count each of fraud over $5,000 and theft over $5,000" (Attawapiskat First Nation website, 31 Jan. 2015).

7 In 2014, a thirteen-year-old Cree girl wore a sweatshirt to school that read "Got Land?" on the front and "Thank an Indian" on the back. She was reportedly told that the message was "racist" and "offensive," but stood her (Treaty 4) ground ("Saskatchewan School Officials").

8 The "scoop-up" or "Sixties scoop" both refer to the practice of taking Aboriginal children from their families and putting them up for adoption outside their

communities. This, like sending them to residential school, fits the UN definition of genocide, Article 2e, "forcibly transferring children of the group to
another group" (United Nations).

9 Johnston survived the abuse he endured at St. Peter Claver Residential School
in Spanish, Ontario. See his interview with Sam McKegney (Johnston, "Indigenous Writing").

10 See also her *The People of the Kattawapiskat River* (2012) about Attawapiskat.
The 2012 federal budget made deep cuts to the budget of the NFB, as well as the
CBC, Library and Archives Canada, and the Department of Canadian Heritage
(see McCuaig). Of course, these agencies support settler-nationalist story-mak-
ing as well; see Regan on the CBC-TV series *Canada: A People's History* (104–5).

11 Indigenous people constantly use the phrase "the youth." Getting the old and the
young together is a vital part of knowledge transmission. Mainstream culture
isolates age groups in day care, school, university, sports teams, and care homes.

12 For example, Rebecca Belmore focused the public gaze during the 1988 Winter
Olympics in Calgary by sitting outside in –22°C cold as "Artifact 671B" in front
of the Thunder Bay Art Gallery. She was supporting the protest of the Lubicon
Cree in northern Alberta against Shell Oil's drilling on their traditional territories. As its contribution to the Olympics, Shell Oil had sponsored a major
exhibit, "The Spirit Sings: Artistic Traditions of Canada's First Peoples." She
used her body to draw attention to how mainstream representations carve off
sport and art from issues of land and resource extraction. The Lubicon land
dispute continues.

13 Phil Fontaine spoke out publicly about his own sexual abuse in a CBC televi-
sion interview in 1990, just before his election as grand chief of the Assembly of
Manitoba Chiefs ("Phil Fontaine's Shocking Testimony").

14 Similarly, the Covenant Chain needed to be regularly "polished," that is, reaf-
firmed (Woo 5). The "living tree" metaphor has been used for the Canadian
Constitution itself (Woo 18). It nicely combines the image of something majestic
and beautiful that grows slowly while changing annually.

15 This notion has more force in areas where treaties were made: only small areas
of British Columbia are covered by treaty.

16 See Long for more detail on the depth of bad faith with which these treaties
were first made and then ignored by Scott and other government officials.
Daniel G. MacMartin represented the province during the Treaty 9 negotiations
in Ontario. He accompanied the two federal treaty commissioners, Duncan
Campbell Scott and Samuel Stewart. His 1905 notebook records that oral promises were made that were not written in the treaty ("Daniel G. MacMartin").

17 See Wiebe, "Mistahimaskwa / Big Bear."

Works Cited

Adams, Howard. *Prison of Grass: Canada from a Native Point of View*. 2nd ed. Saska-toon: Fifth House, 1989. Print.

Akrigg, G.P.V., and Helen B. Akrigg. *British Columbia Place Names*. 3rd ed. Vancou-ver: U of British Columbia P, 1997. Print.

Akwesasne. "The Kaswentha/Two-Row Wampum." *Mohawk Council of Akwesasne*. N.p., n.d. Web. 13 Nov. 2012.

Alfred, Gerald R. *Heeding the Voices of Our Ancestors: Kahnawake Mohawk Politics and the Rise of Native Nationalism*. Don Mills: Oxford UP, 1995. Print.

Alfred, Taiaiake. *Peace, Power, Righteousness: An Indigenous Manifesto*. Don Mills: Oxford UP, 1999. Print.

———.(@Taiaiake). "Six Nations Chiefs Recover 1812 Wampum Belt Sold Off for Per-sonal Profit to American by Poet Pauline Johnson in 1800s" 22 July 2012. Tweet.

———. *Wasasé: Indigenous Pathways of Action and Freedom*. Toronto: U of Toronto P, 2005. Print.

Al-Kassim, Dina. *On Pain of Speech: Fantasies of the First Order and the Literary Rant*. Berkeley: U of California P, 2010. Print.

Anahareo [Gertrude Barnard]. *Devil in Deerskins: My Life with Grey Owl*. 1972. Ed. Sophie McCall. Winnipeg: U of Manitoba P, 2014. Print. First Voices, First Texts.

"Ancient Printing Press Resurrected for Yule." *The Native Voice* Dec. 1965: 4. Print.

Anderson, Benedict. *Imagined Communities: Reflections on the Origin and Spread of Nationalism*. Rev. ed. New York: Verso, 1991. Print.

Anderson, Elizabeth. "Feminist Epistemology and Philosophy of Science." *Stanford Encyclopedia of Philosophy*. Ed. Edward N. Zalta. Fall 2012. Web. 18 Mar. 2015.

Anderson, Mark Cronlund, and Carmen L. Robertson. *Seeing Red: A History of Natives in Canadian Newspapers*. Winnipeg: U of Manitoba P, 2011. Print.

Andrews, Jennifer. "Rethinking the Canadian Gothic: Reading Eden Robinson's *Monkey Beach*." Sugars and Turcotte 205–27.

Angus, Ian. "Louis Riel and English-Canadian Political Thought." *University of Toronto Quarterly* 74.4 (2005): 884–94. Print.

Antwi, Phanuel. "Hidden Signs, Haunting Shadows: Literary Currencies of Blackness in Upper Canada." Diss. McMaster University, 2011. Print.

Archibald, Jo-ann / Q'um Q'um Xiiem. *Indigenous Storywork: Educating the Heart, Body, Mind and Spirit.* Vancouver: U of British Columbia P, 2008. Print.

Arens, William. *The Man-Eating Myth: Anthropology and Anthropophagy.* 1979. New York: Oxford UP, 1981. Print.

Armitage, David. "Literature and Empire." *The Origins of Empire.* Ed. Nicholas Canny. Oxford: Oxford UP, 1998. 99–123. Print. The Oxford History of the British Empire. William Roger Louis, ed. in chief.

———. "The Red Atlantic." *Reviews in American History* 29 (2001): 479–86. Print.

Armour, David A. "Henry, Alexander." *Dictionary of Canadian Biography.* Vol. 6. U of Toronto/U Laval, 2003. Web. 3 Feb. 2013.

Armstrong, Jeannette. "Community: 'Sharing One Skin.'" *Paradigm Wars: Indigenous Peoples' Resistance to Globalization.* Ed. Jerry Mander and Victoria Tauli-Corpuz. San Francisco: Sierra Book Club, 2006. 35–39. Print.

———. "Land Speaking." *Speaking for the Generations: Native Writers on Writing.* Ed. Simon Ortiz. Tucson: U of Arizona, 1999. 175–94. Print.

———. *Slash.* Penticton: Theytus, 1985. Print.

Attawapiskat First Nation. N.p., n.d. Web. 1 Feb. 2015.

Attawapiskat First Nation v. Canada, 2012 FC 948. Web. 26 Jan. 2014.

"Attawapiskat Walkers on the Trail to Ottawa." *NetNewsledger.com.* NetNewsLedger, 16 Jan. 2014. Web. 9 Feb. 2014.

Attenborough, Richard, dir. *Grey Owl.* Perf. Pierce Brosnan. 20th Century Fox, 1999. Feature film.

Atwood, Margaret. "A Double-Bladed Knife: Subversive Laughter in Two Stories by Thomas King." *Canadian Literature* 124–25 (1990): 243–50. Print.

———. "The Grey Owl Syndrome." *Strange Things: The Malevolent North in Canadian Literature.* Oxford: Clarendon, 1995. 35–61. Print.

———. Introduction to *Survival* 2003, and Introduction to *Survival* 2012. "Survival: A Demi-Memoir." *Houseofanansi.com.* House of Anansi Press, n.d. PDF file. Web. 31 Dec. 2013.

———. *Survival: A Thematic Guide to Canadian Literature.* Toronto: Anansi, 1972. Print.

Axtell, James. "Scalps and Scalping." *Encyclopedia of North American Indians.* Ed. Frederick E. Hoxie. New York: Houghton Mifflin, 1996. 570–72. Print.

Backhouse, Constance. *Colour-Coded: A Legal History of Racism in Canada.* Toronto: U of Toronto P for the Osgoode Society for Canadian Legal History, 1999. Print.

Bailey, Norma, dir. *Women in the Shadows*. Prod. Christine Welsh and Signe Johannson. NFB, 1991. Documentary film.

Baker, Marie Annharte. "Borrowing Enemy Language: A First Nations Woman's Use of English." *Tracing the Lines: Reflections on Contemporary Poetics and Cultural Politics*. Ed. Maia Joseph, Christine Kim, Larissa Lai, and Christopher Lee. Vancouver: Talonbooks, 2012. 48–56. Print.

Baker, Mona. *In Other Words: A Coursebook on Translation*. London: Routledge, 1992. Print.

Bakker, Peter. *A Language of Our Own: The Genesis of Michif, the Mixed Cree-French Language of the Canadian Metis*. Oxford: Oxford UP, 1997. Print.

Ballstadt, Carl, ed. *Major John Richardson: A Selection of Reviews and Criticism*. Montreal: Lawrence M. Lande Foundation, McGill University, 1972. Print.

——. *The Search for English-Canadian Literature: An Anthology of Critical Articles from the Nineteenth and Early Twentieth Centuries*. Toronto: U of Toronto P, 1975. Print.

Barman, Jean. "Erasing of Indigenous Indigeneity in Vancouver." *BC Studies* 155 (2007): 3–30. Print.

——. "Race, Greed, and Something More: The Erasure of Urban Indigenous Space in Early Twentieth Century British Columbia." *Making Space: Settler and Colonial Perspectives on Land, Place, and Identity*. Ed. Tracey Banivauna-Mar and Penelope Edmonds. London: Palgrave Macmillan, 2010. 155–73. Print.

——. *Stanley Park's Secret: The Forgotten Families of Whoi Whoi, Kanaka Ranch, and Brockton Point*. Vancouver: Harbour, 2005. Print.

——. "Taming Aboriginal Sexuality." *Native Peoples and Colonialism*. Spec. issue of *BC Studies* 115/16 (1997/98): 237–66. Print.

——. *The West beyond the West: A History of British Columbia*. Rev. ed. Toronto: U of Toronto P, 1996. Print.

Barnholden, Michael. Introduction. *Gabriel Dumont Speaks*. Rev. 2nd ed. By Gabriel Dumont. Trans. Barnholden. Vancouver: Talonbooks, 2009. 11–35. Print.

Bateson, Gregory. *Steps toward an Ecology of Mind*. San Francisco: Chandler, 1972. Print.

Battiste, Marie. "Print Culture and Decolonizing the University: Indigenizing the Page: Part 1." *The Future of the Page*. Ed. Peter Stoicheff and Andrew Taylor. Toronto: U of Toronto P, 2004. 111–23. Print.

Baum, Bruce. *The Rise and Fall of the Caucasian Race: A Political History of Racial Identity*. New York: New York UP, 2006. Print.

Bautz, Annika. *The Reception of Jane Austen and Walter Scott: A Comparative Longitudinal Study*. London: Bloomsbury, 2007. Print.

Baxter v. Canada (Attorney General), 2006 CanLII 41673 (ON S.C.). Web. 17 April 2015.

Beal, Bob. "An Indian Chief, an English Tourist, a Doctor, a Reverend, and a Member of Parliament: The Journeys of Pasqua's Pictographs and the Meaning of Treaty Four." *Canadian Journal of Native Studies* 27.1 (2007): 109–88. Print.

Beasley, David R. *The Canadian Don Quixote: The Life and Works of Major John Richardson, Canada's First Novelist.* Erin: Porcupine's Quill, 1977. Print.

———. "Richardson, John." *Dictionary of Canadian Biography.* Vol. 8. U of Toronto/U Laval, 1985. Web. 10 April 2011.

Beauvoir, Simone de. *The Second Sex.* Trans. Constance Borde and Sheila Malovany-Chevallier. New York: Vintage, 2011. Print.

Benn, Carl. *The Iroquois in the War of 1812.* Toronto: U of Toronto P, 1998. Print.

Bennett, Jo-ann, and John W. Berry. "Cree Literacy in the Syllabic Script." *Literacy and Orality.* Ed. David R. Olson and Nancy Torrance. Cambridge: Cambridge UP, 1991. 90–104. Print.

Bennett, Paula Bernat. *Poets in the Public Sphere: The Emancipatory Project of American Women's Poetry, 1800–1900.* Princeton: Princeton UP, 2003. Print.

Bentley, D.M.R. "John Richardson: *Tecumseh.*" *Mimic Fires: Accounts of Early Long Poems on Canada.* Montreal: McGill-Queen's UP, 1994. 139–53. Print.

———. "Shadows in the Soul: Racial Haunting in the Poetry of Duncan Campbell Scott." *University of Toronto Quarterly* 75.2 (2006): 753–70. Print.

Berger, Carl. *Imperialism and Nationalism, 1884–1914: A Conflict in Canadian Thought.* Toronto: Copp Clark, 1969. Print.

Berkes, Fikret. *Sacred Ecology.* 2nd ed. New York: Routledge, 2012. Print.

Bhabha, Homi. "The Other Question: Stereotype, Discrimination, and the Discourse of Colonialism." *The Location of Culture.* London: Routledge, 1994. 66–84. Print.

Billinghurst, Jane. *Grey Owl: The Many Faces of Archie Belaney.* Vancouver: Greystone, 1999. Print.

Binnie-Clark, Georgina. *Women and Wheat.* 1914. Toronto: U of Toronto P, 1979. Print.

Birney, Earle. "Can. Lit." *The New Oxford Book of Canadian Verse.* Ed. Margaret Atwood. Toronto: Oxford UP, 1982. 116. Print.

Bitzer, Lloyd. "The Rhetorical Situation." *Philosophy and Rhetoric* 1 (1968): 1–14. Print.

Blake, Lynn. "Le Jeune, Jean-Marie-Raphaël." *Dictionary of Canadian Biography.* Vol. 15. U of Toronto/U Laval, 2005. Web. 5 Jan. 2014.

Blake, William. *The Marriage of Heaven and Hell.* 1790. *William Blake Archive.* Web. 12 Dec. 2013.

Blatchford, Christie. "Inevitable Puffery and Horse Manure Surrounds Hunger Strike while Real Aboriginal Problems Forgotten." *National Post* [Toronto]. Postmedia, 27 Dec. 2012. Web. 27 Jan. 2014.

Boone, Elizabeth Hill, and Walter D. Mignolo, eds. *Writing without Words: Alternative Literacies in Mesoamerica and the Andes*. Durham: Duke UP, 1994. Print.

Bordo, Jonathan. "Picture and Witness at the Site of the Wilderness." *Critical Inquiry* 26.2 (2000): 224–47. Print.

Borrows, John. *Canada's Indigenous Constitution*. Toronto: U of Toronto P, 2010. Print.

———. *Recovering Canada: The Resurgence of Indigenous Law*. Toronto: U of Toronto P, 2002. Print.

Borrows, John / Kegedonce. *Drawing Out Law: A Spirit's Guide*. Toronto: U of Toronto P, 2010. Print.

Bourdieu, Pierre. "The Force of Law: Towards a Sociology of the Juridical Field." *Hastings Law Journal* 38.5 (1987): 814–54. Print.

Boyden, Joseph. *The Orenda*. Toronto: Penguin, 2013. Print.

Brant, Beth. "The Good Red Road: Writing as Homecoming in Native Women's Writing." 1994. *New Contexts of Canadian Criticism*. Ed. Ajay Heble, Donna Palmateer Pennee, and J.R. (Tim) Struthers. Peterborough: Broadview, 1997. 175–87. Print.

Braun, Bruce. *The Intemperate Rainforest: Nature, Culture, and Power on Canada's West Coast*. Minneapolis: U of Minnesota P, 2002. Print.

Bray, Matt, and Ashley Thomson, eds. *Temagami: A Debate on Wilderness*. Toronto: Dundurn, 1996. Print.

Braz, Albert. *The False Traitor: Louis Riel in Canadian Culture*. Toronto: U of Toronto P, 2003. Print.

———. "The Modern Hiawatha: Grey Owl's Construction of His Aboriginal Self." *Auto /Biography in Canada: Critical Directions*. Ed. Julie Rak. Waterloo: Wilfrid Laurier UP, 2005. 53–68. Print.

———. "St. Archie of the Wilderness: Grey Owl's Account of his 'Natural' Conversion." *Other Selves: Animals in the Canadian Literary Imagination*. Ed. Janice Fiamengo. Ottawa: U of Ottawa P, 2007. 206–26. Print.

———. "The White Indian: Armand Garnet Ruffo's *Grey Owl* and the Spectre of Authenticity." *Journal of Canadian Studies* 36.4 (2001–2): 171–87. Print.

Brewer, Anthony. "Adam Smith's Stages of History." *Bristol Economics Discussion Papers* 08/601. University of Bristol, March 2008. Web. 19 Jan. 2014.

British Columbia. *Nisga'a Final Agreement*. Ministry of Aboriginal Relations, 9 Dec. 2013. Web. 16 Feb. 2014.

British Columbia. *Papers Connected with the Indian Land Question, 1850–1875*. Victoria: Government Printer, 1875. Rpt. with supplement, *Papers Connected with the Indian Land Question, 1877*, 1987. Print.

———. *Papers Relating to the Commission Appointed to Enquire into the Condition of the Indians of the North-West Coast*. Victoria: Government Printer, 1888. Web. 8 July 2014.

British Columbia Treaty Commission. BCTreaty.ca, n.d. Web. 9 July 2011.

Brizinski, Peggy. *Knots in a String: An Introduction to Native Studies in Canada*. 2nd ed. Saskatoon: University of Saskatchewan Extension, 1993. Print.

Brody, Hugh. *Maps and Dreams: Indians and the British Columbia Frontier*. Vancouver: Douglas and McIntyre, 1981. Print.

Brotherston, Gordon. *Book of the Fourth World: Reading the Native Americas through Their Literature*. Cambridge: Cambridge UP, 1992. Print.

Brown, Chester. *Louis Riel: A Comic-Strip Biography*. 1999–2003. Montreal: Drawn and Quarterly, 2006. Print.

Bruyneel, Kevin. "Exiled, Executed, Exalted: Louis Riel, *Homo Sacer* and the Production of Canadian Sovereignty." *Canadian Journal of Political Science* 43.3 (2010): 711–32. Print.

Buell, Lawrence. *The Environmental Imagination: Thoreau, Nature Writing, and the Formation of American Culture*. Cambridge: Harvard UP, Belknap, 1995. Print.

Bumsted, J.M. *Louis Riel v. Canada: The Making of a Rebel*. Winnipeg: Great Plains, 2001. Print.

Burke, Edmund. *On the Sublime and the Beautiful*. New York: P.F. Collier & Son, 1909–14. Vol. 24, Pt. 2. Harvard Classics. Bartleby.com, 2001. Web. 12 Dec. 2013.

Burton, Gideon. *Sylva Rhetoricae / The Forest of Rhetoric*. Brigham Young University, 2007. Web. 28 July 2012.

Butler, Judith. *Gender Trouble: Feminism and the Subversion of Identity*. New York: Routledge, 1999. Print.

———. Interview with Peter Osborne and Lynne Segla. *Radical Philosophy* 67 (1994). Web. 18 Jan. 2013.

Calder et al. v. Attorney-General of British Columbia, [1973] S.C.R. 313. Web. 15 Dec. 2012.

Calloway, Colin G. *White People, Indians, and Highlanders: Tribal Peoples and Colonial Encounters in Scotland and America*. Oxford: Oxford UP, 2008. Print.

Campbell, Maria. *Halfbreed*. Toronto: McClelland & Stewart, 1973. Print.

———. *Stories of the Road Allowance People*. Penticton: Theytus, 1995. Print.

Canada. "The Battle at Duck Lake, March 26, 1885." *Virtual Museum of Canada*. Canadian Museum of History, n.d. PDF file. Web. 24 Jan. 2014.

Canada. [Dominion Lands Act, 1872] An Act Respecting the Public Lands of the Dominion. *Acts of the Parliament of the Dominion of Canada.* Ottawa: Brown Chamberlin, 1874. Print.

Canada. "First Nations Involvement in the 1885 Resistance." *Virtual Museum of Canada.* Canadian Museum of History, n.d. Web. 24 Jan. 2014.

Canada. [Indian Act] An Act to Amend and Consolidate the Laws Respecting Indians. 1876. Aboriginal Affairs and Northern Development. Web. 22 March 2015.

Canada. Manitoba Act. 33 Victoria c. 3, 1870. *Wikisource.* Wikimedia Foundation, n.d. Web. 6 Mar. 2014.

Canada [The Province of Canada]. An Act to Encourage the Gradual Civilization of Indian Tribes in this Province, and to Amend the Laws Relating to Indians. 5th Parl., 3rd sess. 1857. *Wikisource.* Wikimedia Foundation, n.d. Web. 14 Dec. 2012.

Canada. Aboriginal Affairs and Northern Development. *Canada's Statement of Support on the United Nations Declaration on the Rights of Indigenous Peoples.* Ottawa: Aboriginal Affairs and Northern Development Canada, 12 Nov. 2010. Web. 30 Mar. 2014.

———. *The Government of Canada's Approach to Implementation of the Inherent Right and the Negotiation of Aboriginal Self-Government.* Ottawa: Aboriginal Affairs and Northern Development Canada, 15 Sept. 2010. Web. 10 April 2011.

———. *Report of the Royal Commission on Aboriginal Peoples.* Ottawa: The Commission, 1996. Web. 17 April 2015.

———. [White Paper, 1969] *Statement of the Government of Canada on Indian Policy.* Ottawa: Queen's Printer, 1969. Web. 17 April 2015.

Canada. Citizenship and Immigration. "Towards the Canadian Citizenship Act." *Forging Our Legacy: Canadian Citizenship and Immigration, 1900–1977.* 1 July 2006. Web. 23 April 2015.

Canada. Statistics Canada. *Aboriginal Statistics at a Glance.* Catalogue no. 89-645-X. Ottawa: Statistics Canada, 21 June 2010. Web. 11 Jan. 2014.

———. "An Increasingly Urban Population." *2006 Census: Aboriginal Peoples in Canada in 2006: Inuit, Métis and First Nations.* Ottawa: Minister of Industry, 2008. Web. 13 April 2015.

Cardinal, Harold. "A Canadian What the Hell's It All About." *The Rebirth of Canada's Indians.* Edmonton: Hurtig, 1977. 7–16. Print.

———. *The Rebirth of Canada's Indians.* Edmonton: Hurtig, 1977. Print.

———. *The Unjust Society: The Tragedy of Canada's Indians.* Edmonton: Hurtig, 1969. Print.

Cardinal, Harold, and Walter Hildebrandt. *Treaty Elders of Saskatchewan: Our Dream Is that Our Peoples Will One Day Be Recognized as Nations.* Calgary: U of Calgary P, 2000. Print.

Cariou, Warren. "Dances with Rigoureau." *Troubling Tricksters: Revisioning Critical Conversations*. Ed. Deanna Reder and Linda M. Morra. Waterloo: Wilfrid Laurier UP, 2010. 157–67. Print.

———. *Lake of the Prairies: A Story of Belonging*. Toronto: Doubleday, 2002. Print.

Carlson, Keith Thor. "Aboriginal Diplomacy: The Queen Comes to Canada, and Coyote Goes to London." *Indigenous Diplomacies*. Ed. J. Marshall Bier. Hampshire: Palgrave MacMillan, 2009. 155–70. Print.

———. "The Indians and the Crown: Aboriginal Memories of Royal Promises in Pacific Canada." *Majesty in Canada: Essays on the Role of Royalty*. Ed. Colin MacMillan Coates. Toronto: Dundurn, 2006. 68–95. Print.

———. "Orality about Literacy: The 'Black and White' of Salish History." *Orality and Literacy: Reflections across Disciplines*. Ed. Carlson, Kristina Fagan, and Natalia Khanenko-Friesen. Toronto: U of Toronto P, 2011. 43–69. Print.

———. *The Power of Place, the Problem of Time: Aboriginal Identity and Historical Consciousness in the Cauldron of Colonialism*. Toronto: U of Toronto P, 2010. Print.

———. "Rethinking Dialogue and History: The King's Promise and the 1906 Aboriginal Delegation to London." *Native Studies Review* 16.2 (2005): 1–38. Web. 22 March 2015.

Carpenter, Cari M. "'A Woman to Let Alone': E. Pauline Johnson and the Performance of Anger." *Seeing Red: Anger, Sentimentality and American Indians*. Columbus: Ohio State UP, 2008. 54–147. Print.

Carter, Sarah. *The Importance of Being Monogamous: Marriage and Nation Building in Western Canada to 1915*. Edmonton: U of Alberta P, 2008. Print.

———. Introduction. *Two Months in the Camp of Big Bear*. By Theresa Delaney and Theresa Gowanlock. Ed. Carter. Regina: Canadian Plains Research Center, U of Regina, 1999. vii–xxxviii. Print.

Casselman, Alexander Clark. Introduction. *Richardson's War of 1812*. 1842. Toronto: Historical, 1902. v–lviii. Print.

Cassidy, Oliver. "B.C.'s Treaty Process in Limbo after Premier Resets Table." *Province* [Vancouver]. Postmedia Network, 27 March 2015. Web. 17 April 2015.

Castellano, Marlene Brant, Linda Archibald, and Mike DeGagne, eds. *From Truth to Reconciliation: Transforming the Legacy of Residential Schools*. Rev. ed. Ottawa: Aboriginal Healing Foundation, 2011. Print.

Castillo, Susan. *Colonial Encounters in New World Writing, 1500–1786: Performing America*. New York: Routledge, 2006. Print.

Castricano, Jodey. "Learning to Talk with Ghosts: Canadian Gothic and the Poetics of Haunting in Eden Robinson's *Monkey Beach*." *University of Toronto Quarterly* 75.2 (2006): 801–13. Print.

Catapano, Andrea Lucille. "The Rising of the Ongwehònwe: Sovereignty, Identity, and Representation on the Six Nations Reserve." PhD diss. Stony Brook University, 2007. Print.

Chamberlin, J. Edward. *Harrowing of Eden: White Attitudes to North American Natives*. Toronto: Fitzhenry & Whiteside, 1975. Print.

———. *If This Is Your Land, Where Are Your Stories? Finding Common Ground.* Toronto: Knopf, 2003. Print.

Chambers, Lori. *Married Women and Property Law in Victorian Canada*. Toronto: U of Toronto P for Osgoode Society for Canadian Legal History, 1997. Print.

Chapin, David. "Gender and Indian Masquerade in the Life of Grey Owl." *American Indian Quarterly* 24.1 (2000): 91–109. Print.

Charland, Maurice. "Constitutive Rhetoric: The Case of the *Peuple Québécois*." *The Quarterly Journal of Speech* 73.2 (1987): 133–50. Print.

———. "Louis Riel's *Ethos* and the *Différend*." *Riel's Defence: Perspectives on His Speeches*. Ed. Hans V. Hansen. Montreal: McGill-Queen's UP, 2014. 264–79. Print.

Charlebois, Peter. *The Life of Louis Riel*. Toronto: NC, 1975. Print.

Chartrand, Paul L.A.H. *Manitoba's Metis Settlement Scheme of 1870*. Saskatoon: Native Law Centre, University of Saskatchewan, 1991. Print.

Chen, Mel Y. *Animacies: Biopolitics, Racial Mattering, and Queer Affect*. Durham: Duke UP, 2012. Print.

Chiefswood National Historical Site. 10 April 2013. Text on informational display.

Chow, Rey. *The Protestant Eth(n)ic and the Spirit of Capitalism*. New York: Columbia UP, 2002. Print.

"Civilization." *Oxford English Dictionary*. 3rd ed. Oxford University Press, n.d. Web. 15 Feb. 2014.

Clarke, C.K. "A Critical Study of the Case of Louis Riel." Pt. 1. *Queen's Quarterly* 12.4 (1905): 379–88. Pt. 2. *Queen's Quarterly* 12.5 (1905): 14–25. Print.

Clifford, James, and George E. Marcus, eds. *Writing Culture: The Poetics and Politics of Ethnography*. Berkeley: U of California P, 1968. Print.

Coe, Michael D. *Breaking the Maya Code*. 3rd ed. London: Thames and Hudson, 2012. Print.

Coleman, Daniel. "Epistemological Crosstalk: Between Melancholia and Spiritual Cosmology in David Chariandy's *Soucouyant* and Lee Maracle's *Daughters Are Forever*." *Crosstalk: Canadian and Global Imaginaries in Dialogue*. Ed. Diana Brydon and Marta Dvorák. Waterloo: Wilfrid Laurier UP, 2012. 53–72. Print.

———. *White Civility: The Literary Project of English Canada*. Toronto: U of Toronto P, 2006. Print.

Colley, Linda. *Captives: Britain, Empire and the World, 1600–1850*. London: Jonathan Cape, 2002. Print.

Comeau-Vasilopoulos, Gayle M. "Oronhyatekha." *Dictionary of Canadian Biography*. Vol. 13. U of Toronto/U Laval, 1994. Web. 10 Nov. 2012.

Conrad, Joseph. *Heart of Darkness*. 2nd ed. Ed. D.C.R.A. Goonetilleke. Peterborough: Broadview, 1999. Print.

Cooper, James Fenimore. *The Last of the Mohicans*. 1826. Harmondsworth: Penguin, 1986. Print.

Cooper, Karen Coody. *Spirited Encounters: American Indians Protest Museum Policies and Practices*. Lanham: AltaMira, 2008. Print.

Copway, George. *The Life, History, and Travels of Kah-Ge-Ga-Gah-Bowh (George Copway), a Young Indian Chief of the Ojebwa Nation*. Albany: Weed and Parsons, 1847. *Internet Archive*. Web. 12 Jan. 2014.

Coulthard, Glen S. "Subjects of Empire: Indigenous Peoples and the 'Politics of Recognition' in Canada." *Contemporary Political Theory* 6 (2007): 437–60. Print.

"Cree Youth from Northern Quebec Reach Ottawa after 1500km Trek." *Globe and Mail* [Toronto]. Globe and Mail, 25 March 2013. Web. 9 July 2014.

Cronk, Douglas. Introduction. *Wacousta or, The Prophecy: A Tale of the Canadas*. By John Richardson. Ottawa: Carleton UP, 1987. xvii–lvi. Print. Centre for Editing Early Canadian Texts, 4.

Cruikshank, Julie. "Invention of Anthropology in British Columbia's Supreme Court: Oral Tradition as Evidence in Delgamuukw v. BC." *BC Studies* 95 (1992): 25–42. Print.

———. *The Social Life of Stories: Narrative and Knowledge in the Yukon Territory*. Vancouver: U of British Columbia P, 1998. Print.

Culhane, Dara. *The Pleasure of the Crown: Anthropology, Law and First Nations*. Vancouver: Talonbooks, 1998. Print.

Curtis, Edward S. *The North American Indian*. 1907–1930. *Northwestern University Digital Library Collections*. Web. 5 Aug. 2012.

Curtis, James M. "Marshall McLuhan and French Structuralism." *Boundary 2* 1.1 (1970): 134–46. Print.

Daly, Richard. *Our Box Was Full: An Ethnography for the Delgaamukw Plaintiffs*. Vancouver: U of British Columbia P, 2005. Print.

"Daniel G. MacMartin." *Wikipedia*. Wikimedia Foundation, n.d. Web. 5 Jan. 2014.

Daschuk, Peter. *Clearing the Plains: Disease, Politics of Starvation and the Loss of Aboriginal Life*. Regina: U of Regina P, 2013. Print.

Davey, Frank. Introduction. *From There to Here: A Guide to English-Canadian Literature since 1960*. Erin: Porcepic, 1974. 11–25. Print. Our Nature, Our Voices, Vol. 2.

———. "Surviving the Paraphrase." *Canadian Literature* 17 (1976): 5–13. Print.

David, Johnny. *"Hang on to These Words": Johnny David's Delgamuukw Evidence.* Ed. Antonia Mills. Toronto: U of Toronto P, 2005. Print.

Davidson, William McCartney. *Louis Riel 1844–1885.* Calgary: The Albertan, 1995. Print.

Dawson, Carrie. "The 'I' in Beaver: Sympathetic Identification and Self-Representation in Grey Owl's *Pilgrims of the Wild.*" *Five Emus to the King of Siam: Environment and Empire.* Ed. Helen Tiffin. Amsterdam: Rodopi, 2007. 113–29. Print.

———. "Never Cry Fraud: Remembering Grey Owl, Rethinking Imposture." *Essays on Canadian Writing* 65 (1998): n. pag. Web. 3 Dec. 2012.

Daymond, Douglas, and Leslie Monkman. Introduction. *Tecumseh: A Poem in Four Cantos.* By John Richardson. 1828. London: Canadian Poetry, 1992. xi–xlviii. Print.

Dean, Misao. *Inheriting a Canoe Paddle: The Canoe in Discourses of English-Canadian Nationalism.* Toronto: U of Toronto P, 2013. Print.

Deleuze, Gilles, and Félix Guattari. *Anti-Oedipus: Capitalism and Schizophrenia.* Trans. Robert Hurley, Mark Seem, and Helen R. Lane. New York: Viking, 1977. Print.

Delgamuukw v. British Columbia, [1997] 3 S.C.R. 1010. Web. 14 Dec. 2012.

Deloria, Philip. *Playing Indian.* New Haven: Yale UP, 1998. Print.

Deloria Jr., Vine. "Marginal and Submarginal." *Indigenizing the Academy: Transforming Scholarship and Empowering Communities.* Ed. Devon Abbott Mihesuah and Angela Cavender Wilson. Lincoln: U of Nebraska P, 2005. 16–30. Print.

Derrida, Jacques. *Limited Inc.* Trans. Samuel Weber and Jeffrey Mehlman. Evanston: Northwestern UP, 1988. Print.

———. *Of Grammatology.* Trans. Gayatri Spivak. Baltimore: Johns Hopkins UP, 1976. Print.

Deur, Douglas, and Nancy J. Turner, eds. *Keeping It Living: Traditions of Plant Life and Cultivation on the Northwest Coast of North America.* Seattle: U of Washington P, 2005. Print.

Dewar, Jonathan R. "Fringes, Imposture, and Connection: Armand Garnet Ruffo's *Grey Owl: The Mystery of Archie Belaney* and 'Communitist' Literature." *Creating Community: A Roundtable on Canadian Aboriginal Literature.* Ed. Renate Eigenbrod and Jo-ann Episkenew. Penticton: Theytus, 2002. 255–73. Print.

Dewart, Edward Hartley. Introduction. *Selections from Canadian Poets.* Montreal: Lovell, 1864. ix–xix. *Early Canadiana Online.* Web. 6 Mar. 2014.

Dickason, Olive P. *The Myth of the Savage and the Beginnings of French Colonialism in the Americas.* Edmonton: U of Alberta P, 1984. Print.

Dickson, Lovat. *The Green Leaf: A Tribute to Grey Owl.* 2nd ed. London: Lovat Dickson, 1938. Print.

——. *Wilderness Man: The Strange Story of Grey Owl.* 1973. Toronto: General, 1991. Print.

Dorion, Leah, and Darren Préfontaine. Introduction. *Metis Legacy.* Regina: Pemmican, 2000. 13–36. Print.

Dorland, Michael, and Maurice Charland. *Law, Rhetoric and Irony in the Formation of Canadian Civil Culture.* Toronto: U of Toronto P, 2002. Print.

Dowd, Gregory Evans. *War under Heaven: Pontiac, the Indian Nations, and the British Empire.* Baltimore: Johns Hopkins UP, 2002. Print.

Drake, Benjamin. *Tecumseh and His Brother the Prophet with a Historical Sketch of the Shawanoe Indians.* Cincinnati: Morgan, 1841. *Internet Archive.* Web. 17 April 2015.

Duff, Oliver, and Harry Stoneley. "Brothers Reunited: The Fabulous Attenborough Boys." *Independent* [London, UK]. Independent Print, 14 July 2006. Web. 28 Dec. 2012.

Duffy, Dennis. *A Tale of Sad Reality: John Richardson's* Wacousta. Don Mills: ECW, 1991. Print.

——. *A World under Sentence: John Richardson and the Interior.* Don Mills: ECW, 1996. Print.

Dumont, Marilyn. *A Really Good Brown Girl.* London: Brick, 1996. Print.

Dunlop, H.F. *Andy Paull: As I Knew Him and Understood His Times.* Vancouver: Standard, 1983. Print.

"Durham Report." *Canadian Encyclopedia.* Historica Foundation, 7 Feb. 2006. Web. 8 Jan. 2014.

"Ecosystem." *Oxford English Dictionary.* 3rd ed. Oxford University Press, n.d. Web. 15 Dec. 2013.

Edwards, Brendan F.R. "'I Have Lots of Help Behind Me, Lots of Books to Convince You': Andy Paull and the Value of Literacy in English." *BC Studies* 164 (2009–10): 7–25. Web. 13 Feb. 2012.

Edwards, Brendan Frederick R. *Paper Talk: A History of Libraries, Print Culture and Aboriginal Peoples in Canada before 1960.* Lanham, MD: Scarecrow, 2004. Print.

Edwards, Justin D. *Gothic Canada: Reading the Spectre of a National Literature.* Edmonton: U of Alberta P, 2005. Print.

Edwards, Mary Jane. "Drummond, William Henry." *Dictionary of Canadian Biography.* Vol. 13. U of Toronto/U Laval, 2003. Web. 3 Nov. 2012.

"Edward S. Curtis." *Wikipedia.* Wikimedia Foundation, n.d. Web. 17 Dec. 2013.

Ellingson, Ter. *The Myth of the Noble Savage.* Berkeley: U of California P, 2001. Print.

Epp, Roger. "We Are All Treaty People: History, Reconciliation, and the 'Settler Problem.'" *We Are All Treaty People: Prairie Essays.* Edmonton: U of Alberta P, 2008. 121–41. Print.

Erickson, Bruce. *Canoe Nation: Nature, Race and the Making of a Canadian Icon.* Vancouver: U of British Columbia P, 2013. Print.

Fabian, Johannes, and Matti Bunzi. *Time and the Other: How Anthropology Makes Its Object.* 1983. New York: Columbia UP, 2002. Print.

Fagan, Kristina. "Tewatatha:wi: Aboriginal Nationalism in Taiaiake Alfred's *Peace, Power, Righteousness: An Indigenous Manifesto." American Indian Quarterly* 28.1/2 (2004): 12–29. Print.

———. "'Well Done Old Half Breed Woman': Lydia Campbell and the Labrador Literary Tradition." *Papers of the Bibliographical Society of Canada* 48.1 (2010): 49–76. Print.

Farrell, David R. "Askin, John." *Dictionary of Canadian Biography.* Vol. 5. U of Toronto/U Laval, 2003. Web. 10 April 2011.

"Fate of the Red Man." *Ottawa Daily Free Press* 21 June 1894: 3.

"Feds Aware of Attawapiskat Crisis for Years." *CBC News.* CBC/Radio-Canada, 3 Dec. 2011. Web. 27 Jan. 2014.

Fee, Margery. "English-Canadian Literary Criticism, 1890–1950: Defining and Establishing a National Literature." PhD diss. U of Toronto, 1981. Print.

———. "Publication, Performances, and Politics: The 'Indian Poems' of E. Pauline Johnson / Tekahionwake (1861–1913) and Duncan Campbell Scott (1862–1947)." *Anthologizing Canadian Literature: Theoretical and Cultural Perspectives.* Ed. Robert Lecker. Waterloo: Wilfrid Laurier UP, 2015. 51–77. Print.

———. "Rewriting Anthropology and Identifications on the North Pacific Coast: The Work of George Hunt, William Beynon, Franz Boas and Marius Barbeau." *Australian Literary Studies* 25.4 (2010): 17–32. Print.

———. "Romantic Nationalism and the Image of Native People in Contemporary English-Canadian Literature." *The Native in Literature: Canadian and Comparative Perspectives.* Ed. Thomas King, Cheryl Calver, and Helen Hoy. Toronto: ECW, 1987. 15–33. Print.

———. "The Trickster Moment, Cultural Appropriation and the Liberal Imagination in Canada." *Troubling Tricksters: Revisiting Critical Conversations.* Ed. Deanna Reder and Linda Morra. Waterloo: Wilfrid Laurier UP, 2010. 59–76. Print.

Feit, Harvey A. "Recognizing Co-Management as Co-governance: Visions and Histories of Governance at James Bay." *Anthropologica* 47 (2005): 266–88. Print.

Fenton, William N. "Return of Eleven Wampum Belts to the Six Nations Confederacy on Grand River, Canada." *Ethnohistory* 16.4 (1989): 392–410. Print.

Fidler, Dick. "Red Power in Canada." *Socialist History Project: Documenting the Revolutionary Socialist Tradition in Canada.* South Branch Publishing, n.d. Web. 27 Aug. 2012.

"Films on Grey Owl." *Canadian Film Encyclopedia.* Film Reference Library, Toronto International Film Festival, n.d. Web. 16 Feb. 2014.

Findlay, L.M. "Extraordinary Renditions: Translating the Humanities Now." *Retooling the Humanities: The Culture of Research of Canadian Universities*. Ed. Daniel Coleman and Smaro Kamboureli. Edmonton: U of Alberta P, 2011. 41–57. Print.

Finnegan, Ruth H. "Not by Words Alone: Reclothing the 'Oral.'" *Technology, Literacy, and the Evolution of Society: Implications of the Work of Jack Goody*. Ed. David R. Olson and Michael Cole. Mahwak, NJ: Erlbaum, 2006. 265–87. Print.

Flanagan. Thomas. Introduction. *The Collected Writings of Louis Riel/Les écrits complets de Louis Riel*. 5 vols. Ed. George F.G. Stanley. Edmonton: U of Alberta P, 1985. xxxv–lii. Print.

———. *Louis "David" Riel: "Prophet of the New World."* Rev. ed. Toronto: U of Toronto P, 1996. Print.

———. "Louis Riel: Was He Really Crazy?" *1885 and After: Native Society in Transition*. Ed. F. Laurie Barron and James B. Waldram. Regina: U of Regina, Canadian Plains Research Center, 1986. 105–20. Print.

———. *Riel and the Rebellion: 1885 Reconsidered*. 2nd ed. Toronto: U of Toronto P, 2000. Print.

Fontaine v. Canada (Attorney General), 2014 ONSC 5292 (CanLII). Web. 17 April 2015.

Foot, Paul. *Red Shelley*. London: Sidgewick and Jackson, 1980. Print.

Foster, Hamar. "'We Are Not O'Meara's Children': Law, Lawyers, and the First Campaign for Aboriginal Title in British Columbia, 1908–1928." Foster, Raven, and Webber 61–84. Print.

Foster, Hamar, Heather Raven, and Jeremy Webber. *Let Right Be Done: Aboriginal Title, the Calder Case, and the Future of Indigenous Rights*. Vancouver: U of British Columbia P, 2007. Print.

Foucault, Michel. *The Archaeology of Knowledge and the Discourse on Language*. Trans. A.M. Sheridan Smith. New York: Pantheon, 1972. Print.

———. *Discipline and Punish: The Birth of the Prison*. 2nd ed. Trans. Alan Sheridan. New York: Random House Vintage, 1995. Print.

———. *The Foucault Reader*. Ed. Paul Rabinow. New York: Pantheon, 1984. Print.

Fox, L. Chris. "Geometries of Nation-Building: Triangulating Female Homosociality in Richardson's *Wacousta*." *Studies in Canadian Literature* 27.2 (2002): 5–28. Web. 15 July 2014.

Francis, Daniel. *The Imaginary Indian: The Image of the Indian in Canadian Culture*. Vancouver: Arsenal Pulp, 1992. Print.

Freeman, Victoria. *Distant Relations: How My Ancestors Colonized North America*. Toronto: McClelland & Stewart, 2000. Print.

Friesen, Gerald. Rev. of *The Collected Writings of Louis Riel*. *Canadian Historical Review* 69 (1985): 89–93. Print.

Frye, Northrop. *The Bush Garden: Essays on the Canadian Imagination*. 1971. 2nd ed. Introd. Linda Hutcheon. Toronto: Anansi, 1995. Print.

———. "Sharing the Continent." 1977. *Divisions on a Ground*. Ed. James Polk. Toronto: Anansi, 1982. 57–70. Print.

Fulford, Timothy. *Romantic Indians: Native Americans, British Literature, and Transatlantic Culture, 1756–1830*. Oxford: Oxford UP, 2006. Print.

Fulford, Timothy, and Kevin Hutchings. "The Indian Atlantic." Introduction. *Native Americans and Anglo-American Culture, 1750–1850*. Ed. Fulford and Hutchings. Cambridge: Cambridge UP, 2009. 1–38. Print.

Gagnon, Monika Kin. *Other Conundrums: Race, Culture and Canadian Art*. Vancouver: Arsenal Pulp, 2000. Print.

Gallagher, William. Rev. of *Grey Owl* (1999). *BBC Movie Reviews*. British Broadcasting Corporation, 31 Oct. 2000. Web. 19 Dec. 2012.

Garroutte, Eva Marie. *Real Indians: Identity and the Survival of Native America*. Berkeley: U of California P, 2003. Print.

Gaudry, Adam. "The Métis-ization of Canada: The Process of Claiming Louis Riel, Métissage, and the Métis People as Canada's Mythical Origin." *Aboriginal Policy Studies* 2.2 (2013): 64–87. Print.

Gentner, Dedre, and Susan Goldin-Meadow, eds. *Language in Mind: Advances in the Study of Language and Thought*. Cambridge: MIT P, 2003. Print.

George III. "Royal Proclamation." 1763. *Wikisource*. Wikimedia Foundation, n.d. Web. 6 Mar. 2014.

Gerson, Carole. *Canadian Women in Print, 1750–1918*. Waterloo: Wilfrid Laurier UP, 2011. Print.

———. "'The Most Canadian of All Canadian Poets': Pauline Johnson and the Construction of a National Literature." *Canadian Literature* 158 (1998): 90–107. Print.

———. "Postcolonialism Meets Book History: Pauline Johnson and Imperial London." *Home-Work: Postcolonialism, Pedagogy, and Canadian Literature*. Ed. Cynthia Sugars. Ottawa: U of Ottawa P, 2004. 423–39. Print.

———. *A Purer Taste: The Writing and Reading of Fiction in Nineteenth-Century Canada*. Toronto: U of Toronto P, 1989. Print.

Gerson, Carole, and Veronica Strong-Boag. Introduction. *E. Pauline Johnson / Tekahionwake: Collected Poems and Selected Prose*. Ed. Gerson and Strong-Boag. Toronto: U of Toronto P, 2002. xiii–xliv. Print.

Gibb, Sandra. *The Covenant Chain: Indian Ceremonial and Trade Silver*. Ottawa: National Museums, 1980. Print.

Gibbons, Luke. "'Subtilized into Savages': Edmund Burke, Progress and Primitivism." *The South Atlantic Quarterly* 100.1 (2001): 83–109. Print.

Gill, Harold B. Jr. "Colonial Germ Warfare." *Colonial Williamsburg*. Colonial Williamsburg Foundation, 2004. Web. 13 Feb. 2013.

Gilmore, Scott. "Out of Sight, Out of Mind: Canada Has a Race Problem Worse than America's. Why Is This Not a National Crisis?" *Maclean's* 2 Feb. 2015. 24–25. Print.

Giltrow, Janet. "Ironies of Politeness in Anita Brookner's *Hotel du Lac*." *Ambiguous Discourse: Feminist Narratology and British Women Writers*. Ed. Kathy Mezei. Chapel Hill: U of North Carolina P, 1996. 215–37. Print.

Gingell, Susan. "Teaching the Talk That Walks on Paper: Oral Traditions and Textualized Orature in the Canadian Literature Classroom." *Home-work: Postcolonialism, Pedagogy, and Canadian Literature*. Ed. Cynthia Sugars. Ottawa: U of Ottawa P, 2004. 285–300. Print.

Gingell, Susan, and Wendy Roy. "Opening the Door to Transdisciplinary, Multimodal Communication." Introduction. *Listening Up, Writing Down and Looking Beyond: Interfaces of the Oral, Written and Visual*. Ed. Gingell and Roy. Waterloo: Wilfrid Laurier UP, 2012. 1–50. Print.

Gleeson, Kristin L. "Blazing Her Own Trail: Anahareo's Rejection of Euro-Canadian Stereotypes." *Recollecting: Lives of Aboriginal Women of the Canadian Northwest and Borderlands*. Ed. Sarah Carter and Patricia Cormack. Edmonton: AU, 2011. 287–311. Print.

Goddard, Ives, ed. *Languages*. Washington: Smithsonian, 1997. Print. Handbook of the American Indian, Vol. 17.

Godlewska, Anne, Jackie Moore, and C. Drew Bednasek. "Cultivating Ignorance of Aboriginal Realities." *Canadian Geographer* 54.4 (2010): 417–40. Print.

Goldberg-Hiller, Jonathan, and Noenoe K. Silva. "Sharks and Pigs: Animating Hawaiian Sovereignty against the Anthropological Machine." *South Atlantic Quarterly* 110.2 (2011): 429–46. Print.

Goldie, Terry. *Fear and Temptation: The Image of the Indigene in Canadian, Australian, and New Zealand Literatures*. Montreal: McGill-Queen's UP, 1989. Print.

Goldman, Marlene. *Dispossession: Haunting in Canadian Fiction*. Montreal: McGill-Queen's UP, 2012. Print.

Gough, Barry M. *Gunboat Frontier: British Maritime Authority and Northwest Coast Indians, 1846–1890*. Vancouver: U of British Columbia P, 1984. Print.

Goulet, George R.D. *The Trial of Louis Riel: Justice and Mercy Denied. A Critical Legal and Political Analysis*. Calgary: Tellwell, 1999. Print.

Grace, Sherrill E. *Canada and the Idea of North*. Montreal: McGill-Queen's UP, 2002. Print.

Graff, Harvey J. *The Literacy Myth: Cultural Integration and Social Structure in the Nineteenth Century*. Rev. ed. New Brunswick, NJ: Transaction, 1991. Print.

Grant, George. *Lament for a Nation: The Defeat of Canadian Nationalism*. Toronto: McClelland & Stewart, 1965. Print.

Gray, Charlotte. *Flint and Feather: The Life and Times of E. Pauline Johnson*. Toronto: HarperFlamingo, 2002. Print.

Greensmith, Cameron. "Pathologizing Indigeneity in the Caledonia 'Crisis.'" *Canadian Journal of Disability Studies* 1.2 (2012): 19–42. Print.

Grey Owl [Archibald Belaney]. *The Men of the Last Frontier*. 1931. Toronto: Macmillan, 1989. Print.

———. *Pilgrims of the Wild*. 1935. New York: Scribner's, 1971. Print.

———. *Tales of an Empty Cabin*. 1936. Toronto: Macmillan, 1989. Print.

Griffiths, Linda, and Maria Campbell. *The Book of Jessica: A Theatrical Transformation*. Toronto: Coach House, 1989. Print.

Groarke, Paul. "Reconstructing the Substantive Argument in Louis Riel's Address to the Jury." *Riel's Defence: Perspectives on His Speeches*. Ed. Hans V. Hansen. Montreal: McGill-Queen's UP, 2014. 204–23. Print.

Grosswiler, Paul, ed. *Transforming McLuhan: Cultural, Critical, and Postmodern Perspectives*. New York: Peter Lang, 2010. Print.

Groulx, Patrice. *Pièges de mémoire: Dollard des Ormeaux, les Amerindiens, et nous*. Gatineau: Vents d'Ouest, 1998. Print.

Guerin v. The Queen, [1984] 2 S.C.R. 335. Web. 28 Mar. 2015.

Gunew, Sneja. "Between Auto/Biography and Theory: Can 'Ethnic Abjects' Write Theory?" *Comparative Literature Studies* 42.4 (2005): 363–78. Print.

———. "Culture, Gender and the Author-Function: 'Wongar's *Walg*.'" *Southern Review* 20.3 (1987): 261–70. Print.

———. *Haunted Nations: The Colonial Dimensions of Multiculturalisms*. London: Routledge, 2004. Print.

———. "Performing Ethnicity: The Demidenko Show and Its Gratifying Pathologies." *Canadian Ethnic Studies* 28.3 (1996): 72–84. Print.

Gwyn, Richard. *Nation Maker: Sir John A. Macdonald. His Life, Our Times*. Vol. 2: 1867–1891. Toronto: Random House, 2011. Print.

Hagan, Helene E. "The Plastic Medicine People Circle." *Institute of Archetypal Ethnology Newsletter*. N.p., 1992. Web. 11 Aug. 2012.

Haggerty, Liam. "nehiyawak (Plains Cree) Leadership on the Plains." *Our Legacy*. University of Saskatchewan Archives and University of Saskatchewan Library, 2008. Web. 5 August 2012.

Haida Nation v. British Columbia (Minister of Forests), [2004] 3 S.C.R. 511, 2004 SCC 73. Web. 2 May 2011.

Haig-Brown, Mary. "Arthur Eugene O'Meara: Servant, Advocate, Seeker of Justice." *With Good Intentions: Euro-Canadian and Aboriginal Relations in Colonial Canada*. Ed. Celia Haig-Brown. Vancouver: U of British Columbia P, 2005. 258–96. Print.

Hale, Horatio. Rev. of *The White Wampum*, by E. Pauline Johnson. *The Critic* [New York] 4 June 1896. 4–5. Print.

Halliday, M.A.K., and Ruqaiya Hasan. *Cohesion in English*. London: Longman, 1976. Print.

Hallowell, A. Irving. "Ojibwa Ontology, Behavior, and World View." *Culture in History*. Ed. Stanley Diamond. New York: Columbia UP, 1960. 18–49. Print.

Hamilton, Michelle A. *Collections and Objections: Aboriginal Material Culture in Southern Ontario, 1791–1914*. Montreal: McGill-Queen's UP, 2010. Print.

Hansen, Hans V. "Preface to the Texts of Louis Riel's Addresses to the Court and the Jury." *Riel's Defence: Perspectives on His Speeches*. Ed. Hansen. Montreal: McGill-Queen's UP, 2014. 19–24. Print.

Haraway, Donna. *Companion Species Manifesto: Dogs, People, and Significant Otherness*. Chicago: Prickly Paradigms, 2003. Print.

———. "The Promises of Monsters: A Regenerative Politics for Inappropriate/d Others." *Cultural Studies*. Ed. Lawrence Grossberg, Cary Nelson, and Paula A. Treichler. New York: Routledge, 1992. 295–337. Print.

———. "Situated Knowledges: The Science Question in Feminism and the Privilege of a Partial Perspective." *Feminist Studies* 14.3 (1988): 575–99. Print.

Harding, Sandra, ed. *The Feminist Standpoint Theory Reader: Intellectual and Political Controversies*. New York: Routledge, 2003. Print.

———. *Sciences from Below: Feminisms, Postcolonialities, and Modernities*. Durham: Duke UP, 2008. Print.

Harring, Sidney L. *White Man's Law: Native People in Nineteenth-Century Canadian Jurisprudence*. Toronto: U of Toronto P, 1998. Print.

Harris, Cole. "How Did Colonialism Dispossess? Comments from an Edge of Empire." *Annals of the Association of American Geographers* 94.1 (2004): 165–82. Print.

———. *Making Space: Colonialism, Resistance, and Reserves in British Columbia*. Vancouver: U of British Columbia P, 2002. Print.

Heartfield, James. *The Aborigines' Protection Society: Humanitarian Imperialism in Australia, New Zealand, Fiji, Canada, South Africa and the Congo, 1836–1909*. New York: Columbia UP, 2011. Print.

Henry, Alexander. *Travels and Adventures in Canada and the Indian Territories between the Years 1760 and 1776*. 1809. New ed. Boston: Little, Brown, 1901. *Internet Archive*. Web. 10 April 2011.

Highway, Tomson. *The Rez Sisters*. Calgary: Fifth House, 1988. Print.

Hill, Rick. *Haudenosaunee War of 1812 Wampum Belts*. Six Nations Legacy Consortium. June 2012. Web. 1 Nov. 2012.

Historica Canada. Black History Canada. Timeline. Historica Dominion Institute, n.d. Web. 25 Jan. 2015.

———. "Grey Owl." *Heritage Minute*. Video. Historica Canada, n.d. Web. 6 Aug. 2012.

"History." Canadian Sikh Heritage.ca Khalsa Diwan Society, Abbotsford. N.p., n.d. Web. 20 April 2015.

"Honorary Witness." *Truth and Reconciliation Commission of Canada*. N.p., n.d. Web. 11 Feb. 2015.

Hood, Glynnis A., and Suzanne E. Bayley. "Beaver (*Castor canadensis*) Mitigate the Effects of Climate on the Area of Open Water in Boreal Wetlands in Western Canada." *Biological Conservation* 141.2 (2008): 556–67. Web. 7 June 2013.

Hookimaw-Witt, Jaqueline. "Keenebonanoh Keemoshominook Kaeshe Peemishikhik Odaskiwakh/ We Stand on the Graves of Our Ancestors." MA thesis, Trent University, 1998. Print.

Hudson, Nicholas. "From 'Nation' to 'Race': The Origin of Racial Classification in Eighteenth-Century Thought." *Eighteenth-Century Studies* 29.3 (1996): 247–64. Web. 3 July 2011.

Hudson's Bay Company. "James and Maud Watt: Protectors of the Beaver." *Our History: People: Associates*. Hudson's Bay Company, n.d. Web. 2 Feb. 2014.

Hulan, Renée. *Northern Experience and the Myths of Canadian Culture*. Montreal: McGill-Queen's UP, 2003. Print.

Hulme, Peter, and Neil L. Whitehead, eds. *Wild Majesty: Encounters with Caribs from Columbus to the Present Day. An Anthology*. Oxford: Clarendon, 1992. Print.

Hurley, Mary. *Aboriginal Title: The Supreme Court of Canada Decision in Delgamuukw v. British Columbia*. Parliamentary Information and Research Service. Library of Parliament. Rev. ed. 2000. Web. 28 Dec. 2013.

Hurley, Michael. *Borders of Nightmare: The Fiction of John Richardson*. Toronto: U of Toronto P, 1992. Print.

Hutcheon, Linda. Introduction. "The Field Notes of a Public Critic." *The Bush Garden: Essays on the Canadian Imagination*. By Northrop Frye. Toronto: Anansi, 1995. xvii–xx. Print.

———. *The Politics of Postmodernism*. London: Routledge, 1989. Print.

Hyvärinen, Matti, Lars-Christer Hydén, Marja Saarenheimo, and Maria Tamboukou. *Beyond Narrative Coherence*. Amsterdam: John Benjamins, 2010. Print.

Indigenous Foundations. Faculty of Arts, University of British Columbia, n.d. Web. 13 Feb. 2013.

Johnson, E. Pauline. "A Cry from an Indian Wife." *The Week*. 18 June 1885. *Early Canadiana Online*. Web. 12 Nov. 2012.

———. "My Mother." *The Moccasin Maker*. Toronto: Ryerson, 1913. 23–85. Print.

———. *E. Pauline Johnson / Tekahionwake: Collected Poems and Selected Prose*. Ed. Carole Gerson and Veronica Strong-Boag. Toronto: U of Toronto P, 2002. Print.

———. *The Shaganappi*. Toronto: William Briggs, 1913. *Project Gutenberg Canada*. Web. 14 April 2015.

Johnson, Evelyn H.C. *Memoirs*. Ohsweken: Chiefswood Board of Trustees, 2009.

Johnston, Basil H. *Indian School Days*. Toronto: Key Porter, 1988. Print.

———. "Indigenous Writing and the Residential School Legacy." Interview with Sam McKegney. *Studies in Canadian Literature* 34.2 (2009). Web. 9 Feb. 2013.

———. "Is That All There Is? Tribal Literature." *Canadian Literature* 128 (1991): 54–62. Print.

———. *The Manitous: The Supernatural World of the Ojibway*. Toronto: Key Porter, 1995. Print.

———. *Think Indian: Languages Are Beyond Price*. Wiarton: Kegedonce, 2010. Print.

Jones, Manina. "Beyond the Pale: Gender, 'Savagery,' and the Colonial Project in Richardson's *Wacousta*." *Essays on Canadian Writing* 54 (1994): 46–59. Print.

Josephy, Alvin M. Jr., Joane Nagel, and Troy Johnson, eds. *The American Indians' Fight for Freedom*. 2nd ed. Lincoln: U of Nebraska P, 1999. Print.

Justice, Daniel Heath. "Go Away Water: Kinship Criticism and the Decolonizing Imperative." *Reasoning Together: The Native Critics Collective*. Ed. Craig S. Womack, Daniel Heath Justice, and Christopher B. Teuton. Norman: U of Oklahoma P, 2008. 147–68. Print.

Kalant, Amelia. *National Identity and the Conflict at Oka: Native Belonging and Myths of Postcolonial Nationhood in Canada*. New York: Routledge, 2004. Print.

Keeshig-Tobias, Lenore. "The Magic of Others." *Language in Her Eye: Writing and Gender*. Ed. Libby Scheier, Sarah Sheard, and Eleanor Wachtel. Toronto: Coach House, 1990. 173–77.

———. "Stop Stealing Native Stories." *Globe and Mail* [Toronto] 26 Jan. 1990: A7. *Canadian Newsstand*. Web. 27 Jan. 2013.

———. "The White Man's Burden." *An Anthology of Canadian Native Literature in English*. 3rd ed. Ed. Daniel David Moses and Terry Goldie. Don Mills: Oxford UP, 2005. 262–67. Print.

Keller, Betty. *Pauline: A Biography of Pauline Johnson*. Vancouver: Douglas & McIntyre, 1981. Print.

Kerzer, Jonathan. *Worrying the Nation: Imagining a National Literature in Canada*. Toronto: U of Toronto P, 1998. Print.

King, Thomas. "Godzilla vs. Postcolonial." 1990. *Unhomely States: Theorizing English-Canadian Post-colonialism*. Ed. Cynthia Sugars. Peterborough: Broadview, 2004. 181–90. Print.

———. *Green Grass, Running Water*. New York: Bantam, 1993. Print.

———. *The Inconvenient Indian: A Curious Account of Native People in North America*. Toronto: Doubleday Canada, 2012. Print.

———. Introduction. *All My Relations: An Anthology of Contemporary Canadian Native Fiction*. Ed. King. Toronto: McClelland & Stewart, 1990. ix–xvi. Print.

———. *The Truth about Stories: A Native Narrative*. Toronto: Anansi, 2003. Print.

———. "You're Not the Indian I Had in Mind." *The Truth about Stories: A Native Narrative*. Toronto: Anansi, 2003: 31–60. Print.

Kino-nda-niimi Collective, ed. *The Winter We Danced: Voices from the Past, the Future and the Idle No More Movement*. Winnipeg: Arbeiter Ring, 2014. Print.

Kipling, Rudyard. "The White Man's Burden." 1899. *Modern History Sourcebook*. Fordham University, 1997. Web. 2 Feb. 2013.

Klinck, Carl F. Biographical Introduction. *Journal of Major John Norton, 1809–16*. By John Norton (Teyoninhokarawen). Ed. Klinck and James J. Talman. Toronto: Champlain Society, 1970. xiii–xcii. Print.

———. Introduction. *The Canadian Brothers; or, The Prophecy Fulfilled: A Tale of the Late American War*. 1840. Toronto: U of Toronto P, 1976. vii–xxiv. Print.

———. "John Norton." Ross 15–22.

Kolodny, Annette. *The Lay of the Land: Metaphor as Experience and History in American Life and Letters*. Chapel Hill: U of North Carolina P, 1975. Print.

Konkle, Maureen. *Writing Indian Nations: Native Intellectuals and the Politics of Historiography, 1827–1863*. Chapel Hill: U of North Carolina P, 2004. Print.

Konnikova, Maria. "The Psychology of Online Comments." *New Yorker* 24 Oct. 2013. Web. 28 Jan. 2014.

Kovacs, Sasha. "Tekahionwake (Double Wampum): E. Pauline Johnson's Performances of/with Treaty." Hemispheric Institute Encuentro. Concordia University, Montreal. 23 June 2014. Working Group Presentation.

Kramer, Jennifer. "'Fighting with Property': The Double-Edged Character of Ownership." *Native Art of the Northwest Coast: A History of Changing Ideas*. Ed. Charlotte Townsend-Gault, Jennifer Kramer, and Ki-ke-in. Vancouver: U of British Columbia P, 2013. 720–56. Print.

Krech, Shepard III. *The Ecological Indian: Myth and History*. New York: Norton, 1999. Print.

Krupat, Arnold. *Ethnocriticism: Ethnography, History, Literature*. Berkeley: U of California P, 1992. Print.

Kuokkanen, Rauna. "Alter-Native Nations and Narrations in the Work of DeWitt Clinton Duncan (Too-qua-stee), Charles A. Eastman (Ohiyesa) and E. Pauline Johnson." *Indigenous Nations Studies Journal* 1.2 (2000): 51–71. Print.

Ladino, Jennifer. "Longing for Wonderland: Nostalgia for Nature in Post-Frontier America." *Iowa Journal of Cultural Studies* 5 (2004). Web. 30 Jan. 2013. Print.

Lambertus, Sandra. *Wartime Images, Peacetime Wounds: The Media and the Gustafsen Lake Standoff*. Toronto: U of Toronto P, 2004. Print.

Lampman, Archibald. "At the Long Sault, 1660." *At the Long Sault and Other New Poems*. Ed. Duncan Campbell Scott and E.K. Brown. Toronto: Ryerson, 1943. 1–4. Print.

Lang, George. *Making Wawa: The Genesis of Chinook Jargon*. Vancouver: U of British Columbia P, 2008. Print.

LaRocque, Emma. *When the Other Is Me: Native Resistance Discourse, 1850–1990*. Winnipeg: U of Manitoba P, 2010. Print.

Latour, Bruno. "An Attempt at a Compositionist Manifesto." *New Literary History* 41 (2010): 471–90. Print.

———. *The Politics of Nature: How to Bring the Sciences into Democracy*. Trans. Catherine Porter. Cambridge: Harvard UP, 2004. Print.

———. *We Have Never Been Modern*. Trans. Catherine Porter. New York: Harvester Wheatsheaf, 1993. Print.

———. "Why Has Critique Run Out of Steam? From Matters of Fact to Matters of Concern." *Critical Inquiry* 30.2 (2003): 225–48. Print.

Laugrand, Frédéric. "Peck, Edmund James." *Dictionary of Canadian Biography*. Vol. 15. U of Toronto/U Laval, 2005. Web. 10 Jan. 2014.

Laurier, Wilfrid. *House of Commons Debates 1910–11*. 11th Parliament, 3rd Session. Vol. 4. 19 April 1911: 7249. Library of Parliament. Web. 28 Mar. 2015.

Lawrence, Bonita. *Fractured Homeland: Federal Recognition and Algonquin Identity in Ontario*. Vancouver: U of British Columbia P, 2012. Print.

———. *Real Indians and Others: Mixed-Blood Urban Native Peoples and Indigenous Nationhood*. Vancouver: U of British Columbia P, 2004. Print.

Lawrence, Bonita, and Enakshi Dua. "Decolonizing Antiracism." *Racism, Colonialism, and Indigeneity in Canada*. Ed. Martin J. Cannon and Lina Sunseri. Don Mills: Oxford UP, 2011. 19–28. Print.

Lecker, Robert. *Keepers of the Code: English-Canadian Literary Anthologies and the Representation of Nation*. Toronto: U of Toronto P, 2013. Print.

Lee, Dennis. "Cadence, Country, Silence: Writing in Colonial Space." *Unhomely States: Theorizing English-Canadian Postcolonialism*. Ed. Cynthia Sugars. Peterborough: Broadview, 2004. 43–60. Print.

Lee, SKY. *Disappearing Moon Café*. Vancouver: Douglas & McIntyre, 1990. Print.

Leitner, Rick. "Bicentennial Marks Broken Promise for First Nations." *Hamilton News*. Metroland, 24 May 2012. Web. 2 Feb. 2014.

Levack, Brian P. *The Witch Hunt in Early Modern Europe*. Toronto: Pearson/Longman, 2006. Print.

Lévi-Strauss, Claude. *The Savage Mind*. Chicago: U of Chicago P, 1966. Print.

Liebersohn, Harry. *Aristocratic Encounters: European Travellers and American Indians*. Cambridge: Cambridge UP, 1998. Print.

Lighthall, W.D., ed. *Songs of the Great Dominion*. London: Walter Scott, 1889. *Archive.org*. Web. 6 Mar. 2014.

Lindberg, Tracey. "The Doctrine of Discovery in Canada." *Discovering Indigenous Lands: The Doctrine of Discovery in the English Colonies*. By Robert J. Miller, Jacinta Ruru, Larissa Behrendt, and Tracey Lindberg. Oxford: Oxford UP, 2010: 89–170. Print.

Ljunggren, David. "Every G20 Nation Wants to Be Canada, Insists PM." *Reuters*. 25 Sept. 2009. Web. 29 March 2014.

Locke, John. *Second Treatise on Government*. 1690. *Project Gutenberg*. Web. 4 Jan. 2014.

Long, John. *Treaty No. 9: Making the Agreement to Share the Land in Far Northern Ontario in 1905*. Montreal: McGill-Queen's UP, 2010. Print.

Loo, Tina. *States of Nature: Conserving Canada's Wildlife in the Twentieth Century*. Vancouver: U of British Columbia P, 2006. Print.

"Louis Riel (Comics)." *Wikipedia*. Wikimedia Foundation, n.d. Web. 17 Feb. 2015.

Lukács, Georg. *The Historical Novel*. 1937. Trans. Hannah and Stanley Mitchell. Harmondsworth: Penguin, 1962. Print.

Lutz, John Sutton. *Makúk: A New History of Aboriginal-White Relations*. Vancouver: U of British Columbia P, 2008. Print.

Lux, Maureen. *Medicine That Walks: Disease, Medicine and Canadian Plains Native People, 1880–1940*. Toronto: U of Toronto P, 2001. Print.

Mackenzie, Anne. "A Short History of the United Empire Loyalists." *United Empire Loyalists' Association of Canada*. UELAC, 2008. PDF file. Web. 15 Feb. 2013.

Mackey, Eva. *The House of Difference: Cultural Politics and National Identity in Canada*. London: Routledge, 1999. Print.

Macklem, Patrick. *Indigenous Difference and the Constitution of Canada*. Toronto: U of Toronto P, 2001. Print.

MacLulich, T.D. "The Colonial Major: Richardson and *Wacousta*." *Essays on Canadian Writing* 29 (1984): n. pag. Web. 10 April 2011.

Makmillen, Shurli. "Land, Law and Language: Rhetorics of Indigenous Rights and Title." PhD diss. University of British Columbia, 2010. Print.

Manitoba. *Report of the Aboriginal Justice Inquiry of Manitoba*. [Winnipeg: Aboriginal Justice Implementation Commission], 1999. Web. 28 Dec. 2013.

Manuel, George. *Fourth World: An Indian Reality*. Don Mills: Collier Macmillan, 1974. Print.

Maracle, Lee. "The Postcolonial Imagination." *Unhomely States: Theorizing English-Canadian Post-colonialism*. Ed. Cynthia Sugars. Peterborough, ON: Broadview, 2004. 204–8. Print.

———. Preface. "You Become the Trickster." *Sojourner's Truth and Other Stories.* Vancouver: Press Gang, 1990. 11–13. Print.

———. "Yin Chin." *Sojourner's Truth and Other Stories.* Vancouver: Press Gang, 1990. 65–72. Print.

Margolis, Rebecca. "Jewish Immigrant Encounters with Canada's Native Peoples: Yiddish Writings on Tekahionwake." *Journal of Canadian Studies* 43.3 (2009): 169–93. Print.

Marshall, Robert. "The Dark Legacy of Carlos Castenada." *Salon.* Salon Media Group, 12 April 2007. Web. 30 Dec. 2012.

Mathews, Robin. "The Wacousta Factor." *Canadian Literature: Surrender or Revolution.* Ed. Gaile Dexter. Toronto: Steel Rail, 1978. 13–25. Print.

Maud, Ralph. *A Guide to B.C. Indian Myth and Legend.* Vancouver: Talonbooks, 1982. Print.

———. *Transmission Difficulties: Franz Boas and Tsimshian Mythography.* Vancouver: Talonbooks, 2000. Print.

Mawani, Renisa. *Colonial Proximities: Crossracial Encounters and Juridical Truths in British Columbia, 1871–1921.* Vancouver: U of British Columbia P, 2009. Print.

———. "Legal Geographies of Aboriginal Segregation in British Columbia: The Making and Unmaking of the Songhees Reserve, 1850–1911." *Isolation: Places and Practices of Exclusion.* Ed. Carolyn Strange and Alison Bashford. London: Routledge, 2003. 170–90. Print.

Mbembe, Achille. "Necropolitics." *Public Culture* 15.1 (2003): 11–40. Print.

McCall, Sophie. *First Person Plural: Aboriginal Storytelling and the Ethics of Collaborative Authorship.* Vancouver: U of British Columbia P, 2011. Print.

McClintock, Anne. "Family Feuds: Gender, Nationalism, and the Family." *Feminist Review* 44 (1993): 61–80. Print.

McClung, Nellie L. *The Stream Runs Fast: My Own Story.* Toronto: Thomas Allen, 1945. *Project Gutenberg.* Web. 29 April 2013.

McCuaig, Amanda. "One Month Later: How the Federal Government Impacts the Arts." *Art Threat* (2 May 2012): n. pag. Web. 29 Jan. 2012.

McKegney, Sam. "'pain, pleasure, shame. Shame': Masculine Embodiment, Kinship, and Indigenous Reterritorialization." *Canadian Literature* 216 (2013): 12–33. Print.

McLachlin, Beverley. "Louis Riel: Patriot Rebel." *Manitoba Law Journal* 35.1 (2011): n. pag. Web. 19 July 2012.

McLaren, I.S. "*Wacousta* and the Gothic Tradition." Ross 49–62.

McLeod, Neal. *Cree Narrative Memory: From Treaties to Contemporary Times.* Saskatoon: Purich, 2007. Print.

McNab, David T. *No Place for Fairness: Indigenous Land Rights and Policy in the Bear Island Case and Beyond.* Montreal: McGill-Queen's UP, 2009. Print.

McNab, Miriam. Revised by Anne-Marie Pederson. "Aboriginal Women's Issues." *Canadian Encyclopedia*. Historica Foundation, Dec. 2013. Web. 6 Mar. 2014.

McNally, Michael D. "The Indian Passion Play: Contesting the Real Indian in Song of Hiawatha Pageants, 1901–1965." *American Quarterly* 58.1 (2006): 105–36. Print.

McRaye, Walter. *Pauline Johnson and Her Friends*. Toronto: Ryerson, 1947. Print.

Midgley, Mary. *The Essential Mary Midgley*. Ed. David Midgley. London: Taylor and Francis, 2005. Print.

———. *Science and Poetry*. New York: Norton, 2001. Print.

Miki, Roy. "What's a Racialized Text Like You Doing in a Place Like This? Reforming Boundaries, Negotiating Borders in English and CanLit Studies." *Broken Entries: Race, Subjectivity, Writing*. Toronto: Mercury, 1998. 160–80. Print.

Miller, Bruce Granville. *Oral History on Trial: Recognizing Aboriginal Narrative in the Courts*. Vancouver: U of British Columbia P, 2011. Print.

Miller, Carolyn R. "Genre as Social Action." *Quarterly Journal of Speech* 70 (1984): 151–67. Print.

Milloy, John S. *A National Crime: The Canadian Government and the Residential School System, 1879 to 1986*. Winnipeg: U of Manitoba P, 1999. Print.

Mills, Antonia. *Eagle Down Is Our Law: Witsuwit'en Law, Feasts, and Land Claims*. Vancouver: U of British Columbia P, 1994. Print.

Milne, Brad. "The Historiography of Metis Land Dispersal, 1870–90." *Manitoba History* 30 (1995): n. pag. Manitoba Historical Society. Web. 13 January 2013.

Mitchell v. Minister of National Revenue. 2001. Supreme Court of Canada. 1 SCR 911. Web. 12 Dec. 2013.

Moeran, J.W.W. *McCullagh of Aiyansh*. 2nd ed. London: Marshall, [1923]. Print.

Monkman, Leslie. *A Native Heritage: Images of the Indian in English-Canadian Literature*. Toronto: U of Toronto P, 1981. Print.

Montaigne, Michel de. "Of Cannibals." *Essays of Michel de Montaigne*. Trans. Charles Cotton. Ed. William Carew Hazlitt. 1877. *Project Gutenberg*. Web. 10 April 2011.

Montrose, Louis. "The Work of Gender in the Discourse of Discovery." *New World Encounters*. Ed. Stephen Greenblatt. Berkeley: U of California P, 1993. 179–80. Print.

Monture, Rick. "'Beneath the British Flag': Iroquois and Canadian Nationalism in the Work of Pauline Johnson and Duncan Campbell Scott." Spec. issue on race. Ed. Daniel Coleman and Donald Goellnicht. *Essays on Canadian Writing* 75 (2002): 118–41. Print.

———. "Teionkwakhashion Tsi Niionkwariho:ten: 'We Share Our Matters': A Literary History of Six Nations of the Grand River." PhD diss. McMaster University, 2010. Print.

————. *We Share Our Matters: Two Centuries of Writing and Resistance at Six Nations of the Grand River*. Winnipeg: U of Manitoba P, 2014. Print.

Moodie, Susanna. *Roughing It in the Bush or, Life in Canada*. New ed. London: Bentley, 1857. Print.

Moore, Patrick. "Archdeacon Robert McDonald and Gwich'in Literacy." *Anthropological Linguistics* 49.1 (2007): 27–53. Print.

————. "Poking Fun: Humour and Power in Kaska Contact Narratives." *Myth and Memory: Stories of Indigenous-European Contact*. Ed. John Sutton Lutz. Vancouver: U of British Columbia P, 2007. 69–89. Print.

Morley, Alan. *Roar of the Breakers: A Biography of Peter Kelly*. Toronto: Ryerson, 1967. Print.

Morriseau, Norval. *Legends of My People: The Great Ojibway*. Ed. Selwyn Dewdney. Toronto: Ryerson, 1965. Print.

Morton, Desmond, ed. *The Queen v. Louis Riel*. Toronto: U of Toronto P, 1974. Print.

Moses, Daniel David. *Brébeuf's Ghost*. Toronto: Exile, 2000. Print.

Mosionier, Beatrice Culleton. *In Search of April Raintree*. 1983. Critical ed. Winnipeg: Portage and Main, 1999. Print.

Moss, John. *Patterns of Isolation in English Canadian Fiction*. Toronto: McClelland & Stewart, 1974. Print.

Muehlbauer, Jeff. "Animacy in Plains Cree, or Why Cree Is More Calvin and Hobbes than Pocahontas." *That Môniyâw Linguist*. Blog. 23 Dec. 2011. Web. 17 Feb. 2015.

Muñoz, Jose Esteban. *Disidentifications: Queers of Colour and the Performance of Politics*. Minneapolis: U of Minnesota P, 1999. Print.

Murray, David. *Indian Giving: Economies of Power in Indian-White Exchanges*. Amherst: U of Massachusetts P, 2000. Print.

Neu, Dean, and Richard Therrien. *Accounting for Genocide: Canada's Bureaucratic Assault on Aboriginal People*. Winnipeg: Fernwood, 2001. Print.

Newhouse, David R., Cora J. Voyageur, and Dan Beavon. *Hidden in Plain Sight: Contributions of Aboriginal Peoples to Canadian Identity and Culture*. Toronto: U of Toronto P, 2005. Print.

Nichols, John D. "The Cree Syllabary." *The World's Writing Systems*. Ed. Peter T. Daniels and William Bright. New York: Oxford UP, 1996. 599–611. Print.

Nicks, Trudy. "Dr. Oronhyatekha's History Lessons: Reading Museum Collections as Texts." *Reading Beyond Words: Contexts for Native History*. Ed. Jennifer S.H. Brown and Elizabeth Vibert. Peterborough, ON: Broadview, 1996. 483–510. Print.

Norman, Emma Spencer. "Point Grey Pre-University (Pre-1890)." *Recovering the University Fabric*. University of British Columbia, n.d. Web. 12 Dec. 2011. Print.

Northey, Margot. *The Haunted Wilderness: The Gothic and Grotesque in Canadian Fiction*. Toronto: U of Toronto P, 1976. Print.

Norton, John (Teyoninhokarawen). *Journal of Major John Norton, 1809–16*. Ed. Carl F. Klinck and James J. Talman. Toronto: Champlain Society, 1970. Print.

Obeyesekere, Gananath. "'British Cannibals': Contemplation of an Event in the Death and Resurrection of James Cook, Explorer." *Critical Inquiry* 18 (1992): 630–54. Print.

Obomsawin, Alanis, dir. *Is the Crown at War with Us?* NFB, 2002. Documentary film.

———. *Kanehsatake: 270 Years of Resistance*. NFB, 1993. Documentary film.

———. *The People of the Kattawapiskat River*. NFB, 2012. Documentary film.

O'Hagan, Howard. "Grey Owl." *Wilderness Men*. Vancouver: Talonbooks, 1978. 95–116. Print.

Oliver, Kelly. *The Colonization of Psychic Space: A Psychoanalytic Theory of Oppression*. Minneapolis: U of Minnesota P, 2004. Print.

Ong, Walter J. *Orality and Literacy: The Technologizing of the Word*. 1982. London: Routledge, 2002. Print.

Ontario. *The Algonquin Land Claim*. Queen's Printer for Ontario, 23 Dec. 2013. Web. 3 Feb. 2014.

Ontario. *The Ipperwash Inquiry*. Ipperwash Inquiry, 31 May 2007. Updated 6 June 2007. Web. 28 Jan. 2014.

Owens, Margaret E. *Stages of Dismemberment: The Fragmented Body in Late Medieval and Early Modern Drama*. Delaware: Associated University Presses, 2005. Print.

Pacey, Desmond. "A Colonial Romantic: Major John Richardson, Soldier and Novelist." Part I. *Canadian Literature* 2 (1959): 20–31. Part II. *Canadian Literature* 3 (1960): 47–56. Print.

"Pacific Scandal." *Canadian Encyclopedia*. Historica Foundation, 7 Feb. 2006. Web. 14 August 2012.

Pagden, Anthony. "The Struggle for Legitimacy and the Image of Empire in the Atlantic to c. 1700." *The Origins of Empire: British Overseas Enterprise to the Close of the Seventeenth Century*. Ed. Nicholas Canny. Oxford: Oxford UP, 1998. 34–54. Print. Vol. 1 of *The Oxford History of the British Empire*. Wm. Roger Louis, ed. in chief.

Palmer, Andie Diane. *Maps of Experience: The Anchoring of Land to Story in Secwepemc Discourse*. Toronto: U of Toronto P, 2005. Print.

Papaschase First Nation #136. Papaschase.ca, 2014. Web. 4 August 2014.

Parkinson, Edward. "That 'Ere Ingian's One of Us!': Orality and Literacy in 'Wacousta.'" *Studies in the Novel* 29.4 (1997): 453–75. Print.

Patterson, E. Palmer III. "Andrew Paull and the Early History of British Columbia Indian Organizations." *One Century Later: Western Canadian Reserve Indians Since Treaty 7*. Ed. Ian A.L. Getty and Donald B. Smith. Vancouver: U of British Columbia P, 1978. 43–54. Print.

Paul, Daniel N. *We Were Not the Savages: Collision between European and Native American Civilizations*. 3rd ed. Halifax: Fernwood, 2006. Print.

Paul, Philip Kevin. *Taking the Names Down from the Hill*. Roberts Creek: Nightwood, 2003. Print.

Perkel, Colin. "Residential School Hearings Come to a Close." *Globe and Mail* [Toronto] 31 Mar. 2014: A3.

Petrone, Penny, ed. *Northern Voices: Inuit Writing in English*. Toronto: U of Toronto P, 1988. Print.

Peyer, Bernd. *The Tutor'd Mind: Indian Missionary-Writers in Antebellum America*. Amherst: U of Massachusetts P, 1997. Print.

"Phil Fontaine's Shocking Testimony of Sexual Abuse." CBC *Digital Archives*. CBC/ Radio-Canada, 2015. Web. 17 Feb. 2015.

Piatote, Beth. *Domestic Subjects: Gender, Citizenship and Law in Native American Literature*. New Haven: Yale UP, 2013. Print.

"Plaint of the Siwash: Reason Why Chiefs Will Seek to See King." *Granby Leader-Mail*, N.p., 10 Aug. 1906. Web. 5 Feb. 2013.

Polk, James. Introduction. *Men of the Last Frontier*. 1931. By Grey Owl. Toronto: Dundurn, 2011. 7–23. Print.

Potter, Tiffany. Introduction. *Ponteach, or The Savages of America*. By Robert Rogers. 1766. Toronto: U of Toronto P, 2010. 3–54. Print.

Povinelli, Elizabeth A. "The Governance of the Prior." *Between Subalternity and Indigeneity*. Ed. Jodi A. Byrd and Michael Rothberg. Spec. issue of *Interventions: International Journal of Postcolonial Studies* 13.1 (2011): 13–30. Print.

Pratt, E.J. *Brébeuf and His Brethren*. Toronto: Macmillan, 1940. Print.

———. *Towards the Last Spike*. Toronto: Macmillan, 1952. Print.

Pratt, Mary Louise. "Arts of the Contact Zone." *Profession* 1991: 33–40. MLA. JSTOR. Web. 15 Feb. 2014.

———. *Imperial Eyes: Travel Writing and Transculturation*. London: Routledge, 1992. Print.

Pritchett, John Perry. "The So-Called Fenian Raid on Manitoba in 1871." *Canadian Historical Review* 10 (March 1929): 23–43. Print.

Quaife, Milo M. Introduction. *The John Askin Papers*. Ed. Quaife. Vol. 1. Detroit: Detroit Library Commission, 1928. 1–24. Print.

Queen vs. Louis Riel. Ottawa: Queen's Printer, 1886. *Peel's Prairie Provinces*. University of Alberta, n.d. Web. 19 July 2012.

Radical Dramaturgy Unit. *Sinking Neptune*. Optative Theatrical Laboratories, n.d. Web. 16 Feb. 2014.

Raibmon, Paige. *Authentic Indians: Episodes of Encounter from the Late-Nineteenth-Century Northwest Coast*. Durham: Duke UP, 2006. Print.

Rak, Julie. "Double-Wampum, Double-Life, Double Click: E. Pauline Johnson by and for the World Wide Web." *Textual Studies in Canada* (2001): n. pag. Web. 2 Feb. 2012.

Ramsay, William M. *Four Modern Prophets: Walter Rauschenbusch, Martin Luther King, Jr., Gustavo Guttierez, and Rosemary Radford Reuther*. Louisville: Westminster John Knox, 1986. Print.

Ray, Arthur J. *Telling It to the Judge: Taking Native History to Court*. Montreal: McGill-Queen's UP, 2011. Print.

Razack, Sherene H. "The Murder of Pamela George." *Race, Space and the Law: Unmapping a White Settler Society*. Ed. Razack. Toronto: Between the Lines, 2002. 121–56. Print.

Reaney, James. Afterword. *Wacousta*. 1991. Toronto: McClelland & Stewart, 2008. 585–89. Print. New Canadian Library.

———. *Wacousta! A Melodrama in Three Acts with a Description of Its Development in Workshops*. Toronto: Porcépic, 1979. Print.

Reder, Deanna, and Linda Morra, eds. *Troubling Tricksters: Revisioning Critical Conversations*. Waterloo: Wilfrid Laurier UP, 2010. Print.

Reder, Deanna Helen. "âcimisowin as Theoretical Practice: Autobiography as Indigenous Intellectual Tradition in Canada." PhD diss. University of British Columbia, 2007. Print.

Reford, Alexander. "Smith, Donald Alexander, 1st Baron Strathcona and Mount Royal." *Dictionary of Canadian Biography*. Vol. 14. U of Toronto/U Laval, 1998. Web. 4 Feb. 2004.

Regan, Paulette. *Unsettling the Settler Within: Indian Residential Schools, Truth Telling, and Reconciliation in Canada*. Vancouver: U of British Columbia P, 2010. Print.

Reid, Basil A. *Caribbean Archaeology and Ethnohistory: Myths and Realities of Caribbean History*. Tuscaloosa: U of Alabama P, 2009. Print.

Reid, Jennifer. *Louis Riel and the Creation of Modern Canada: Mythic Discourse and the Postcolonial State*. Albuquerque: U of New Mexico P, 2008. Print.

Renan, Ernst. "What Is a Nation?" Sorbonne, Paris. 11 March 1882. Lecture. Web. 11 April 2011.

"Report Finds Mohawk Warrior Responsible for Policeman's Death." *Windspeaker* 13.5 (1995): 2. Web. 1 Feb. 2015.

Revie, Linda. "Pauline Johnson's Sapphic Wampum." *torquere: Journal of the Canadian Lesbian and Gay Studies Association* 4–5 (2002–2003): 38–62. Print.

Reynolds, James I. *A Breach of Duty: Fiduciary Obligations and Aboriginal Peoples.* Saskatoon: Purich, 2005. Print.

Richardson, Boyce. *Strangers Devour the Land.* Post Mills: Chelsea Green, 1991. Print.

Richardson, John. *The Canadian Brothers; or, The Prophecy Fulfilled: A Tale of the Late American War.* 1840. Ed. Donald G. Stephens. Ottawa: Carleton UP, 1992. xvii–lxxxii. Centre for Editing Early Canadian Texts, 9. Print.

———. *Eight Years in Canada.* Montreal: Cunningham, 1847. *Archive.org.* Web. 16 Feb. 2014.

———. *Richardson's War of 1812.* 1842. Ed. Alexander Clark Casselman. Toronto: Historical, 1902. Web. 13 Feb. 2011.

———. *Tecumseh: A Poem in Four Cantos.* 1828. Ed. Douglas Daymond and Leslie Monkman. London: Canadian Poetry, 1992. Print.

———. "A Trip to Walpole Island and Port Sarnia." 1849. *Major John Richardson: Short Stories.* Ed. David Beasley. Penticton: Theytus, 1985. 113–31. Print.

———. *Wacousta or, The Prophecy: A Tale of the Canadas.* 1832. Ed. Douglas Cronk. Ottawa: Carleton UP, 1987. Print. Centre for Editing Early Canadian Texts, 4.

———. *Wau-nan-gee; Or, the Massacre at Chicago: A Romance of the American Revolution.* New York: H. Long, 1852. *Internet Archive.* Web. 13 Feb. 2011.

Richter, Daniel K. *Facing East from Indian Country: A Native History of Early America.* Cambridge: Harvard UP, 2001. Print.

Riel, Louis. *The Collected Writings of Louis Riel / Les écrits complets de Louis Riel.* Ed. George F.G. Stanley. 5 vols. Edmonton: U of Alberta P, 1985. Print.

———. "Last Memoir." *Hold High Your Heads: History of the Metis Nation in Western Canada.* By A.-H. de Tremaudan. Trans. E. Maguet. Winnipeg: Pemmican, 1982. 200–10. Print.

Rifkin, Mark. *When Did Indians Become Straight? Kinship, the History of Sexuality, and Native Sovereignty.* New York: Oxford UP, 2011. Print.

Robinson, Eden. *Monkey Beach.* Toronto: Vintage, 2001. Print.

———. *The Sasquatch at Home: Traditional Protocols and Modern Storytelling.* Edmonton: U of Alberta P, 2011. Print.

Robinson, Harry. *Living by Stories: A Journey of Landscape and Memory.* Comp. and ed. Wendy Wickwire. Vancouver: Talonbooks, 2005. Print.

———. *Nature Power: In the Spirit of an Okanagan Storyteller.* Comp. and ed. Wendy Wickwire. Vancouver: Douglas and McIntyre, 1992. Print.

———. *Write It on Your Heart: The Epic World of an Okanagan Storyteller.* Comp. and ed. Wendy Wickwire. Vancouver: Talonbooks/Theytus, 1989. Print.

Rogers, Shelagh. "Reflections on Being an Honorary Witness." *CBC News*. CBC/Radio-Canada, 29 Mar. 2014. Web. 30 Mar. 2014.

Roppolo, Kimberly. "Samson Occom as Writing Instructor: The Search for an Intertribal Rhetoric." *Reasoning Together: The Native Critics Collective*. Ed. Craig S. Womack, Daniel Heath Justice, and Christopher B. Teuton. Norman: U of Oklahoma P, 2008. 303–24. Print.

Ross, Catherine Sheldrick, ed. *Recovering Canada's First Novelist: Proceedings from the John Richardson Conference*. Erin: Porcupine's Quill, 1984. Print.

Roth, Christopher F. "'Without Treaty, without Conquest': Indigenous Sovereignty in Post-*Delgamuukw* British Columbia." *Wicazo Sa Review* 17.2 (2002): 143–65. Print.

Roy, Susan. "A History of the Site: The Kitsilano Indian Reserve." *Digital Natives: Other Sights for Artists' Projects*. Ed. Lorna Brown and Clint Burnham. Vancouver: City of Vancouver Public Art Program, 2011. 86–93. Print.

———. *These Mysterious People: Shaping History and Archaeology in a Northwest Coast Community*. Montreal: McGill-Queen's UP, 2010. Print.

Rubin, Gayle. "The Traffic in Women: Notes on the 'Political Economy' of Sex." *Toward an Anthropology of Women*. Ed. Rayna Reiter. New York: Monthly Review, 1975. 157–210. Print.

Ruffo, Armand Garnet. *Grey Owl: The Mystery of Archie Belaney*. Regina: Coteau, 1996. Print.

Ruoff, A. LaVonne Brown. Introduction. *The Moccasin Maker*. 1913. Norman: U of Oklahoma P, 1998. 1–22. Print.

R. v. Marshall, [1999] 3 S.C.R. 456 and R. v. Marshall, [1999] 3 S.C.R. 533. Web. 3 Feb. 2013.

R. v. Powley, [2003] 2 S.C.R. 207, 2003 SCC 43. Web. 13 Jan. 2012.

R. v. Sparrow, [1990] 1 S.C.R. 1075. Web. 28 Mar. 2015.

Sahlins, Marshall. "Cannibalism: An Exchange?" *New York Review of Books* 22 March 1979: 46–47. Print.

Sarris, Greg. *Keeping Slug Woman Alive: A Holistic Approach to American Indian Texts*. Berkeley: U of California P, 1993. Print.

"Saskatchewan School Officials Backtrack on 'Got Land? Thank an Indian' Hoodie." *National Post* [Toronto]. Postmedia, 15 Jan. 2014. Web. 16 Feb. 2014.

Satzewich, Victor. "Indian Agents and the 'Indian Problem' in Canada in 1946: Reconsidering the Theory of 'Coercive Tutelage.'" *Canadian Journal of Native Studies* 17.2 (1997): 227–57. Print.

Saul, John Ralston. *A Fair Country: Telling Truths about Canada*. Toronto: Viking Penguin, 2008. Print.

Schorcht, Blanca. *Storied Voices in Native American Texts: Harry Robinson, Thomas King, James Welch and Leslie Marmon Silko*. New York: Routledge, 2003. Print.

——. "The Storied World of Harry Robinson: Emerging Dialogues." *BC Studies* 135 (2002): 145–62. Print.

Schweninger, Lee. "'Back When I Used to Be Indian': Native American Authenticity and Postcolonial Discourse." *Native Authenticity: Transnational Perspectives on Native American Literary Studies*. Ed. Deborah L. Madsen. Albany: State U of New York P, 2010. 69–85. Print.

Scollon, Ronald, and Suzanne B.K. Scollon. *Linguistic Convergence: An Ethnography of Speaking at Fort Chipewyan, Alberta*. New York: Academic, 1979. Print.

Scott, Duncan Campbell. *Selected Poetry*. Ed. Glenn Clever. Ottawa: Tecumseh, 1974. Print.

Scott, F.R. "All the Spikes but the Last." *Selected Poems*. Toronto: Oxford UP, 1966. 64. Print.

Sedgewick, Eve Kosofsky. *Between Men: English Literature and Male Homosocial Desire*. New York: Columbia UP, 1985. Print.

Seibt, Johanna. "Process Philosophy." *Stanford Encyclopedia of Philosophy*. Ed. E.N. Zalta. Stanford: Stanford University, 2012. Web. 5 Jan. 2013.

Seigworth, Gregory J., and Melissa Gregg. "An Inventory of Shimmers." Introduction. *The Affect Theory Reader*. Ed. Gregg and Seigworth. Durham: Duke UP, 2010. 1–25. Print.

Seton, Ernest Thompson. Introduction. *The Shaganappi*. By E. Pauline Johnson. 1913. *Project Gutenburg*. Web. 1 Sept. 2012.

Shaw, Patricia A. "Language and Identity, Language and the Land." *BC Studies* 131 (2001): 39–55. Print.

Shrive, Norman. "What Happened to Pauline?" *Canadian Literature* 13 (1962): 25–38. Print.

Shyla. "Imaginary Indian, 10th Anniversary Redesign." *Arsenalia*. Arsenal Pulp Press, 27 June 2011. Web. 30 Sept. 2012.

Silva, Denise Ferreira da. *Towards a Global Idea of Race*. Minneapolis: U of Minnesota P, 2007. Print.

Silver, Peter. *Our Savage Neighbors*. New York: Norton, 2009. Print.

Sioui, George E. *For an Amerindian Autohistory*. Trans. Sheila Fischman. Montreal: McGill-Queen's UP, 1992. Print.

Six Nations Lands and Resources. *Land Rights: A Global Solution for the Six Nations of the Grand River*. Six Nations Lands & Resources Department, n.d. Web. 24 May 2013.

Six Nations Legacy Consortium. Wampum Belts associated with the War of 1812. *Six Nations Legacy Consortium: In Our Own Words*. Six Nations Legacy Consortium, 2014. Web. 4 Aug. 2014.

Slaney, Frances M. "Harper's History Museum Betrays First Nations." *CAUT Bulletin* 61.4 (2014): n. pag. Web. 6 Mar. 2014.

Sloan, Kerry. "'A New German-Indian World' in the North-West: A Métis Deconstruction of the Rhetoric of Immigration in Louis Riel's Trial Speeches." *Riel's Defence: Perspectives on His Speeches*. Ed. Hans V. Hanson. Kingston: McGill-Queen's UP, 2014. 166–203. Print.

Smith, Andrea. *Conquest: Sexual Violence and American Indian Genocide*. Cambridge, MA: South End, 2005. Print.

Smith, Donald B. *From the Land of Shadows: The Making of Grey Owl*. Vancouver: Douglas & McIntyre, 1991. Print.

Smith, Graham Hingangaroa. "Indigenous Struggle for the Transformation of Education." Alaskan Federation of Natives Convention. Anchorage, Alaska. October 2003. Keynote Address. Web. 13 Nov. 2012.

Soyinka, Wole. "From a Common Backcloth: A Reassessment of the African Literary Image." *American Scholar* 32.3 (1963): 387–96. Print.

Spielmann, Roger. *Anishinaabe World: A Survival Guide for Building Bridges between Canada and First Nations*. Sudbury: Your Scrivener, 2009. Print.

Spivak, Gayatri Chakravorty. *A Critique of Postcolonial Reason: Toward a History of the Vanishing Present*. Cambridge: Harvard UP, 1999. Print.

———. "Who Claims Alterity?" *Remaking History: Dia Art Foundation Discussions in Contemporary Cultures No. 4*. Seattle: Dia Art Foundation, 1989. 269–92. Web. 27 June 2011.

Sprague, D.N. *Canada and the Métis 1869–1885*. Waterloo: Wilfrid Laurier UP, 1988. Print.

Stacey, Robert David. "State of Shock: History and Crisis in Hugh Maclennan's *Barometer Rising*." *National Plots: Historical Fiction and Changing Ideas of Canada*. Ed. Andrea Cabajsky and Brett Grubesic. Waterloo: Wilfrid Laurier UP, 2010. 53–66. Print.

Staines, David, ed. *The Canadian Imagination: Dimensions of a Literary Culture*. Cambridge: Harvard UP, 1977. Print.

Stanley, George F.G. *The Birth of Western Canada: A History of the Riel Rebellions*. Toronto: Longman, 1936. Print.

"Statement Gathering: Frequently Asked Questions." *Truth and Reconciliation Commission of Canada*. Truth and Reconciliation Commission of Canada, n.d. Web. 17 Feb. 2015.

Steel, Debora. "SUN News Reports." *Windspeaker* 30.8 (2012): n. pag. Web. 22 Jan. 2014.

Stephens, Donald G. "Editor's Introduction." *The Canadian Brothers; or, The Prophecy Fulfilled* by John Richardson. Ottawa: Carleton UP, 1992. xvii–lxxxii. Centre for Editing Early Canadian Texts, 9. Print.

Sterling, Shirley. *My Name Is Seepeetza*. Toronto: Groundwood, 1992. Print.

———. "Seepeetza Revisited: An Introduction to Six Voices." *On-line Issues* 3.1. Centre for the Study of Curriculum and Instruction, University of British Columbia, 1995. Web. Feb. 2013.

Stoehr, Catherine Murton. "Nativism's Bastard: Neolin, Tenskwatawa, and the Anishinabeg Methodist Movement." *Lines Drawn upon the Water: First Nations and the Great Lakes Borders and Borderlands*. Ed. Karl S. Hele. Waterloo: Wilfrid Laurier P, 2008.175–90. Print. Aboriginal Studies Series.

Stonechild, Blair, and Bill Waiser. *Loyal until Death: Indians and the North-West Rebellion*. Calgary: Fifth House, 1997. Print.

Strange, Carolyn. "Capital Punishment." *The Oxford Companion to Canadian History*. Ed. Gerald Hallowell. Vol. 1. Toronto: U of Oxford P, 2004. 115. Print.

Stromberg, Joseph. "Starving Settlers in Jamestown Colony Resorted to Cannibalism." *Smithsonian.com*. Smithsonian Institution, 1 May 2013. Web 8 Jan. 2014.

Strong-Boag, Veronica, and Carole Gerson. *Paddling Her Own Canoe: The Times and Texts of E. Pauline Johnson*. Toronto: U of Toronto P, 2000. Print.

"Success, One Student at a Time." *Maclean's* 7 Nov. 2011: 72–78. Print.

Sugars, Cyntha. *Canadian Gothic: Literature, History, and the Spectre of Self-Invention*. Cardiff: U of Wales P, 2014. Print.

Sugars, Cynthia, and Gerry Turcotte, eds. *Unsettled Remains: Canadian Literature and the Postcolonial Gothic*. Waterloo: Wilfrid Laurier UP, 2009. Print.

Sugg, Richard. "'Good Physic, but Bad Food': Early Modern Attitudes to Medicinal Cannibalism and Its Suppliers." *Social History of Medicine* 19.2 (2006): 225–40. Print.

Surtees, Robert J. *Treaty Research Report: Manitoulin Island Treaties*. Treaties and Historical Research Centre, Indian and Northern Affairs Canada, 1986. *Aboriginal Affairs and Northern Development Canada*, 2010. Web. 25 Jan. 2015.

Sutherland, Stuart R.J., Pierre Tousignant, and Madeleine Dionne-Tousignant. "Haldimand, Frederick." *Dictionary of Canadian Biography*. Vol. 5. U of Toronto/U Laval, 1983. Web. 10 April 2011.

Suttles, Wayne. *Musqueam Reference Grammar*. Vancouver: U of British Columbia P, 2004. Print. First Nations Languages.

Szeman, Imre. *Zones of Instability: Literature, Postcolonialism and the Nation*. Baltimore: Johns Hopkins UP, 2003. Print.

Tate, Henry Wellington. *The Porcupine Hunter and Other Stories*. Ed. Ralph Maud. Vancouver: Talonbooks, 1993. Print.

Taylor, Charles. "The Politics of Recognition." *Multiculturalism: Examining the Politics of Recognition*. Ed. A. Gutmann. Princeton: Princeton UP, 1994. 25–73. Print.

Taylor, Diana. *The Archive and the Repertoire: Performing Cultural Memory in the Americas*. Durham: Duke UP, 2003. Print.

Taylor, Drew Hayden. "Pretty Like a White Boy: The Adventures of a Blue-Eyed Ojibway." *An Anthology of Canadian Native Literature in English*. Ed. Daniel David Moses and Terry Goldie. Toronto: Oxford UP, 1992. 504–7. Print.

Tema-Augama Anishnabai. "The Native Dimension: Key Dates." Bray and Thomson 147–51.

Temagami First Nation. *Official Site of Temagami First Nation*. Temagami First Nation, 2011. Web. 15 February 2014.

Telling It Collective. *Telling It: Women and Language across Cultures*. Vancouver: Press Gang, 1990. Print.

Tennant, Paul. *Aboriginal People and Politics: The Indian Land Question in British Columbia, 1849–1989*. Vancouver: U of British Columbia P, 1990. Print.

Terralingua. *Terralingua: Unity in Biodiversity*. Terralingua, n.d. Web. 24 Jan. 2013.

Theriault, Madeline Katt. *Moose to Moccasins: The Story of Ka Kita Wa Pa No Kwe*. Toronto: Natural Heritage/Natural History, 1992. Print.

Thérien, Gilles. *Les figures de l'Indien*. Montréal: Hexagone, 1993. Print.

Thom, Brian. "The Paradox of Boundaries in Coast Salish Territories." *Cultural Geographies* 16 (2009): 179–205. Print.

Thomson, Duane. "Clexlixqen, Louis (Xlexxle'xken, Klicktickkun, Tlihtlihen, Hatakun, Little Louis, Petit Louis)." *Dictionary of Canadian Biography*. Vol. 14. U of Toronto/U Laval, 1998. Web. 20 June 2011.

Titley, Brian E. *Narrow Vision: Duncan Campbell Scott and the Administration of Indian Affairs in Canada*. Vancouver: U of British Columbia P, 1986. Print.

Townsend-Gault, Charlotte. "Art Claims in the Age of Delgamuukw." *Native Art of the Northwest Coast: A History of Changing Ideas*. Ed. Townsend-Gault, Jennifer Kramer, and Ki-ke-in. Vancouver: U of British Columbia P, 2013: 865–77. Print.

Tracy, Andrew, and Cle-alls (Dr. John Medicine Horse Kelly). "Secrets of Sound." Introduction. *Native Drums*. Carleton University, 2005. Web. 27 Jan. 2011.

Tremaudan, A.-H. de. *Hold High Your Heads: History of the Metis Nation in Western Canada*. Trans. E. Maguet. Winnipeg: Pemmican, 1982. 200–10. Print.

Trevor-Roper, Hugh. "The Invention of Tradition: The Highland Tradition of Scotland." *The Invention of Tradition*. Ed. Eric Hobsbawm and Terence Ranger. Cambridge: Cambridge UP, 1983. 15–41. Print.

Trigger, Bruce G. *Natives and Newcomers: Canada's "Heroic Age" Reconsidered*. Montreal: McGill-Queen's UP, 1985. Print.

Troniak, Shauna. *Addressing the Legacy of Residential Schools*. Background Paper 2011-76-E. Ottawa: Library of Parliament, 1 Sept. 2011. Web. 15 Dec. 2013.

Trumpener, Katie. *Bardic Nationalism: The Romantic Novel and the British Empire*. Princeton: Princeton UP, 1997. Print.

Tsilhqot'in Nation v. British Columbia, 2007 BCSC 1700. Web. 12 Dec. 2013.

Tsilhqot'in Nation v. British Columbia, 2014 SCC 44, [2014] 2 S.C.R. 256. Web. 30 July 2014.

Tsing, Anna Lowenhaupt. *Friction: An Ethnography of Global Connection*. Princeton: Princeton UP, 2005. Print.

Turcotte, Gerry. *Peripheral Fear: Transformations of the Gothic in Canadian and Australian Fiction*. Brussels: Peter Lang, 2009. Print.

Turk, James L. "Whose History on Display at New Museum?" *Toronto Star*. Toronto Star Newspapers, 9 Dec. 2012. Web. 5 Mar. 2014.

"[Two-hundred]-year-old Wampum Belt Finally Returned to Six Nations Community." *Telegraph Journal* [Saint John, NB]. Brunswick News, 24 July 2012. Web. 24 Aug. 2012.

United Nations. *Convention on the Prevention and Punishment of the Crime of Genocide*. UN General Assembly, 9 Dec. 1948. Web. 15 Feb. 2014.

US Department of the Interior. Census Office. *Report on Indians Taxed and Indians Not Taxed in the United States Except Alaska*. 11th Census 1890. 1894. Rpt. 1994. *Googlebooks*. Web. 23 April 2013.

Vancouver. Motion: Protocol to Acknowledge First Nations Unceded Traditional Territory. *City of Vancouver*. City of Vancouver, 24 June 2014. Web. 29 Aug. 2014.

Van den Brink, J.H. *The Haida Indians: Cultural Change Mainly between 1876–1970*. Leiden: Brill, 1974. Print.

Van der Horst, Pieter W. "Jewish Cannibalism: The History of an Antisemitic Myth." *Telos* 144 (2008): 106–28. Print.

Vandervort, Bruce. *Indian Wars of Mexico, Canada and the United States, 1812–1900*. New York: Routledge, 2006. Print. Warfare and History.

Van Kirk, Sylvia. *Many Tender Ties: Women in Fur Trade Society, 1670–1870*. Winnipeg: Watson and Dwyer, 1980. Print.

———. "Tracing the Fortunes of Five Founding Families of Victoria." *Native Peoples and Colonialism*. Spec. issue of *BC Studies* 115/16 (1997/98): 148–79. Print.

Venne, Sharon Helen. *The Indian Act and Amendments 1868–1975: An Indexed Collection*. Saskatoon: Saskatoon Law Centre, 1981. Print.

Victoria Heritage Foundation. "Songhees First Nation Village, 1853–1911." *Victoria Heritage Foundation*. VHF, n.d. Web. 10 Dec. 2011.

Viehmann, Martha L. "Speaking Chinook: Adaptation, Indigeneity, and Pauline Johnson's British Columbia Stories." *Western American Literature* 47.3 (2012): 259–85. Print.

Viswanathan, Gauri. *Masks of Conquest: Literary Study and British Rule*. New York: Columbia UP, 1989. Print.

Vowel, Chelsea. "Attawapiskat: You Want to Be Shown the Money? Here It Is." *Huffington Post*. The HuffingtonPost.com, 6 Dec. 2011. Web. 27 Jan. 2014.

———. "The Truth Is, Attawapiskat Was Never Financially Mismanaged." *Huffington Post*. TheHuffingtonPost.com, 2 Aug. 2012. Web. 27 Jan. 2014.

Wa, Gisday, and Delgam Uukw. *The Spirit in the Land: The Opening Statement of the Gitksan and Wet'suwe'en Hereditary Chiefs in the Supreme Court of British Columbia, May 11, 1987*. Gabriola: Reflections, 1989. Print.

Wah, Fred. "Half-Bred Poetics." *Faking It: Poetics and Hybridity. Critical Writing 1984–1999*. Edmonton: NeWest 2000. 71–96. Print. The Writer as Critic 7.

Walkem, Ardith, and Halle Bruce, eds. *Box of Treasures or Empty Box: Twenty Years of Section 35*. Penticton: Theytus, 2003. Print.

Warrior, Robert. *Tribal Secrets: Recovering American Intellectual Traditions*. Minneapolis: U of Minnesota P, 1995. Print.

Weatherford, Jack. *Indian Givers: How the Indians of the Americas Transformed the World*. New York: Fawcett Columbine, 1988. Print.

Weaver, Jace. *The Red Atlantic: American Indigenes and the Making of the Modern World, 1000–1927*. Chapel Hill: U of North Carolina P, 2014. Print.

Weaver, John C. *The Great Land Rush and the Making of the Modern World, 1650–1900*. Montreal: McGill-Queen's UP, 2003. Print.

Weinstein, John. *Quiet Revolution West*. Calgary: Fifth House, 2007. Print.

Welsh, Christine. "Voices of the Grandmothers: Reclaiming a Metis Heritage." *Canadian Literature* 131 (1991): 15–24. Print.

"White." *Oxford English Dictionary*. 3rd ed. Oxford University Press, n.d. Web. 14 Jan. 2013.

White, Richard. *The Middle Ground: Indians, Empires, and Republics in the Great Lakes Region, 1650–1815*. Cambridge: Cambridge UP, 1991. Print.

"White Flag." *Wikipedia*. Wikimedia Foundation, n.d. Web. 10 April 2011.

Whitlock, Gillian. *The Intimate Empire: Reading Women's Autobiography*. London: Cassell, 2000. Print.

Wickwire, Wendy. "Driving, Wandering, Recollecting: The Legacy of Coyote's Twin Brother." *BC Studies* 131 (2001): 29–38. Print.

———. Introduction. Robinson, *Living by Stories* 7–33.

———. Introduction. Robinson, *Nature Power* 1–22.

———. Introduction. Robinson, *Write It on Your Heart* 11–28.

———. "Stories from the Margins: Towards a More Inclusive British Columbia Historiography." *Journal of American Folklore* 118.470 (2005): 453–74. Print.

———. "To See Ourselves as the Other's Other: Nlaka'pamux Contact Narratives." *Canadian Historical Review* 75.1 (1994): 1–20. Print.

Widder, Agnes Haigh. "The John Askin Family Library: A Fur-Trading Family's Books." *Michigan Historical Review* (Spring 2007): n. pag. Web. 10 April 2011.

Wiebe, Rudy. "Mistahimaskwa." *Dictionary of Canadian Biography*. Vol. 11. U of Toronto/U Laval, 1982. Web. 13 Feb. 2013.

Wiebe, Rudy, and Bob Beal, eds. *War in the West: Voices of the 1885 Rebellion*. Toronto: McClelland & Stewart, 1985. Print.

Wiegman, Robin. *Object Lessons*. Durham: Duke UP, 2012. Print.

Williams, Glen. *Blood Must Tell: Debating Race and Identity in the Canadian House of Commons: 1880–1925*. WillowBX Press, 2014. E-book.

Willig, Timothy D. *Restoring the Chain of Friendship: British Policy and the Indians of the Great Lakes, 1783–1815*. Lincoln: U of Nebraska P, 2008. Print.

Willmott, Glenn. "Modernism and Aboriginal Modernity: The Appropriation of Products of West Coast Native Heritage as National Goods." *Essays on Canadian Writing* 83 (2004): 75–139. Print.

Wilson, J. Donald. "'No Blanket to Be Worn in School': The Education of Indians in Nineteenth-Century Ontario." *The Legacy*. Ed. Jean Barman, Yvonne Hebert, and Don McCaskill. Vancouver: U of British Columbia P, 1986. 64–83. Print. Vol. 1 of *Indian Education in Canada*.

Winks, Robin. *The Blacks in Canada: A History*. Kingston: McGill-Queen's UP, 1997. Print.

Womack, Craig. *Art as Performance, Story as Criticism: Reflections on Native Literary Aesthetics*. Norman: U of Oklahoma P, 2009. Print.

Woo, Grace Li Xiu. *Ghost Dancing with Colonialism: Decolonization and Indigenous Rights at the Supreme Court of Canada*. Vancouver: U of British Columbia P, 2011. Print.

Wright, Ronald. *Stolen Continents: The "New World" through Indian Eyes*. Toronto: Penguin, 1993. Print.

Yonson, Neal. "Courts Uphold Transfer of University Golf Course to Musqueam." *UBC Insiders*. UBC Insiders, 26 Aug. 2011. Web. 7 Jan. 2014.

York, Lorraine. *Literary Celebrity in Canada*. Toronto: U of Toronto P, 2007. Print.

Yuxweluptun, Lawrence Paul. "Lawrence Paul Yuxweluptun." *Native Art of the Northwest Coast: A History of Changing Ideas*. Ed. Charlotte Townsend-Gault, Jennifer Kramer, and Ki-ke-in. Vancouver: U of British Columbia P, 2013. 878–79. Print.

Zapf, Hubert. "Literary Ecology and the Ethics of Texts." *New Literary History* 39.4 (2008): 847–68. Print.

Index

abjection, 41, 54, 63, 86, 109, 125. *See also* suicide

Aboriginal Justice Inquiry of Manitoba, Report, 23

Aborigines Protection Society, 204

academy, 16, 22, 35, 184, 251n30; as adversarial arena, 223. *See also* anthropology; disciplines, academic

adoption/foster care, 36, 53, 257–58n8; enforced, 31, 257n8; foster children, Indigenous, 216; Indigenous, 74, 131, 236n15, 244n8

affect, 31, 65, 134, 148, 218, 248n2; theory, 134

Ahenekew, Edward ("Old Keyam"), 113–14

Alfred, Taiaiake, 35, 114, 140–41, 164, 227n2; *Peace, Power, and Righteousness*, 142–43

Algonquin. *See* land

Al-Kassim, Dina: *On Pain of Speech*, 85–86

Allied Indian Tribes of British Columbia, 201, 254–55n17

allies, Indigenous men as military, 14, 42, 43, 45, 47, 50, 51, 55, 61, 66, 68, 69–70, 74, 130; British controversy over, 69

"all my relations," 114, 148–49, 222. *See also* animism

American Revolution, 13, 41, 47, 55, 69, 74, 79, 84, 125, 233n19, 236n13

Americans, negatively depicted, 9, 29, 44, 59, 67, 73; fellow Britons and, 47, 69, 85; as morally inferior to Canadians, 83–85, 87, 216; as racist, 46–47, 61, 79, 237–38n1; as savages, 73

Amherst, Jeffery, 60, 61, 237n23

Anahareo (Gertrude Bernard), 150, 152, 160, 170, 171, 174, 249n3, 250n17, 251n26, 251n28; *Devil in Deerskins*, 180. *See also* Belaney, Archibald

ancestry, 3, 30, 31, 32, 53, 137, 138–39, 140, 142, 143, 152, 154, 163, 246n20. *See also* blood quantum

Anderson, Benedict, 227n1, 229n11

Andrews, Jennifer, 53, 235n8

Andrews, Lynn, 163, 250n18

Angus, Ian, 117

animals, 149, 151, 160, 166–67, 170, 171, 173, 174–77, 178, 222, 226. *See also* beavers

animism, 151, 160, 179. *See also* "all my relations"

Anishinaabe. *See* Ojibwa, Mississauga

anthropology, 15, 22, 33, 36–37, 181–82, 184, 207, 234n26; salvage, 33

Delgaamukw v. British Columbia, 23,
191, 208, 231n4, 233n18, 254n13. *See
also* law; legal cases
Derrida, Jacques, 184, 208–9, 234n22.
See also deconstruction
development, 168, 213, 222
Dewar, Jonathan, 154–55, 167, 224
Dewart, Edward Hartley, 5, 227n1; *Selections from the Canadian Poets*, 4
Dickson, Lovat, 151, 158, 177
diplomacy, 16, 25, 26, 60, 62, 191–92,
222, 226
disciplines, academic, 15, 16, 164, 172,
191, 222; English, 22; formation of,
34; history, 22; humanities 20, 92;
identity-based, 34; interdisciplinarity, 22, 37, 222; literary studies, Canadian, 16, 38; narrative disciplines,
20, 22; philosophy, 22; queer studies,
35; science, 22–23; science and technology studies, 38; social sciences,
172; women's studies, 34. *See also*
anthropology
discourse, 32, 37, 41, 94, 108, 137; "atrocity" discourse, 21, 69, 73, 104, 164;
biopolitical, 228n5; cannibalism
and, 75, 77; civilization as, 105–6;
dominant, 9, 12, 13, 19, 21–22, 24, 28,
31, 80, 85, 92, 95, 104, 107, 109, 121,
125, 134; discourse/reality, 77, 179,
215; Foucault's concept of, 27; God as
anchor for, 135; identity and, 3, 34–35,
36, 44, 45, 89, 156, 164; Indigenous,
7, 111, 114, 226, 243n30; Judith Butler
and, 145; land and, 2; literature
and, 22; nationalist, 9, 11, 12, 73, 117,
252n35. *See also* criticism, literary
discovery, doctrine of, 6, 12, 23, 58,
188–89
disidentification, 14, 120–21, 122, 134,
145, 153, 156, 236n16. *See also* Muñoz,
José Esteban

distinction, 27–28, 31, 42, 46–47, 49,
67, 79, 181, 216, 237n21, 257; chain of
alterity and, 29. *See also* binaries
Dollard des Ormeaux, Adam, 74, 238n8
Dominion Lands Act (1872), 240–
41n12
Dorion, Leah, 106
Dorland, Michael, 92, 99, 115–16
Douglas, James, 204, 205, 206, 256n32;
marriage to Amelia Connolly, 127
Duffy, Dennis, 45, 50–51, 60, 66, 237n23
Dumont, Gabriel, 95, 112, 243n33
Dumont, Marilyn: "Leather and
Naugahyde," 30–31, 32, 137; "Not Just
a Platform for My Dance," 8
Durham, Lord (John Lambton, 1st
earl), 235n3, 238n2

ecology, 148, 172,178, 213; activism and,
159; cultural, 37; eco-critical theory,
38; knowledge of, 175; literature
and, 180. *See also* Anahareo (Gertrude Bernard); "all my relations";
Belaney, Archibald; conservation;
wildlife management
education, unequal funding for reserve
schools, 190. *See also* residential
school
Edward VII, 127, 183, 197–98, 199, 200
Egwuna, Angele, 148, 165
Egwuna, John, 148, 250n20
Ellingson, Ter, 27
employment. *See* jobs (employment)
enfranchisement, 32, 185, 254n7. *See
also* voting rights
Engel, Marian, 163, 165
English language, 4; ability to speak
or write, 26, 44, 92, 94, 98, 181–82,
185, 186, 188, 190–91, 192, 203, 207,
244n5, 244n8; accent, 54; direction
(compass) and, 187, non-standard,
of storytellers, 15, 255n20

BOOKS IN THE INDIGENOUS STUDIES SERIES PUBLISHED BY WILFRID LAURIER UNIVERSITY PRESS

Blockades and Resistance: Studies in Actions of Peace and the Temagami Blockades of 1988–89 / Bruce W. Hodgins, Ute Lischke, and David T. McNab, editors / 2003 / xi + 276 pp. / illus. / ISBN 0-88920-381-4

Indian Country: Essays on Contemporary Native Culture / Gail Guthrie Valaskakis / 2005 / x + 293 pp. / illus. / ISBN 0-88920-479-9

Walking a Tightrope: Aboriginal People and Their Representations / Ute Lischke and David T. McNab, editors / 2005 / xix + 377 pp. / illus. / ISBN 978-0-88920-484-3

The Long Journey of a Forgotten People: Métis Identities and Family Histories / Ute Lischke and David T. McNab, editors / 2007 / viii + 386 pp. / illus. / ISBN 978-0-88920-523-9

Words of the Huron / John L. Steckley / 2007 / xvii + 259 pp. / ISBN 978-0-88920-516-1

Essential Song: Three Decades of Northern Cree Music / Lynn Whidden / 2007 / xvi + 176 pp. / illus., musical examples, audio CD / ISBN 978-0-88920-459-1

From the Iron House: Imprisonment in First Nations Writing / Deena Rymhs / 2008 / ix + 147 pp. / ISBN 978-1-55458-021-7

Lines Drawn upon the Water: First Nations and the Great Lakes Borders and Borderlands / Karl S. Hele, editor / 2008 / xxiii + 351 pp. / illus. / ISBN 978-1-55458-004-0

Troubling Tricksters: Revisioning Critical Conversations / Linda M. Morra and Deanna Reder, editors / 2009 / xii+ 336 pp. / illus. / ISBN 978-1-55458-181-8

Aboriginal Peoples in Canadian Cities: Transformations and Continuities / Heather A. Howard and Craig Proulx, editors / 2011 / viii + 256 pp. / illus. / ISBN 978-1-055458-260-0

Bridging Two Peoples: Chief Peter E. Jones, 1843–1909 / Allan Sherwin / 2012 / xxiv + 246 pp. / illus. / ISBN 978-1-55458-633-2

The Nature of Empires and the Empires of Nature: Indigenous Peoples and the Great Lakes Environment / Karl S. Hele, editor / 2013 / xxii + 350 / illus. / ISBN 978-1-55458-328-7

The Eighteenth-Century Wyandot: A Clan-Based Study / John L. Steckley / 2014 / x + 306 / ISBN 978-1-55458-956-2

Indigenous Poetics in Canada / Neal McLeod, editor / 2014 / xii + 404 pp. / ISBN 978-1-55458-982-1

Literary Land Claims: The "Indian Land Question" from Pontiac's War to Attawapiskat / Margery Fee / 2015 / x + 318 pp. / illus. / ISBN 978-1-77112-119-4